Constructing The Self, Constructing America

Constructing

THE SELF,

Constructing

AMERICA

A Cultural History

of Psychotherapy

PHILIP CUSHMAN, PH.D.

ADDISON-WESLEY PUBLISHING COMPANY

READING, MASSACHUSETTS   MENLO PARK, CALIFORNIA
NEW YORK   DON MILLS, ONTARIO
WOKINGHAM, ENGLAND   AMSTERDAM   BONN
SYDNEY   SINGAPORE   TOKYO   MADRID   SAN JUAN
PARIS   SEOUL   MILAN   MEXICO CITY   TAIPEI

Many of the designations used by manufacturers and sellers to distinguish their products are claimed as trademarks. Where those designations appear in this book and Addison-Wesley was aware of a trademark claim, the designations have been printed in initial capital letters (i.e., Chevrolet).

Photographs on page 51 are from Dailey Paskman and Sigmund Spaeth, *"Gentlemen, Be Seated!"* (Garden City, N.Y.: Doubleday, Doran & Co., 1928).

Library of Congress Cataloging-in-Publication Data

Cushman, Philip.
    Constructing the self, constructing America : a cultural history of psychotherapy / Philip Cushman.
        p.   cm.
    Includes bibliographical references and index.
    ISBN 0-201-62643-8
    1. Psychotherapy—Social aspects—United States.   2. United States—Civilization—Psychological aspects.   3. Psychotherapy—Moral and ethical aspects.   4. Identity (Psychology)—United States.   5. Individualism—United States.   I. Title.
    [DNLM: 1. Psychotherapy—history—United States.   2. Sociology. WM 11 AA1 C9c 1995]
    RC443.C84   1995
    616.89'14'0973—dc20
    DNLM/DLC
    for Library of Congress   ⸙   94-33066
                                                                              CIP

Jacket design by Suzanne Heiser
Text design by Barbara Cohen Aronica
Set in 10.5-point Stemple Schneidler by Pagesetters, Inc.
1 2 3 4 5 6 7 8 9-MA-98979695
First printing, January 1995

To my Grandmothers Rose and Sara:
one sang to me,
and one confided in me that, had she been
born a man, she would have been a philosopher

To Szmuel Zygelbojm, who fought in the Warsaw Ghetto uprising, served on the parliament of the exiled Polish government, was imprisoned, and then miraculously made his way to England in order to persuade the Western Allies to intervene against the genocide. But no one listened. On May 12, 1943, in protest and despair, he committed suicide on the steps of 10 Downing Street. He was forty-eight years old.

To Dr. Abraham Zygielbaum, Szmuel's youngest brother, actor, poet, beloved teacher, and dear man. He survived the Holocaust, married Tema, immigrated to America after the war, and taught for many years at Hebrew Union College. He fought fascism his own way, through stories and songs, which he thought were the most powerful weapons of all. He was my teacher.

Contents

ACKNOWLEDGMENTS

This strange, unorthodox book is framed by several academic disciplines and communal traditions, informed by many currents and yet peacefully at home in none. It was not produced during a sabbatical, a lessened teaching load, or research and writing grants, nor can I thank institutions, institutes, or research assistants. Instead, this book was written in the trenches of a full-time private practice: between patients, during precious midday hours purposely left unscheduled, in (very) late nights, and on weekend and vacation writing marathons. It was written because many people talked with me, wrote to me, and shared their ideas, confusions, stories, and enthusiasms. It was written because people I never met sacrificed in their own ways in order to write and contribute to our common body of shared understandings; I learned from them, was inspired by them, and was encouraged to add my thoughts to theirs. Their names can be found in the quotations and citations interspersed throughout the following pages. Some of them are contemporaries of mine, some lived decades and centuries ago; I may not have known them, but I am forever indebted to them.

Most of all, this book is a product of the influence of many good people: friends, professors, therapists, supervisors, consultants, patients, colleagues, and family. Their impact on me has made this book possible; quite literally, it would have been inconceivable without them. I would like to mention a few of them to acknowledge their invaluable help. To begin, three groups of colleagues have been instrumental in the writing and editing of this book: First, my longtime peer consultation group in Berkeley—Jane Burka, Jules Burstein, Leah Potts Fisher (from the Center for Work and the Family), Margaret Guertin, and Alice Wilkens—read and critiqued several chapters; their comments, as always, were uncommonly insightful and helpful. The task was time-consuming, I know, and I am grateful. My American Psychological Association colleagues—Betty Bayer, John Christopher, Blaine Fowers, Laurel Furumoto, Charles Guignon (not really in APA, but included nonetheless), Rachel Hare-

Mustin, Suzanne Kirschner, Jeanne Maracek, Jill Morawski, Isaac Pri-lleltensky, Frank Richardson, Louis Sass, and Jamie Walkup—have helped me, step by-step, to understand the world, and the issues confronting our discipline, in a more nuanced, complex manner. Their work has brought a richness and depth to my thinking, and their friendship and encouragement a comradeship that I feel blessed by. I am especially indebted to Blaine, Jill, Frank, and Louie, not only for their scholarly assistance but also for their generosity and warmheartedness. My Bay Area hermeneuticist colleagues—Nathan Adler, Hilde Burton, the world famous Terence O'Hare, Bruce Johnston, Steven Joseph, Edward Sampson, Margaret Thaler Singer, Tony Stigliano, and Larry Wornian—read and comment on most everything I write, which is fitting, considering that they have taught me much of it. I would like especially to thank Hilde and Ed, who lead the way intellectually and politically and are unfailingly helpful. Nathan, recently deceased, was in the great gadfly tradition of intellectual scholarship: disturbing, probing, and challenging. Poet, maverick analyst, and political radical, he carefully edited several chapters of this manuscript and was eagerly awaiting the next installments. He died at eighty-three, far too soon.

I would also like to thank Donald Freedheim, Stanley Messer, and Paul Wachtel for encouraging me to write the first iteration of this project; John Demos, Dave Hitchens, Chuck Strozier, and John Toews, good friends and good historians; psychologists Joel Crohn, Lane Gerber, Susan Hales, and Bill Lax; and Jack Mitchell, my first supervisor and dear friend. Thanks to my patients, who continue to teach even though I am slow to learn. Finally, a loving appreciation to Melanie O'Hare, Phyllis Johnston, the Reverend Robby Cranch, reference librarian/design consultant/agent-for-life Jim Cooke, Roni Summers, Mary Lanier, Michael Lisman, Steve and Judy Lawrence, Jim Cotter, Rich Lewycky, Wayne Johnson, Robert Gay, Elizabeth Adler, and Marya Martas; they help me laugh.

Several longtime teachers and friends helped me develop the capacity to write this book: Rabbis Bill Cutter, Richard Levy, and Leonard Beerman; Cantor Bill Sharlin; Dr. Abraham Zygielbaum; my good buddies Joel Rosenberg, Jerry Winston, David Ben-Veniste, and the invisible David Colloff; Drs. Joseph Boskin, Ken Lincoln, David Lindsay, and Joe Collier; Drs. Carl Faber and Ira Nathanson, Rev. Don Hartsock, and old friends Roger Cox, Judy Jones Ritchie, Judy Wilson-Wilson, Kevin and Marcie West, Don (or Gloria) Angelo, Bari (Magenta) Polansky, Lenny Borer, Dov Geller, Dick Whitney, and Wilson Fetting Humphries, Jr.; Oregon colleagues John Haugse and Kathleen McLaughlin; and Dr. Paul Erickson (eighth-grade history teacher and steadfast friend), coaches Bob Stout and

Paul Beck, and friends Richard Shrock, Stevie Jo Beitscher, and Bob Cuthbert.

I owe a hearty thanks to the people who labored to make this book appear: Addison-Wesley's Nancy Miller has been a friendly, knowledgeable editor and had the courage to take a chance with this strange project; production coordinator Tiffany Cobb displayed admirable patience in the face of many difficulties; copy editor Maggie Carr produced a thoughtful, clear-sighted (and remarkably Heideggerian) reading; my agent, James Levine and his staff—Pat Hersch, Melissa Rowland, and Arielle Ekstut—made the submission phase of this adventure relatively painless; and the reference librarians of the Berkeley Public Library and the University of California came through with last-minute heroics. Thank you all for your hard work.

This book has been a great joy to write, but the process has been difficult for my family: my wife Karen, daughter Leah, brother Edward, his wife Sharon, their children David and Yael, my in-laws Loretta, Art, Duffy, and C.J., and especially my parents Frances and Alvin, who helped mightily and continue to do so in many ways. Thank you for your love, patience, and encouragement.

There is one who deserves special thanks. Although it is traditional to thank one's significant other at the end of the acknowledgments, in my case the tradition seems upside down. I want to thank Karen, novelist and educator: my intellectual partner, traveling companion, and fellow conspirator; my editor, my inspiration, my lover, my wife. We have traveled many roads together, you and I. Despite the strange twists and turns, we have dreamed, labored, shifted, rethought, dreamed again, and, it seems, survived. The seasons are indeed passing, but I do not think even a *mad* god could have anticipated the sweetness, sorrows, and richness of these many years. Like your novels, my book is brought to light by the framework we have made together. Dear Karen, I could not have done this, I would not have begun this, without you.

"I assume that history is not a well-ordered city . . . but a jungle. . . . The only thing I am really sure of is that we who plunge into the jungle need to think about what we are doing, because there is somewhere we want to go."

—HOWARD ZINN, 1970
THE POLITICS OF HISTORY

Constructing
THE SELF,
Constructing
AMERICA

CHAPTER ONE

Psychotherapy, The Impossible Bridge

*Life is a very narrow bridge
between two eternities—
do not be afraid.*
—*RABBI NACHMAN OF BRASLAV*

We take psychotherapy for granted today. It is such a normal, everyday aspect of our lives that we rarely look at it, wonder about it, question it. It is certainly true that we criticize psychotherapy and make jokes about it, but we criticize it as we would the weather. For late twentieth-century urban Americans, psychotherapy is a given; it is an unquestioned part of our world.

When social artifacts or institutions are taken for granted it usually means that they have developed functions in the society that are so integral to the culture that they are indispensable, unacknowledged, and finally invisible. So, then, what *are* psychotherapy's sociopolitical functions? What part does psychotherapy play in the complicated cultural landscape of late twentieth-century America? How does psychotherapy either add to or challenge the status quo—by affecting current understandings of what it means to be human, or influencing standards of normality and criminality, trends in educational and advertising theory, the content of popular culture, the conduct of election campaigns, concepts of health and illness, and the particulars of moral understandings, everyday language, fashion trends, and leisure activities? Vast historical changes in the last 500 years in the West have slowly created a world in which the individual is commonly understood to be a container of a "mind" and more recently a "self" that needs to be "therapied," rather than, say, a carrier of a divine soul that needs to be saved, or simply an element of the communal unit that must cooperate for the common good. There were, of course, sociopolitical reasons for these changes, and there must be groups and institutions that currently profit from the changes. How does psychotherapy fit with this new configuration?

Psychotherapy—and its relationship to the United States—is anything but simple; it is one of the most complex, colorful, and strange artifacts of the modern era. It is a social institution with many theoretical frameworks, ideologies, and guilds. It features some of the most varied and creative ideas of the last 150 years. Its practitioners have developed some of the most unusual social practices of our time, yet they often hold their theories with a certainty and true belief that rivals religious conviction. It is thought of as a scientific practice, yet it is anything but standardized or empirical, and it has not yet developed a disciplinewide consensus about how to think about patients or what to do with them. It is thought of as a medical practice, yet it has an enormous social and political impact. Most psychotherapy theories dictate that the therapist can and must remain objective throughout the therapy, yet a close examination clearly shows that these theories are founded on social ideologies and value structures that by definition are not objective.

None of this is meant to insinuate that psychotherapy is necessarily counterproductive or dangerous. Nor is it to say that creativity, conviction, moral values, or political influence are wrong, or that psychotherapy is bad. Not at all. In fact, over the course of this book I will argue that many of these qualities are necessary, in fact unavoidable, when one is operating in the social realm. In many ways the theories and practices of psychotherapy are helpful, perhaps even indispensable, to our late twentieth-century world. But there is much to question, much to wonder about. Psychotherapy is, in fact, an extremely puzzling phenomenon to practitioners and patients alike. It is such an integral part of our everyday world that we do not often wonder about its function in American society, its reason for being, its impact. We do not often question the assumptions of many of its theories, such as the underlying ideology of self-contained individualism or the valuing of "inner" feelings or the unquestioned assumption that health is produced by experiencing and expressing those feelings.

We don't often think about psychotherapy in these broad sociopolitical terms, but we would gain a great deal by doing so. If we could, we might be better able to understand our own problems, both personal and national, because we would have a broader, more encompassing perspective on the historical and economic forces that frame and shape them. We might be better able to grapple with current issues and anticipate future dilemmas if we could get a better grasp on the dynamics of our social system and how it both creates and closes off opportunities and alternatives. Much would open to us if we could inquire broadly and critically into the functions and impact of psychotherapy in our late twentieth-century urban world.

One way of beginning such a critical inquiry is to situate psychotherapy in the history and culture of its time and place. That is the intent of this book. Contrary to a current California joke, the history of psychotherapy did not begin one day in the early sixties in Marin County when Alan Watts said to Werner Erhard, "Go with that feeling." But neither does psychotherapy's history reach back to shamans, ancient seers, or Druid priests. Therapists are not shamans; shamans are shamans. At the heart of this book is an interpretive perspective that looks at each era in terms of its local truths and local medicines. Each era has a predominant configuration of the self, a particular foundational set of beliefs about what it means to be human. Each particular configuration of the self brings with it characteristic illnesses, local healers, and local healing technologies. These selves and roles are not interchangeable or equivalant. Each embodies a kind of unique and local truth that should not be reduced to a universal law, because such reductions inevitably depend on a particular cultural frame of reference, which in turn inevitably involves an ideological agenda. This book explores the social construction of several schools of American psychotherapy by drawing out and interpreting some of their historical antecedents, economic constituents, and political consequences. The ultimate intent is to further interpret the era in which we live and the many activities and encounters that are called psychotherapy.

Of course, the accomplishment falls short of the intent. The attempt to write a comprehensive cultural history of psychotherapy is a lofty goal too grand to be accomplished by this book, which is more a coordinated series of studies in the cultural history of psychotherapy than an encyclopedic approach to the history of the profession. For instance, behavior therapy, cognitive therapy, family therapy, and Jungian psychoanalysis are not discussed in great detail. Certain events and schools of psychotherapy are discussed at length because they illuminate cultural and political issues that I think are central to our current dilemmas as a nation. We struggle to face the problems of our time by developing a way of being that aids in our survival and yet is consistent with our beliefs and worthy of our ideals. In the process, perhaps we can develop new ways of thinking about psychotherapy that will lead us to new therapeutic practices, and develop ways of thinking about our larger society that will move us to a new, slightly shifted way of conceiving of the self and of arranging ourselves socially and politically. Psychotherapy—like it or not—has been and will continue to be instrumental in that struggle.

There seems little question that psychotherapy is one of the most significant cultural artifacts of our time, reflecting and shaping the central themes of the last 150 years. There is something about the field of psychology and the practices of psychotherapy that is particularly emblematic of the texture of twentieth-century American middle-class life. The history of psychotherapy is intertwined with America's history: its promise, optimism, and vitality; its corruptions, collusions, and destructiveness. America's history is a grand history, filled with new beginnings and unlimited opportunities; yet it is also a history of oppression, exploitation, and profound betrayal. Most of all it is a history of a mixture of peoples who attempt to live together without an indigenous, inclusive tradition of shared meanings in a rapidly changing world of powerful social and economic forces—industrialization, urbanization, immigration, and secularization. It is the story of religious institutions and moral philosophers that, confronted with economic and political pressures to conform and accommodate, have had difficulty maintaining authority and developing viable alternatives to sociopolitical trends. It is the story of small communities that have been culturally overwhelmed and geographically engulfed by the tremendous growth of urban life. It is the story of increasingly lonely people trying to live decently in a world of growing complexities, confusions, and dangers. As a result, over the last 150 years America's history has become a history of the modern ills of isolation, uncertainty, and doubt. It was into this world that psychotherapy was born.

This book is based on the belief that in order to understand American psychotherapy, we must study the world into which it was born and in which it currently resides. Concurrently, in order to understand the sociopolitical dynamics of American life, we must study how psychotherapy not only reflects but also constructs the social field. This type of scholarly tacking back and forth between the part and the whole is what is referred to as the "hermeneutic circle" and is an important aspect of the type of historical research sometimes referred to as "cultural history"; both concepts will be discussed at length in chapter two. However, this contextual approach to psychotherapy is more critical than mainstream approaches; as a result it might seem confusing to some readers and perhaps even hostile to many therapists. This is an understandable response, since mainstream theorists and historians of psychology consistently portray psychology as an apolitical, transhistorical science removed from the power struggles of history and the vicissitudes of everyday social life. Some cultural historians, in fact, have accused the mainstream of developing a sanitized, fanciful version of the discipline's beginnings, an "origin myth" instead of a critical history. Origin myths are covert attempts by a historian to legitimize a discipline by allying the discipline with high status individuals, factions, or accepted social practices. Origin myths also describe the origins of the discipline in such a way as to demonstrate the discipline's utility for those in positions of power. This means that mainstream historians will shy away from portraying psychology as critical of the status quo and will avoid including within their work a critical exploration of the sociopolitical frame of reference in which the discipline is embedded. In order to avoid a critical approach, mainstream historians usually portray the origin of a discipline as the creation of individual genius or the incremental but inevitable progress of the neutral scientific process.

Rather than restricting a history of the field to the isolated influence of one psychotherapist upon another, the hermeneutic approach used in this book seeks to place the entire enterprise of psychotherapy within history. It is an attempt to guard against developing a celebration, a panegyric, rather than a critical history. Celebrations in the guise of history are inaccurate and sometimes politically dangerous. In the case of psychotherapy, a celebratory history would be disastrous, because psychotherapy is central to our culture and important to the functioning of our late twentieth-century social institutions. Without a critical historical perspective we would be unable to resist colluding with the political and economic forces in control of our society. "A science without memory," Franz Samelson once said, "is at the mercy of the forces of the day."[1] In fact, the most common way historians of psychotherapy celebrate rather than critically interpret their subject is by decontextualizing it. By failing to situate the various theories and practices of psychotherapy within the larger history and culture of their respective eras, some historians treat psychotherapy as though it is a transhistorical science that treats universal illnesses. These historians imply that because psychotherapy is a science, its findings are akin to facts, and because it is a transhistorical technology, its practices are apolitical. Current thinkers in interpretive social science and the sociology of knowledge have argued that that stance is philosophically impossible and politically dangerous. Again, these issues will be more fully discussed in chapter two. Chapter three, "The Self in America," will put the contextual approach to use by describing my view of the historical contexts in which American psychotherapy was created.

Considering the fact that modern medical psychotherapy did not really emerge until the second half of the nineteenth century, psychotherapy's rise to power has been rapid and pervasive. Especially in the last hundred years in the United States, there has been an amazing advance in its prevalence, status, and influence. In the early 1890s Sigmund Freud set out on the marvelous adventure now known as the first psychoanalysis. It was a *self*-analysis because at that time there was no such thing as a psychoanalyst. In 1994 in California alone there were approximately 6,500 psychiatrists, 13,800 clinical psychologists, 13,000 clinical social workers, and 21,600 marriage, family, and child therapists![2] What does this tremendous growth mean?

I do not think it means that psychotherapy has perfected its "science." It means that psychotherapy, somehow, is so accurately attuned to the twentieth-century cultural frame of reference that it has developed an intellectual discourse and provides human services that are crucial, perhaps indispensable, to our current way of life. Psychotherapy has become emblematic of the post–World War II era. It is the historian's job to interpret psychotherapy in such a way as to illuminate this new configuration, to speculate about the functions and influences of psychotherapy so that we can better understand the world in which we live. If, as I shall argue, the role of the psychotherapist has been creator and caretaker of the realm of the "interior," then we can ask a host of questions regarding the nature and function of personal interiority, how it is constructed, and what cultural, political, and economic roles it plays in our society.

Psychotherapy has had many faces and utilized many ideologies during its stay in America. Several schools, such as nineteenth-century mesmerism, were considered in their time to be undeniably scientific and remarkably, almost magically, effective. Currently, the field continues to have its trends, its scientific claims, and its occasional superstars. The post–World War II era is the product of an individualism no longer leavened by a moral tradition of political discourse and communal values. American individualism, bereft of its once vibrant commitment to communalism, and under the enormous pressures of industrial capitalism, has all too often been used as a tool to promote consumerism and to bust unions. In the course of this book I will argue that the current configuration of the self is the empty self. The empty self is a way of being human; it is characterized by a pervasive sense of personal emptiness and is committed to the values of self-liberation through consumption. The empty self is the perfect complement to an economy that must stave off economic stagnation by arranging for the continual purchase and consumption of surplus goods. Psychotherapy is the profession responsible for treating the unfortunate personal effects of the empty self without disrupting the economic arrangements of consumerism. Psychotherapy is permeated by the philosophy of self-contained individualism, exists within the framework of consumerism, speaks the language of self-liberation, and thereby unknowingly reproduces some of the ills it is responsible for healing. None of this is an accident. The self is a product of the complex, awe-inspiring cultural process that weaves together various elements of a society in order to perpetuate the status quo. The empty self is configured to fit *our* particular culture; it makes for a great deal of abundance and stimulation, isolation and loneliness.

Notice that I am treating psychotherapy as a cultural artifact that can be interpreted, rather than as a universal healing technology that has already brought a transcendent "cure" to earthlings. As a matter of fact, nothing has cured the human race, and nothing is about to. Mental ills don't work that way; they are not universal, they are local. Every era has a particular configuration of self, illness, healer, technology; they are a kind of cultural package. They are interrelated, intertwined, interpenetrating. So when we study a particular illness, we are also studying the conditions that shape and define that illness, and the sociopolitical impact of those who are responsible for healing it.

Chapters four through eight discuss in detail the historical development of various psychotherapy theories and the historical contexts in which they are embedded. Unfortunately, the vast majority of psychotherapy theories do not take into consideration the sociohistorical conditions that shaped the illnesses they are responsible for healing. Theorists often hold ideas aloof from any social context, claiming a privileged epistemological position uncontaminated by the rough and tumble of the local values and politics of their respective eras. With all the promise and optimism that accompanies new theories, they have not been able to affect the sociopolitical conditions that cause or shape mental distress. The socioeconomic structures of Western society and the power relations of ethnicity, race, class, and gender have not been transformed because of psychotherapy. In fact, several writers have argued that the structures and relations of our era have often been unknowingly reinforced rather than challenged by therapy.

Decontextualized approaches to psychotherapy, that is, approaches that imply that therapy is a healing technology that transcends the politics and culture of its era, fail because they promise the impossible. They cannot explore the synchrony of the social institution, its social practices, and the larger cultural frame of reference. Without appreciating the synchrony, they cannot shift the old loop. They cannot free themselves to comment directly on the structural causes of local emotional ills, grasp their unintended involvement in the perpetuation of those ills, or devise therapeutic practices that would attempt to heal those ills without simultaneously reproducing them. Most object relations, humanistic, cognitive, and addiction therapies, for instance, however effective in producing behavior change or emotional experiences in the short run, inevitably reproduce the very causes of the ills they treat by implicitly valorizing and reproducing the isolated, empty individual. This argument is spelled out in detail in chapters four through eight and used in chapter nine to suggest the beginnings of new therapeutic practices that do not so completely recycle the ills of our age. Even though there are myriad therapy theories currently abroad, the fundamental miseries of twentieth-century Westerners remain in some ways more pronounced or entrenched than ever.

So what are we to do?

I would like to offer three brief stories in response to the question. First I use a scene from a book by J. H. Van den Berg, the Dutch psychiatrist, that likens psychotherapy to a bridge that cannot succeed. Another is the story surrounding a quotation from the Hasidic rabbi Nachman of Braslav, a statement that was set to music and sung by the Jewish resistance in Auschwitz. However, the one I'd like to start with is not so literary. I have chosen a quote from one of Hollywood's campiest spoofs, *Love at First Bite*, because it captures in a few words one half of what I am about to take an entire book to argue. The time is the late 1970s in New York City. A goofy psychiatrist, Jeffery Rosenberg (played by Richard Benjamin), is standing in a hotel room staring at a coffin. George Hamilton, as Count Dracula, is sleeping inside the coffin. Dr. Rosenberg, the only person in New York City who is aware of Dracula's presence, is trying to decide whether or not to seize the moment, incinerate the coffin, and kill Dracula. However, Rosenberg is timid, self-absorbed, indecisive, and prone to overintellectualizing. He stares at the coffin, then looks at the gasoline can and matches. His indecision initiates a soliloquy that is at once the funniest, most ridiculous, and most noble moment in the movie. He stares into the camera and wonders: "Can I really do this? A Freudian wouldn't do this. A Jungian would do this. A Reichian would do this—But I'm a Freudian. . . ."

Then, in the middle of his twentieth century effete paralysis, a new thought occurs to him: "But wait! I'm also a Van Helsing!" It turns out Rosenberg's grandfather—Fritz Van Helsing—fought against this same Count Dracula in London generations ago. It is his inheritance to act. "In the name of all the Van Helsings who ever lived . . . 'Burn, baby, burn!'" Amidst much drama, Rosenberg pours out the gasoline and ignites it.[3]

Of course, the good (?) doctor's attempt fails, and Dracula gets the girl, but that's not the point here. What's important for this book is that when faced with the necessity of taking action in the world, action that will either protect or threaten what he values most, Rosenberg, like the vast majority of twentieth-century Americans, does not know where to stand or how to act, even in an emergency. We are morally confused. We do not have a mutually agreed upon tradition that guides our daily practices, gives us a sense of moral certainty, and informs our life with meaning and courage. When push comes to shove, the "universal truth" claims of decontextualized social science theories do not help much. In fact, they are not an integral part of us, they disavow moral authority, and we do not know quite where they fit into our lives.

This is the tragedy of the twentieth century. Our dedication to the philosophical frame of reference of the physical sciences has helped us develop the power to manipulate the physical world in undreamed of ways. But that same frame of reference has within it a built-in paradox: By conceiving of a world that is based on doubt and irrevocably separates "inner" from "outer," body from mind, science from superstition (see chapter two and the appendix), the physical science framework makes it nearly impossible to use traditional ideas, philosophical thinking, and a sense of moral authority—and thus to take a moral stand. We have no way of developing shared moral understandings that would help us cooperate in using our newfound power for the betterment of human-kind. The very framework that has made it possible for us to develop our power has made it difficult for us to determine how to use it wisely.

Instead of having vibrant, authoritative communities and moral traditions to guide us, we are faced with a multiplicity of scientific theories, a cacophony of voices, one more dogmatic and self-righteous than the next. Each promises a universal truth, a magical technology, and some type of certain deliverance from the vicissitudes and illnesses of twentieth-century living. A societywide consensus, a shared sense of right and good and true, simply does not exist in our time. It has been shattered by historical forces, military events, and intellectual trends. This is the problem Rosenberg was having as he shuffled through the major theories of his field, a kind of adoptive culture. These theories were fine in the abstract, but they did not help him to live and act meaningfully in the everyday.

Those charged with the responsibility of treating the emotional difficulties of others, especially psychotherapists, often experience a par-ticular kind of confusion and despair. We confront, embodied in our patients, the consequences of four centuries of increasing urbanization, secularism, and industrialization. It is tempting at these times to turn to a self-sealing doctrine that presents an airtight ideology and a rigid technol-ogy. At times of panic, ahistorical theories that proclaim a universal truth may be somewhat comforting, not only to the patient but particularly to the practitioner.

But the quieting of the therapist's anxiety and despair is not, theo-retically, the major purpose of psychotherapy. What if, in the course of soothing the psychotherapist, these grand theories were actually to con-tribute to the very suffering that they are meant to alleviate, precisely because of their universal claims? Then we have a big problem. And I think we do.

Dr. Rosenberg solved his dilemma by finding guidance in the traditions and values of his family history. When events called on him to act, the decontextualized theories of the modern social sciences were of little use to him. Ultimately, he was able to act because he had a past. *Love at First Bite* has (no doubt unwittingly) demonstrated one of the main points of this book: The first step in ceasing to reproduce the nihilism and violence of our era is for us to learn how to situate ourselves within human history and draw from our moral traditions.

In *The Changing Nature of Man*, J. H. Van den Berg suggests that psychotherapy is an attempt to connect by a man-made bridge two bodies of land that were once one.[4] At times in human history the individual and the community were not experienced as separate. Van den Berg describes the unity and coherence of some eras past, the organic whole of shared understandings, cultural meanings, and sacred rituals. We do not have such unifying influences today. And as a result of this brokenness, people are confused, anxious, despairing, and in need of guidance.

Researchers have chronicled the many influences on the cultural brokenness of our time, in particular the urbanization, industrialism, and secularism that have come about in the modern era. Another important element of our brokenness has been the intellectual discourse of self-contained individualism: the ideal of the masterful, bounded self and its antecedents, the Cartesian splits and oppositions between mind and body, reason and passion, subject and object, individual and community.

But this book is not just about brokenness and absence. If it were it would be flat and one-dimensional—only one half of the story. Human life is not that simple. Our current problems are not caused solely by absences. They are also the product of certain presences: the coercive influence of dominant traditions; the exercise of power by various communities, ethnic groups, and socioeconomic classes; the rage and greed of particular individuals. Individualism wasn't simply a coincidence, a mutation that popped out of the Zeusian forehead of some late medieval poet. It is a slow-building, centuries-old phenomenon that has developed in part because of the oppressiveness of certain traditions, the stifling inertia of life in small communities, and the compelling decision to resist the old, the given, the unjust, and to be creative, unique, and unusual. Viewed in this way, individualism is itself a Western tradition, a response to the economic arrangements, moral understandings, and political constrictions of feudal life.

The remarkable fit between a psychotherapy theory and its historical era, the exquisite interrelationship between a cultural artifact and the cultural frame of reference in which it is embedded, is not the product of one half of the equation. Psychotherapy and our isolated individualism are not solely the products of the loss of community and tradition. In order to capture the poetry of history, we have to understand that communities can be mean-spirited and traditions oppressive. Individualism was influenced not only by the *absence* of religion and stability but also by the *presence* of the various interests and forces that socially constructed a certain type of individual with certain kinds of wishes, urges, ambitions, and proclivities. Immense sociohistorical movements like individualism cannot be easily explained; they emerge and fade because of vast happenings that seemingly have no one cause, no clear beginning or end. As a cautionary note to Dr. Rosenberg's epiphany regarding the helpfulness of tradition, let us remember a scene from *Adventures of Huckleberry Finn*. In this pre–Emancipation Proclamation scene Huck, a young white boy, and his friend Jim, an African-American slave, are traveling on the Mississippi River on a large raft. Jim is trying to escape, and Huck is wrestling with his conscience about whether to turn Jim in to the authorities.

> Conscience says to me, "What had poor Miss Watson done to you, that you could see her nigger go off right under your eyes and never say one single word? What did that poor old woman do to you, that you could treat her so mean? ..." I got to feeling so mean and so miserable I most wished I was dead. ... [Jim] was saying how the first thing he would do when he got to a free State he would go to saving up money and never spend a single cent, and when he got enough he would buy his wife ... and then they would both work to buy the two children, and if their master wouldn't sell them, they'd get an Ab'litionist to go and steal them.
>
> It almost froze me to hear such talk. ... Here was this nigger which I had as good as helped to run away, coming right out flat-footed and saying he would steal his children— children that belonged to a man I didn't even know; a man that hadn't ever done me no harm.
>
> I was sorry to hear Jim say that, it was such a lowering of him.[5]

Huck, of course, somehow found it within himself to choose his friendship with Jim over his certain belief that allowing a slave to go free was wrong. But his inability to see Jim in any frame other than as a piece of property, despite his friendship and affection for Jim, illustrates the profound power of a cultural frame of reference. If culture completely determines us, then how do groups or individuals ever resist specific practices, trends, laws? There is more to the exercise of power than overt coercion and repression, more to the ills of our age than the absence of community and tradition. The current configuration of the self, what I call the empty self, will be discussed at length in later chapters. We must keep in mind, however, that the essence of that self is caused not only by a loss of a sense of communal certainty, but also by the exercise of power through certain "positive" forces within the social realm, such as advertising, federal monetary and banking policies, intellectual theories and their attendant social practices, moral understandings, and popular culture. This is the message Michel Foucault taught us: The configuration of the self, even a configuration composed of an absence, is socially constructed by those in power. The self is always a product of a specific cultural frame of reference, configured out of moral understandings and local politics. There are reasons and functions to most social phenomena, even if seemingly benign or obscure.

It is precisely the reasons for and the functions of psychotherapy that are featured in the chapters that follow. Earlier we have noticed how Van den Berg suggested that psychotherapy is an attempt to unify two bodies of land, the individual and the community, that were once one. Because the task of unification is, in our era, an impossible one, what are psychotherapists and patients to do? We will find that psychotherapy in our era has unknowingly helped perpetuate self-contained individualism, certain era-specific moral frameworks, and the political status quo. If that is so, what is still possible for us? How do we construct an increasingly impossible bridge?

An eighteenth-century Hasidic rabbi, Nachman of Braslav had many thoughts about absences, abysses, and dilemmas. He also knew a thing or two about bridges. He once made a statement about a bridge that his followers remembered and set to music. Generations later, the song was sung by Jewish prisoners in the death camps at Auschwitz. He taught that "Life is a very narrow bridge between two eternities—do not be afraid." I am not sure what Nachman meant by his statement. But I can tell you what occurs to me when I listen to it. Many years ago, when I first heard this song, I imagined that Nachman was alluding to what he believed to be a heavenly eternity before and after death. Never being particularly interested in heaven, I didn't think much about it at the time. But more recently, I had a new idea. I thought about our countless ancestors, who stretch out behind us into the eternity of the past. And I thought of the countless number of our as yet unknown offspring, our children's children's children, who stretch out in front of us into the eternity of the future. And I thought perhaps Reb Nachman was helping us to see that we, the living, are the only link, the only bridge, between those who have come before us and those who will come after us. One of our main tasks is to keep the connection alive by respecting the past, studying it, being challenged by it, rejecting some of it, seeing the possibilities in it, reshaping it, situating ourselves and our practices within in, making meaning from it.

Another of our tasks, Nachman might be telling us, is to keep the connection alive by valuing the future, by living and working for the survival of our communities, traditions, our species, our environment, our earth. This would, of course, necessitate a flexibility and a creativity in relationship to the varying, intersecting moral traditions in which we are embedded. So we live, balancing on this narrow bridge. We are poised between a past that we can only reach, dimly, through study and imagination, and a future that we can never partake of and that we can secure only at great cost and through difficult struggle. Perhaps we can extrapolate from this that only by situating psychotherapy and the larger American political experience within their historical contexts (which would connect us to the past), and only by developing a value-laden, activist set of therapeutic practices (that would help secure a future) can we develop a psychotherapy bridge that can keep us above the abyss for a while longer.

One way of bringing these commitments to life in the therapy hour is to conceive of psychotherapy as taking place within a larger cultural space, or "terrain." This is a terrain that emerges out of the parameters of the shared philosophical and moral understandings, language, gender roles and identities, customs, rituals, and political and economic structures of the particular historical era in which the therapy takes place. The parameters of the patient's terrain are determined by these dominant cultural understandings, and by more local understandings formed from community, neighborhood, affinity group, and family traditions and experiences. The sum of these understandings determine what is possible within a given terrain, what is permissible and incorrect, desirable and disgusting; these rules are "embodied" and experienced through the senses as "emotions." The parameters, or horizons (see chapter two), of the cultural terrain then allow certain things to emerge within the terrain and exclude other things from appearing. The horizon both enables and limits. Therapeutic change could then be conceived of as the ability of the patient to *shift* the parameters of the terrain. Chapter nine will discuss this idea in some detail.

The particulars of that shift, for the most part, will always be beyond our understanding. But if it is true that the embodied cultural terrain is fundamentally a moral terrain, then we could conceive of psychotherapy as an activity that brings into being a new or renewed moral ground upon which the patient may stand. This ground is constructed, I will argue in chapter nine, in part through the implicit moral understandings developed and enacted within the therapy hour, and in part through renewed access to a committed, creative relationship with hitherto unacknowledged or dismissed aspects of the intersecting moral traditions that make up the patient's life. By directly acknowledging the central role of moral discourse within psychotherapy, therapeutic practices will have the opportunity to be less the exercise of a "disguised ideology,"[6] and thus less an unknowing instrument of those forces that have shaped the arrangements of power, privilege, and meaning predominant in our late twentieth-century society. It is to the carrying out of this task that this book is dedicated.

CHAPTER TWO

Selves, Illnesses, Healers, Technologies

Billy couldn't read Tralfamadorian,
of course, but he could at least see how
the books were laid out—in brief clumps of
symbols separated by stars. Billy
commented that the clumps might be
telegrams. . . .

"There are no telegrams on
Tralfamadore. But you're right: each
clump of symbols is a brief, urgent
message—describing a situation, a scene.
We Tralfamadorians read them all at once,
not one after the other. There isn't any
particular relationship between all the
messages, except that the author has
chosen them carefully, so that, when
seen all at once, they produce an image of
life that is beautiful and surprising and deep.
There is no beginning, no middle, no end, no
suspense, no moral, no causes, no
effects. What we love in our books
are the depths of many marvelous
moments seen all at one time."
    —KURT VONNEGUT, JR.
    SLAUGHTERHOUSE FIVE

Unlike the Tralfamadorians, it is not easy for us to put into words the multilayered richness of paradox, humor, mystery, terror, awe, and tragedy that is life in human culture. But that is what each of the current critical approaches to the social sciences and the humanities—variously referred to as social constructionism, cultural history, cultural psychology, feminist theory, and philosophical hermeneutics—is trying to do, each within the limitations of its respective discipline, and each with its overmatched (that is, un-Tralfamadorian) research language. The driving force behind this book is the belief that to develop historically and culturally situated interpretations of our activities, systems, and institutions—by writing cultural history in ways that imitate, however crudely, the instantaneous, multilayered approach of a Tralfamadorian novel—and to grasp the remarkable interrelatedness of a culture—to sense for an instant how the disparate pieces of the social fabric are woven into the whole, how they politically reinforce, reproduce, collude with, resist, and reshape one another, to understand the innocence, the cynicism, the terror, and the brave fiction of it all—that is the task of interpretive, cultural history.

By experiencing history in this way, we will be forced to develop an understanding of the precariously constructed foundation upon which human social life is built. Simply acknowledging that our most cherished beliefs and institutions are constructions, and not reality itself, that chaos lurks just beneath our various constructions is potentially too disorienting for us to often tolerate. From my own work I am sure of one thing: Historians and psychologists who use the interpretive, cultural history approach will inevitably find themselves at the edge of an awe-inspiring and terrifying abyss. An old Bloom County cartoon comes to mind:

Oliver Wendell Jones, the prepubescent scientist-computer hacker genius, is sitting on the roof of his house, gazing at the heavens through his powerful telescope. But even though he is a genius, he is still only a young child, and after a short time he is overcome by the terrible complexity of space and the insignificance of human life. He drops the telescope, runs into his room, and dives into bed for comfort. For a while he just shakes. Later he staggers to the kitchen to wallow "in the welcome mundanity of a chocolate chip cookie."[1] The reality of it all is just too much for Oliver, but he does see the majesty of it, if only for a moment. We should all be so lucky.

I hope, during the course of this book, that we might have a moment or two like that together. If there is any current subject likely to stir up that response, it is the fit between psychotherapy and the historical eras in which it flourishes. To lessen the confusion inherent in this project, for the most part I will use the terms *social constructionism* and *philosophical hermeneutics* in order to refer to the perspective that guides this book, even though these two approaches do have their differences.[2] What is important is not what the approach is called but what it stands for: a determination to focus on the everyday, lived *context* of whatever, or whoever, one is studying. This approach focuses on situating one's object of study in the cultural and historical context in which it is embedded. People and things exist only within a certain political and moral context, and they are not understandable outside of it. Studying humans by abstracting them from their cultural context and observing them in a dispassionate, putatively objective manner in the psychological laboratory is more akin to removing a fish from water than picking up a rock from its resting place. Studying people in a scientistic way renders them lifeless. Individuals and their context form a dialogical, interpenetrating *unit*. By studying one, the researcher inevitably studies the other. Also, in undertaking a research project, the researcher brings his or her own cultural frame of reference into the picture, which continually and unavoidably frames and shapes the process.

I hope that by studying the interpenetrating relationship between psychotherapy and Western—particularly American—society in eras past, we will be able to develop interpretations about their current relationship, and our current era.

SOCIAL CONSTRUCTIONISM

The social constructionist argument can be simply stated through eight basic propositions. One, humans do not have a basic, fundamental, pure human nature that is transhistorical and transcultural. We are incomplete and therefore unable to adequately function unless we are embedded in a specific cultural matrix composed of language, symbols, moral understandings, rituals, rules, institutional arrangements of power and privilege, origin myths and explanatory stories, ritual songs, and costumes.

Two, the cultural matrix "completes" humans by explaining and interpreting the world, helping them to focus their attention on or ignore certain aspects or potential aspects of their environment, instructing and forbidding them to think and act in certain ways. Culture infuses individuals through the social practices of the everyday world, shaping and forming in the most fundamental ways how humans conceive of the world and their place within it, how they see others, how they engage in a moral framework of mutual obligations and responsibilities, where they are located in a hierarchical structure of local power relations, and how they use all of this to determine their own behavior and make choices.

Thus culture is not indigenous "clothing" that covers the universal human; rather it is an integral part of each individual's psychological flesh and bones. In Maurice Merleau-Ponty's famous phrase, culture, through everyday social practices, is "sedimented" in the body. This is what is meant by the social "construction" of the individual. For instance, an "accent" is an example of how a social practice, language, sediments a culture in the body of the speaker. Each language requires the production of certain sounds, while other sounds are never used; the Xhosa click, or the Hebrew letter *chet* are just two among a multitude of examples. Although the human speech apparatus is initially capable of performing all human sounds, after years of performing only certain sounds, a speaker experiences increasing difficulty making sounds particular to other languages, and in fact may find it impossible. It is as if the mouth has been trained in such a way that it loses its capacity to accomplish what it was once capable of. The physical body has thus been shaped by the language it performs: It has been constructed by social practices.

Three, the material objects we create, the ideas we hold, and the actions we take are shaped in a fundamental way by the social framework in which we have been raised. They have been created out of the particular perspective of a specific historical and cultural situation and therefore they express that perspective. They are cultural artifacts.

Four, these cultural artifacts, however, are not only the reflection or expression of an era. They are the immediate "stuff" of daily life, and as such they shape and mold the community's generalized reality orientation in subtle and unseen ways. One can see the quiet, everyday influence of artifacts in cultural differences pertaining to language (using the active or passive voice); clothing (wearing a two-piece swimsuit or a chador); the marking of time (using the seasons, the phases of the moon, or a wristwatch); the concept of the self (conceiving of the individual as simply part of the larger communal whole or as the isolated, autonomous self); religious rituals (speaking to the gods or feeding them through animal sacrifices, praying three times each day or once a week, singing communally or whispering in private); monetary exchange (reading a price tag, bartering, or public bargaining); and eating utensils (using chopsticks, fingers, or a knife and fork).

One of the most complex examples of the influence of the social realm is the social construction of gender. Feminist constructionists have developed a body of research studying issues such as the cultural definitions of gender, the development of gender identity, the varieties of sexual choice, the political meanings of psychopathology commonly attributed to females—such as hysteria, borderline personality disorder, depression, and eating disorders; and the influence of the power relations of gender on therapeutic activities such as transference-counter-transference dynamics, conceptualizations of "healthy" or "functional" family systems, and statements pertaining to "universal" maleness or femaleness and "normal" child development.

Five, owing to the dual nature of cultural artifacts (that is, that they both reflect and reproduce their era), one task of human science is to develop understandings about the contextual meanings and functions of these artifacts. The researcher's job is not to describe an artifact as an end in itself, a reified "thing" that has an existence and meaning apart from what is imputed to it by the culture, but rather to discuss the artifact in such a way as to interpret the particular social construction of the era and culture in which it was produced. Seen in this way, the research task is to interpret the multitudinous and conflicting ways in which various worlds are constructed and human meanings developed.

Six, because cultural artifacts express aspects of the society from which they are created, they also reinforce and reproduce the constellations of power, wealth, and influence that dominate in that society. Artifacts are not benign, apolitical coincidences; they are part of very subtle and effective social contrivances that keep human communities functioning and surviving.

Seven, researchers should concentrate on describing and explaining how the particular social constructions of a specific society are communicated to the individuals who are born and raised within it, as well as (a) how artifacts are produced by certain social constructions, and (b) how artifacts in turn reproduce current social constructions and reinforce current understandings of the good and concomitant arrangements of power and wealth. This means that the researcher's task is to define in each culture what constitutes the broad cultural framework, the institutional structures, and finally the everyday artifacts that instruct, influence, and shape the individual's moment-by-moment perspective and experiences. Having done that, it will be easier for the researcher to interpret (a) how the cultural framework is communicated to the community, (b) how the community's artifacts express, represent, or shift the framework, and (c) how those artifacts in turn influence the community, slightly change the existing social construction of the era, or in general continue the status quo.

For instance, the character of U.S. society in the twentieth century reveals itself in part through the broad concept of the masterful, bounded, isolated individual who has what has been called "a richly furnished interior." This broad concept is then translated into and expressed by smaller and more easily transmittable cultural units such as psychological theories (developmental theories that describe "psychological separation" as inevitable and "individuation" as inherently desirable); architecture that emphasizes private, enclosed areas and ignores public, open spaces; pop culture that teaches the value of cosmetic beauty and individual competitiveness and acquisitiveness (T.V. soap operas, game shows, commercial advertisements) that treat these values as "normal" and "good"; current language usage ("the *real* you," "your *inner* life"); psychotherapy practices (individual therapies that stress the development of the "true" as opposed to the "false" self; or mass-marathon psychology training sessions that help participants get in touch with their "true," "inner" feelings). These cultural artifacts in turn have an impact on the era's character, which again is expressed in broad cultural concepts. And the cycle continues.

Eight, because the West's concept of the bounded, autonomous self is an expression of the current historical era, that concept of the self plays certain roles in the reinforcement and reproduction of that era, serving whatever forces may benefit from the current configuration of power and wealth. Because the dominant dynamic of our era is consumerism, the preeminence of the isolated, autonomous self is probably, somehow, both a consequence of that dynamic and a means of reinforcing and reproducing it. Following the constructionist perspective we could ask How is the current Western concept of the self communicated to individuals? and How does it fit the dominant moral themes of our era, thereby reinforcing the current political constellation of power and wealth? These questions would lead to an examination of how the current configuration of the self creates in individuals compliance with the rules related to the current vision of the good; the power relations of race, gender, and class; and the absences and desires that fuel the insatiable consumer wish for a continuing stream of new items, calories, experiences, role models, and identities.

PHILOSOPHICAL HERMENEUTICS

Martin Heidegger and Hans-Georg Gadamer argued that it is not possible to exist as a human being outside of a cultural context.[3] People can exist only within a cultural framework that is carved out of the sensory bombardment of potential perceptions and possible ways of being. The carving out is done through the use of cultural artifacts during the exercise of social practices, especially that of language. The bombardment of perceptions and possibilities is like a forest, and the carved out space is like a "clearing" in the forest. The clearing of a particular culture is created by the components of its conceptual systems and transmitted from one individual to the next and one generation to the next through their communal traditions of shared understandings and linguistic distinctions. It is only within the clearing that things and people "show up" in certain shapes and with certain characteristics. The paradox of the clearing is thought to be caused by its horizonal nature: Horizons are created by the culture's particular way of perceiving. The placement of the horizon determines what there is "room for" and what is precluded from view. That is, the clearing is both liberating, because it makes room for certain possibilities, and limiting, because it closes off others. Horizons are thought to be perspectival, and therefore moveable. For instance, what shows up as a chair in one culture might show up in another as firewood, or what shows up as a fork might in another culture show up as a weapon.

To use a more complicated example, the modern era in Western society, usually thought to have begun in the sixteenth century, slowly developed an intense belief in rationality and the scientific practices of quantification and objectification. As a result, many extraordinary things "show up" in this modern clearing, such as electricity, the internal combustion engine, modern medicine, and space travel. However, the West has been unable to develop room for a moral discourse that can keep pace with its scientific practices.[4] As a result, the West continues to make marvelous scientific discoveries but has difficulty using them for the common good, because it cannot develop a consensus about what *is* the common good. So, although many wonderful tools show up in the clearing of the West, the moral understandings and authority that are needed to use these tools have little room to appear.

Thus there is good news and bad new about the clearing: The good news is that the cultural clearing is constructed by social practices, and therefore its horizons of understanding are somewhat moveable. The bad news is that the horizons of the clearing are difficult for any tradition to move quickly under any circumstances, and because horizons are tied to the moral vision, economic structures, and power relations of the society, certain individuals and groups will forcefully resist any attempt at change.

Heidegger and Gadamer are the two foremost proponents of philosophical hermeneutics. I resisted using the concepts of the clearing and the horizon in this chapter because they are unusual turns of the phrase, and as a result they sound like jargon. But I decided to bring them into the discussion because they are useful terms that can aid in developing other ideas that are essential to understanding the history of psychotherapy. *Hermeneutics* is itself a word that sounds strange to many of us. It is a philosophical term that refers to a tradition in the humanities that at first related to the careful textual analysis of sacred books. It was originally thought that God's precise ideas and intentions could be deciphered because they were concretely signified in the text. Thus the ancient rabbis poured over the Hebrew Bible, trying to find explanations for why a specific word in Genesis might be misspelled or incorrectly conjugated or pluralized. They viewed these anomalies as clues to God's opinions and used them as opportunities to interpret God's hidden messages.[5] In the nineteenth century in Europe, certain philosophers, drawing from the earlier hermeneutic tradition, developed ways of analyzing texts and studying people that were in opposition to the physical science approach that up to that point was dominant in the humanities and social sciences. These thinkers claimed that social science had to be an *interpretive* science, that to understand people one had to use methods that were different from the objectivism and scientism of the modern age.

During the twentieth century, Heidegger and Gadamer, among others, have argued that there is no single truth to be found when studying humans—that there are many truths, depending, among other things, on the historical and cultural context of the observed and the observer. Because humans are always embedded in a particular historical and cultural frame of reference, Gadamer has argued that it is impossible to attain objectivity, and in fact the pursuit of objectivity will only lead to concealment of the clearing's inevitable political and moral framework. A research agenda, he argued, is *always* framed by the shared understandings and limits of the researcher's clearing: There is nowhere else to stand. As a result, researchers can only understand an object by attempting to place it within its larger context, and they can only understand the whole by studying its elements. Thus, research is unavoidably a process of tacking between the part and the whole, between the researcher's context and the object's context, between the familiar and the unknown. This is the hermeneutic circle, and it is basic to the research process. What is familiar is always, first and foremost, what has been given to the researcher by his or her culture—the possibilities and limitations of the understandings that constitute the clearing. Gadamer has called these understandings "prejudices." This idea is crucial to Gadamer's vision. Understandings or prejudices constitute the parameters of the clearing— without them, there is no horizon, and without a horizon, there is no clearing. This is why Gadamer decried the "prejudice against prejudice" that is characteristic of the scientific worldview. He believed that prejudice has obscured the fundamental importance of the researcher's perspective. The study of any cultural artifact or any individual or group, Gadamer argued, is unavoidably the study of the *source* of its being, its cultural context.

HERMENEUTICS AND THE SELF

Currently one of the most discussed and yet most elusive of psychological concepts is "the self." Psychotherapy theories in particular often speak of the self, treating it as a transhistorical, universal human complex of qualities without ever adequately defining it. In this book, however, I will not use the concept of the self to imply some universal human experience of subjectivity. Instead I will use the interpretive hermeneutic definition of the self: the concept of the individual as described by the indigenous psychology of a particular cultural group and the shared moral understandings within a particular culture of what it means to be human.[6] The self embodies what the culture believes is humankind's place in the cosmos—its limits, talents, expectations, and prohibitions. In this hermeneutic sense the self is an integral aspect of the horizon of shared understandings. There is no universal, transhistorical self, only local selves; there is no universal theory about the self, only local theories.

Studying the self of a particular era in this way allows us to put into play a basic tenet of interpretive hermeneutics: the process of studying humans is not the same as "reading" persons as "texts,"[7] but more like standing behind them and reading over their shoulder the cultural text from which they themselves are reading.[8] That is what I am suggesting we do when studying the configuration of the self: read over our subjects' shoulders. It is difficult to get a perspective on the concept of the self precisely because it is such a central aspect of the horizon. We have trouble imagining the self in any other way than the way we have configured it in our era, or to consider it a legitimate subject for study. Also, because a hermeneutic study of the self might expose various political and economic issues that would potentially threaten mainstream institutions and activities, such as the cultural dominance of consumerism, mainstream researchers are often hesitant to undertake such projects. But as difficult and risky as it is, studying the self is also a crucial element in interpreting an era. When it comes to a discussion of the psychotherapy of an era, the configuration of the self is an indispensable element of the puzzle.

THE SELF AND ITS ERA:
A FOUR-PART PROPOSAL

Psychotherapists might not like thinking historically, but we must; and eventually, we will. The question is not so much a matter of *if*. With the pressures from the constructionist critique and the epistemological crisis within psychology, thinking historically is ultimately unavoidable. The question is more a matter of *how*. By what processes and through which philosophical frameworks are therapists to undertake a historical examination of the field? History is no more a giant camera or microscope than any other discipline. There is no single, true history waiting to be discovered by the objective, removed historian. The same issues and problems apply to the attempt to situate psychotherapy as to the attempt to study any human experience. If we seek to understand psychotherapy not as an objective, inert thing that exists apart from history and culture but as a reflection and shaper of the eras in which it is embedded, then we will be attempting to *interpret* psychotherapy's history, not find and reflect on the one pure truth about it. We will be seeking to develop contextual histories of psychotherapy, histories that attempt to articulate its historical antecedents, economic constituents, and political consequences.

The goal of a contextualized history of psychotherapy, as I imagine it, would be to develop understandings about the subtle interplay between the culture and its artifacts, between America and what it means to be an American, between what it means to be an American and what it means to be human, between the construction of the self and the construction of the country. Our goal would be to understand psychotherapy by understanding America, and vice versa. That is what I am trying to begin. If we do not situate psychotherapy in its historical context, I am concerned that we will not do justice to the brave and creative effort that it is, nor will we be able to see our way to new constructions of theory and practice that will extend the therapist's capacity to help others. Because we have not yet been able to develop that kind of a history, we have had difficulty realizing when our practices collude with, support, and even reproduce the institutions and social practices that cause the very psychological ills we try to heal. However, if we situate psychotherapy historically, we might be able to develop social practices that will shape a slightly new configuration of the self, one that will be composed of new moral understandings and be capable of developing new political and economic structures, structures that could lessen the country's capacity to injure and destroy its own citizens and those of other nations.

I would like to suggest that we use four signposts to interpret particular eras and cultures—according to historical and cultural judgments indigenous to each era or culture: (1) the predominant configuration of the self of a particular cultural or historical "clearing"; (2) the illnesses with which that self was characteristically afflicted; (3) the institutions or officials most responsible for healing those illnesses; and (4) the technologies that the particular institutions or practitioners have used in order to heal that self's characteristic illnesses.

When undertaking such a task, it is important to remember that the predominant configuration of the self of our current era is not universal and transhistorical. The self has been configured in order to conform to the requirements of a particular time and place. Just as the Athenian playwright healed the communal self of classical Greece, and just as the hand-to-hand combat of a holy crusade healed the self by solidifying the Christian knight's relationship with his feudal lord and with God, so in our world it is psychotherapy that is one of the institutions responsible for healing the illnesses of the masterful, bounded twentieth-century self.

The central idea about this four-part proposal for the study of the self is that eras or cultures form a unit. There are not universal illnesses any more than there is a universal self. The self of a specific era is constructed by the clearing of that era and thus develops certain particular characteristics. It is, for instance, strong in certain areas and weak in others, unaffected by certain emotional problems, and quite vulnerable to others. A particular, local self will thus develop certain illnesses and likewise be welcoming and hopeful about a particular healer, the person or institution who "shows up" in the clearing as a gifted, powerful doctor. This local healer will, of course, be trained in the healing arts of the local community, and the healing technology will fit with the local frame of reference. It would make little sense if the healer "saw" a different illness than the patient thought he suffered from, or if the healer performed a medical or religious practice, or prescribed a medicine, that the patient thought was dangerous, repugnant, humiliating, ridiculous, or immoral. These things appear as packages; each element is part of the unit.

Cultural packages like selves, illnesses, healers, technologies can tell us a good deal about a culture if we can remember that they are local and not universal. To unquestioningly or glibly equate the self-package of one culture with that of another, or to analyze the self-package of one culture solely through the distinctions and understandings of another is to show disrespect toward or to commit a kind of psychological imperialism against a local community. However, let us also remember that philosophical hermeneutics suggests that it is not possible to be objective and neutral while trying to understand a different culture. Researchers do not "see" or "discover" the one, reified truth of a culture; they construct a truth through the process of collecting, studying, and analyzing. What researchers construct is always, in part, a product of their cultural frame of reference, and therefore the moral and political agenda they are trying to prove or justify. Since prejudices are unavoidable, and in fact, indispensable to our ability to "see" and analyze *anything*, we have to become comfortable with a central paradox of the constructionist, interpretive enterprise: we should not impose the notions or prejudices of our cultural clearing, and yet we cannot help but do so. The trick, I suppose, is to be *aware* of what we are doing. As Gadamer, Martin Packer and Richard Addison, and Anthony Stigliano have suggested, the tacking between the detail and the unit, and the other and the familiar, is the essence of the hermeneutic circle.[9] The two are in a comparative or dialectical relationship: you can't know one without the other. Somehow if we are going to be curious and inquisitive in the world, we will have to learn how to tolerate the paradoxes inherent in being culturally and historically embedded beings. We will have to learn how to develop a sense of humor about the impossible position of being human, about being apart from and a part of, uninitiated and knower, stranger and landsman.

THE SELF IN CULTURAL AND HISTORICAL PERSPECTIVE

For those of us educated in the social sciences, or the "great books" perspective in the humanities, a hermeneutic study of the self across time and culture can be something of a shock. We in the West are accustomed to thinking that humans are all basically the same underneath our different cultural clothing, that the concerns the middle class struggles with in contemporary society are at bottom the same concerns with which all other classes, societies, and cultures struggle. To glimpse the possibility that that is not so comes as an unwelcome surprise. The idea that we are not all identical "under the skin" strikes at the heart of the liberal heritage in the West that began with the modern era. It rightly causes us to question some fundamental ideas we have held regarding humankind's place in the universe, our responsibilities to others, the fragility of life as we know it. In short, it causes us to question anew what it means to be human.

Information from non-Western cultures and earlier eras in the West regarding their particular configurations of the self, the illnesses that plague those selves, the identities of those responsible for healing those ills, and the healing technologies they use to heal offers an array of evidence that seems to support the constructionist, hermeneutic argument. Space does not permit a detailed discussion of such evidence,[10] but I would like to briefly mention two examples of non-Western configurations of the self. The first is the Maori concept of what Jean Smith calls the "organs of experience."[11] When Smith studied the Maori, an indigenous Polynesian people of New Zealand, in the early 1970s, they believed that, no matter what one's status or station in life, one is only someone within a kinship group; the Maori believed that one would lose the status of being human once separated from kin. The Maori's first responsibility was to the group, not to themselves.

The Maori did not believe that feelings were caused by psychological conflicts or problems that could be rationally understood and then modified or controlled. Organs were thought to generate a certain way of being that unfolded over time. The Maori believed that various organs were responsible for certain feelings. When an organ was invaded by an outside force, the force stimulated the organ to release the emotions with which that organ was identified; when the intrusion stopped, the emotion subsided.

The Maori experienced emotions—such as fear before battle, grief and mourning, or personal confusion, insecurity, and indecision—as intrusions from the outside, attacks upon the various organs responsible for the specific emotion or mental state. The organs of experience were thought to become invaded for various reasons, usually related to external causes such as the anger of the ancestral gods (often on account of an unacceptable performance of a ritual) or an attack by one's enemies from another village. Healing rituals also used powers external to the inflicted individual, such as rituals to appease the gods, or the activity of passing close by the organs of another member of the village, especially the vagina, which were considered to possess a powerful curative force. Interestingly, the Maori believed that functions of the mind such as memory, cognition, volition, which the West locates in the brain, resided in the intestines.

The Maori did not take responsibility for their feelings; feelings were thought to happen to them. According to the Maori, the self, then, possessed a much more fluid or porous personal boundary than does the Western self. Feelings were conceptualized as being "in" individuals, but not "of" them.[12]

The second example is from the Lohorung Rai, a Mongol hill tribe in East Nepal studied extensively by Charlotte Hardman in the years 1976–79.[13] The Lohorung Rai lived a life that revolved around their community and especially their felt obligations to ancestors and traditions. They believed that humans are related not only to their immediate social group but also to a wider physical and spiritual world. Their relationship to spirits of the dead, their community's ancestors, and primeval beings determined their mental and physical states. The Lohorung Rai believed that the body was intimately involved with the ancestors through three spiritual but physical substances: *niva* (mind), located primarily in the stomach and secondarily in the head; *saya* (ancestral substance), also located in the head; and *niwa* (the soul or essence of life), located throughout the body. *Saya*, the ancestral substance, was the direct connection with the forebears. When the connection between individuals and the tradition was strong, that is, when individuals acted properly (were cooperative and emotionally sensitive to others) and were respectful and attentive to the traditions, it was said that their *saya* was "high." Then they manifested the qualities of strength, courage, and vitality, and they prospered physically and financially. When they were not properly attentive to the traditions, their *saya* became depleted; they became weak, apathetic, nervous, physically ill, depressed, socially withdrawn, and financially poor. It was said that one's *saya* could be imagined as a flower in the world of the ancestors. If *saya* was high, the flower bloomed; if *saya* was low, the flower wilted and drooped. *Saya* was in constant need of attention, revitalization, lifting.[14]

Again, as in the Maori, we can see how the Lohorung Rai self was much more a communal self than the individualistic self of the West. It was a self much less boundaried and much more influenced by others and particularly by the vitality of its connection with the ancestors. This idea is movingly captured by the image of the *saya* flower that lives in the world of the ancestors. Interestingly, the soul (*niwa*) was thought to be built, or constructed, during the time the child was educated and initiated into the traditional stories and moral understandings of the culture. In this way, we might say that an adult *niwa*, the soul, was communally built.

In the West, there have been many pre-twentieth century configurations of the self. I have included in the appendix a summary of various historical eras in Western society, giving particular attention to the selves, illnesses, healers, and healing technology framework described above. Our contemporary idea of what it means to be human, of what is the proper and natural way of being, was probably not shared by our ancestors, and it certainly is not shared by peoples of other cultures. This might help us better understand why the current configuration of the self, the masterful, bounded self of the twentieth century, is considered an aberration by many other cultures and would have been considered unthinkable (literally) by Westerners in earlier times, say six hundred, a thousand, or two thousand years ago. In reading the appendix one can see how several configurations of the self, as Shakespeare wrote, strutted and fretted their "hour upon the stage" and then were heard no more. There was the "nondeep" self of the ancient Greeks; the self of the Hebrews that was a communal, equal partner with God; the empty, self-loathing Augustinian self; the crusading Christian self of the Middle Ages, container for the immortal soul, which lived in a circular, enchanted world, and which healed through obedience to warrior vows and by delivering death and destruction to the infidel; the Renaissance self with a foot in both the feudal and the about-to-dawn modern era; the rational, logical self of the Enlightenment era, intent on separating from the Church and local folkways; the romantic self that valorized the autonomous, all-powerful artist-genius who naturally contained the pure truth of the universe interiorly; and the Victorian self, the culmination of the Enlightenment agenda of linearity, deferred gratification, and bourgeois calculation. Each of these selves are part of the heritage of the West. Each of these selves, all sure that they were the one, proper way of being human, all sure that their way of arranging the power relations of gender, race, community, and age was the one natural arrangement, all sure that their God was the only true God, are the antecedents of our current self. It is a humbling, disorienting vision.

It is difficult for us to grasp the medieval experience of life, to experience ourselves and our world as being held in the hand of God, to be more identified with the corporate feudal community, the group self, than with a separate, unique self; to regard a person's sociocommunal *position* as more important than the person who occupies it. The modern era, of course, began to shift that perspective. In the appendix, I use historian Natalie Zemon Davis' *The Return of Martin Guerre*[15] to illustrate the modern lurch into a more individualistic, competitive, potentially "false" world. But what is so compelling about the story is how it describes individuals who live with one foot in each world. In the story, taken from an event in the early sixteenth century in the Basque region of France, a man claims to be Martin Guerre, who long before had abandoned the rural village of his youth, his wife, and his children. The village, shocked but joyous, welcomes him back, and life goes on, in fact much better than before. However, after several years, the man is thought to be an impostor, two trials take place, and the impostor Arnaud finally confesses and is killed. Bertrande, the wife, is spared. I argue in the appendix that without the medieval concept of the self as placeholder and without the legal reality of male privilege, the imposture would not have been needed (Bertrande could have inherited and managed Martin's estate, been free to remarry, and so on); but also, without the Renaissance concept of self-fashioning and imposture, the deed could never have been conceived of and carried through. I also argue that without the growing popularization of the experience of romantic love, Bertrande and Arnaud would never have been able to carry the deceit through to its final conclusion. It is a story conceived of, enacted, and concluded in the paradoxes characteristic of the two eras it straddles.

By the time of the Enlightenment, a concept of the self as an entity independent of the corporate entanglements of Church, communal identity, and feudal vow had become a distinct possibility. But then new problems arose. The Enlightenment era philosophers, ancestors of the social scientist, grappled with questions pertaining to the meaning of truth, the attainment of certainty, and the determination of the good in a world increasingly distanced from God's presence, His all-protecting hand, and the authoritative guidance of His embodiment on earth, the Church. These questions emerged in the early modern era owing in part to the vast socioeconomic changes brought on by the growth of individualism and capitalism, which in turn caused the fall of the feudal structure and increasing urbanization, the Reformation, and (slowly) a secularization of the population. These political changes then increased the population's readiness to accept the new philosophy. Much later, of course, the continuing advances of the new empirical sciences brought about the industrialization of Europe and the New World, which increased and multiplied the aforementioned trends.

However, the philosophers not only answered questions; they also *created* questions. They were not simply dispassionate, "objective" truth-seekers; they were *directly* involved in the political struggles of their era. Central to the struggle was the configuration of the self. If the feudal institutions of Church and community had weakened, then who would come forward to help configure and guide the new self that was emerging? Why, the philosophers, of course. And they did, indeed, grapple with questions related to the meaning and attainment of truth, the definition of personal and political freedom, and the exercise of rationality, logic, and individual choice.

But the philosophers did more than that. They exercised power by establishing the frame of reference for the era. They not only filled the vacuum created by the fall of the Church; they helped *cause* the vacuum. Descartes based all knowledge on universal doubt. He put forth a radical idea: The material world, far from the enchanted world of the Middle Ages, was in fact *devoid* of God. It was made by God, of course, but then abandoned by Him. The spiritual, on the other hand, was graced by the spirit of God, but it was a realm separated from the material realm by an unbridgeable gulf. In the natural scheme of things, human abilities situated in the immaterial or spiritual realm—such as logic and reason—were capable of understanding, manipulating, and then ultimately dominating the material realm. Descartes's formulation of two distinct and separate worlds was eagerly embraced and extended by Locke, Hume, and a horde of empiricists. If the material world was devoid of God, then centuries of accumulated Church knowledge had lost its unquestioned authority, and the Monarchy its divine warrant. Knowledge about the material world could only be discovered through the exercise of objective scientific processes, which were not influenced by ecclesiastical authority, military might, or folk traditions. Knowledge, in turn, was the fulcrum by which the material realm was moved. Interpreted in this way, the Enlightenment era philosophers had used intellectual discourse to exercise political power. By setting the frame of reference in this way, they raised doubts about the authority of the Church, the power of the Monarchy, and the salience of communal folkways. Under the guise of objective, apolitical science, they initiated, reflected, promoted, and carried out a revolution in thinking and authority. They became the sole owners of the scientific process, the only true path to knowledge.

Who then could determine what was right and wrong, good and bad, what ways of being were proper and improper—in other words, the correct configuration of the self? Why, those trained in the new empiricism and the exercise of logic, answered the philosophers. Indeed, empiricists such as Locke and Hume argued that the self was not created fully formed by God. It had to be fashioned and formed—not by the Church, or the traditional folkways of the medieval community, but by the careful formulations of logic and the empirical "truth" determined by the sciences. The self ceased to be the container of the God-given soul, the material world ceased to be the territory that God created and over which He actively presided, and the Church ceased to be the owner of certainty and truth. Instead, the self became constituted by rationality and the scientific empirical process, the material world became the realm properly controlled and dominated by humankind, and the new empirical science became the vehicle of domination and the measure of all things. In future chapters I often refer to the theories of the philosophers as the "power agenda" of the Enlightenment, because their ideas advanced the political shift in power from the Church to secular institutions.[16]

Not all the philosophers, of course, were entirely pleased with the implications of the empirical line of reasoning. Kant, for instance, was concerned by the absence of morality in the empiricists' formulations. He argued that if one takes the empiricist argument to its extreme conclusions, as did Hume, one can know very little except that which one discovers in each moment of observation. Ultimately, Kant argued, this tells one nothing about developing a personal identity, understanding causal relationships, anticipating the future, or making moral choices. That was intolerable to Kant. In response he decided that inherent in each individual were certain mental *structures* that allowed one to "see" life in a certain way. These structures worked like the lenses in a pair of spectacles or, better yet, a pair of sunglasses: They "colored" one's perceptions, provided an invisible framework within which perceptions and mental categories could emerge and take form. In this way, Kant believed, humans could develop an ongoing identity, perceive categories such as causality, and use logic to determine how to live a moral life. Given the discoveries of modern science and the arguments of the radical empiricists, and unable (or unwilling) to discuss the social realm as an adequately powerful shaper of the frame of reference, Kant had to invent inherent or a priori mental categories in order to attend to and explain what the empiricists thought unimportant or unexplainable. In this way, the philosophical movement known as structuralism was born. Several current psychotherapy theories—most notably Freudian and Jungian psychoanalysis, Melanie Klein's object relations theory, and forms of cognitive therapy—are indebted to structuralist notions of the mind.

Later in the modern era, especially with the romantic movement of the late eighteenth and early nineteenth centuries, some philosophers and literary figures rebelled against the Enlightenment emphasis on science, rationality, objectivity, and logic. The romantics instead sought truth in the artistic, the subjective, and the emotional. But the Enlightenment era frame of reference was so well established that even the romantics never challenged modern individualism. In fact, in some ways the romantics valued a kind of hyperindividualism even more than did the empiricists. Whereas the Enlightenment thinkers made a god out of science, the romantics deified the subjectivity and beauty of nature and the heroic, artistic self. The self, they believed, had an inherent, perfect nature that would grow, organically, if simply left alone by Church, state, and society.

The Victorian era was in many ways the culmination of the Enlightenment philosophers' power agenda. Victorians believed that the material world could be quantified, objectively measured, and logically manipulated and dominated for personal gain by a masterful, bounded individualism. For instance, laissez-faire capitalism, justified by Adam Smith's belief that unrestricted selfishness would ultimately lead to the perfection of society and be to the benefit of all, reached its prominence at this time.[17] Some historians have argued that once the external world was thought to be entirely quantifiable, controllable, and thus understandable, it was a short step to locating the unknowable within the interior of the self-contained individual.[18] Thus the Freudian unconscious was "discovered" during this era. The struggles and conflicts Freud located within the unconscious were, in retrospect, not unlike the fierce political conflicts, such as the imperialist wars, anti-Semitism, and gender oppression that showed up in Europe throughout this era. The political oppression of women, which they were unable to express directly in words, often took the form of psychosomatic symptoms, which the medical profession attributed to the inherent nature of the untameable female body, especially its reproductive organs. The Victorian self was conceptualized as containing secret, mysterious, and dangerous urges for sex and aggression. These urges were controllable by various defense mechanisms such as repression; but too much repression, Freud argued, caused neurosis. Rational self-domination, brought to consciousness through introspection, was one aspect of Freud's solution. Too little rational self-domination, however, would mean the destruction of civilization. The European Victorian self was caught, to paraphrase novelist Edgar Allan Poe, between the pit and the pendulum.

This is merely a brief exploration of Western history. The appendix, however, contains an expanded discussion of these eras and configurations of self. Even this brief look at Western history brings up many troubling questions regarding the configuration of the self. How are we to decide how to live, if we cannot think that our current configuration of the self is the one, true, universal self? How can we decide how to live when we are not embedded in the kind of enfolding, all-encompassing indigenous tradition that many Western eras were informed by? This is indeed a troubling—no terrifying—dilemma. This dilemma is our fate, but perhaps it is also our opportunity, if we can embrace it.

CHAPTER THREE

The Self in America

*[G]radually I became aware of the old island
here that flowered once for Dutch sailors'
eyes—a fresh, green breast of the new
world. Its vanished trees, the trees that had
made way for Gatsby's house, had once
pandered in whispers to the last and greatest
of all human dreams; for a transitory
enchanted moment man must have held his
breath in the presence of this continent . . .
face to face for the last time in
history with something commensurate to his
capacity for wonder. . . . I thought of
[Gatsby's dream]. . . . He did not know that
it was already behind him, somewhere back in
that vast obscurity beyond the city, where
the dark fields of the republic rolled on under
the night. Gatsby believed in the green light,
the orgiastic future that year by year recedes
before us. It eluded us then, but that's no
matter—tomorrow we will run faster,
stretch out our arms farther. . . .
And one fine morning—
So we beat on, boats against the current,
borne back ceaselessly into the past.*
          —F. SCOTT FITZGERALD
          THE GREAT GATSBY

Living as we do now, in the bustling, secular, densely populated, highly alienating urban centers of late twentieth century America, it is difficult to remember that a relatively short time ago the early American colonies, and then later the antebellum South and the western frontier were worlds substantially different from the world in which we live today. Because the people of those times lived in different worlds, they were different people than we are today. "The past," L. P. Hartley once remarked, "is a foreign country. They do things differently there."[1] However, who they were and the social arrangements they constructed still influence us. The horizons of their worlds continue to have an impact on the overall cultural framework of our world; their political structures and ways of being are selectively used by us in various ways. Groups vie for political power by invoking the heritage of earlier times, by claiming to be the inheritors of a certain moral tradition, by telling historical stories in such a way as to develop an "origin myth" about a particular geographical area, a political party, or a professional guild. These origin myths are used to justify claims such as land ownership, political legitimacy, or a place in the economic (or scientific) marketplace.

We all tell historical stories, and by doing so we all take certain moral positions that have political consequences and are meant to further political agendas. In other words, we all have an axe to grind. Mine, as you will see, is to argue that the configuration of the American self has changed over time, that there have been several healing professions that used various healing technologies in order to create, shape, and maintain a particular historical self, that all of these selves have had important political and economic functions within their eras, and that each profession responsible for healing the self has put forth the claim that the self of its era is the only proper self, that its technologies are the one true healing, and that its technologies have a transcendent warrant, usually from God, from natural law, or from the natural sciences.

Using an interpretation of American history I argue that there is no single, seamless stream of progressive healing traditions, and that current forms of psychological healing are as historically situated, and thus as morally opinionated and politically involved, as were all the earlier forms of healing. My ideas are presented in order to persuade and enlist agreement. I want to convince readers that there are good things and bad things about any sociohistorical era. I want readers to agree that there is no single, transcendent truth that can be used by humans to heal in any perfect, universal, apolitical way. I suggest that most healing technologies in the United States have been subtly complicit in the sexism, racism, and economic injustice of their eras, and that we must be vigilant in analyzing the technologies of our current era in order to acknowledge and understand their moral, political, and economic consequences. This is not a pleasant thought, especially for those of us who are either the practitioners or the patients of current healing practices. But we must do this in an effort to better understand our world, and the role we play in its construction and maintenance.

In the seventeenth century the American colonies were small, primitive, and very poor. Life centered on the Puritans' religious mission, their belief that God had intended that they find a new promised land, and the certainty that the hard work and piety of the elect would be rewarded by God in the afterlife. But with the slow but steady changes that the eighteenth century brought, life in the New World began to take on a cast that would remain throughout the nineteenth and twentieth centuries. In the eighteenth and nineteenth centuries two major issues emerged and gained increasing prominence: capitalism and the individual greed it encouraged, and racism and the political oppression it engendered. These two problems would take root and flourish in the new colonies, becoming stronger, more influential, and more disruptive with the passing decades, until they would come to dominate and eventually transfigure the political process. Both capitalism and racism can be understood in part as aspects of a fledgling immigrant nation searching for its identity— that is, as part of a people's attempt to configure the self—in a time of rapid and disorienting sociohistorical change.

In this chapter I will briefly examine several historical phenomena as a means of exploring how the self was configured in the eighteenth, nineteenth, and twentieth centuries in the United States. Jonathan Edwards's tent revival meetings in the 1730s and 1740s, known as the First Great Awakening, demonstrate the conflict between the communal Puritan self submerged in piety and compliance, and a growing entrepreneurial individualism. Negro minstrelsy, a type of popular theater in the mid-nineteenth century, and Congress's "Peace Policy" to subdue the Sioux (as enacted in the Indian Appropriations Act of 1871) demonstrate attempts by the dominant white population to define the self by determining what it *was not*: "the other." A section on the turn of the century concept of "personality" and the uses of national advertising illustrates the important changes the self is going through at that time, and highlights the emergence of "the therapeutic" as a healing metaphor. The mental hygiene movement, in combination with a recently imported Freudian psychoanalysis, is discussed in order to notice important new changes in America during the first half of the twentieth century. Finally, the post–World War II era and its new configuration of the self—the empty self—is used to demonstrate the impact of the economic force of consumerism.

THE GREAT AWAKENING:
PROTESTANT REVIVAL MEETINGS AS A TECHNOLOGY OF THE SELF

In the 1730s and 1740s a religious renewal movement swept through the New England colonies. It featured revival meetings held in large tents, itinerant preachers, fire-and-brimstone rhetoric, and a straightforward, unapologetic appeal to the emotions. Although some mainstream ministers, such as Jonathan Edwards, joined the "New Lights" group, for the most part the new preachers were young antiestablishment charismatic performers. They attracted thousands of common folk and incited dissatisfaction with mainstream churches and their usually staid, overly rational ministers. New churches sprang up, new doctrines were professed, and a whole new worship process was developed. Worshippers were thought to experience "conviction" and then "conversion." Conviction was the emotional experience within each worshipper that he or she was a sinner, corrupt, and despised by God. Conversion, of course, was the surrender of oneself to God in all one's sinfulness, and the experience of the sense of love, acceptance, and salvation that comes about through being engulfed by God. Moaning, grieving, sobbing, publicly confessing, writhing on the floor, crying out for and pleading with God were some of the more common activities under the revival tents. Although the First Great Awakening had a significant effect on American religion, by the 1750s its influence had lessened.

Surprisingly, given the emotional excesses of the revival meetings, the early modern philosopher John Locke seems to have had an important influence on Edwards's fire-and-brimstone sermons. Historian Richard Bushman has argued that one can see Locke's influence on Edwards in the central importance the revival meetings placed on using the senses to perceive the empirical truth of the glory of God. The senses could also help converts directly experience their personal "helplessness" and the emotional joy produced from the indwelling of God.[2] The tent meetings also demonstrated the influence of what would become known as a particularly American trait: colonists became *proactive* and emotionally *expressive* in their pursuit of salvation. Rather than sit passively, hoping for a sign of election, the colonists began to actively "prepare" and thus implicitly promote God's presence in their lives. Indeed, American tent revivals were known for their noisy, emotional, chaotic style. Personal "sharing" was another aspect of the meetings; Americans were more expressive and revealed more personal feelings than did their European counterparts, even at this early stage in their history. They were also more democratic; the sharing of emotions was done in the context of the nonhierarchical tent meeting, which brought together "rich and poor, men and women, powerful and weak, old and young alike."[3]

The Great Awakening played an important part in the struggle over the shaping of the mid-eighteenth century Colonial self. The economic changes that accompanied the progression of the eighteenth century set off a moral conflict that eventually caused a crisis of the self. After the influx of new colonists and with the initial taming of the severe New England wilderness in the 1600s, the colonists began to get a glimpse of the economic opportunities that the New World provided. The population expanded, the number of settlements increased, and therefore the opportunity for commercial ventures soared.[4] But to take advantage of these opportunities, colonists had to start thinking less like humble parts of a communal whole and more like ambitious separate, individual entrepreneurs. They had to think less like pious believers consumed by a wish for eternal salvation and more like separate individuals bent on the accumulation of wealth and power. As a result, for the first time in the short history of the colonies, the religious mission upon which the colonies were founded, and the people's unquestioned dedication to a life of piety and hard, honest labor in service to the community was seriously challenged. The colonies appeared confused as to how to evaluate these wishes for riches and notoriety. Were they falling prey to the sins of pride and covetousness or simply following the "natural" workings of the marketplace? This is a question about the configuration of the self, a question about what it means to be human.

In response to this crisis about the self, Edwards used the revival tent to reconstruct the Puritan communal self. He preached that only a complete renunciation of the self and a total surrender to God would be acceptable to Him. Edwards demanded that his parishioners search their souls and sacrifice themselves entirely to God; not one iota of self should be left for the individual. Conversion in the tent meetings meant a "willingness to obliterate selfishness and give all to God."[5]

The unmediated experience of God through the use of the senses and the lack of social hierarchy within the tent meetings demonstrate the early modern empiricists' power strategy in action, although in an unlikely place. The Lockean emphasis on the production of scientific truth through empirical means, as we have seen, furthered the delegitimation of the authority of the Church in Europe, which was characteristic of the modern era, and promoted early forms of individualism. Ironically, in America Edwards promoted using the senses at tent meetings to reinforce the communal, nonindividual self. Although the intention of the tent meetings was the opposite of the intention of the philosophers of the new science during the Enlightenment, empiricism was used in both contexts to oppose one way of being and support another: to promote a particular configuration of the self. In a complex way, the Puritan agenda and the early modern philosopher's agenda shared some common understandings. As a result, the change from the proactive, emotional, non-hierarchical leveling of the Great Awakening communal self to the proactive, optimistic, ambitious individualism of the entrepreneurial self of the nineteenth century was an easier transition than we might imagine. In fact, soon after the triumph of the communal self brought on by the Great Awakening, the victory was undone. As the tides of capitalism crept in and then flowed through the colonies and later the fledgling Republic, the moral frame reflected in the socioeconomic leveling of the tent meeting subtly shifted. Initially the small communities were based on self-renunciation and dedicated to a God who demanded the obliteration of individualist proclivities. But as the communities grew and became towns they were based on individual self-preservation and self-advancement and dedicated to a God who expected his flock to take personal initiative and fend for themselves and their families by acquiring wealth, knowledge, and material possessions. The democratic leveling of the tent meetings was transformed into the admonition that each individual was capable of—in fact, responsible for—economic independence and achievement. If all were equal, then each individual had an equal opportunity to fend for oneself and acquire what one could in order to insure a good life. In retrospect, it is amazing how quickly the communal self could be undone when faced with the temptations of New World wealth.

IDENTITY AND "THE OTHER" IN THE NINETEENTH CENTURY

The nineteenth century, of course, was a time of enormous change in the United States. Industrialization began in earnest, creating for the first time higher concentrations of citizens and one-dimensional, repetitive factory work. An increase in urban, European-style cities in turn brought with it a loss of community, an increase in crime, and a worsening of alienation. Waves of European immigrants poured into the East Coast ports, often from Central and Eastern European countries bringing with them languages and customs vastly different from those of the original colonies. Secularization grew, brought on by a continuation of the Enlightenment era belief in the new science and its attack on the Church in particular and organized religion in general. The triumph of the Puritan communal self over capitalism and entrepreneurial individualism during the First Great Awakening had already been shaken by cultural changes. A healthy dose of religious utopianism, usually in the form of agrarian communes, was influential but ultimately not persuasive enough to stem the tide of nineteenth-century individualism and industrial capitalism.

The growing urbanization, industrialism, secularism, and immigration combined to produce a disorientation and confusion regarding the nature and proper expression of the good. Individuals were increasingly alienated, uncertain, isolated, and frightened of the future. The shared understandings of rural colonial life no longer seemed to hold. The configuration of the self would from this century to the present be a "problem"[6] and a source of confusion and discomfort for the American public.

Two of the prime factors that shaped the nineteenth century and its configuration of the self were the struggles over slavery and the acquisition of western lands. The social arrangements pertaining to the delegation of political power and economic resources had to be continually renegotiated in the new nation. The question of the moral status and the political uses of slavery became a focal point for several important issues of the century. The Civil War, a war waged for many reasons, was one of the first of the modern wars of mass destruction. Because it was a war between different segments of the same country, its violence, bloodshed, and destruction were particularly devastating; it dealt another blow to the sense of shared understandings about the moral values and social agreements of a unified people. The Indian wars were likewise complex affairs, combining moral struggles with an unsatiable hunger for land. In the nineteenth century urban factories added to the moral confusion, disorientation, and personal sense of unreality and unworthiness settling onto the middle classes. These events—motivated by racism and greed—troubled the conscience of the nation and had a psychological impact on the population in a variety of ways.

Neither of these two wars, nor the class conflict of East Coast industrialism, could have been engaged in with quite the same misunderstandings, misrepresentations, violence, corruption, and fervor, were it not for American society's confusion over what it was to be a proper human being: over the American configuration of the self. The growing socioeconomic pressures of the nineteenth century and the increased alienation characteristic of the modern era combined to cause severe confusion about identity in the white population. The moral uncertainty about the proper way to be human moved the white population to desperate measures in an attempt to define the self of their era. The nineteenth-century American white identity strategy was based on the psychological processes used to define "the other." It was difficult for the young, increasingly diverse nation to develop a consensus as to what the self was. It was easier to develop a sense of what the self was not— the supposedly lazy, stupid Negro or the supposedly heathen, savage Indian. The white self was defined as being unlike the Negro slave and unlike the untamed Indian; it was *not* lazy, stupid, savage, and unciv- ilized. Of course, in order to use African Americans and Native Ameri- cans to help define the white self, these racial groups had to be actively redefined in specific ways. Whites accomplished this particular definition through the vehicles of popular theater and political discourse. The minstrel stage and popular and intellectual conceptions of the "wild west" served as technologies of the self. These were the vehicles by which the middle-class white self was configured.

Popular Theater and the Uses of "The Other": Negro Minstrelsy as a Technology of the Self

In 1828, during the intermission of a local drama, a small-time white actor named Jim Rice shuffled onto a stage at the Louisville Theatre. Dressed in the rags, speaking dialect, and made up in the color of an old black man he had spied upon, Rice limped and sang a tune that catapulted him into theater immortality. The song was named "Jim Crow," supposedly after the man whom Rice was imitating. It went like this:

> First on de heel tap, den on de toe,
> Ebery time I wheel about I jump Jim Crow.
> Wheel about and turn about an do jis so,
> And every time I wheel about I jump Jim Crow.[7]

A stereotypical caricature of the African American had been used before as comic relief on the American stage, but this was the first time that the caricature had stood alone as the focal point of an act. It was not, as before, a small, inconsequential bit part in a larger performance. This time it *was* the performance. For the first time, Sambo—that grotesque, clownish caricature of the black man—or rather Sambo's function, was so important to the white audience, so central to the life and thought of white America, that it commanded the very center of its cultural stage.[8] Negro minstrelsy had begun. From this humble beginning, minstrelsy was to grow until it became a dominant force in popular culture at mid- century.

A cultural movement of this size and importance had a significant impact on the feelings and thoughts of the American people. Coming as it did at a critical time in the race relations of the young country, directly before and after the Civil War, it both expressed and molded the opinions of a sizeable number of white Americans. Since most Northern whites had little direct personal contact with African Americans, the images they turned to were, out of necessity, secondhand—stories, jokes, and songs about people they did not know well and events they had never witnessed. The white man, for various reasons, had a system of racist folklore about African Americans. One of the most effective disseminators of this system of folklore was the minstrel stage.

Rice's "Jim Crow" act was a creative new idea, and it was received as such. It was an instant success, in the North perhaps even more than in the South. In New York City in 1832 Rice "probably drew more money into the box office than any American performer in the same period of time," and the "Jim Crow" song swept the country.[9]

As a testament to Rice's success, he soon had a great many imitators, all white. They, like Rice himself, always performed alone between acts of a play or circus performances. It was not until 1843, over a dozen years after Rice first performed, that the performance began to resemble what we now know as a "real" Negro minstrel show. In 1841 the four Virginia Minstrels strutted onto the stage of the Bowery Amphitheater, sat in a semicircle, wore flashy costumes complete with long, swallowtail evening coats, and played unusual instruments (violin, banjo, bones, and tambourine). They joked, sang, and jigged, ending with a song and dance breakdown to close the show.[10]

The new format and instruments were unfamiliar to audiences, and it took a while for the group performance to catch on. But catch on it did, and many groups flourished in imitation of the Virginia format. In 1847, E. P. Christy's Ethiopian Minstrels began a stand at Mechanics Hall on Broadway in New York City that played for ten years. Christy became "the unchallenged leader of his profession,"[11] and along the way his performances developed the rather strict, stereotyped format that Negro minstrelsy thereafter closely followed. The performances had two distinct sections, a first part taken from the Virginia Minstrel format, and a second, or "Olio" part. The first part consisted of a series of songs, dances, jokes, and repartee, performed by the interlocutor (the master of ceremonies and straight man) and the end men. It would end, usually before an hour was up, with either another drill, or a "walk-around" that was referred to as a "grand finale." The "Olio" consisted of a series of variety acts, in which each member of the cast performed his specialty. The show closed with a farce or a song and dance in which the whole cast would participate.

In the new format the shows continued to gain in popularity, reaching their heyday from 1850 to 1870; in the early 1880s there were at least thirty traveling companies in existence at any one time.[12] Although their popularity tapered off after that, they continued to draw crowds long after the turn of the century. It was only at this time that African-American entertainers were allowed to perform in the shows, although they were forced to black-up in order to perpetuate the stereotypical appearance of the characters. In 1926 the last of the large popular troups, the Al G. Field Minstrels, suddenly and unexpectedly closed its doors, and professional minstrelsy ended.

The foremost characteristic of the African-American male in minstrelsy (as played by the white man) was that he was always clownish and foolish, in all important ways inferior to the white man. The audience was constantly bombarded with foppish, absurd costumes, corny, low-quality jokes and puns, and exaggerated comic behavior, all in the guise of exhibiting African-American culture. Frank Dumont, describing the personality of end men in 1899, graphically illustrates the one-dimensional character of the image: "One end-man may represent the enlightened, sarcastic darkey; another, the dense fellow—jolly, but ignorant. Still another, the imitative or declamatory darkey . . . then again, you can have a sleepy, blundering fellow, mispronouncing words and totally at sea concerning ettiquette [sic] or history."[13] All of Dumont's characters, despite their differences, shared the common traits of exaggeration, inferiority, and foolishness.

Carl Wittke explained how makeup and folklore combined to portray the minstrel caricature: "The Black man was distinguished by an unusually large mouth and a peculiar kind of broad grin; he dressed in gaudy colors and in a flashy style; he usually consumed more gin than he could properly hold; and he loved chickens so well that he could not pass a chicken-coop without falling into temptation."[14] Drawings and pictures of the time depict clownish figures with absurd hairdos, enormous ears and lips, extremely wide eyes, and huge feet. Even the interlocutor, distinguished and supposedly intelligent, was unable to escape the comic role.

The primary African-American character the white audience saw was a comic, foolish, empty-headed idiot: the Sambo of white folklore. Each act was framed by the taken-for-granted understanding that the white race was inherently superior, intellectually and morally, to the black race. The minstrel characters were judged entirely by how poorly they adjusted to (that is, imitated) the dominant white culture. The most obvious example of the African American's failure to adopt the "superior" culture was his misuse of the white man's language. He either mispronounced or he uttered malaprops; either way his linguistic butchery sent his audience into fits of laughter. He wrestled with the tense of verbs and the meaning of large, impressive nouns:

Int: Pickles is beautiful! That is nice grammar.
Bones: *That is a little tough grammar; it sounds very Schenectady. I wrote back to my mother and told her neber to say "is beautiful," but always say "am beautiful." You know, Sam, a person should neber put an adverb where a semi-colon will take the place of an interrogation point.*[15]

Malapropism is intimately connected with an important trait of the minstrel character: the compulsive but unsuccessful attempt to imitate the white man. Often the most prominent symbol of imitation was the way blacks did their hair—often resorting to painful straightening and bleaching treatments for the sake of appearing like the whites.

Jake, what is the matter with your hair?
Nofin', Pete. Why?
It looks as if you had had a fever, and lost the greater part
of it.
Oh, no. I had it cut.
Cut?
Yes, it's fashionable to hab it cut de way mine is.
And how in the world could the barber cut it so short?
Wall, Pete, I'll tell you; he fust cut it wid de scissors, en he put my head in a wice, and filed it, and de way he finished it was by gibin' it a good sand-paperin'.[16]

Clothing was another favorite target of minstrelsy. The African-American male, so the story went, loved expensive, impressive, eye-catching clothes. He was enamored with the snobbery of the ever-changing fashion scene, but because the minstrel character had neither the sense nor the good taste to select his clothes wisely, the result was inevitable: his clothing was flashy, garish, grotesque, and clashing.

Romantic courtship was another arena in which the minstrel character made a deliberate attempt to imitate white culture. Predictably, he fell flat on his face. Sounding like someone from King Arthur's court, the blacked-up minstrel pranced and fawned his way across the stage in bombastic courtship rites. Because he was so inherently skilled in music, song, and dance, the minstrel character used those tools to gain his heart's true affection. He also tried his hand at poetry, but poetry is an exercise of language and intellect, so the minstrel character had to be made to fail. Thus his poems were absurd and comical.

> O you sweet and lubby Dinah!
> Dare are nofin any finer;
> Your tongue is sweeter than a parrot's.
> Your hair hanga like a bunch of carrots,
> And though of flattery I'm a hater,
> I lubs you like a sweet potater![17]

Sambo was a failure in work as well as in love. Minstrelsy portrayed only two kinds of African-American business ventures: stealing by the lower classes or cheating by the upper classes, but both, of course, failed in the end.

> M: I dare say you have reformed in a great many things. You do not
>   steal any more chickens?
> E: *No indeed. I've joined church.*
> M: Nor any turkeys?
> E: *No, sir. I tell you I've reformed.*
> M: Nor any geese?
> E: *No sir; no geese.*
> M: I am glad to hear that.
> E: *(to minstrel next to him) If he had said ducks he'd a had me.*[18]

As in business and the arts, so too in religion. Here again one finds the minstrel character desperately trying to imitate white culture and failing miserably. The minstrel character tried to be pious, but his "natural" emotions and impulses just made him look clownish and hypocritical.

> E: But say, I lost my umbrella [in church] that day, but I didn't make
>   a fuss over it. I just got up and said, "Brethern, and sistern, I've lost
>   my umbrella. I know who took it. If my umbrella isn't returned to
>   me by next Sunday, I'll get up here and mention the name of the
>   man that stole my umbrella."
> *M: What was the result?*
> E: Next morning my yard was full of umbrellas.[19]

Minstrelsy portrayed African Americans as happy-go-lucky. Their nature dictated that they be in good spirits all the time, regardless of their economic or political situation.

> Gay is the Life of a Colored Man,
>   He is bound to be happy wherever he can,
> This darkey is a gay boy, he lives the right way,
>   He's as happy as happy can be.[20]

They were happiest, of course, when they were singing and dancing and entertaining white folks.

> You've often heard of the Southern nigs,
> And what they all can do;
> . . . And when we sling our feet around,
> Just watch how we keep time.
> . . . And when we sling our feet around,
> We're happy as can be.[21]

Cheerfulness was an important quality for the minstrel character to have. Perhaps the violent oppression of African-American slaves and freed men would have been more difficult for white audiences to ignore without the minstrel claim of African-American happiness. Cheerfulness and another minstrel trait, immorality, seemed to go hand-in-hand on the minstrel stage. F. P. Gaines described the stereotypical African-American male as "cheerfully but irredeemably outside the place of moral account-ability."[22] It is that same constitutional flaw that caused him to dance and show off. The white culture's mores held humility as perhaps the greatest virtue, yet the minstrel character was grotesquely, comically vain. He held a very high opinion of himself, and his white audience delighted in his strutting.

> I've often heard it said ob late, Dat Souf Ca'lina
> Was de state, Whar handsome nigga's bound to shine,
> Like Dandy Jim of Caroline,
> For my old massa tole me so,
> I'm de best looking nigga in de country
> Oh, I look in de glass, an' I found it so,
> Just as massa tell me, oh.[23]

But all was not sweetness and light in the African-American community that was portrayed on the minstrel stage. Racial group self-hatred was an ever present component of minstrel performances. This self-hatred was expressed by the actors through dialogue laced with disparaging references to the physical attributes of African Americans, such as nappy hair, darker skin color, and also with a great deal of name-calling. The words *coon, nigger, darkey, brackman, culled pu'son, nig,* and *pick'ninny,* were essential to minstrel dialogue, sometimes comprising the entire joke or punch line. Abusive language expressing African-American self-contempt and self-hatred might have played an important function for the white audience. Perhaps it served to justify white contempt for Africans Americans and thus exonerated white-on-black discrimination and violence, and assuaged white guilt.

Besides the vast amount of minstrel material on the male African American, there is also a great deal of material about the female African American as portrayed in the Negro minstrels, about the relationship between male and female African Americans, about the relationship between higher and lower socioeconomic classes of African Americans, and, of course, about the relationship between whites and African Americans. Female African Americans were portrayed as slow-witted, lazy, ugly, vain, unclean, crude, and very sexual. They loved to dance, wear flashy clothes, and eat strange "Negro" foods such as raccoon, possum, and eel. They also ate prodigious amounts of ice cream and drank their dates under the table. They were made up to have funny hair, large ears and feet, a strangely shaped head, and a wide nose and big lips. They loved to be courted by the African-American male, and they were easily won over. They were focused on one thing: manipulating men into buying clothes and food, and proposing marriage.[24]

Given these descriptions, it should not be difficult to imagine that the relationship between males and females portrayed onstage was a stormy one. Marriages were shown as being controlled by the woman. She was the responsible one, worrying about the bills, food for the children, and holes in the roof. She also used the male, forcing him into debt and emotional depression. The male was pictured as a worthless degenerate, an irresponsible husband and father. The female minstrel character became a nagging, deceitful, and sometimes violent wife. Marital infidelity was common.[25]

The minstrel shows also portrayed the relationship between socioeconomic classes in the African-American community as a battle, a scene of constant recrimination. The conflict was enacted through constant repartee between the interlocutor, who was pretentious and aristocratic, and the clownish, moronic end men, such as Bones or Sambo. The interlocutor was portrayed as lighter skinned than the end men; he was self-centered, self-righteous, self-conscious, outrageously fickle and inconsistent, snobbish, and afraid of the lower classes. The end men were darker, poorer, more confused, openly dishonest, and untrustworthy.[26] This portrayal of the African-American community probably had a calming effect on white consciences: How could whites be faulted for doing to African Americans no more than what they did to one another? Also the African-American community was portrayed as comically apolitical, constantly divided, and in continual intragroup conflict. This must have calmed and relieved white audiences, who, one imagines, were at least occasionally worried about the possibility of slave rebellions and/or guilty about the inequities of northern institutional racism.

The relationship between African Americans and whites was not addressed as directly as the relationship between the African-American sexes or socioeconomic classes, but the performance was saturated with the implied political relationship between the races. Besides covert, indirect political messages, minstrelsy also used a more direct approach to air views about the decisions that had to be made regarding slavery, the Civil War, and Reconstruction. Perhaps the most popular example of political material was Dan Emmett's famous song "Dixie," created expressly for the minstrel stage. It began:

> I wish I was in de land ob cotton,
> Cimmon seed 'an sandy bottom—
> In Dixie's Land whar I was born in,
> Early on one frosty mornin,
>
> Chor: Look away—look away—Dixie Land.
> Chorus: Den I wish I was in Dixie,
>   Hooray—Hooray!
> In Dixie's Land we'll took our stand
> To lib and die in Dixie.
> Away—away down south in Dixie?[27]

Here one can see one of the strongest themes of the political material in minstrelsy: African Americans loved the South, and they didn't want to leave. African Americans were shown to be empty-headed subhumans who needed the institution of slavery to survive; they loved the South, the massa, and manual labor.

These songs portrayed the life of the slave as easy in the South, where dancing, singing, drinking, and an occasional odd job or two was all there was to life. However, much of the minstrel material was published during and after the Civil War. Although emancipation had been declared, during the years of Reconstruction (1865–1877) the pro-South forces were attempting to regroup, consolidate their power, and retain economic control of the newly freed African-American workforce. Their strategy was to sabotage and finally destroy Radical Reconstruction (the Republican strategy to enfranchise and empower the African-American population in the South). Songs that spoke of blacks who had left their homes during the war and who missed their old plantations and the easy slave life spoke to this issue:

> Oh, here you see before you a nigger old and grey. . . .
> I used to work among the sugar cane,
> But since them happy times I've had to roam. . . .
> Soon the cruel war broke out and I was forced to go
> From that sunny land that's always dear to me. . . .
> So all I ask and crave is that I may find a grave,
> Way down in my Louisiana home.[28]

African Americans were pictured as semihelpless beings who were starving in the North because they couldn't get along without the master's help. Some were portrayed as having disagreed with the war in the first place, and now that they had been forced away from their plantations they were homesick and afraid of the abolitionists:

> Once more we're in danger ob destruction,
> For dars traitors in de Souf, and some hot heads in de Norf,
> Dat am tired ob dis happy land of Canaan. . . .
> De surf ob Abolition and de breakers ob Secession
> Am arollin' o'er dis happy land ob Canaan.[29]

And they questioned the wisdom of their own emancipation:

> I'm a saucy nig from Tenesee, I want you all to know,
> I'll gib you my opinion ob de matters as they go. . . .
> Some say de niggers shall be slaves, some say dey shall be free—
> I'd like to know what difference all dis trouble makes to me;
> Freedom may be well enough, likewise emancipation,
> But I guess dat i is better off down on de old plantation.[30]

What was probably the most damaging material against the cause of the Radical Reconstructionists was the direct appeal to patriotic compromise and the plea to let white Southerners and ex-slaves work out their differences without interference:

> There is one thing more I'd like to state, and
> I guess its not too late,
> It am about the colored population;
> Just leave them all alone, in their present Southern home,
> That's the way to save this great and glorious nation.[31]

Minstrel ideology was clearly on the side of pro-Southern forces who wished to retain control of their region through economic control of the ex-slaves. It supported the old slave/master mythology that served as moral justification both for slavery during antebellum days and for the strategic absence of federal pro-black legislation during Reconstruction, which was responsible for the ultimate failure of Reconstruction.

During the confusing, sad days surrounding the Civil War, and especially during the decisive years of Reconstruction, the times demanded either a wholesale reexamination of the racial beliefs of the nation, or a hasty retreat to the racist mythology of the past. Reappraisal would have been a painful, difficult job requiring dedication, vision, and a great deal of help from social institutions. Retreat, on the other hand, was a comforting sanctuary, complete with self-justification and expiated guilt. No new, revolutionary institution was required for guiding the populace; any popular outlet that had credibility with the people would be sufficient. Sadly, Radical Reconstruction was sabotaged and defeated, and the old power relations were restored—changed, but again triumphant. Negro minstrelsy was tailor-made for the role of the communications medium of retreat. Minstrelsy contained all the old racist elements, it was already a great favorite of whites, and it was adaptable. Most important, its operational medium—laughter—was painless and effective.

But this was not all there was to the success of minstrelsy. It was an extremely complicated psychological phenomenon; race usually is in America, especially when masquerade is involved. And this was masquerade of the most profound type. The white actors pretended to be a figure whose characteristics were popularly believed to be the antithesis of excellence. As historian Joseph Boskin points out, "From his beginnings, Sambo was an integral part of colonial life. His existence created an important contrast—that of the opposite—to all that the white master aspired to be. . . . On virtually every level, Sambo was fashioned to be the contrast of the white man. . . . [He] was the antithesis of the American success-symbol, the Individualist."[32]

The white actors and audiences were apparently unable to admit that they had certain propensities and that they yearned to pursue them—for instance, loving music, relaxing, dancing, clowning, and sex. Such behavior was permitted for African Americans, at the periphery of the clearing, but not for whites. Because of the shape of the cultural clearing, the complex social negotiations of the mid- and late nineteenth century, these characteristics were not available to the white Victorian bourgeoisie in the United States. In the complex social negotiations of the mid- and late nineteenth century, whites were unable to own these characteristics *as whites*. For various sociopolitical reasons, probably related to the needs of the new industrial economy and the national imperative to settle the western wilderness, the characteristics depicted on the Negro minstrel stage were not considered to be included in the definition of what it was to be human. So whites used the minstrel stage to define negatively the configuration of the white self and to experience, either directly or vicariously, a different way of being, the way of "the other."

The mask of burnt cork allowed the white actors to use their artistic talents to act out a lifestyle that would have been considered socially unacceptable, were it not for the fiction of the mask, to embody attitudes and behaviors that were not permitted by the restraints of race and class. The mask also allowed the white audience to unknowingly identify with the characteristics of a complete social outcast, the most imperfect of characters. It allowed the audience to experience vicariously some of the forbidden fruits of a different way of being—and yet not be discovered. They were protected from detection (and self-awareness) by the ridicule of their own laughter.

Minstrelsy disguised whites and protected them from their own unacknowledged wishes. It also "protected" their society, a society held together by a mythology of racial difference. If it had been acknowledged that whites yearned to act like they thought African Americans acted, the foundation of the clearing would have been threatened. That whites were forced to act one way in public, yet allowed to act quite another when pretending to be someone else, is graphically demonstrated by this picture of Billy Emerson, posing as his two different personaes.

Looking upon the dualism of Billy Emerson, one is moved to remember the social confusions of the nineteenth century. Whites used the minstrel stage to actually dip into, to embody, the particular mysteries of

Two faces of the Victorian male: The proper bourgeois gentleman Billy Emerson, and his on-stage portrayal of "Big Sunflower"

the forbidden, the African-American "other." In response to the confusions and absences of the Victorian American self, minstrelsy was a technology of the self, an attempt *to heal* the white self of Victorian illnesses such as personal rigidity, loneliness, isolation, and lack of imagination, humor, and creativity. The emotional illnesses particular to the Victorian era, especially neurasthenia, were characterized by a lack of will and vitality, a kind of paralysis, brought about by the stresses and demands of white middle-class work, what physician George Beard in 1881 called "brainwork."[33] It is true that the minstrel character suffered from many problems, but none of them could have been considered neurasthenia. Whatever it was that went into the makeup of the minstrel's character, white neurasthenics could certainly have used a judicious dose or two. That is exactly what they received from the good Dr. Sambo.

This way of interpreting minstrelsy, not only as a political force but also as a technology of the self, is reinforced by the manner in which some scholars have viewed the encounter between Jim Rice and Jim Crow. They believe that the old black man, Jim Crow, was not "dancing and singing to himself," as traditional white scholarship maintained; instead, Jim Crow was actually ridiculing white society. They believe that he was imitating what he thought to be the foolish, comical customs of whites, who he thought danced in a stiff, constricted, absurd manner. If this is the case, what Rice did on the stage of the Louisville Theatre was not imitate an African American; rather, what he did was imitate an imitation of himself. Sambo was not the African American; he was the white man, or rather he embodied aspects of human living in which the white man could not partake. The white audience, so prim and proper, was never really laughing at the African American. It was ridiculing (and indulging in) its own inclinations and wishes, long denied, that were allowed to venture out only in the darkness of the minstrel stage.

The Sioux Nation and the Uses of "The Other": The Frontier as a Technology of the Self

The minstrel stage helped the actors and vicariously the audience to embody a different way of being and the white middle classes to define the configuration of the self a bit more clearly, while at the same time putting forth a racist mythology that had a direct impact on one of the most important political debates of its era, slavery and Radical Reconstruction. In the same way, continual westward migration to the receding frontier, the Indian wars it necessitated, and the intellectual and literary discourse surrounding the wars helped the settlers embody a different way of being (one people believed was more real, more connected with the earth, and more physically vigorous) and the nation to define the configuration of the self a bit more clearly through casting Native Americans as "the other." The myth of the frontier accomplished all this, while at the same time putting forth a racist mythology that had a direct impact on the acquisition and use of the western frontier, one of the most important political debates of its era, and an indirect impact on the definition of and control over the newly created urban working class, another important political debate.

Minstrelsy and the myth of the frontier were similar because as technologies of the times both provided moral and political guidance to a nation facing enormous and unfamiliar political decisions and lacking the help of credible traditions and institutions. The technology had to be administered within a socioeconomic climate that necessitated the justification (and mystification) of the capitalist agenda of the uprooting and exploitation of urban labor, the rapid utilization (and consequent despoliation) of natural resources, and the progressive alienation of everyday life. Practitioners of both minstrelsy and frontier mythology— probably unintentionally—accomplished these goals by using popular culture (that is, the theater and the popular and intellectual press) to influence political decisions. Those who influenced popular culture probably didn't do so consciously, but they accomplished political ends by developing racist practices that shifted the configuration of the self, that altered how the populace conceived of themselves and those who were considered "different."

Much of this complex process of acquiring and settling the western wilderness was reflected in the Indian Appropriations Act passed by the House of Representatives in 1871. During the shaping and debating of this bill, the 41st and 42nd Congresses articulated some of the most important features of the frontier myth, the government's Indian policy, and the overall racial politics of the nineteenth century. One of the primary focuses of the 1871 Congressional debate was the Sioux nation: its definition, its location, its rights, its identity, its future. The plight of the Sioux epitomized that of other Native American nations as they were invaded and finally overrun by the stampede of white Europeans to the frontier.

A BRIEF HISTORY OF THE SIOUX NATION In the late seventeenth century in the Minnesota area, the Sioux nation split; some of the tribes gradually migrated westward, where they found the herds of wild horses that had been migrating north for centuries after being brought to the New World by the Spanish. The Sioux and the horse met on the High

Plains in the first half of the eighteenth century and established a partnership responsible for one of the most colorful and vibrant cultures of the indigenous peoples of North America. The Sioux settled in the Powder River-Black Hills area of what is today South Dakota and Montana and there developed a nomadic way of life based in part on a deep religious connectedness with the natural world and an economic dependence upon the great bison herds of the Great Plains. As the whites moved into these areas from the east, they acquired land by subduing, driving westward, and finally destroying the peoples indigenous to the continent. In the mid-nineteenth century the whites' westward migration began to encroach upon the Sioux's Powder River land. The Union Pacific Railroad was built directly through Sioux land, the U.S. Cavalry appeared, roads were constructed, and white farmers began trying to homestead; finally, in 1874 gold was discovered in the Black Hills, the sacred mountain "church" of the Sioux. The Sioux resisted the encroaching settlements, the whites fought, lied, and swindled their way onto the land, and the Sioux retaliated with increasing violence. The U.S. Cavalry protected the settlers, the Sioux organized and mounted a sustained guerrilla campaign, the East Coast newspapers whipped up national "pride" and popular support for increased military action, and Congress blustered and appropriated money for new Indian campaigns.

This familiar cycle of invasion, war, and victory, which had been enacted many times on the East Coast and in the Midwest, was seen once again in the 1860s with the Sioux. Except in 1868 the Indians were victorious. Yet over the course of the next sixteen years, the government lied, cheated, and stole the land back and in the process decimated the Sioux. A nation had been nearly destroyed, and the Great Plains had been won.[34]

A BRIEF HISTORY OF THE PEACE POLICY The story of the fight over the Black Hills is full of dishonesty, death, and personal tragedy. But set against this scene was the government's *official* position. Throughout the war, and the fragile peace that followed, officials kept speaking like this to the Sioux: "The Great father said that his heart was full of tenderness for his red children, and he selected this commission of friends of the Indians that they might devise a plan . . . in order that the Indian nations might be saved, and that . . . they might become as the white man has become, a great and powerful people."[35] This speech, by Bishop Wipple, contained language that was almost identical to the professions of friendship and assistance that had been a general feature of the 1871 Indian Appropriations Act. The language and some of the ideas of the Indian

Appropriations Act were the direct result of a broad philosophical movement called the Quaker or Peace Policy. This policy appeared to show compassion for the Indian nations and professed to save them from destruction and from their own worst traits. In later years, in fact, the Sioux were often used as proof that the Peace Policy was working splendidly.

The Indian Appropriations Act did not appear out of nowhere; it evolved decades before it became law. A small minority had pressed for humanitarian action for the Indian nations early in the history of the United States. For instance, in 1820 John Calhoun argued that the Indians "must be brought gradually under our authority and laws, or they will insensibly waste away in vice and misery."[36] Calhoun neglected to mention other forces that threatened them, such as starvation, disease, and murder. However, early in his first term in office President Ulysses Grant was able to recognize the possibility of genocide. He saw only two solutions, extermination or a reservation system that would "protect" the Indian from white settlers and white railroads.[37] Under the influence of abolitionist-type reformers, Grant inaugurated an Indian policy that was designed to root out corruption within the ranks of the Indian agents and replace corrupt agents with men picked from various religious organizations. The Quaker or Peace Policy's central aim was to view the Indian not as an inferior savage whom a Christian country ought to *kill*, but rather as an inferior savage whom it ought to *save*.

An expanded Peace Policy was the philosophical basis upon which the entire 1871 Indian Appropriations Act rested. The Peace Policy was an attempt to remove Indian nations from their hunting areas, which were being swallowed up by white settlers, and to place the Indians in reservations from which they would not be able to leave. The government would then pay them a certain fixed amount for the land, which was to be paid annually in the form of food, shelter, and clothing. The Indians needed all that support because the land the government bought from them was invariably their old hunting areas.

Salvation was to be accomplished through education, religious training, and especially by isolating and confining the Indians. Grant thought that this could be done through the reservation system, and therefore from 1869 to 1871 his administration sent into the battlegrounds scores of "peace commissions" that were charged with securing treaties with the still hostile Plains Indians.[38] But there were problems with this policy. Many times Native Americans were forced into selling land that was vital to their survival. Sometimes they signed fraudulent documents. Sometimes they did not understand what the treaties really meant. Sometimes they were tricked by corrupt translators. Sometimes the treaties were changed after the fact by the Senate without the consent of the tribes. Sometimes the government corruption was so complete that the Indians on the reservations never received their allotments and were forced into either stealing or starvation. The list of abuses is endless.

Unfortunately, many congressmen, encouraged by Grant administration spokesmen, viewed the allotments as a *gift* to the Indians that would bribe them into peace.

> Sargent: The Apaches of New Mexico are at war with the United States—the money alloted to them is in reality also for the whites—for if they are bribed into peace (like the Sioux) everybody benefits, but if we don't give them the money, they stay at war.
>
> *Taffe: Do you want to pay them for being at war?*
>
> Sargent: We shall say to them "the people of the United States . . . are willing to act toward you with humanity if you will go upon the reservations and stay there, and conduct yourself peaceably."
>
> *Garfield: You propose to buy a peace?*
>
> Sargent: Yes. . . . [I]t was cheaper as well as more human to feed the Indians than to fight them.[39]

Obviously, many congressmen neglected to remember that the money paid to the Indians could not be legally withheld or debated, because it was payment for land purchased from the Indians. In fact, the mistaken idea that Congress could actually withhold the promised allotments from the Indians was exceedingly popular in Congress and became a cornerstone of the new Peace Policy. Indeed, the theory that Congress could decide to withhold the allotments from the Indians became the most powerful weapon the government possessed during the fight over the Black Hills. After the Indian Appropriations Act, Congress decided it had complete control over the distribution of money to the Indians; therefore it didn't bother with elaborate legal rationalizations or explanations, as it had before the act was passed. Representative James R. McCormick was quite direct about the issue:

> McCormick: The Indians should get money only if they stay on their reservation and don't get hostile. It's when they are allowed to come and go at will that they cause trouble. If they stay on the reservation people won't mind the reservation system. . . .
>
> *Sargent: . . . While relief was carried to the Indians in one hand, there*

was in the other a sword which would punish ... wanton hostility committed upon our people. The Sioux of the Dakota are the best example of the peace policy. ... Now they are beginning to cultivate their fields. ...

Garfield: One element that will control the savage, be he an American Indian, an African Hottentot, or an Asiatic Mongolian, that is first, to be right with him, and second, make him fear you.[40]

The few Congressmen sympathetic to the Sioux were afraid that, ultimately, the army would exterminate them. But their alternative to genocide was to "reform" the Indian: "Are we to civilize, domesticate, Christianize these barbarians, or is the old policy to continue, of annihilation and obliteration?"[41] This argument is reminiscent of the Abolitionists' arguments against slavery. The reformer wanted an end to extreme and public abuses, but only if solutions could be found that left the larger sociopolitical system intact. Solutions that could only be implemented by significant changes in the larger system held little interest for the Indian reformer. Congress was perfectly willing to "save" the Indians by obtaining Indian land through treaty and other provisions, and then by attempting to "civilize" and "Christianize" them. But once the land was gone and once the Indians refused to be "civilized," no one but the army knew what to do with them.

True to the trends of the modern era in general and the nineteenth century in particular, the central piece of Congress's plan to save the Indians by "civilizing" them was to break up the tribal unit and reconstruct tribe members into separate *individuals*. The strategy involved dividing Indian land into individual family plots, which each family would be responsible for farming. It was a common belief in Congress at this time that as long as Native Americans held their land in common, they would continue to be barbaric. "Keeping the Indians in tribes," Senator William M. Stewart explained, "only fosters and cultivates dependence [on the tribal structure]."[42] The plan to divide and distribute tribal land was referred to as "severalty"; it was an important ideological force in the Indian Appropriations Act debate. Severalty was later expanded and made into law in the infamous Dawes Severalty Act of 1887, perhaps *the* most efficient means invented for extracting land from the Indian. During the 1871 debate, Senator Henry Dawes explained the purpose behind severalty: "planting the Indian upon the soil in severalty, giving him an idea of the rights of property and all ... the associations which gather around the few acres that ... is associated with the name of home. ... Let us make a home for the Indian in severalty, and hold it in trust for him, but at least let each one of them know that this spot is his ... to be adorned and beautified by him and cultivated, in that cultivating cultivating himself and his family. Through that civilization comes."[43]

Senator James Nye agreed, citing the experience of his home state as a model: "In . . . Nevada the tribe of Washoe Indians was the first tribe in the state among whom white civilization found in their way, and today there are not a hundred of that tribe who wear a blanket or dress in Indian costume. They dress as the white dress, they eat as the white eat, and they work as the white work. What has caused it? It is because they came in contact with that civilization and Christianity which improve by example every day."[44]

What Senator Nye meant by "work as the white work" is especially important to the whole debate over the Indians' future. Perhaps Representative McCormick helped define what his colleague Nye meant as he explained his own amendment that stipulated that male Indians must be made to work for their allotment money. Here he quotes from a letter from a Bishop Salpointe of Arizona: "[W]e must begin to instruct them in the arts of labor. . . . '[I]t would render them a great service, and would teach them to provide for and maintain themselves hereafter by their labor, while rewards gratiously bestowed only serve to stimulate their vices and to leave them continually at the point of degradation.' "[45] "The arts of labor" is a strange term to use for hard manual work. A further explanation is given by Senator William M. Stewart: "[E]very dollar appropriated for Indians tends to demoralize the Indians and the whites, tends to prevent Indians from becoming civilized . . . and demoralizes the country. I do not believe Indians will ever become civilized without labor. . . . This system of appropriating money for Indians and taxing white men . . . to feed the Indians is the radical evil at the bottom of this whole business. . . . You keep a few aristocratic big Indians, big Indian chiefs, drunk, swaggering, and oppressing the weak."[46] One must by this time wonder who all those working Native Americans were going to be working for, and who would actually benefit from their work as individual farmers and manual laborers. "Civilizing" begins to appear to be a way of turning a cohesive, unified Indian nation into an isolated, inexpensive, easily controlled workforce. Congress wanted tribal Indians to give up hunting, live close to town, dress and act like whites, and most of all, cease living and working cooperatively; in other words, to become isolated, self-contained, bourgeois individuals.

The policy of taking Native American land was justified in part by Congress's view of the Indian as the antithesis of the individualistic Anglo-Saxon yeoman farmer. Senator Timothy O. Howe asked, "What have we taken from the Indian race? That which was worthless to them;

land which they did not know how to cultivate, and would not learn how to cultivate. . . . It was possession which . . . was worthless to them, but worth everything to humanity if once possessed by civilization, by education, by capacity."[47] But a few Congressmen, such as Senator Eugene Casserly, understood that the dependency provision of the Indian Appropriations Act "is the beginning of the end in respect to Indian lands. It is the first step in a great scheme of spoilation, in which the Indians will be plundered, corporations and individuals enriched, and the American name dishonored in history. . . . Their [the Indians'] misfortune is not that they are red men; not that they are semi-civilized. . . . [T]heir misfortune is that they hold great bodies of rich lands, which have aroused the cupidity of powerful corporations and of powerful individuals."[48]

In the struggle over the Black Hills, and in the Congressional debate over the 1871 Indian Appropriations Act, we can see the echoes of past ideological struggles in Western society and the seeds of future issues. Congress's stereotypic description of the aboriginal Indian, its insistence on using a bourgeois standard of behavior as the yardstick of civilization, and its insistence that the white man take responsibility to reform the Indian and thus remake the Indian in the white man's own image—these characteristics all serve to remind us what century, and what era, we are studying. The Victorian era—what historian Donald Lowe referred to as the bourgeois perception—was the culmination of the Enlightenment agenda.[49] It was characterized by a belief in progress, individualism, the values and prerogatives of the entrepreneurial middle class, linear thinking and calculation, and a belief in the quantification and scientizing of the external world. Sloth, fear, apathy, confusion, hopelessness, mysticism, sexuality, and communalism were held in disdain. Characteristics from both the early modern era and the reign of the bourgeoisie can be detected in the language used by the 41st and 42nd Congresses in the 1871 debate. Indians were portrayed as inadequate bourgeoisie: savage, ignorant, lazy, dishonest, communal. They survived on the Great Plains by hunting, rather than by individual initiative, personal achievement, and the calculation and utilization of the labor of others. They were unaware of Western science, the concept of linearity, or the inevitability of progressive development. They appeared unable to delay gratification, save money, or accumulate capital. In other words, they were the antithesis of bourgeois values.

THE MYTH OF THE FRONTIER Yet at the same time that Native Americans were being portrayed as an inadequate, incompetent version of the white bourgeoisie, another curious cultural artifact was in bloom: the myth of the frontier. Historian Richard Slotkin has noted that the myth, which had been popularized by journalistic accounts, artists, and intellectuals, conceived of the world as divided into three parts: (1) The metropolis, which was pictured as the seat of Old World tradition and aristocratic privilege; (2) the pristine wilderness, which was pictured as the seat of natural goodness, abundance, and savage purity; and (3) the frontier, which was pictured as a boundary and interface between the two.[50] It was thought that progress was made by separating from one's tradition-bound homeland, surviving the attacks of wilderness savages, harvesting the natural bounty of the wilderness through personal initiative and sacrifice, and finally achieving personal wealth and self-transformation. Historian Frederick Jackson Turner developed "The Frontier Thesis."[51] Turner's frontier was envisioned as a bourgeois outpost, in opposition to both the tradition and privilege of the metropolis and the savage, untamed but bountiful wilderness. If the frontier partakes too much of the metropolis, it gets bogged down in tradition and loses its creativity, vitality, and daring. If it partakes too much of the wilderness, it gets engulfed in savagery and loses its ability to calculate, objectify, and thereby exact a profit. In an important move, the frontier mythmakers argued that progressive development is a *universal* process that is constituted by the metropolis-frontier dynamic: civilization is always "fed" by being connected to the wilderness through the frontier.

Slotkin has noted that at the time the frontier myth was at its height of intellectual popularity, frontier expansion had already reached an end. Why then did the myth have such strength? He argued that the myth functioned not only to justify the destruction of Native American nations and the acquisition and exploitation of their land, but also to explain and justify the oppression of the working class of new European immigrants in the East Coast factories. In Slotkin's words, the myth "represent[s] a displacement or deflection of social conflict into the world of myth." The "class war [in the metropolis] was projected outward to racial war on the borders,"[52] and conversely the racial war was projected into the cities. The use of the term "white savages" to refer to these immigrants who served as the cheap labor supply of nineteenth-century American capitalism was thus not simply an insult; it also served to situate immigrant workers in the cultural terrain of their era. They were like the Indian: ignorant, savage, lazy, untrustworthy—in short, uncivilized. By defining the urban proletariat in this way, the frontier myth implied that these men and women were not human; they were the equivalent of natural resources, and thus their place in the natural scheme of things was to be exploited, used in the maintenance of the metropolis and the accumulation of capital by the bourgeoisie.

The putative law of supply and demand, an important ideological component of industrial capitalism, was described as a universal, scientific law and was symbolized by the two opposite worlds of frontier abundance (that is, supply) and metropolis scarcity (that is, demand). In other words, the frontier myth functioned to mask the exploitative practices of industrial capitalism in the New World. Class war was removed to the wilderness and reframed as a *natural* process, a benign but important aspect of the march of scientific, civilized progress. Once this intellectual sleight of hand took place, it was but a short step to justifying the exploitation of Native Americans and their land, and thus by extension the exploitation of the newly emigrated and their labor. "By accepting the treatment of the Indian as an aspect of the world of resources," Slotkin explains, "the [white] citizen consents to the commodification of humanity, the reduction of human values—including his own—to the calculus of capitalism."[53] Slotkin suggests that the stereotypic characterization of the Indian was a feature of the larger ideology of the frontier myth. The myth functioned in such a way as to favor the entrepreneurial bourgeoisie and grease the wheels of industrial capitalism by mythologizing (and thus depoliticizing) class conflict and frontier genocide.

The economic functions of the myth were all the more influential because the dichotomy between the civilized, individualistic, entrepreneurial bourgeois and the savage, lazy, sexual, communal Native American ("the other") was embedded in the ongoing confusion in America about the proper configuration of the white middle-class self. In the same way that whites embraced the descriptions of the African-American "other" as depicted on the minstrel stage, they embraced the descriptions of the Indian "other" as depicted in the debate over the 1871 Indian Appropriations Act and the frontier myth. They did so in part so that they could gain some small measure of definition about who they themselves were. There may have been little consensus about what the white self was during this time of enormous socioeconomic change, but at least they were able to develop some understandings about what it was *not*. The stereotypic visions of the African American and the Native American were, of course, psychopolitical prisons from which these oppressed groups could not escape. But these depictions also provided a way of disseminating a flawed, ill-defined configuration of the white self. For the time being, it had to suffice.

The configuration of the white bourgeois self was one that was fairly restrictive and rigid. What the whites were not supposed to be like, therefore, was mysteriously attractive to them. Characteristic bourgeois illnesses such as hysteria and neurasthenia were reflective of qualities of the self that proper bourgeois selves were prohibited from experiencing. These illnesses, and their psychological cures, will be discussed in more detail in later chapters. Suffice it to say that the bourgeoisie could only embody certain qualities of the self by acting the Negro on the minstrel stage, by migrating to the wilderness and living the life of a frontiersman "gone native," or in certain circumstances discussed in later chapters, by becoming psychologically ill. In other words, Negro minstrelsy and life on the frontier were technologies of the self. It was through participation in the roles of "the other," through the dynamic of vicarious masquerade and disavowal, that middle-class whites could configure the self.

Just as the minstrel stage provided a means by which whites could not only define but also act out, in masquerade, what they were not, so too did the frontier myth provide a kind of stage: the actual frontier. One of the attractions of going west was to live out a different lifestyle, one portrayed by the myth as more down-to-earth, real, and honest than that afforded in the evil city. Life on the frontier was thought to build character, provide physical health and vigor, and cure Victorian middle-class ills such as neurasthenia. Life on the frontier, and especially in the wilderness, was portrayed as heroic, more virtuous, and purer than city living. It was a kind of Victorian "work" cure (as opposed to the "rest cure," discussed in chapter four). By living close to, and in ways copying the lifestyle and survival wisdom of the Indian, whites could act out some of the forbidden ways of being.

Those who partook *directly* of the masquerade, such as the white minstrels or frontier settlers, were allowed to engage in activities and assume personalities (that is, to live out a configuration of the self) from which they were otherwise prohibited. Those who partook *vicariously* of the masquerade, like the white audience or the white urban readership of frontier articles and books, were allowed to imagine being "the other." And for the entire bourgeoisie, actors or voyeurs alike, the definition of the despised "other," and the psychological mechanism of disavowal, helped them define their bourgeois self with a bit more self-righteous clarity and certainty.

To summarize, the nineteenth-century American bourgeois self was a self that was individualistic, hardworking, moralistic, frugal, and emotionally restricted. It was a self dedicated to the building of (its own version of) civilization and the taming of the wilderness through hard work, the postponement of gratification, and the calculated use of the labor of others. Characteristic bourgeois illnesses, such as laziness, cowardice, hopelessness, excessive pride, sexuality, or communal sympathies, or the lack of inhibitions, initiative, entrepreneurial ambition, and individual competitiveness were the property of "the other." Such illnesses were treated by the minstrel stage, the frontier experience, and the new psychological cures discussed in later chapters.

PERSONALITY, THE NATIONAL PRESS, AND "THE THERAPEUTIC": ADVERTISING AS A TECHNOLOGY OF THE SELF

The turn of the century in the United States, from about 1890, witnessed one of the great sea changes in American cultural life. "On or about December 10, 1910," Virginia Woolf once deadpanned, "human character changed." The cultural confusion of the nineteenth century, brought on by the increased industrialization, urbanization, European immigration, and secularization of the age, combined with the moral conflicts caused by slavery and the Indian Wars, and the horror that was the Civil War, came to a head at the turn of the century. As Robert Park put it, "the 'cake of custom' had been broken,"[54] and it could never be put back together again. The power strategy first developed by the early modern and Enlightenment philosophers had reached an extreme expression in the unrelieved individualism, pragmatism, and communal isolation of the bourgeois American as the twentieth century began.

The confusion and uncertainty brought about by the lack of tradition, authority, and institutional bedrock was becoming a serious problem, as was the new mix of personality traits that made for economic and social success in the new century. The lack of guidance from tradition, the loss of religious certainty, and the effect of new business and social pressures combined to produce new personality traits and new psychological symptoms, such as new psychosomatic symptoms, a sense of unreality, and an experience of alienation and nihilism that could be seen as an eerie foreshadowing of the emptiness and narcissism of our current era.

Mesmerism, a strange mix of hypnosis and philosophy, was brought from France to the United States in 1836 (see chapter five). It soon developed a decidedly American character and evolved into a popular and influential secular cure. Its popularity with the middle classes foreshadowed the important changes in the self and its ills that became so obvious by the turn of the century. Mesmerism and its heirs, such as positive thinking and mind cure philosophy, were the first secular psychotherapies. The healing of the secular soul, the psyche, had begun in earnest. What once could have been conceived of as sociopolitical problems began to be conceived of in psychological terms. The "therapeutic ethos" was beginning to emerge. Mesmerism will be discussed in detail in later chapters. It is important to simply note that mesmerism and its heirs were a response to the cultural confusions of the time. "America in the late 1800s," Robert Fuller explains "was a culture without a core." Even the disavowal-masquerade dynamic, a vicarious commerce with "the other," could not save the old bourgeois self. Historians such as Warren Susman and T. J. Lears have noticed a drastic change in the configuration of the self at this time in U.S. history.[55] As the Victorian self bent under its internal inconsistencies, its failures, and the strain of a newly emerging sociocultural constellation, a new configuration began to take shape.

In order to understand the nineteenth century Susman studied the advice manuals spanning the second half of the century. These small broadside publications, usually written by the semi-intellectual physician/preacher/writer common at the time, were quite influential. Susman noticed that for most of the second half of the nineteenth century, the advice manuals seemed to describe the self in a manner that was radically different from the manner in which the self was described in the advice manuals of the turn of the century. For much of the nineteenth century the self was thought to consist primarily of Victorian "character." Character, a kind of moral toughness and integrity, could be "strengthened" through hard work, self-sacrifice, religious observance, adherence to strict moral laws, the postponement of gratification, frugality, the rejection of overweening pride and self-congratulation. In this cultural terrain, Susman argued, individuals could admire and try to emulate persons of high morality and learning who had contributed something of value to the community, who had led through example, or who had humbly and selflessly risen to the occasion in time of crisis. These persons, Susman argued, were rightly called heroes. Heroes were made, not born; heroism was achieved through sacrifice and hard work, not stumbled upon by luck.

Sometime around 1890, Susman discovered, the advice manuals abruptly changed. The primary ingredient of the self ceased to be character. Instead, a new quality became prominent: personality. Personality meant the ability to be attractive to others, to stand out in a crowd. "Personality," Henry Laurent suggested, "is the quality of being Somebody."[56] Personality was cultivated by carefully attending to the details of one's public performance. Personal style could be "built," usually by developing unique, personal qualities that attracted others. Personality was shaped by attending to and manipulating others, not by following moral codes or adhering to religious ideals. Poise and charm, rather than adherence to a moral code; personal grooming and health, rather than hard work and self-sacrifice, were the important behaviors to learn.

These were all qualities that were best learned during leisure time and were usually linked to the consumption of various consumer items. Personality, since it made one attractive to others, led to business success as well as personal success. Success in business was predicated on the ability to sell—not only goods, but oneself as well. Social performance, not hard work, became the key to wealth and power.

Naturally, this changed configuration of the self was not conducive to the production of heroes. Instead, celebrities became the order of the day. Celebrities became famous by performing, by doing something that caused them to stand out from the crowd, something unusual, uncommon, even bizarre or illegal. Celebrities were not admired for their moral character, but envied for their personal skills, inherited wealth, or good luck. One did not try to *be* like a celebrity, but instead one tried to *get* what they had, to acquire what they possessed: fame and fortune.

The shift from character to personality obviously reflected a profound change in the cultural terrain of the era. The self was in the process of being configured into a radically different shape. Perhaps the focus on this new self was a response to the condition of being lost in the crowd, overlooked in the crush of humanity recently assembled in the large cities. In the turn-of-the-century world, individuals appeared to be feeling lonely and isolated, hungry for attention and positive regard. There was a pervasive sense that others would not find one interesting or attractive unless one worked at it. So social interactions became transformed into a series of entertainments or sales performances. Each encounter became an opportunity to be "discovered," to be turned into a star, or conversely, to be ignored and humiliated.

The business applications of this new configuration of the self soon became clear. Capitalism was moving into a new phase of its history. An emphasis on producing goods through hard work and honest labor was being replaced by an emphasis on the sales and consumption of goods and services, predicated upon the effectiveness of a sales technique and/ or the attractiveness of the individual salesperson. Personal magnetism replaced craftsmanship; technique replaced moral integrity. Over the course of the next several decades the means to proper living were redefined: leisure activities and the consumption of goods and services began to replace work, learning, and the production of goods and services. The cultural clearing was shifting, the shape of the economy was changing, and as a result the configuration of the self, including the most fundamental aspects of common-sense truths, also changed. One's sensations and even the most intimate sense of one's self and one's "natural" needs changed in order to fit the new clearing.

Obviously, one of the main aspects of the new turn-of-the-century self was its confusion. What was a problem for the mid-nineteenth-century self had become an epidemic by the 1890s and the early years of the twentieth century. With the loss of tradition and community, the waning of religious authority and the banalization of religious thought, with the disorientation resulting from science's new claims and discoveries, and with the disruptions of immigration, urbanization, and the Civil War came the loss of certainty and centeredness. In 1887, Reverend Theodore T. Munger wrote that modern doubt "envelops all things in its puzzle—God, immortality, the value of life, the rewards of virtue, and the operation of conscience."[57] Rollo Ogden, writing for the *Nation* in 1891, reported that educated citizens everywhere seemed "distracted, wavering, [and the victims of] confused thought."[58] Vida D. Scutter revealed his difficulties in the *Atlantic Monthly* in 1902. "I lately found myself questioning if it were worth while to have any convictions about anything, when everybody differs from everyone else."[59] Individuals, trying to adjust to a rapidly changing, complex, and damaged world, sought authoritative guidance. However, because they were increasingly distrustful of claims to truth, they seemed unable to accept guidance when they did receive it. *Neurasthenia*, a term coined by Dr. George Beard to indicate "nervous exhaustion," described a multitude of symptoms, particularly those clustered around a paralysis of the will. Lears characterized neurasthenics as being "tortured by indecision and doubt."[60] This condition reached near epidemic proportions in large East Coast cities: "On every street," H. Addington Bruce wrote in the *North American Review*, "at every corner, we meet the neurasthenics."[61]

Another characteristic of middle- and upper-class selfhood was also important at the turn of the century: its "weightlessness" or "unrealness." Lears argues that in a society of bureaucratic corporations, massive secularization, and continual "other directedness," the self became "fragmented, diffuse, and somehow 'unreal.' "[62] Cut off from "the hard, resistant reality of things,"[63] the educated bourgeoisie searched desperately for a more solid sense of reality and meaning. A secure sense of self was difficult to find because it seemed as though doubt had turned the ground to "quicksand under every step."[64] "Doubt," Reverend Munger warned the reader, "destroys the sense of reality."[65] Doubt was becoming more prevalent, Lears reminds us, because at the turn of the century America was becoming increasingly secular; the search for transcendence was in the process of being removed from the communal realm and relocated *within* the individual. The turn of the century search for personal transcendence extended the early modern era's construction of the individual, autonomous self; by the turn of the century, for many educated bourgeoisie, "harmony, vitality, and the hope of self realization"[66] could *only* be located within the self-contained individual.

The configuration of the turn-of-the-century self could be described as lonely, undervalued, "unreal," fragmented, diffuse, obsessed with gaining personal recognition, and lacking in guidance. But how could individuals achieve physical and psychological vitality? In the first two decades of the twentieth century, science and medicine were becoming powerful sources of influence; the public was becoming preoccupied with health, and in their minds physical and mental health were closely linked. The "evils" of city life—especially the lack of fresh air, country scenery, and physical activity—were thought to lead inevitably to emotional distress. Mesmerists and their heirs, utilizing perhaps the most popular secular mental treatment of the nineteenth and early twentieth centuries, based their practices on the belief that illness was caused by a loss of contact with the electrical force of the universe that flows through the body of each individual. Franklin Roosevelt overcame childhood polio through a regime of will, physical exercise, and the outdoor life, thereby exemplifying the healing connection between physical and emotional health. His physical ailments were said to be cured by the force of his will, and his mental resources redoubled by his growing physical health. But how was physical and psychological vitality to be achieved? How could one live in such a way as to be vital and real, to stand out from the crowd, to transcend the mundane and the commonplace? Lears argues that it was at this time that a new sociohistorical phenomenon, the "therapeutic ethos," emerged and became a central player in the new clearing.

The new ethos grew out of the medical practices of the modern era. *Therapy* means the cure of illness through the application of science. As "the therapeutic" began to be applied to psychological maladies, it took on the linguistic sense of curing patients in order to return them to normal society. Philip Rieff describes the goal of "the therapeutic" in the twentieth century as creating "an intensely private sense of well-being."[67]

A fundamental change of focus in the entire cast of our culture has come about, Rieff suggests, because "a sense of well-being has become the end, rather than a by-product of striving after some superior communal end."[68] Individuals ceased to be thought of as public *citizens* whose behavior was evaluated according to an external moral standard; instead citizens began to be thought of as individual *patients* whose behavior was an uncontrollable manifestation of medical illness. The trend toward ignoring sociopolitical causes of personal suffering was reflected throughout mesmerist doctrine. Mesmerism developed a healing theory that depended on an extreme belief in interiority and the powers of the mind over external circumstance. Inappropriate behavior was therefore thought to be remedied through medical-like procedures enacted upon isolated individuals, not moral reevaluation and the application of the will, nor political analysis and group action. Personal well-being (and, later in the century, personal gratification), not communal salvation, became the ultimate goal of life.

Into the institutional void of the turn of the century stepped two quite new therapeutic activities: psychotherapy and advertising. How was advertising "therapeutic"? Around this time, advertising agencies began to promise consumers that they could improve their social and business success by purchasing and consuming the proper products. Over a period of time, advertisements began to prey on (and further construct) the consumer's hunger for a sense of realness, practical guidance, and personal transcendence. Ads promised to transform the consumer's life (and hinted at the lost opportunities or downright disasters that would follow without the proper purchase). Agencies persuaded consumers to buy by associating their products with "imaginary states of well being."[69] Ads featured individuals who had been "transformed," who had found a richer, healthier, fuller life because they had consumed the proper product.[70]

In this way, Lears suggests, advertising furthered the burgeoning "therapeutic ethos" that was so much a part of the turn-of-the-century era: now healing could be accomplished through the purchase of consumer goods. In a world in which structures of meaning had collapsed, Rieff writes, "nothing [is] at stake beyond a manipulative sense of well-being."[71] And manipulate advertisers did. The public became inundated with national advertising campaigns promising health, vitality, cleanliness, social grace, and business success. Parents were chided for not buying early for Christmas, husbands for not providing enough life insurance, wives for not properly feeding the children or scientifically washing the bathroom. The answer to all problems related to health, identity, and enhancement could be found through purchasing the right product.

Above all, national advertising transformed America's concept of the individual from citizen to consumer. The public life of concerned, active citizens was consistently devalued "in favor of a leisure world of intense private experience"[72] facilitated by the purchase and consumption of goods and services. The pursuit of the good, which had been found by Plato in the contemplation of the True Forms, by Augustine in confession to God, by the Enlightenment philosophers in rationality and science, had been transformed by advertising into the pursuit of the good life, or rather the good *things* in life. The way to personal salvation, health, wealth, and popularity could be achieved through consuming. The self-contained individualism of such a vision is obvious. The individual is portrayed as standing outside the communal, sociopolitical world. One's allegiance is to oneself in the striving after individual health and revitalization. A liberation is promised, but it is an entirely isolated, apolitical, individual liberation, which at bottom, of course, is no liberation at all.

One of advertising's first great successes was the campaign that manipulated women into cigarette smoking. Advertising's ability to create a specific desire for a product is well illustrated by this achievement. The campaign reflected one of the functions of advertising in twentieth-century corporate capitalism: the deflection of political activity into the quest for leisure activities and sensuous experiences, into the revitalization and transcendence of the individual self. The influence of advertising, Lears argues, has had a negative effect on the feminist movement, preoccupying women with the perfectionist pursuit of cleanliness in the middle-class home and the ambitious pursuit of a life of sensuality and glamour in the celebrity spotlight. The tragic irony of advertising's victory was captured in Lucky Strikes' gift to women: the freedom to smoke. In a similar move, in 1920 Goddard Corsets noted that women now had the freedom to purchase "natural" corsets. Throughout the history of advertising one can see the trivialization and then exploitation of feminist protest, brought to its nadir in our own era by the famous 1970s Virginia Slims slogan "You've come a long way, baby!" This slogan equates political gains by women with the social acceptance of women's smoking in public, thus trivializing political efforts by putting them in the same category as individual, private, sensuous consuming.

MENTAL HYGIENE AND THE EARLY TWENTIETH-CENTURY SELF

It seems obvious at this point that the turn-of-the-century concept of "personality" has begun to sound suspiciously similar to the current psychological concept of narcissism. Indeed, there do seem to be similarities; after all, both concepts are a product of the same century. Personality was thought to be composed of the qualities embodied by celebrities: Douglas Fairbanks and Clara Bow were stunningly "magnetic." Celebrities were people who stood out in a crowd; they were obsessed with drawing attention to themselves, shamelessly self-centered and self-absorbed. They appeared unwaveringly self-assured in public yet were often painfully insecure and self-hating in private. Perhaps this was due, in part, to how intent they were on pleasing others—if they would fail, or think they were failing, they would be devastated. This highlights the basic paradox of turn-of-the-century celebrity: stars were thought to be attractive because they were "unique," but their uniqueness was dependent on their ability to attract others. A famous art critic, in a scathing 1894 social critique, complained that "we have grown so morbidly self-conscious, so enamored of ourselves, that we are dissatisfied if our [artistic] explorations bring us face to face with any image but our own."[73] Currently, some of the diagnostic criteria for narcissistic personality disorder are (1) grandiose self-importance or uniqueness; (2) preoccupation with fantasies of unlimited success, power, brilliance, beauty; (3) exhibitionism; (4) marked feelings of rage, inferiority, shame, humiliation or emptiness in response to criticism or the indifference of others; (5) entitlement; (6) interpersonal exploitativeness; (7) relationships that alternate between overidealization and devaluation; and (8) lack of empathy.[74] The similarities seem marked. However, the late twentieth-century constellation of narcissistic traits was not constructed overnight. The development from Victorian hero to post–World War II narcissist has taken time, despite the rapid sociohistorical changes of our present century.

After the turn of the century, popularized forms of psychology and religion began to offer ever more cogent and "scientific" advice on how to impress others, become popular, and achieve monetary success and "peace of mind." The practices of mind cure, especially through the popularity of one of its influential successors, abundance theory, were expanding in both medical and practical applications (see chapter five for a detailed discussion). "The therapeutic" began to diversify and in the process claimed more and more territory. Concepts of the secular psyche, such as "mind" and "the subconscious," and social interactions, such as "relationship," and "healthy-mindedness," moved into colloquial language. At the same time, advertising was continuing to craft its strategy. "By the 1920s," Roland Marchand explains, "advertisers had come to recognize a public demand for broad guidance ... about taste, social correctness, and psychological satisfaction. ... Advertising men had now become broader social therapists who offered ... balms for the discontents of modernity."[75] Cleanliness and personal "hygiene" became an overriding concern in the new century and were often portrayed as the solutions to many social problems.

In the meantime, the field of psychiatry witnessed two events in the first decade that were to have an immense impact on the country and on one another. First, Freud came to America. He was invited to lecture at Clark University in Worcester, Massachusetts, in order to introduce psychoanalysis to the United States. Second, the mental hygiene movement, started by an ex–mental patient, first led to reforms in mental hospitals and then made an impact on the entire field of psychotherapy. It began as a volunteer organization and expanded to become a professional association with powerful members and strong ties to the federal government (see chapter six for more details). It stressed *preventive* mental health practices, likening the mind to other physical organs of the body and psychotherapy to everyday hygienic practices. Some researchers, Joel Kovel[76] in particular, believe that in the long run this "mental hygiene" view of psychological healing subverted psychoanalysis's critical political stance by reducing the unconscious to a bourgeois container of urges that could be easily "sanitized" by a conformist therapy. By factoring out any sociohistorical influences, and by medicalizing and individualizing psychological problems, Kovel argues the early mental hygiene movement added to the banalization of psychoanalysis and moved it to collude with capitalism and the growing consumerization of the era. For instance, by using cleansing and sanitation metaphors, the movement developed a concrete, material conception of the mind. It was then easier to quantify medical-like procedures and thus develop understandings about the exchange value of those practices. This process made it possible for psychoanalysis to be understood as a set of procedures that could be assigned a dollar amount. (See chapter six for more details.) Suffice it to say that the twentieth century was beginning to view psychological problems as being situated *within* the individual, as being *medical* in nature, and as being *preventable* through the practice of hygienic activities that would necessarily lead to health and happiness. This view of psychoanalysis erased the critical political stance begun by Freud (see chapter six), objectified emotional ills, and made it possible to integrate psychoanalysis into the approved medical activities of the capitalist marketplace. This in turn allowed for the cooperation between the mental health profession and the corporate business world.

Indeed, in the 1920s and 1930s psychologists began to forge an alliance with corporate management that enhanced both partners: big business became more adept at manipulating consumers and controlling the workforce, and psychology's status as an independent social science discipline was enhanced. In the workplace an emphasis on health, individual feelings, and interpersonal relationships, as opposed to earlier, more mechanistic understandings of management technique and social influence, became more prominent as mid-century approached. In line with psychology's emphasis on "the whole person" came an emphasis on "the whole worker." Psychologists in the workplace, hired by management, portrayed workers as being more concerned with peer pressure, personal feelings, and individual expressiveness than with the situational conditions of their labor. By psychologizing the workplace, psychologists helped management reduce worker complaints to psychological symptoms, mystify class conflict, and develop psychological manipulations that controlled labor more effectively. The famous Hawthorne experiments, usually described as a watershed in the field of organizational development, have been touted as examples of scientific techniques that "discovered" the importance of the emotional life of the workforce. Instead historian Richard Gillespie has argued that they were not the product of objective science and were transparently influenced by management's wish to control the worker.[77] The way the experiments were written up and used make them a type of "origin myth" for the history of organizational development. In any event, they led to an increasing alliance between big business and psychology. As corporations began to glimpse the utility of using psychologists to boost profits, maximize worker productivity, undermine worker solidarity, and influence consumers, new subfields of academic and applied psychology emerged. None of this could have been possible during the Victorian era, wherein the concerns and strategies of management involved mechanization and quantification. Of course, "scientific" laboratory work in the new fields of marketing, advertising, and personnel not only reflected the needs of big business and the growing ethos of personal feelings and expressiveness but also produced and shaped them as well.

The waning of Victorian values in the first three decades of the twentieth century slowed somewhat during the Great Depression and World War II. The concrete problems of unemployment and hunger took precedence over the cynical and reckless self-absorption of the 1920s. Then World War II effectively ended the Depression and provided an inescapable sense of "realness" in the self, even for the middle and upper classes. For a moment the ennui of the turn of the century and the early twentieth-century self, which the therapeutic ethos had tried to cure, receded as the life-and-death struggles of starvation and war came to the fore.

At first the unprepared U.S. military was pounded by the fascist Axis forces and was of little help to its beleaguered British and French allies. Slowly, however, the fortunes of war began to turn as the managers of big business and government learned how to work together to develop and focus America's industrial power for the war effort. The tide of battle began to shift, and it became clear that the allies would be victorious. With the development and use of the atom bomb, again through an alliance between science, big business, and the state, Hiroshima and Nagasaki were reduced to rubble, and the Axis was defeated. A sense of the power and affluence that the United States would generate in the unknown postwar future began to emerge in the national consciousness. A new era was about to dawn.

ADVERTISING AND THE EMPTY SELF: THE POST–WORLD WAR II ERA

On December 22, 1949, a rumpled, friendly Uncle Walt Wallet—an inaugural character in the comic strip *Gasoline Alley* and reluctant patriarch of the Wallet clan—sat back in his easy chair and looked directly into the reader's eyes. In a move uncharacteristic of the folksy, unself-conscious comic strip, Walt took a moment from the Christmas rush to speak directly to his longtime audience. By the time these four small panels were completed, Uncle Walt had reflected the mood of a country leaving behind the traumas of the Great Depression and World War II, and stepping off into a brave new postwar world. In a few well-chosen words, he evoked an America that was at first naive and un-involved, then committed and productive, and finally, by the eve of 1950, fruitful, reasonably safe, well off, and above all hopeful. It was Christmas 1949; for a moment, the emerging postwar era problems receded from view. Uncle Walt smiled and said: "Yes, when I was a bachelor my motto was, 'I know when I'm well off.' I didn't want to hop into matrimony, but somebody pushed me. I had Skeezix, but now I have Phyllis, and Corky and Judy and Nina, and Chipper, too. Clovia and Hope have just been added and we are all together for Christmas. Am I a lucky guy!"[78]

Indeed, Uncle Walt felt safe and proud, as did most Americans. The war had been won, the boys were back home again, business was good, new families were starting up, suburban housing developments were appearing, business was good, ex-servicemen were going to college, the United States stood alone as the most powerful military force in the world, business was good, it looked like the beloved "Ike" might run for president in 1952, and business was good. For a moment, even with all the uncertainties and rough spots at home and abroad, Americans took a moment and enjoyed a sigh of relief.

Walt Wallet was aptly named. The originator and artist of the strip, Franklin King, named his protagonist after two twentieth-century American preoccupations: money and identity. And indeed, Walt was like an old wallet: well-worn, overstuffed, a bit tattered at the corners, the once soft leather dry and shiny with overuse. Like an old wallet, Walt was a monument to procrastination: full of good intentions such as business cards, notes from old friends, and endless lists of things to do. There was something about old Walt that was small-town life, solid middle-class identity, and a no-nonsense trustworthiness and reliability. He was stuffed to overflowing with a good heart, a reluctant, individualistic sense of civic and familial duty, and a bemused but hopeful confusion about the future. He was identity and security—a Wallet through and through. And now the new, young Wallets—the battle-hardened and resourceful Skeezix and his wife Nina, the strange new "teenagers" Corky, his bride Hope, and his sister Judy, and the about to emerge postwar generation embodied by Clovia, blessed with peace, the glimmering of prosperity, and above all luck—What would *they* be like?

It would take decades for the postwar story to unfold, but in the meantime, *Gasoline Alley* stopped its readership for a moment, and helped the country count its blessings. It was a myopic, self-serving, all-too-brief personal accounting, as most celebrations are, but it was also a well-deserved moment of relief. The country had weathered some severe storms, it had been courageous and unbowed, and now it paused before plunging on.

Gasoline Alley was a popular newspaper cartoon that began in August 1919. It presented a neighborly, unthreatening celebration of middle-class American values, featuring soft, rounded figures and modulated colors, evocative of a slower, more innocent rural America that was rapidly disappearing during the postwar years. The strip's most distinctive feature was the innovative use of temporality: the characters aged realistically and struggled with mundane problems day by day. For these reasons *Gasoline Alley* became a kind of pretelevision soap opera. Between the years 1920 and 1950 the strip was one of the most popular cartoons in newspaper history, represented by the most prominent cartoon syndicate of its time, and carried by seven to eight hundred papers.[79] The writer-artist, King, was particularly accurate in portraying everyday material culture such as clothing, furniture, and hairstyles, and the strip's themes and overall look seem to have been fairly representative of the interests and concerns of the white middle classes in the years leading to mid-century.

The Post–World War II Middle-Class Terrain

In 1949 the country was trying to return to normalcy, and the populace was going about the business of accommodating the newly returned soldiers and their new families. There were veterans to be mourned, doctored, or put through college, babies to be born, and educated, houses to be built, industry to be strengthened. The country was proud, optimistic, yet cautious. Americans had seen events that were terrifying, evil that would shake the innocence of even the most confirmed "cockeyed optimist" from Little Rock, Arkansas, as the 1949 play *South Pacific* portrayed Nurse Nellie Forbush. But beneath the promising postwar exterior lurked many unresolved problems that would rear their ugly heads in the ensuing years. The allies had fought against the fascist regimes of Germany and Italy, which were founded on a racist ideology, yet the American forces were themselves still segregated according to race, and the Jim Crow laws of racial segregation and oppression in the South were still the law of the land. How would a more cosmopolitan, sophisticated America deal with the issue of race? Women had played an essential role in the wartime economy. What jobs would they hold when the men returned home? The Depression, which had caused enormous suffering, had been put on hold by the war and the necessity of a managed economy. Would the horror of worldwide depression return again once the war was over? The world had witnessed the most despicable war crimes in human history. How would the United States respond to the world's anti-Semitic indifference, the Japanese violations of the Geneva accords, and the devastation committed by the massive Allied air strikes such as the firebombing of Dresden? The war had barely ended when the fragile alliance between the Western democracies and the Soviet Union began to show signs of crumbling. Would the new peace hold? The old enemies had finally and at great cost been vanquished. From which corner of the globe would the next threat come? The final victory over Japan was brought about by the use of the new atom bomb. It was the most hideous and destructive weapon ever conceived of by humankind, and it was in the sole possession of the United States. To what use would it be put, and who would be next to possess it?

By 1949 these questions had not been answered yet, but some of them were becoming increasingly pressing. In September the USSR exploded its first nuclear device, three years ahead of U.S. predictions; a new, "cold" war began. Also, questions about the economy were beginning to come into focus: what President Dwight Eisenhower was later to call the military-industrial complex, together with a continuous wartime need for goods and services, had combined in the managed wartime economy to defeat the Depression. The need for military goods, of course, was not as great in peacetime; what would take its place in the new postwar economy, and who would manage it? In a world that was about to be introduced to the television and the two-car garage, something was about to change forever. *Gasoline Alley*, its finger ever on the pulse of middle-class life, described the moment.

In 1949 the comic strip ran a series of story lines in which its loyal, self-reliant small-town characters struggled to come to terms with a new world that featured a self-aggrandizing, sometimes corrupt, urban approach to the postwar age. Skeezix Wallet, the all-American boy soldier, the embodiment of American ingenuity, returned to his hometown after the war and started a (what else?) fix-it shop. His new business partner (someone who had weaseled out of soldiering) was corrupt and eventually betrayed him,[80] and the new fast-paced, advertising-oriented business economy seemed too complex for Skeezix.[81] He yearned to farm and return to a yeoman self-sufficiency he imagined in an idealized past.[82] His wife Nina convinced him to stay in the city (actually the new suburbs) by forcing him to face what life would be like without all the modern "conveniences" that were starting to be produced by the postwar economy.[83]

In the end, Skeezix stayed in the new postwar world, although he was disgusted by the overcrowding, the new suburbs, and the lack of traditional, prewar values. His brother and sister, too young to be in the war, were wearing strange clothes, performing strange dances, and acting insolent and rebellious.[84] Poor Skeezix could understand none of this. But he persevered, he and Nina settled down, and she became pregnant. In an important event that foreshadowed the future of the postwar era, Nina got stuck in traffic on the way to the hospital and was forced to give birth in a taxi.[85] On the infant's wrist was a birthmark in the shape of a four-leaf clover.[86] She was named Clovia, the embodiment of a new, *lucky* postwar America, born in a car.

Many of the aspects of the immediate postwar era with which the characters of *Gasoline Alley* struggled have now become familiar, highly developed features of the current American landscape. The inevitable products of war, such as Uncle Walt's fear and occasional paranoia, became manifest in the early postwar years through the mass paranoia evident in the domestic Red-baiting of the House Un-American Activities Committee hearings and the cold war. Uncle Walt and Skeezix had some difficulty accepting the new housing developments and the loss of unpopulated countryside, the faster pace of larger cities, the shift from a rural or small-town economy to urban industry, and especially the new economy's demands that businessmen be acquisitive, highly competitive, and well-versed in promotional activities such as advertising and marketing. The new focus on the acquisition of goods and the gratification of the individual consumer, the emphasis on personal "freedom," the growing importance of the automobile, and the early beginnings of a youth rebellion, all present in *Gasoline Alley* in 1949, were showing up throughout the country with increasing frequency.

Historians have described America at mid-century as highly urbanized and industrialized. In 1940 the urban population composed 77 percent of the whole; by 1970 it composed 95 percent.[87] Writers such as Fromm and Lasch have described postwar America as a society in which flash was valued over substance, opportunism over loyalty, salesmanship over integrity, and mobility over stability.[88] The car transformed urban living, and postwar industrialization brought with it new business capacities and new technologies, such as enormous advances in electronics, which fueled a demand for the electronic communications media, especially television. Increasingly some musicians and actors, using the promotional possibilities of the new media, began marketing themselves as the embodiment of personal freedom, self-expression, and sexual liberation.

More and more in the twentieth century the focus has come to rest on the isolated, self-contained individual.[89] People began to live ever more secluded and secular lives, forsaking even the shrinking nuclear family. The percentage of American households of seven or more persons declined from 35.9 percent in 1790, to 20.4 percent in 1900, to 5.8 percent in 1950. At the same time, households with only one person rose from 3.7 percent in 1790 to 9.3 percent in 1950—and to 18.5 percent in 1973. Households with two persons rose from 7.8 percent in 1790 to 28.1 percent in 1950.[90] Coincident with the decline of the extended family, the individual self came to be seen as the ultimate locus of salvation: the self was ever evolving, constantly changing, on a never-ending search for self-actualization and "growth."[91] Even today personal fulfillment is seen as residing primarily *within* the individual, who is supposed to be self-sufficient and self-satisfied.[92] For this self there are supposed to be no limits to achievement and enjoyment.

The Peacetime Economy, Buying on Credit, and the Self-Contained Individual

For the United States, one of the tasks of the 1950s was to convert its powerful international war machine into a viable international peacetime economy. This was not an easy task, and at times the country floundered in recessions, with the specter of the Great Depression never far from consciousness. But in the decades immediately following World War II, the U.S. economy learned one of the economic lessons of the war: in order to stay out of a depression, twentieth-century capitalism had to base its economy on the continual production and consumption of goods and services. Yet because it was now peacetime, enormous quantities of goods and services were not as essential nor as quickly used up as in wartime. Therefore, big business had to develop ways of selling goods that were not essential or well-made. In other words, the nation was now dependent on producing and selling nonessential and quickly obsolete products, services, and experiences that consumers could not save enough to afford. In order to allow consumers to purchase these products, banks had to develop new forms of easy credit. Personal credit, business credit, and government credit made it possible for the new economy to develop. But credit for what?

Because this new type of purchasing was foreign to most Americans, they had to be enculturated into a new way of thinking about themselves and thinking about the *meaning* of the process of purchasing and consuming. Just as *Gasoline Alley*'s Nina learned about the new postwar modern conveniences from radio, magazine, and newspaper ads, so too did the increasingly powerful print and electronic media unleash a flood of opinions about how postwar families should handle their finances (that is, spend their money). Just as large suburban housing developments began transforming the countryside in *Gasoline Alley*, countless ads, radio shows, and TV situation comedies portrayed a nation of postwar families that needed new homes. As ads portrayed a nation of new families, just like the Wallets, who needed modern electronic household gadgets in order to stay "scientific," healthy, and modern, new appliances appeared on the market and transformed household chores. Homes and products were expensive, and young middle-class families, fresh from the war effort and the G.I. Bill-financed university, could not save enough cash to purchase them. Thus credit became indispensable.[93] The percentage of after-tax income that Americans have saved decreased from a high of 25.5 percent in 1944 to less than 2 percent by 1986.[94] In contrast, the Japanese rate of savings is currently at 30 percent of after-tax income. During that same span of time, the volume of consumer installment loans rose from 5 percent of personal income in 1949, to 15 percent in 1979, to a record 20 percent by 1987.[95] Purchasing, rather than saving; indulging, rather than sacrificing, became the predominant style. In order to accomplish the enculturation into purchasing and consuming, a new cultural clearing with a new configuration of the self had to be constructed. And indeed, in the miraculous way these sea changes come about, through the intersection of various sociohistorical forces and events, a new self did begin to emerge.

The new cultural terrain was now oriented to purchasing and consuming rather than to moral striving; to individual transcendence rather than to community salvation; to isolated relationships rather than to community activism; to an individualistic mysticism rather than to political change. But this exclusive focus on the self-contained individual and on "personal," emotional relationships between individuals was something that was quite new in the West. As we saw in chapter two, the bounded, masterful self, which emerged slowly and unevenly in Western history, is a self that has specific psychological boundaries, a sense of personal agency that is located interiorly, and a wish to manipulate the external world for its own personal ends. In the post–World War II era in the United States the shape of the cultural landscape has configured the self of the middle and upper classes into a particular kind of masterful, bounded self: the empty self. By this I mean a self that experiences a significant absence of community, tradition, and shared meaning—a self that experiences these social absences and their consequences "interiorly" as a lack of personal conviction and worth; a self that embodies the absences, loneliness, and disappointments of life as a chronic, undifferentiated emotional hunger. It is this undifferentiated hunger that has provided the motivation for the mindless, wasteful consumerism of the late twentieth century. The post–World War II self thus yearns to acquire and consume as an unconscious way of compensating for what has been lost, and unknowingly it fuels the new consumer-orientated economy: the self is empty, and it strives, desperately, to be filled up.

Without the empty self, America's consumer-based economy (and its charismatically oriented political process) would be inconceivable. New fields such as advertising and psychology have responded to and further developed the new configuration of the empty self.[96] However, practitioners in both fields are placed in the position of being responsible for guiding and/or healing the empty self without being allowed to address the historical causes of the emptiness. Therefore they are placed in an impossible bind, one that makes their responsibilities difficult and problematic. In chapter nine we will examine evidence of the empty self in current psychological discourse about narcissism and borderline states, pop culture's emphasis on consuming, political advertising strategies that emphasize soothing, attunement, and charisma instead of critical thought, and the nationwide difficulty in maintaining intimate personal relationships.

Americans in the post–World War II era came to pursue self-improvement in a form and to a degree unknown before. As the individual's growth, enjoyment, and fulfillment putatively became the single most valued aspect of life,[97] several industries grew up to minister to the newly created needs: the cosmetics industry, the diet business, the electronic entertainment industry, preventive medical care, and the self-improvement industry (including mainstream psychotherapy, pop psychology, and pop religion). The technological advances in these fields have been astronomical, as has their increasing power to influence and control the mainstream of American life.

But how does this new self-improvement/self-gratification industry work? What makes this network possible? Why do Americans "need" these items and experiences now to a greater degree than they ever did before? Again, the formation of the empty self has made this situation possible; a sense of meaninglessness and absence feeds these businesses. Personal emptiness may be expressed in many ways, such as in low self-esteem (the absence of a sense of personal worth), values confusion (the absence of a sense of personal convictions), eating disorders (the compulsion to fill the emptiness with food, or to embody the emptiness by refusing food), drug abuse (the compulsion to use drugs to produce chemically induced sensory or emotional experiences, or the attempt to deaden all feeling including emptiness), and chronic consumerism (the compulsion to fill the void by acquiring consumer items and the need to experience "receiving" something from the world). Personal emptiness may also take the form of an absence of a sense of personal meaning. This can manifest as a hunger for spiritual guidance, which sometimes takes the form of a wish to be instantly filled up by the spirit of God, by a simpleminded, exclusive religious "truth," or by the power and personality of an authoritarian leader or guru.[98] For instance, one of the most au courant of New Age therapies is channeling, an experience in which an individual is said to be entered by the soul or spirit of another "entity," usually thought to be a god, who then speaks "important truths." The wish to be spiritually filled up and guided can make the individual vulnerable to the deceptive practices of restrictive religious cults or mass marathon psychology trainings,[99] or the destructiveness of charismatic political leaders,[100] unethical psychotherapists,[101] or even highly authoritarian and controlling romantic partners.[102]

The Empty Self and the Lifestyle Solution: Commercials, Celebrities, and Psychotherapists

In the second half of the twentieth century the configuration of the empty self has made it much easier for advertising to exert influence and control; and advertising, in turn, has been instrumental in the construction of the empty self. Because the postwar emptiness is, in part, an absence of communal beliefs and traditions, individuals in this era are particularly vulnerable to influence from cultural institutions such as advertising that emanates authority and certainty. A good case could be made that many current ads (for example, regarding body odor, hair color, or life insurance) are less a type of benign guidance and more a kind of coercive attack. Ads seem to criticize and condemn the average consumer while glorifying the model, extolling a standard of beauty and mastery impossible to achieve. Advertising certainly does not address itself to the underlying causes of the customer's problems (for example, alienating or uncertain employment, loneliness, loss of community); instead it turns to the refuge of what I will refer to as *the lifestyle solution*. Because advertising is unable to effect lasting change by developing political solutions to the problems of modern life, its cures are illusory cures. One common type of ad offers the fantasy that the consumer's life can be transformed into a glorious, problem-free life: the "life" of the model who is featured in the ad. This metamorphosis is accomplished by purchasing and "ingesting" the product. By surrounding themselves with the accoutrements of the model, by ingesting the proper liquid while wearing the proper clothing, all the while exhibiting the proper body shape, consumers seek to "become" the model. Consumers' problems will simply disappear, the ad implies, when the magical transfer takes place. The lifestyle solution is advertising's cure for the empty self.

The accoutrements of a model in an advertisement are, of course, a poor substitute for the tools traditional cultures use for curing the sick. According to anthropologist Clifford Geertz, traditional cultures use a web of meaning, an array of stories, songs, beliefs, traditional folk wisdom, rituals, ceremonial objects, costumes, and potions that heal by teaching the society's cultural frame of reference and applying the culture's traditional folk wisdom to every day problems.[103] In contrast, ads substitute the concept of lifestyle for this workable web of folk meanings: they set forth a kind of mimicry of traditional culture for a society that has lost its own. In this way, lifestyle is used as a pseudoculture—a pseudoculture that promises an instant, illusory cure, a "transformation."

The hope of substituting one identity, one life, for another is used as a sales strategy for many products today. Stuart Ewen has referred to this as "the consumable life, the buyable fantasy."[104] Examples are numerous: the yuppie Lowenbrau models who lift their bottles and say, "Here's to good friends"; the working-class Old Milwaukee buddies who maintain, "It doesn't get any better than this"; the upper-class commercial that portrays a yachting/equestrian "Cadillac style," or the ad that asks, "What kind of man reads *Playboy*?"; cigarette ads that feature the Marlboro Man, Camel's man-beast who is a "smooth character," or the Virginia Slims model who has "come a long way, baby"; and of course toothpaste and deodorant ads that transform models by delivering to them instant sex appeal and popularity. Consumers are customers that buy lifestyle in a vain attempt to transform their lives because their lives are unsatisfying and—without massive societal change—ultimately unfixable. As a salve, advertising can only offer the illusory exchange of one life for another.

But the self is now not only suffering from feeling unreal, and thereby somewhat passively hoping for a cure, as it did at the turn of the century; it is also aggressively, sometimes desperately, acquisitive. It must consume in order to be soothed and satisfied; it must "take in" and merge with a selfobject celebrity, an ideology, or a drug, or it will be in danger of feeling worthless, confused, and despairing.

The use of the image of the masterful, bounded self is everywhere in post–World War II advertising. Marlboro ads, which maintained some of the highest recognition value in postwar television, are a good example. The Marlboro Man, young, ruggedly handsome, and physically strong, is portrayed as calm, competent, and alone. He appears supremely at ease with himself and the wilderness. The message appears to be that this is what a real male should be like: He needs no one, he is afraid of no one, and he is perfectly content in his isolation. He is often accompanied by a horse, and this appears to be the only relationship he requires. On a lighter note, Mug Root Beer commercials use a jingle that portrays another aspect of the individual self—its uniqueness. The cheery singers intone: "Mug Root Beer is just like you: it's one of a kind." The soft drink 7-Up commercials also stress the product's uniqueness. By not being a cola (that is, an "uncola") 7-Up can proudly claim, "There's only one un." The Best Western Hotel chain claims that it is "as individual as America itself." Mastery, another unquestioned quality depicted in advertising, is present in most ads the public is exposed to. Control, manifested through achievements such as social popularity, hygienic excellence, or financial security is constantly reinforced. Toothpaste, clothing, beer and alcohol, and life insurance are all commodities that, once purchased and used, transform consumers into confident, powerful, secure people who are obviously in control of their own destiny.

The portrayal of personal, internal emptiness is another aspect of the postwar cultural clearing, but it is more difficult to notice in ads. In one of the more obvious ads, Snickers sings to us that "There's a hunger inside you that won't go away, grows stronger every day. (Chorus) There's a hunger inside me, a hunger inside you." This blatant statement, however, is the exception. A better measure of the amount of emptiness taken for granted in television ads is to observe how many ads portray individuals who are either searching for something to acquire or consume, are attempting to choose between two or more items they wish to acquire or consume, or are in need of recovering from having acquired or consumed too much. It appears to be a taken for granted assumption in our society that individuals are constantly searching, desiring, grasping, "on the make." We do not consider this type of activity to be remarkable or unusual; in fact, it is the norm.

Another category of ads extoll the importance of credit. In an economy based on the continual production and consumption of nonessential and quickly obsolete goods, the public must both *want* and be *able* to consume nonessentials at moderate to high levels. Credit is only necessary when the individual's wish to buy outstrips his or her accumulated capital. The public has to be instructed as to, or rather, initiated into the importance of consistently spending more money than they have. This has been a difficult task given the relative importance Americans placed on frugality and savings a short two thirds of a century ago. But one effective tool has been the advertising campaigns large banking firms have presented in which credit is depicted as a necessity and perhaps even a virtue. In California, Bank of America developed what it referred to as a "Bankamericard." The concept quickly took off: Credit became an indispensable element in the healing technology of advertising. Since the empty self could be healed by consuming and transformed by commodities, the public had to be able to purchase the commodities.

Two late 1980s MasterCard commercials demonstrate how advertising firms convinced consumers to use credit and to accumulate personal debt. In one, a beautiful young woman (Shari Belafonte) is standing in an empty apartment. She smiles and says, "MasterCard, furnish my flat!" Magically, expensive, brightly colored, perfectly coordinated furnishings appear and are properly arranged by invisible workers. To extend Foucault's historical description of the "deep, richly furnished interior" of the modern self, Belafonte's private space was effortlessly filled up, or "richly furnished," by MasterCard. She didn't have to plan, save, choose, agonize, arrange, or pay for her "furnishings." All she needed was credit.

A second MasterCard commercial features a famous actor (Robert Duvall) in the late 1980s commercial style of the anticommercial format. Duvall just lectures the audience by explaining how in real life he doesn't play a role, he is just himself. He ends the monologue by saying, "MasterCard: Master the possibilities." In this commercial viewers are obliquely criticized for playing roles in life, for not being strong, self-sufficient, authentic individuals who do not need to please others (that is, play roles) and who can do anything on their own. Here we see the twentieth century's characteristic focus on "authenticity," combined with the Marlboro Man's toughness, extreme individualism, and isolation. The implication is that MasterCard (that is, credit) can help consumers transcend all social roles and responsibilities and the need to tailor their behavior so as to please and cooperate with others; it does this by liberating individuals from the limitations of personal cash-and-carry financing. Strong, self-sufficient people like Duvall are not limited by convention; when they want a product or an experience, they simply go out and get it.

MasterCard can help consumers do that by liberating consumers from the social convention of paying for what they want to buy. MasterCard can get them anything, at anytime; and when they acquire and consume these things, they can "master" any occurrence. Note the unquestioned assumption that buying something means mastering it. Here we see the near total commodification of life in the postwar era: Even the most ephemeral aspect of human life, temporality, is made into a commodity. Even that which has not yet happened, the "possibility" of an unknowable future, can be purchased, consumed, and therefore mastered, by using credit. There is something insidious about all this, not the least of which is that the unquestioned assumption is that the highest act to which an individual can aspire is to be the master. Dominance is portrayed as a central value, and it is achieved through purchasing and consuming.

Yet another category of advertisement enshrines the activities of self-aggrandizement and self-improvement. The message is constantly displayed on television commercials, where the motive of keeping up with (rather than cooperating with) the Joneses is treated as an unquestioned value. Merrill Lynch, an investment firm, tells the viewer, "You should know no boundaries." This is a particularly interesting turn of phrase because it is precisely the boundedness of the modern era self that is one of its primary characteristics. The phrase "to know no boundaries" seems to be a direct encouragement to inflate one's sense of entitlement beyond any limit. Michelob Light, another commercial tells us, is for those consumers who "want it all." The U.S. Army promotes enlistment by encouraging viewers with the slogan "Be all that you can be." The ethos of self-aggrandizement must be pretty dominant in a society for an army to be able to use that slogan as a recruiting device. These messages imply that the individual self and its entitlements can be virtually limitless and that the highest value is to get as much as one possibly can, to excell and acquire beyond all standards, to refuse to limit one's power to earn, purchase, and consume.

It is also difficult to watch television for any length of time without seeing commercials that appeal to the unquestioned assumption that the viewer needs to, must be, improved. This taken-for-granted understanding about what it means to be human—that one must be fixed, adjusted, remade, or healed—seems to be so central an aspect of the postwar clearing that it is never really noticed, let alone challenged. Diet plans do not have to persuade viewers that they need to lose weight. Cosmetic products do not need to explain why women require makeup, perfume, perms, or breast implants. Beer commercials that use sex to sell their products do not need to argue to men that they must be made much more dominant and their lives need to be more exciting before they can get dates with young, beautiful, sexy women. Consumers "know," without being told or convinced, that they are not adequate as they are. They appear to be fully aware that they are inadequate, unattractive, incomplete, or inconsequential and must be transformed into different people in order to be happy, loved, and fulfilled. Ads that use this current folk understanding about the self both reflect and reinforce the public's sense of inadequacy and the felt urgency to be fixed or "therapied." Here we see that the mode of self-surveillance, first practiced in the panopticon of the nineteenth century (see chapter four), has become an unquestioned way of life in late twentieth-century America.

Still another way advertising adds to the construction of the current self is by constantly reiterating the message that consuming fills the emptiness of the self and transforms the individual. Crystal Light, a soft drink mix, tells the viewer that it is "Refreshment for body and soul." A popular commercial of the 1980s featured a bright, friendly young man and a cast of many others happily dancing across the stage singing "Be a pepper, drink Dr. Pepper." The verve and well-being of the dancers, clearly the central message of the scene, was implicitly attributed to purchasing and consuming the drink. In the same vein, a Michelob commercial intones "A Michelob night will make your day." This means consuming Michelob beer at night in social situations will make one's life meaningful and worthwhile (it is also a double entendre: "make your day" could be taken to mean having sexual intercourse). Spuds McKensie, a dog featured in Bud Light commercials during the late 1980s and early 1990s, is introduced as "the original party animal" (a play on words referring to a person who consumes a great deal of alcohol and drugs, has a wild time at parties, and is very attractive to members of the opposite sex). Indeed, wherever Spuds goes, several beautiful, scantily clad young women admiringly follow. Why? Because he drinks the correct beer (Bud Light). Or rather because consuming the correct beer has transformed Spuds from the wrong kind of person (a dog) into the perfect kind of person (a "party animal"). That's what consuming can do: It can transform the empty individual into a new, nondepressed, sexy, popular, rich, altogether happy and satisfied person who attracts others.

The ability of commodities to transform the consumer is demonstrated in a great many commercials. For instance, a well-dressed, powerful man in a Cadillac commercial tells us that he drives an Eldorado because "I need to recharge my batteries." In a similar vein, BMW explains that their luxury sedan is "an executive decompression chamber. We think $33,000 isn't too much to pay for an attitude adjustment." Coca-Cola often produces soft drink commercials with a transformational theme. For instance, it's a very hot day at the football field and several NFL stars are out practicing. It's so hot that they start to melt into little puddles of uniform. Boomer Esiason, star quarterback, notices his pals are melting and runs to the soft drink cooler. He reaches in, pulls out several large bottles of Coca-Cola products, and passes them to his buddies, who are by this time simply puddles of red or blue or green with arms and a head. As soon as they consume the soft drink they resume their regular awesome shapes.

The *passive* nature of being transformed through consumption is well illustrated by a Bud Dry ad campaign that features the slogan "Don't ask why, drink Bud Dry." Each ad presents several short dramas in which the problem is so puzzling that it defies comprehension. In one drama a young man is completely baffled by his girlfriend, who is angry with him about something that he does not, and cannot, understand. Men and women are depicted as being "naturally" and inevitably in conflict. The voiceover then intones, "Don't ask why, drink Bud Dry." The ad implies that it is futile for men and women to try to think about, study, and search their respective souls in order to understand their relationship and develop mutually agreeable solutions to their problems. It is impossible for the "war between the sexes" to be understood and resolved; the only possible response is to drink, and thereby avoid discomfort and stress. The solution to interpersonal conflict and confusion is to anesthetize, gratify, and indulge oneself. The anti-intellectual nature of this ad campaign is as objectionable as is its advocacy of passive drug use in service of the fantasy of transformation.

The portrayal of commodities as *the* transformational tool is particularly troubling when one considers the enormous problem of drug use in our society today. It should not be surprising that children and young adults turn to the consumption of drugs (a commodity) when they want to escape a difficult situation, alter how they feel, or even enhance their attractiveness to others. Of course they think that purchasing and ingesting a commodity will transform them; they have seen it happen for years, day in and day out, in television commercials. A good example of this theme is a 1991 soft drink commercial in which a senior citizens center and a college fraternity both throw parties on the same day. Unfortunately, the respective soft drink orders are mistakenly switched and subsequently delivered to the wrong parties. The seniors receive the highly invigorating, youth-inducing Pepsi, and the fraternity boys receive the Coca-Cola, which causes boredom, stupidity, and an early onset of old age. Viewers are treated to scenes of transformed seniors daringly riding skateboards, dancing the latest dances, using the latest youth language, and generally looking ecstatically happy. In the other scene the fraternity boys have been transformed into dull, napping, senile old folks, trying to stay awake during their bingo game. The commodity is all-powerful, and through purchasing and consuming it, the very nature or essence of personal identity of the consumer is transformed. One can see this theme reflected in several psychotherapy addiction theories, where the commodity, drugs, is considered to be able to take over and control the individual. (This will be discussed in more detail in chapters eight and ten.)

Depicting the commodity as the ultimate transformational object is a strategy that naturally leads to a last category of commercials that depict the construction of the empty self. In an increasing number of ads, commodities are actually portrayed as possessing human traits and personalities. In ads of this type, there is little that distinguishes humans from commodities; a qualitative difference no longer seems to exist. Examples of this type of ad are commercials that feature (1) the 7-Up dot, which sings and dances; (2) walking, talking, football-playing beer cans; and (3) a loving "couple" composed of a human and an automobile. The 7-Up dot has progressed from a tiny cameo role to a starring role in which dots sing, dance, play basketball, have ambition (for example, want to win money on a 7-Up sweepstakes contest), and manifest feelings such as hope and anger. The "Bud Bowl" is a serial commercial composed of an imaginary football game played by two kinds of beer, the Bud team and the Bud Light team. Action is depicted through a stop-action technique that makes it appear as though beer cans and bottles are actually moving and talking. Since 1989 this "game" has been "played" during the real Super Bowl, America's most significant and most watched football game of the season. The beer cans have identities and personalities (some shaped to resemble real football players such as Chicago's William "Refrigerator" Perry), and the games revolve around humanlike dramas. If commodities are like humans, then consuming is like relating: it is satisfying, soothing, energizing; it drives away loneliness; and it makes life rich and rewarding.

A 1990 commercial for Kragen Auto Parts was particularly effective in illustrating the humanization of the commodity. The commercial opens in black-and-white. A young man is lovingly washing his car while the song "When a Man Loves a Woman" plays hauntingly in the background. The voiceover explains that the man's girlfriend got impatient with his devotion to his car and forced him to choose between the two. He chose the car, because it "never lets him down." By purchasing the proper automobile parts the young man has constructed the perfect partner, a mechanical lover who will never be demanding or disappointing, and won't ever hurt him. The commercial ends with the loving "couple" (the man and his car) driving off into the sunset together; the film has turned into color. What turns out to be "sexy" in this commercial is not an individual but the sense of total safety and security that is achieved because the proper product is purchased and "consumed." Individuals who have been addicted to a drug often describe their relationship with the drug in a similar way. For instance, taking heroin is sometimes referred to as riding the white lady, and a crack pipe has been likened to a lover.

This same amorous, idealized attachment to the commodity is also expressed in a commercial for Chevrolet, in which a young woman (obviously on a romantic date) sits in front of a new Chevy. She just stares at it, adoringly and silently, as if it were her young lover. Her rapt attention "takes in" her date in all its precious detail as evocative, romantic music plays. The mood is calm and serene, and she is completely satisfied. Given the usual portrayal of male-female relations on television, that is, the battle between the sexes, the obvious difference in the level of satisfaction is striking. Commodities, these ads imply, or at least the *proper* commodities, are much better romantic partners: they are reliable, safe, and transformative.

Historians and the public have often been puzzled by the rather abrupt change in the cultural terrain symbolized by the differences between the 1960s and the 1980s. However, after reviewing the history of the West, and especially of the modern age, the apparent rollback of values from the 1960s to the 1980s seems much more understandable. This is particularly apparent in the baby boomers, the children of the white middle-class born after World War II.

Middle-class whites born during the baby boom after World War II were told that they were the privileged generation of the most privileged and powerful country on earth. As they grew up there were enormous technological advances in the physical sciences, encouraged by a growing postwar middle-class affluence, and the culture's continuing assault on tradition and community combined with a new sense of America's power and influence. These conditions created a new demographic cohort, the baby boom generation, whose themes of liberation, individualism, and relatedness would become at first subversive, then highly influential culturally and politically, and finally easily exploitable by the forces of American business in the second half of the twentieth century. This was the group that most symbolized the 1960 to early 1970s decade, identified with the civil rights movement, antiwar protests, and the counterculture. Although what has been fondly referred to as "the revolution" was indeed a departure from earlier decades in the United States, it was not able to effect a significant shift in the foundational aspect of the cultural terrain that had been five hundred years in the making: the masterful, bounded, and finally empty self.

Baby boomers were a new phenomenon: they were brought up on affluence, rising expectations, a relative absence of international warfare, and television. They were "the Pepsi Generation," young, brash, spontaneous, naive, idealistic, privileged. They went to college in unprecedented numbers, were sent to ride the crest of the postwar economic boom. But what they found at college wasn't what they, or their society, expected. They didn't automatically learn business skills and fit into the new postwar society. Instead they learned about the underside of U.S. history: the lynchings, the Jim Crow laws, disguised class conflict, the oppression of women, and a destructive foreign policy predicated on a cold war that was equal parts paranoia, economic imperialism, and military opportunism. When this group began to rise up in protest, it did so with a naive idealism that was well meaning if not politically effective. It was the war in Vietnam that turned idealistic and often ineffective protest into confusion, disbelief, resolve, effective action, betrayal, rage, and finally chaos. The senseless horror of Vietnam forced the baby boomers to see beneath the veneer of postwar affluence and liberalism. It was this confrontation with the underpinnings of capitalism, racism, and sexism that was too much for them to bear, emotionally, and too complicated for them to change, politically. The antiwar movement could cause the Nixon administration enough trouble to contribute to ending the war, but it didn't sustain the dedication or develop the intellectual acuity to create and then carry out a new, viable program for massive sociocultural change. The task of effecting change was too great for any one group to undertake, even a group as energetic, bright, but ultimately flawed as the baby boomers. The forces at work to prevent such reforms had enormous resources at their command; foremost among these were the seductions of the consumer-oriented economy—and the vulnerability of the baby boomers to just such a strategy. In a few short years the enormity and complexity of the political changes that were required, the hostile, violent opposition they faced, and the physical and emotional dangers resistance entailed created in the movement a despair and a faltering of vision that ultimately proved fatal.

The masterful, bounded, empty self was as much the configuration of the post–World War II baby boomers as it was the rest of the population, perhaps even more so, since the boomers were *the* defining symbol of the postwar era. Ultimately, they were punished for their resistance, and the seductions of wealth and privilege that society held out as a reward for compliance became too much to resist. What was once open rebellion has become nervous consumerism. The baby boom cohort, today in the throws of a serious recession, has accommodated in order to survive. It is overworked, stressed out, and confused. And when the disappointments and despair rise up, it anesthetizes itself with the usual isolating, mind-numbing, counterrevolutionary consumer items: drugs, electronic toys, cosmetics, mass entertainment, corrupt charismatic leaders, and, unfortunately, some problematic forms of therapy. In the end, the construction of the empty self was too strong for a young, naive, proportionally small group of privileged middle-class college graduates to defeat. Significant sociopolitical change in the last decade of the twentieth century will continue to be ineffective unless a political movement can take into consideration the current configuration of the self and develop ways of reconfiguring the self so that it will be at once more socially cooperative and less vulnerable to consumerism, less rigidly masterful and bounded and not as empty as our present configuration.

CHAPTER FOUR

Healing through Self-Domination

CAPITALISM, THE ASYLUM, THE UNTAMED FEMALE BODY, AND FREUD

*Man is born free, and everywhere
he is in chains.*
— JEAN-JACQUES ROUSSEAU
SOCIAL CONTRACT

One of the most remarkable changes occasioned by the modern era has been its particular version of the realm of the mental. Today we accept the mind, "mental illness," and psychotherapy as unexceptional elements of our everyday life. But this was not always so in Western society. The early 1600s witnessed the beginnings of an enormous shift in the European cultural terrain, brought on in large part by the confluence of individualism, capitalism, and the new empirical sciences. The shift can be illustrated by noting the differences between a medieval world in which satanic possession was the problem and exorcism the cure, and a modern world in which "madness" was the problem and medical incarceration and the reestablishment of the domination of rationality over the emotions was the cure.

In the medieval worldview, God had designed the world and remained a continuing participant in it. He was an active agent, speaking to, through, and against elements of the terrain. Using the elements of nature, such as storms, stars, or even the entrails of a pigeon, God made known His pleasure or anger at the behavior of humankind, revealed the future, guided the pious, and punished the evildoer. The medieval natural world was alive with God's presence: it was enchanted. But during the seventeenth century, the terrain that used to be populated with opposing distinctions such as God and the devil, purity and sin, holiness and possession—somehow made room for new opposing pairs such as empiricism and superstition, scientific calculation and folk traditions, logic and the rule of unreason. What had once been an enchanted world designed by God and interpreted by the Church became a *disenchanted* land that could only be properly understood through secular, man-made tools such as empirical study, mathematical calculations, and logic.

The natural world changed from a living reflection of God's truth to a collection of inert "things," from the inexplicable products of God's handiwork (which only the Church could properly understand) to "objects" of scientific study, which could be studied, quantified, counted, and manipulated, according to various scientific principles, and then controlled by the mind of any learned individual (regardless of religious creed or socioeconomic class) who properly exercised the scientific method.

The political implications (and sometimes precursors) of this change, such as the rise of democratic sympathies and the Church's loss of, or at least lessened, status, were reflected in modern era events such as the Reformation and later the massive secularization of the twentieth century. The vision of a world of inert matter controlled by the mind also established a cultural frame of reference that created new relationships that were also expressions of domination, such as humankind over nature, capital over labor, male over female, mind over body, physician over patient. Eventually, even psychological healing showed up as a type of domination. As we shall see, this was more the case in Europe than in America. European domination theory was an important aspect of the early American Colonies: the Puritans, for instance, favored domination-ist ideas in social practices such as child rearing.[1] But in the late eighteenth and throughout the nineteenth-century in America, a radical shift to a liberationist framework emerged. (See chapter five.)

At first, madness was attributed to reason being overwhelmed by wild, irrational emotions; later, with early nineteenth-century moral reforms, it was attributed to a lack of individual discipline, self-control, and proper bourgeois domesticity. But in either case, as the eighteenth century progressed, possession by the devil stopped "showing up" as the major cause of disruptive behavior.[2] In opposition to the place that possession used to occupy, there began to appear a potential space in which modern, psychological madness could show up. Of course, it took well over a century for the everyday meanings of madness to be articulated as illness, a psychological illness, and finally one of *many* psychological illnesses. The point is that a new configuration of the self was coming into being, one that was vulnerable not to an invasion by the devil, but to an attack by the forces of unreason. Later, in the early nineteenth century, further iterations of the new self emerged, one struggling with self-control and self-discipline.

It follows that the priest who could cure through exorcism would be less needed in a world in which disruptive behavior happened not because of the devil but because of the failure of the individual's rationality and will. And even less would the priest be needed in a world in which neurosis was the problem and self-control, logic, and bourgeois domestication the cure. Thus, eventually, the priest gave way to the psychiatrist, the Church to science, and the prescriptions of medieval roles to the exercise of self-control through the practices of self-domination.

ORIGINS AND MEANINGS OF THE ASYLUM

In the course of less than two centuries, the frame of human being underwent a radical shift. What was once a spiritual being who contained a soul and was embedded within a community that was in turn held in the hand of God, had become an early modern individual who contained a mind which was dependent upon the domination of reason and will over the wild emotions of the body. This individual was set adrift amongst a loose-knit network of semi-acquaintances who would, if need be, institutionalize, confine, and dominate him or her in a desperate attempt to protect polite society and, if possible, return the afflicted person to productive labor.[3]

In the new cultural terrain of the modern era, the mind was becoming a thing in its own right, in contact with but separate from the body. This modern mind was not so much a battleground in which God and the devil contended; instead it was an entire *realm* that was governed by the natural laws of science and logic, and it was superior to the body and other aspects of the world of matter. Slowly, the mind began to show up as the most important quality of human being. It was through the mind that logic and science were exercised, and thus through the mind that the world of matter was dominated and controlled. Because domination and control were the order of the day in the emerging capitalist economy, the mind, as the instrument of domination, was becoming the *essential* quality of the self. It was to become the most studied, focused upon, worried over, experimented with, and revered subject of the modern era. Those who were thought to understand it, and were responsible for healing it, became increasingly powerful.

Several historians have traced the many shapes and meanings of

psychiatry and the asylum, from the early warehouse for the incapacitated, to the Bethlem (or Bedlam) "madhouse" of the eighteenth
century, to the York Retreat of the moral reformers in the early
nineteenth century.[4] Before the mid-eighteenth century, there was not a
commonly accepted social category for those members of the English
population whose behavior was disruptive owing to what we would
today call psychological reasons. They were simply part of a large
segment of the population thought to be disruptive: the poor, the sick,
the homeless, the troublesome, the bizarre. They were commonly understood to be the responsibility of their communities and their families. However, as the century advanced, and society became more
industrialized and urbanized, the category of "mad" increasingly was
used as a means of separating and describing a segment of the troublesome population, and the state began to take more responsibility for
defining and confining the insane.[5] Also private institutions, run by
fledgling custodial entrepreneurs, were operated for wealthy families
who were all too willing to secret away their disruptive and embarrass-
ing relatives. Enterprising laymen often ran these private asylums, but
as the asylums became more lucrative, physicians became more involved.[6]

All three types of medical workers at the time—apothecaries,
surgeons, and physicians—became interested in the lunatic. They
claimed that their scientific medical practices, which included secret
herbs, potions, and purging and depleting procedures, all used to balance the humors, were appropriate for the mad. Medical treatment at
this time did not depend on diagnostically determined remedies: all
maladies were treated with the same methods. In the case of the insane,
a special group of practices was added to the usual medical ministrations. The mad were thought to be acting strangely because either their
ideas had gotten trapped in defective or disoriented mental "pathways,"
or their native reasoning abilities were not controlling their emotions.
The mad were without their major controlling faculty and were therefore savage, violent, and ultimately dangerous to individual citizens and
polite society.

It followed that asylum doctors attempted in various ways to
coerce inmates into complying with society's rules. Commonly used
techniques included forced exercise, forced restraint, imprisonment,
purging, vomiting, beatings, public humiliation, blistering of the forehead, bloodletting, water torture such as surprise forced immersions,
and swinging devices (sometimes employed in the dark) that produced
vertigo, nausea, terror, exhaustion, fatigue, convulsions, and "an instant
discharge of the contents of the stomach, bowels, and bladder, in quick

succession."[7] Benjamin Rush, a famous American psychiatrist, devised a restraining chair that he called the Tranquilizer. "It binds and confines," Rush wrote,

> every part of the body. By keeping the trunk erect, it lessens the impetus of blood toward the brain. By preventing the muscles from acting, it reduces the force and frequency of the pulse, and by the position of the head and feet favors the easy application of cold water or ice to the former and warm water to the latter. Its effects have been truly delightful to me. It acts as a sedative to the tongue and temper as well as to the blood vessels. In 24, 12, six, and in some cases in four hours, the most refractory patients have been composed.[8]

Hermann Boerhaave, a Dutch physician, enthusiastically recommended near drowning as an effective treatment. Hidden trapdoors in corridors that suddenly dropped inmates into the "bath of surprise," and submersible coffinlike containers with holes drilled in their sides were just two of the many water-torture devices employed in seventeenth- and eighteenth-century asylums.

A puzzling change occurred in the seventeenth century when some European leper houses were emptied and over time made into warehouses for the poor and the criminal. In the mid-seventeenth century, the king of France established the Hospital General, which took in the poor, the mad, and the indigent. Foucault was moved to inquire as to the meaning of such a change, and he decided that it was part of a turning point in European history. "The great internment" demonstrated a societal preoccupation with the poor and the troublesome. In Adam Smith's terms, the poor—embodying as they did a potential labor force—had become a national treasure, and thus they had to be counted, observed, and categorized in order to be better utilized and controlled. In the Middle Ages, lepers were thought to be punished by God for being sinful; thus leper colonies had to be located so that their inmates would be isolated from the general population while they remained close enough to serve as a reminder of the fate of the sinner. But Foucault argued that as the cultural landscape shifted and as the central distinctions changed from pious and sinful to capital and labor, the function the lepers carried out was no longer needed. Instead what was required were institutions that facilitated the transformation of the able-bodied poor into the working class. This in turn necessitated the classification, counting, and rehabilitation of the able-bodied, and that required a *distinction* between the able-bodied and the nonable-bodied. As the modern era progressed, various groups of scholars-philosophers-criminologists-doctors—the ancestors of the social scientist—began to develop ways of studying and influencing the poor and the working classes.

In the first two centuries of the modern era, the nations of Europe were in the process of attempting to consolidate their power and develop ways of controlling their modern, increasingly individual, populations. The authority of Church and Crown, the value of tradition, and the cooperative comfort of community and family were slowly being undermined and eclipsed by the emergence of the modern scientific, capitalist state. Further, capitalism led to a shift in European and French society from a hierarchy dependent on inherited rank to one based on socioeconomic class. For the lower socioeconomic classes, survival became dependent on the exchange of labor for currency, and families were put in a precarious position: they were usually unable to save enough to subsist during the times family members would be out of work. As Adam Smith explained,[9] the continual fear of starvation and homelessness was thought to be a necessary element in the grand scheme of capitalism, for without the motivating factor of "want," labor would not be sufficiently mobile or productive. Thomas Hobbes's characterization of life as "solitary, nasty, brutish, and short" becomes understandable as one reads accounts of life in the growing urban centers. Therefore, individuals who acted in bizarre, unproductive, or disruptive ways became an increasing drain on the family. First the Elizabethan Poor Laws of 1601, and later the laws pertaining to the forced confinement of the insane, provided for an alternative, institutional solution to the weakening of lower-class families by their noncontributing members. Although the causes of early modern mental disorders are beyond the scope of this book, it seems probable that the enormous disruptions caused by the destruction of traditional community life, immigration to the cities, and the degrading, physically *destructive*, and unreliable nature of employment in an unstable economy often caused the poor to be anxious, afraid, confused, angry, frustrated, and hopeless. Many of the accounts of lunacy during this time describe behavior that might have been linked to the material conditions of the afflicted person's life.

But deviant behavior that led to reduced economic productivity was a drain not only on the family but more importantly on the nation as a whole. The puzzle of the origin and meaning of the asylum becomes more understandable when we realize that in the minds of the ruling class in eighteenth-century England and France, the health of the nation's economy (and the growth of people's personal fortunes) depended upon the ability to distinguish between the able-bodied and the nonable-bodied worker.[10] The importance of this distinction is obvious once one recalls Adam Smith's arguments regarding the motivations of labor. If society does not distinguish between those able and unable to work, relief might be given to *all* nonproductive deviants, including those who simply *chose* not to work. If they were permitted to collect relief simply because they did not wish to work, it was thought, the "natural" motivation of the labor force would be undone, which would in turn unbalance and ultimately destroy the economy. Only when labor is in want, Smith taught, will it be motivated and mobile—that is, available to be exploited. Therefore it was imperative that the state develop the ability to separate the laggards from the truly incapacitated—otherwise there would not be enough of a labor force to pull a budding modern industry.

At first it was assumed that the recently urbanized peasants could be forced to be obedient subjects of the new nation states and workers in the new modern era economies through the application of physical coercion, such as torture and public hangings.[11] However, it became obvious as the modern era progressed that violence was not an adequate strategy for controlling people. It was inefficient, undependable, and too costly given the enormous changes in the modern population, which was increasingly more mobile, independent, and critical. Individuals were required to adapt to radically different ways of thinking and to develop many unfamiliar skills, while they could not rely on folk traditions, former communities, even parents, to instruct them. Somehow the emerging workforce had to be made to conform to the economic requirements of the era automatically and without ongoing, explicit coercion by the government.

Because of the increased value placed on individuality and personal independence, the new population had to be controlled in such a way that the population's growing sense of personal freedom and agency would not be violated. Sufficient compliance was achieved over time by new social practices developed in institutions such as the asylum, the modern prison, and later the school. Central to the new practices was the concept of self-domination, which took decades to develop and centuries to institute and perfect. The new form of control was accomplished through an understanding of the individual that featured self-control. In order to achieve *self*-control it was necessary to view individuals as possessing a mental apparatus that was rational, private, and located *inside* each individual's brain. This apparatus came to be viewed as the battleground on which two important qualities of the mind, rationality and will, would triumph over the "uncivilized" animal instincts of the body.

The asylum was one of several new social structures that emerged in this era and eventually became responsible for constructing the modern self, which was composed of commendable qualities such as self-containment, self-control, individualism, mastery, and boundedness. Prisons, schools, medical health spas, as well as asylums, all evolved into institutions that reshaped the economically unproductive or socially disruptive deviant into the type of individual who was intent upon and capable of constantly "watching" and dominating him- or herself in service of becoming the proper, "normal" laborer or member of the bourgeoisie. These institutions were "quasi-military" training experiences that were designed to instill in the deviant the incentives and the psychological capacity to conduct the kind of continuous self-objectification, self-surveillance, and self-control required of the modern populace.

Jeremy Bentham, creator of the Panopticon, the visionary prison described in chapter two, aptly characterized these early modern institutions as "a mill to grind rogues honest and idle men industrious."[12] Of course, this applies to asylums as well as to prisons: inmates were either cured, and thus made into productive laborers, or found to be incurably insane, and thus forever confined and isolated so as not to disrupt the ordered workings of polite society or be an economic drag on it. Foucault, in a masterful move, used the socialization processes at work in the asylum and prison as a metaphor for the exercise of state power on *all* groups within the modern era population. He thought that the relocation of the coercive element from an external army or religious authority to a "voice" within the individual's private mental interior did not do away with coercion; it merely reframed coercion and thus mystified its source and political function. Thus in Foucault's writing the asylum and prison were not only deemed new forms of socialization; they were also used as a metaphor for illustrating how a new exercise of power could be developed by shifting the cultural frame of reference.

THE MORAL REFORM MOVEMENT

Without the faculty of reason, individuals were not considered completed, fully human persons and thus were not entitled to the same rights as others. Ridicule, humiliation, and torture were therefore not considered unkind or immoral treatments for the lunatic. These practices were simply thought to be scientific attempts to destroy or reorient dysfunctional mental pathways, or to coerce the emotions into submission, to bring them again under the domination of reason and the will. In fact,

Bethlem, the most famous "luney bin" in England, provided opportunities for middle-class visitors to witness the treatment of the insane as one would view animals in the zoo: an outing to Bethlem was considered uproarious, although occasionally terrifying, entertainment. But by the early decades of the nineteenth century this treatment was considered shocking and abusive.

In 1796 William Tuke, an English Quaker, founded the York Retreat in northern England, a small (twenty- to thirty-bed) facility dedicated to the humane treatment of the insane. Asylum reforms also occurred at about this time in France through the efforts of Philippe Pinel. Tuke argued that the insane needed to be treated gently and kindly, needed to be soothed and educated rather than tortured, dominated, and terrified. He suggested that the bizarre and especially violent behavior of the insane was primarily caused by their treatment: if they were treated kindly and "morally," they would be calmed and reeducated and thus brought back into polite society. In general, Tuke's York Retreat seemed to work: he claimed high success rates, and his writing fueled public protests against the practices of asylums. The protests increased in strength, leading to the founding of several institutions modeled after the York Retreat, including three in the United States: the Friends Asylum at Frankfort, Pennsylvania (1817); Bloomingdale Asylum in New York (1821); and the Hartford Asylum in Connecticut (1824). At first, public and professional optimism in both England and the United States was high. Both the Frankfort and Bloomingdale asylums were run by laymen, and the small size of the institutions and the moral fervor of the reformers produced an atmosphere of hope and excitement. Dorothy Dix, for instance, toured the United States, enthusiastically speaking before state legislatures claiming that the cure for insanity was as certain as that of "a cold or a fever."[13]

Unfortunately, early successes in both England and the United States could not be sustained. As the asylums became more popular, and as the financial burden fell more and more heavily on local governments, they appropriated money for increasingly larger asylums in an attempt to cut costs. As the asylums became larger, the quality of care and living conditions deteriorated; this in turn caused the rich to move out into small private institutions or to be relocated into new diagnostic categories less pejorative than insanity so that they would be treated with less violent techniques in more pleasant surroundings. When the rich moved out, the states became increasingly less likely to fund smaller institutions. The population of the asylums grew, the cure rates fell (to eight out of one hundred), and, by the mid-nineteenth century, the medical profession achieved complete control of the asylums and then of mental illness in general. When explaining their dismally poor cure rate, psychiatrists abandoned even the semblance of commitment to the ideas of moral reform and spoke increasingly of organic brain damage, heredity, and moral degeneracy as the causes of madness. At the same time that cure rates dropped and the rich moved out of the public asylums, asylum administrators and psychiatrists were publicly touting the importance of the asylum. Over time, individual working families and small communities became dependent on the institutional solution of the asylum, and family and community care became increasingly less possible. Simultaneously, the belief that asylums were "the essential guarantor of the social order"[14] became deeply ingrained in the middle and upper classes. In other words, the asylum system had created an increased demand at many levels of both English and American society.[15]

By the mid-nineteenth century, the immense asylums were used as training facilities, primary sources of income, and political power bases for the growing profession of psychiatry. The diagnostic criteria for insanity for the lower socioeconomic classes became significantly broadened at this time, leading to what Scull has called an "expansive" conception of madness. The consequences of the combination of increased social dependence on asylums, more liberal diagnostic criteria, and the increased power of the psychiatric establishment were reflected in the asylum's population figures. In 1808 the typical asylum averaged 110 beds, but by the 1840s the size had increased to 300, 600, and even 1,000 beds. In 1844 in England there were 20,809 inmates; by 1904 the figure was 117,200.[16]

Significantly, while the definition of madness expanded to cover more of the poor, it contracted for the middle and especially the upper classes. As the nineteenth century wore on, a variety of new categories such as hysteria, neurasthenia, and the vapors took the place of the perjorative label of "madness" for middle- and upper-class patients. These mental disorders were thought to be quite different from madness, and a new generation of mental healers began to explain the etiology, treatment, and prognosis of the new categories of disorders, using scientific medicine to justify the distinction. Psychiatry increasingly argued that madness was physiological in nature, and usually incurable: the immense Victorian madhouse, the successor to the moral reformers' retreat house, became "a mere refuge or house of detention for a mass of hopeless and incurable cases."[17] Although the worst of the eighteenth-century Bedlam-type abuses were never reinstituted, many of the pre-reform practices, such as purging and bloodletting, were again regularly seen in the dreary, overcrowded wards.

Historians such as Foucault and Scull have understood the moral reforms to be subtle but crucial reflections of the new ways power was exercised in the new era. By culling the better behaved from the unremittingly disruptive, doctors could control the inmates by granting certain privileges to the classes of inmates who were or who could be enticed to become better behaved, and a crude behavior modification program was instituted along with the warm baths and the kind words of the reformers. Most importantly, the reforms instituted practices that were designed to construct in inmates a strong sense of *personal guilt* and *responsibility* for their own actions. Inmates were taught, in the spirit of the philosopher John Locke, to quantify their actions and think of themselves as objects of scientific interest that could be reshaped or remade. In the Quaker Reform program of the York Retreat, Tuke developed behavioral programs that encouraged individual inmates to "objectively" observe and then punish themselves for their disobedience and mistakes. Tuke believed that the new system worked because it made use of the inmates' wish to protect their self-esteem by avoiding disapproval and punishment by the doctors. One of the prime methods of raising self-esteem was a work regime. Labor was thought to teach responsibility and return self-esteem to those heretofore denigrated by idleness. Common among English, French, and American reform practices was the belief that the inmate was a moral subject[18] whose conscience and need for self-esteem could be used to forge moral self-domination. In order to practice self-domination, inmates had to develop the capacity to spy on, discipline, and reward themselves when doctors and orderlies were absent. This is what Foucault meant by the practice of self-surveillance. In the twentieth century this practice is reified and referred to as "having a conscience" and exercising "will power."

It is the unremitting emphasis on the objectification, surveillance, and domination of the self, historians Foucault, Sass,[19] and Scull argue, that was the major element in the new era. It was this unswerving belief in self-discipline that contributed to shaping the nineteenth century into the polite, bourgeois, and psychological world that it became. By removing the bonds of a violent system of torture, asylum reform substituted one exercise of power for another. Like other institutional solutions in the eighteenth and nineteenth centuries, the asylum was emblematic of the modern era's development of control through the interiorization of surveillance and domination. By the twentieth century, the exercise of power through interiorization would become a central element of Western culture, recognized by psychology and given a new, scientific name: internalization.

Women and the Untamed Body

Both of the two major views of madness that framed the practices of the asylum—the loss of reason (in the eighteenth-century madhouses), and the lack of self-discipline (in the nineteenth-century retreat centers and giant custodial asylums)—located the original cause of madness in the body as opposed to in the mind. Afterall, if the mind was the seat of reason, order, and will, only the untamed body, unmoved by embarrassment, loss of esteem, or rational argumentation, could be responsible for madness.

And where, in this view, did the body find its most congenial host? In the female, of course. It was the woman, in the eighteenth and nineteenth centuries, who was thought to be the emblem and exemplar of irrationality. The female stood for emotion, silence, nature, and the body; the male, in contrast, embodied reason, discourse, culture, and the mind.[20] Given the cultural distinctions of the eighteenth and nineteenth centuries, women were cast repeatedly on the wrong or subersive side of the equation. In an age shaped by the power agenda of the Enlightenment philosophers (see chapter two and the appendix), those who could not reason with and control their wild bodies could not be fully human. And women, by definition, were "dominated by . . . [their] uterus and ovaries, and hence by crisis and periodicity,"[21] so their natural place in society was thought to be determined by their reproductive system, the hormones and organs of generation. The female body, dominated by the capacities of conception and birth, was thought to be naturally endowed with a greater ability for love, tenderness, and caregiving. Women, it was thought, were more emotional than rational, more delicate and fragile than men.

As the nineteenth century proceeded, Victorian-era doctors, especially psychiatrists, explained psychological disorders in general and the emotional suffering of their female patients in particular, through biologically based theories. The social conditions of women's lives, their lack of legal standing, their economic dependence on men, the numerous sociopolitical restrictions on female behavior, dress, and speech, and the lack of personal autonomy—all were thought to be the natural order of things and thus could not be sources of female distress. In this way, the nineteenth century's arrangements of gender-based power relations received the "sanction of science. . . . Humanism [in the form of the moral reform movement] had, as its hidden face, new forms of paternalistic domination."[22]

The changes in the public asylum system—especially the decreasing presence of the wealthy, and the expansion of diagnostic criteria for the poor, which resulted in their proportional overrepresentation in the asylums—led certain doctors to be increasingly interested in the emotional distresses of the middle and upper classes, although doctors, for various reasons, did not classify these disorders as forms of madness. The treatments were located in rest homes, water cure centers, and the salons of Anton Mesmer and his ilk. Significantly, the patients of this nonasylum psychiatry were primarily women.

The realm that some of these patients inhabited was what one late nineteenth-century writer aptly called "Mazeland, Dazeland, and Driftland"[23] because of the strange symptoms associated with these female maladies. Hysteria (often thought to be the direct result of female anatomy; the word is derived from the Greek word for uterus), neurasthenia, and anorexia (first created as a diagnostic category in 1873) were three recognized Victorian ills of the middle and upper classes. Female behavior that violated the "natural" boundaries of acceptable female activity— such as aggressive speech or physical activity, too much education, or explicit or excessive sexuality—was thought to be either an indication of the imminent onset, or a partial cause, of one of the new illnesses.

The accepted understandings in the Victorian era of what was proper female behavior remained unexamined by the male doctors. At a time when scientific advances were opening up exciting new vistas of discovery, power, and adventure for Victorian men, Victorian women, many of them increasingly well educated and politically motivated, were forced into constricted and powerless lives. The frustration and anger that were the consequence of these restrictions must have been difficult for women to understand, let alone control. Women were thought to be incapable of rationality and were prohibited from political activity, so their political complaints could for the most part only be expressed through their bodies. "Our bodies," Florence Nightingale once wrote, "are the only things of consequence."[24] Of course, there were some women who could understand what was destroying their lives, and who could articulate the damage done by the gender prescriptions of the era. But many middle- and upper-class women, especially those manifesting the symptoms of the Victorian psychosomatic illnesses, could not articulate their anger and resistance because such reactions were not permitted to "show up" in the cultural terrain. At least their anger and resistance could not show up as *political* complaints against the configuration of gender. Instead these reactions would show up in forms that were accessible within the Victorian horizon of understandings: as somatic symptoms.

Physical symptoms were one of the few avenues of expression available to women within the Victorian terrain: where else could women express the restrictions and frustrations of their roles but in the body, that realm wholly identified with and expressive of their "untamed" nature? That the male doctors did not make the connection between the sociopolitical restrictions from which their female patients suffered and their bizarre physical symptoms simply further attests to the effects of the horizon on the understanding and vision of these who live within it. Sadly, doctors did not make the connection, and the result was the development of a new healing technology, an arsenal of healing techniques that did not address the moral framework and political structures that shaped women's maladies.

The raging fits, the frightening paralysis, the bizarre fugue states and amnesias, the frozen poses, the pelvic gyrations, the frustrating weaknesses and lethargy—all these conditions presented the Victorian medical profession with an overwhelming array of technical challenges (and potential earnings). Fresh from their late eighteenth-century triumph over nonmedical asylum workers, surgeons, apothecaries, and midwives, male doctors turned to the nonpsychotic and primarily psychosomatic complaints of their middle-and upper-class female patients with a renewed confidence and vigor.

To the doctors, new behaviors meant new symptoms, new symptoms required the delineation of new illnesses, and new illnesses, in turn, called out for new technologies of healing. Soon Europe was awash with new theories and techniques. The first malady on the scene and the most prominent in the hearts of the male doctors was the centuries-old standby, hysteria, and its erstwhile cause, the uterus. By the nineteenth century the uterus was no longer thought to travel throughout the female body (as was believed in ancient Greece and the Middle Ages) infecting the other organs wherever it went; the new science had made that idea passé. Still it seemed self-evident in this patriarchal and highly misogynistic culture that the uterus was indeed the cause of many maladies women suffered. But now it was fashionable and scientifically correct for doctors to explain female illness with the concept of the "reflex arc." According to this concept, each internal organ was connected by nerves to the spinal chord and to other organs. The "irritation" or infection of one organ could excite and distort the function of other organs. Thus the problems of the uterus, which were thought to be legion owing to its coarse reproductive nature, were communicated to other organs such as the brain (causing somnambulism and "second states" of consciousness), the stomach and intestines (causing dyspepsia, indigestion, and constipation), the muscles (causing convulsions, fits, and gyrations), and the sensory organs (causing aphonia, blindness, hallucinations, and body pains).

Later in the nineteenth century, between 1862 and 1893, the brilliant young doctor Jean-Martin Charcot became chief physician of the Salpêtrière infirmary in Paris. In this role he developed a slightly different theory about the uterus and hysteria. Hysteria, he taught, was an inherited and ultimately incurable disease of the central nervous system (that is, the brain) caused by invisible lesions; it had specific symptoms, causes, and a course of history, which he codified into a set of "laws." He continued to believe, in good Victorian medical fashion, that psychological and physical "shocks" to the nervous system, such as sexual problems or direct pressure on the ovaries, could trigger a display of symptoms. Twice each week Charcot would hold a grand rounds, open to the entire medical establishment and other prominent guests. During these presentations, several hysteric patients would be brought out for display, observation, and treatment. In this way, Charcot educated his interns, physicians from all of Europe, and curious intellectuals, artists, and politicians and convinced them of the efficacy of his treatment. The patients, under varying degrees of hypnosis, would listen to the master, intently watch (and imitate) one another, and probably play to the audience. Through the use of hypnosis, Charcot could call up the symptoms and, over time, somewhat influence the intensity and course of the illness. Hypnosis could be used on hysterics, Charcot argued, because hypnotic suggestibility was a recognizable symptom of the disease. Much of the French (and European) medical profession was enthralled by Charcot's theory and intimidated by his great presence. It did not occur to them that Charcot's use of hypnosis in the theater of his public demonstrations not only revealed but also constructed his version of hysteria and instructed his patients in the fine art of hysterical patienthood.

But whether the theory was the reflex arc or inherited organic disease, whether the symptoms were expressed in the motor or the sensory modes, the seat of pre-Freudian nineteenth-century hysteria was usually thought to be the female reproductive system. This must be an example of one of the most remarkably unintentional political metaphors of all time. As I have argued earlier in this chapter, the enormous sociohistorical changes brought about by the modern era, and their political restrictions, binds, and oppressions of middle- and upper-class women, were a primary cause of the epidemic of psychosomatic illness referred to in Europe as hysteria. If this interpretation makes sense, then in a strange, metaphorical way the doctors were correct: the uterus *was* the seat of hysteria. Not, however, because it was infected, irritated, or shocked; rather the uterus was the seat of hysteria because, when specific humans possessed one, they were automatically and without reprieve cast into the role of the Victorian female, and thus burdened with all her attendant restrictions, frustrations, double binds, and oppressions. The uterus was the cause of hysteria not because it was diseased, but because the culture in which the uterus was embedded mistrusted, restricted, and in some ways hated those who possessed it.

The rudimentary teachings of self-domination found in the prisons and asylums of the eighteenth century evolved into the therapeutics of the spas, the hypnosis sessions, and the caustic applications, cauterizations, and tresses of the female reproductive system of nineteenth-century psychiatrists and nerve doctors. The practice of self-domination in the lives of the recently dislocated peasants and artisans (transformed into the new labor force), and the self-discipline necessary to work in the dangerous and mind-numbing factories and mines was taught in part by the panopticon-type prisons and the moral reform asylums. The process of self-domination in the lives of the recently transformed bourgeoisie and the self-discipline necessary to work in the boring, tedious white-collar positions such as male clerking or female housewifery and in the tense, hard-driving, dog-eat-dog male world of small entrepreneurship was in part taught and the psychosomatic rebellions treated by nineteenth-century psychiatrists and hypnotists.

However, as the larger cultural terrain of the modern era in Europe became more entrenched, less direct, more subtle forms of control were needed. This was particularly true for the control of women, although the private, individual agonies of Victorian middle-class women were a far cry from the threatened chaos of violent bands of displaced peasants seeking food and money, or poor Bedlam inmates, deranged by grief, confusion, and unfocused rage. Private agonies, especially when linked to unmentionables such as the genitals, were more easily kept hidden in the dark recesses of Victorian bedrooms, inaccessible country spas, and obfuscating medical jargon. When agonies are private they have, in a sense, already been depoliticized. When a typical Victorian physician peered into the vagina of a typical female patient, he viewed, meddled with, and perhaps surgically removed the putative seat of the patient's problems. The uterus might be thought to be infected, irritated (perhaps by too much physical exercise, menstruation, or masturbation), or tipped or turned incorrectly. It might be congenitally weak or just made toxic owing to its coarse nature as the female reproductive organ. In any case, the doctor would be certain, given his scientific knowledge, that the fit, paralysis, catalepsy, or coughing symptoms indicated hysteria or some hysteria-like illness, and that meant the cause was a toxic uterus that was communicating its irritation or infection to other organs through the reflex arc. The other organs, in turn, were signaling distress through unusual behavior. The doctor would then treat the uterus directly by applying caustic substances, by cauterizing it, by manipulating and securing it into its proper position, or in some cases, by surgically removing it. Because some doctors also thought the uterus communicated directly to the spinal column (or vice versa), blistering and draining the back was also a common practice. Doctors who used reflex theory also often prescribed spa visits, complete rest, and/or confinement.

It is perhaps difficult for late twentieth-century readers to believe that Victorian doctors believed that psychosomatic ills were directly caused by the uterus or Charcot's invisible lesions, but they did. The overall effect of their treatment was to reflect and thus contribute to the ongoing construction of women as naturally weak, vulnerable, passive, ultrasensitive, imprisoned by physiology, yet also mysterious, irrational, unpredictable, sexually excessive, and dangerous if not controlled by custom and proper male authority. Female complaints were medicalized and thereby physicalized, individualized, and depoliticized. The individual woman patient, through the help of social custom, her family, and her doctor, was taught how to conquer her female nature, accept her place in society, and thus dominate and control her inherently irrational, potentially dangerous nature.

The emotional reaction produced by the restrictions placed on women found expression where it could—not in political action, which was severely limited or unavailable for most middle-class women, but in the activities allowed to women, such as illness, inactivity, loss of personal agency and autonomy, irrationality, identity confusion, and a murky, dangerous sexuality. The symptoms of the psychosomatic illnesses of the time appear to be either an exaggeration of or a veiled rebellion against the social roles and activities accorded Victorian women. Women expressed their personal and political outrages through "fits" in which they acted out raging, aggressive, convulsive attacks on their husbands, parents, and doctors, embodied paralysis, physical numbing, and blindness, appeared deaf and dumb, comatose, amnesic, half-hypnotized, and even possessed of alternative, more expressive personalities. Some of these symptoms, such as paralysis, catalepsy, amnesia, convulsions, aphonia, and muteness appear to be an *intensification* of the only behavioral roles open to women. Other symptoms, such as hostile fits, automatic writing, somnambulism, and multiple personality appear to be disguised *rebellions* or attempts to enact behaviors or express emotions that were considered to be impolite, immoral, and unacceptable in Victorian society.

The body of the nineteenth-century woman spoke what her mouth could not; sedimented in the body was the grief and anger for which the language had no words and the society no toleration. Male physicians, on the other hand, had a great deal of words available to them, but they spoke in a metaphor which, if politically interpreted, would have revealed their misogyny. The uterus—that is, the designation "woman"—was the cause of emotional suffering. The truth will out, it seems, even if the cultural landscape does not provide the words to say it or the mouth to speak it.

But if the illnesses with which Victorian women were afflicted—hysteria, neurasthenia, and anorexia—were thought to be caused by the natural emotional fragility and lability of women's bodies, what was the nature of the emotional illnesses with which men were afflicted, and were those illnesses thought to be equally caused by the particularities of the *male* body? Although men were thought to be struck by hysteria and neurasthenia, women outnumbered men in these categories. Men's bodies were thought to have something to do with male maladies, but not in the same way that women's bodies determined hysteria and neurasthenia. Women were thought to suffer illnesses determined by their organs or their hormones; whereas men were thought to be influenced by their "natural" urges, such as sex and aggression, but other forces were present in the equation. Chief among these were environmental influences, such as alcohol, rich food, noise, smog, and other pollutants; hereditary influences; and certain social activities such as gambling, the use of coarse language, and sexual perversity.[25] The two psychological illnesses particularly associated with men were sexual perversion and criminal violence. Two French physicians, Benedictin Augustin Morel (1809–1873) and Jacques Joseph Moreau (1804–1884),[26] believed that decadent social behaviors could start a degenerative moral spiral that would eventuate in serious and perhaps even incurable mental illness. Worse still, according to Morel, the illnesses of degeneracy would then be physiologically passed on to the deviate's progeny. This moral-mental disease would be again inherited by the third generation, where it would, in the character of a particularly intelligent but "weak" offspring, cause an incurable and usually perverse madness.

One environmental force thought to have a morally uplifting effect on males was work. This was especially true of the bourgeois activities of scientifically observing, objectifying, quantifying, and calculating profit and loss. In other words, it was thought that accepting the responsibilities and activities of a manager would promote health. The other positive healing force was the exercise of reason and will. Men were thought to embody reason and strength of character in a way women did not; the possession and exercise of reason were thought to be expressions of their maleness. Aggressively carrying on moral and political discourse, engaging in business and physical competition, furthering the scientific discovery of new knowledge—all these were thought to be inherently male activities that men could pursue as a way of keeping their sexual or aggressive urges under control. And, indeed, Victorian doctors and psychiatrists such as Richard Von Kraft-Ebbing, Charcot, Mesmer, and even Sigmund Freud, to varying degrees, used direct and indirect suggestions and moral exhortation regarding the healing exercise of reason and will as antidotes to the primal male passions.

Whereas men were thought to be able to call on the powerful healing capacities of work, reason, and the will, women were thought to be imprisoned by their untamed bodies. Men could turn to work that was public, competitive, political, and moral—work that was valued. Women, however, turned to work at their own peril: it was, in a way, the very source of the original problem, since women's work was thought to be the work of biological reproduction and domestication. The woman's realm was the realm of organs and hormones and the body. It was private, sacrificing, quiet, restrictive. In fact, when men did fall victim to emotional illnesses such as neurasthenia, they were often prescribed "natural" male activities such as strenuous physical activity, work, or an extended stay on the frontier, or vigorous travel abroad. Women patients, however, were confined to bed; refused visitors, books, or writing materials; immobilized if necessary; and force-fed. Although men's primal urges were powerful, they were not thought to inevitably overwhelm their other capacities; but women's natural work, childbearing, necessarily triggered the primitive, unreasonable body. It was a bind that could not be transcended within the normative cultural horizons.

FREUD AND SELF-DOMINATION

In Victorian times, self-control was an essential aspect of the cultural landscape. Middle- and upper-class Victorians were indeed a controlled, and controlling, people. They raised objectification and quantification of the human spirit, and the calculations of everyday life, to an art form, especially in the realm of business and commerce. Nineteenth-century capitalism, of course, was a system built on domination and exploitation—of capital over labor, property rights over human rights, hunger over the poor. At the same time, new scientific discoveries led to an increased ability to predict and control the material world (and to a lesser degree, the behavior of humans) to a degree previously unknown in human history.

Little wonder, then, that medical theories about the reflex arc and the poisonous effects of the uterus, for instance—and later psychoanalysis—showed this frame of reference by reflecting ideas of domination. And little wonder that middle- and upper-class males became titillated and tortured by sexual fantasies of women with spiked heels, leather pants, whips and chains. These men were speaking, in the symbols of the power relation of gender, their mother tongue: domination and submission. It is also little wonder that a few Victorian women, courageous and politically aware, began to dabble in cross-dressing, and others began to manifest psychological symptoms that expressed through their bodies the bondage, constriction, and agony that they experienced as a part of their everyday lives. Images and activities reflecting domination and control were prevalent in the cultural landscape.

Sigmund Freud, of course, saw through the sham of Victorian sexual propriety. He understood that within the cultural terrain the roles available for men and women, and the activities assigned to them, did not fully capture the everyday thoughts and activities—nor the capabilities—of the players. Through a courageous self-exploration, he came to develop understandings about the conflicts, self-deceptions, and inabilities to see or speak the obvious, and these insights eventually changed the way Western society thought about everyday life. He conceived of a realm of thought and feeling that is not apparent in everyday consciousness, urges and wishes that go against the rules of polite society. He decided that behind the facade of solid, common-sense, bourgeois propriety and self-control lurks an underside of dividedness, lust, hatred, possessiveness, dependence, fragmentation, and incoherence. He thought the unthinkable, and uttered the unspeakable; no one was safe from his gaze, not mothers, not even children. Paul Ricoeur has called psychoanalysis a "hermeneutics of suspicion," and for good reason. Freud saw psychopathology as a product of urges, conflicts, and self-deceptions common to all persons, regardless of social class, race, religion, or gender. According to Freud's theory, if people's inherent physiological drives are not repressed by the "internalized" norms of society, acts of violence or sexual perversity would destroy society. But the repression, in turn, causes its own problems, which are manifested through various psychological symptoms: what is repressed "returns" in creative but ultimately self-destructive or dangerous behavior. Society teeters on the brink of violence, chaos, or pathological rigidity and repression, plagued by either wildly destructive behavior or compromise formulations such as compulsions, dissociation, depression, or hysteria. Through the development of insight—by bringing the conflict between drives and social norms into consciousness—or through the creative use of the drives in nondestructive activities, Freud thought the conflict could be rationally managed.

Some recent hermeneuticists think that Freud's early writing, which named the drives as the first and most important quality of the psyche, was an attempt to find an aspect of human life that was primary to (that is, preceded and more important than) the coercions of culture (the superego) and the political status quo (the ego). The drives, in this reading, are implicitly the seat of political resistance. See chapter seven for a more detailed discussion of the political implications of the drives. But Freud did not include the larger sociopolitical field in his vision, so he was forced to speak of envy and wounding in terms of the penis, of assertiveness in women in terms of the wish to be a man, and of political control solely in terms of restriction and repression. In other words, Freud saw some things and was unaware of or partially aware of others.

One thing that was difficult for him to see was the historically situated nature of domination, first ushered in by the Enlightenment era philosophers (with their emphases on the domination of the material world by logic and empiricism), and later by capitalism (with its emphasis on the domination of capital over labor). For him, the particular domination of Victorian capitalism was a universal. Therefore, when he looked at Oedipus he saw the power relations of gender in the Victorian family; when he looked at history he saw *The Golden Bough's*[27] Victorian fantasy of "the primal horde" killing the father-king each season, the story of the submissive rising up to revenge themselves against the dominator. In order for civilization to continue, Freud thought, the untamed body and its drives (the id) and the repressive forces of tradition and religion (the superego) have to be balanced by the forces of reason (the ego). In Freud's early theory, before he articulated the three-part structural theory of id, ego, and superego, he conceived of domination processes in terms of the conscious mind controlling the unconscious through repression and various other psychological mechanisms such as displacement, projection, and disavowal. Once again we can see, this time in Freud's formulations, a reflection of the cultural frame of reference popularized by Descartes and the Enlightenment-era philosophers. Just as the philosophers undermined the authority of the Church and folk traditions in favor of rationality, so too did Freud attempt to control the superego and the id through the exercise of the rational ego. The domination of the body by the mind, folk "superstition" by the new science of empiricism, capital by labor, and female behavior by medical technologies, all attest to the pervasiveness of the social dance characteristic of the Victorian era.

By the end of the Victorian era, Europe had completed the convulsive shift from the feudal to the modern era. The free market, empirical science, industrial factories, large cities, the proletariat, the accumulation of capital, the quantification of human labor, world travel, modern warfare, and secularization were all in place by the end of the nineteenth century; they were unquestioned, everyday aspects of the cultural terrain. It was no longer possible to contrast, and thus provide an alternative to, everyday modern life by presenting an instance of a living experience or recent memory of the more communal past. The romantics tried to develop a rebellion by evoking the glories of the ancient world, but that was a short-lived diversion for the wealthy few. The Luddites tried to roll back the industrial inventions and business applications of science—all to no avail. Reactionary rebellion was futile; the new world of urban, industrialized, bourgeois capitalism had become a permanent feature of late nineteenth- and early twentieth-century Europe.

It was in the context of this Victorian world that Sigmund Freud was trained and initiated.[28] Over the years spanning the last decade of the century, in the cosmopolitan, diverse, urban center of Vienna, Freud drew together his personal suffering, broad intellect, compassion, grandiosity, competitiveness, and compulsive rationality into a brilliant, creative synthesis.

Freud's theory was forever in creative flux through the last days of his life in the twentieth century. Perhaps the most accurate and salient thing that can be said about Freud's psychoanalysis is that, along with Marx's social theory, it was at once the grandest reflection of and the most profound challenge to the Victorian era that bore and nourished it. At first glance Freud's psychoanalysis was quintessentially Victorian: it appears to be a paean to rationality, quantification, and civilization. It was founded on Enlightenment era individualism, the Cartesian split between mind and body, the Rousseauian opposition of person and culture, the romantic naturalization of passion, and the Lockean belief in empirical science. For instance, Freud could not have located "the unknown" *inside* the individual and called it "the unconscious" unless he took for granted the belief that everything *outside* the individual could be scientifically quantified, calculated, and thus finally understood. He also could never have interiorized the unknown unless he believed that there was a psychological interior within each individual. Freud's ideas about human nature, in part, were anchored in the interplay of domination and submission that was characteristic of the capitalism and scientism of the modern era in Europe. This dynamic was reflected in his theory: rationality must control the drives, and id and superego submit to the ego.

However, at the same time that Freud seemed Victorian, his psychoanalysis also challenged and rebelled against his era. To his credit, he understood that the frame of domination was itself problematic: too much domination caused neurosis as surely as too much uncontrolled libido created chaos and disaster. Freud named and denounced sexual hypocrisy. He also shocked society when he argued that children are sexual beings, that the emotional and geographic closeness of the Victorian family was in part the source of neurosis, and that self-deception is at the heart of the process that creates neurosis. His theory was built on the awareness that the body could *not* entirely be dominated by the mind, emotions by rationality, sexuality and aggression by the will, and the physiological integrity of the individual by social contrivance and custom. Unlike many of his followers, Freud often held both sides of the dialectic.

Importantly, Freud's innovative technique, free association, seems to have been the antithesis of a Victorian control tactic. To some degree, his practices implied that the self is not only or even primarily rational, coherent, unified, consistent—in short, in control; the self is also divided, irrational, inconsistent, fragmented, conflicted—buffeted about by unconscious forces difficult to even detect, let alone control. In fact, some recent writers, such as Adler, Barrett, Loewenstein, and Ogden[29] follow Jacques Lacan in arguing that Freud's work implied that the coherent, unified self is a fiction, constructed out of absence, an unconscious collusion with the unspoken demands and desires of others.

This reading of Freud's work brings out a less rigid, more nuanced view of the mind versus body, ego versus id battle. One way of interpreting Freud's theory is that he refused, ultimately, to favor one intrapsychic force over the others. He suggested that illness and chaos, or rigid compliance and deadness, are the result of the continual dominance of one of the forces over the others. There are aspects of Freud that resist the Victorian, dominationist worldview, although they are sometimes difficult to find, given the patriarchal voice in which Freud spoke and the empirical approach he used when attempting to gain acceptance in the medical establishment.

When Freud held opposing ideas, feelings, and theoretical positions at the same time, developed the innovative use of narrative in medicine, devised free association, and displayed an ability to (sometimes) admit his theoretical mistakes, he undermined by example the Victorian emphasis on the ideal of the unitary, univocal, bourgeois male self.

FREUD'S THEORY OF THE UNCONSCIOUS

Freud's theory was a vast departure from the other psychiatric theories of the era. It is true that Paul Mobius, Adolf Strumpell, Hack Tuke, Hippolyte Bernheim, Frederick van Eeden, Paul Dubois, Jules-Joseph Dejerine, and Wilhelm Griesinger were using some form of verbal encouragement, education, and personal warmth with patients,[30] but none of them thought it helpful, let alone indispensable, to investigate in detail the events, feelings, and consequences of neurotic symptoms, as did Freud. None of them could imagine that events in childhood and the subsequent psychological reactions of the child might be the central *cause* of adult distress. None of them theorized that even more important than the actual event itself, the child's *wish* about the moment is the crucial element in the formation of the symptom; that equally important to the content of what is remembered is what has been *forgotten*; that equally important to the content of the wishes and feelings of the past that the patient communicates *to* the doctor, is the patient's wishes and feelings *about* the doctor. These were all revolutionary creations.

The centerpiece of Freud's early theory was his theory of the unconscious. It was "a stretch of new country," he was proud to say, "which has been reclaimed from popular belief and mysticism."[31] It was a remark that today sounds surprisingly hermeneutic in its spatial metaphor (see chapter nine for some therapeutic uses of the metaphor). He came to believe that the underside of the human experience was situated in the unconscious, and that it was the psychological, and not the physiological, world of his patients that caused their emotional distress. Within the unconscious, hidden from view, the prohibited and disavowed primitive wishes and fantasies, lusts and hatreds, urges and drives of humankind festered and boiled, moving individuals to the best and worst of human actions.

Unmediated, these drives are, in Freud's mind, uncontestably destructive to "civilization." In order to "not know" that they have these undifferentiated and uncontrollable urges, individuals have to repress conscious knowledge of the urges. To accomplish that, they would also have to repress events, people, memories, and activities that would remind them of the urges. Taken to an extreme such repression would mean that too much of life would have to be "forgotten" or "unknown," disavowed and consigned to the unconscious, displaced onto other topics or activities, projected onto others, or too much vitality would have to be stifled or lost altogether.

Freud conceived of the mind as a kind of interior battleground for the three modern forces of the human condition: instincts, rationality, and culture. Life is a constant contest, a struggle to determine which aspect of the mind would dominate and which suffer from the consequences of submission. One can readily see that the history of the centuries of bloody European wars and revolutions were not lost on Freud.

Therefore, Freud came to believe that it is the inner, psychological life of the individual, the psychological *processes* of human being, and not a specific recent or remembered trauma nor an irritated body organ, that is the initial source of hysteria and other neuroses. For this reason his treatment was the talking cure, a form of dialogue that would allow the patient to lift the repression by saying whatever came to mind. By carefully watching every clue, symbol, dream, slip of the tongue, joke, nickname, absence, omission, and angry response, the analyst could piece together the puzzle and help the patient uncover the sexual and/or aggressive sources of his or her symptoms and moderate the excessive demands or punishments meted out by the superego. By uncovering how the *content* of desire is shaped, and how the *object* of desire is constructed, Freud's analysis had the potential to become a deconstructive practice— thus the analyst, by virtue of discrediting the cultural fiction of self-contained individualism, becomes a subversive political agent. Then, with the knowledge of (some of) his or her unconscious life in hand, the patient could rationally manage the balancing of ego processes with the id and superego in a much more effective and less hypocritical manner. The more individuals could be aware of their own dishonesty and hypocrisy, and the effects of exterior, punitive moralizing—free from personal and societal illusions—the closer they would be to the ideal of psychological liberty. The more one could channel (sublimate) the drives into benign, creative, constructive, and especially relational, pursuits, the more productive and less troubled one would be. This, then, was the cure: to know, and thus to better manage and utilize the drives through rational self-domination and creative sublimation.

In some forms of psychoanalysis, especially ego psychology, we can see the crucial importance played by a sophisticated, subtle form of self-domination. In this understanding of psychoanalysis, the ego becomes a "thing" that must be made "free" to do its work, which is to control the id and superego. This is what it will take, these theorists imply, for the middle and upper classes to live well in the late modern era. The constant self-observation, the inquiry into personal motives, the self-surveillance of speech and behavior, the self-analysis of dreams, the rational control of the natural drives—all of this and more has become a necessity, a prerequisite, to functioning in the twentieth century.

Freud's goal, as he explicitly stated it, was to reduce neurotic misery to common everyday unhappiness. This takes on a greater meaning, I think, when something more is considered. Freud's implied goal was the maintenance of stability and peace within the Austrian nation and throughout the whole of Europe. Civilization, Freud believed, could not survive without the harnessing of the impulses. Without some form of self-domination, sons would kill their fathers; polymorphous perversity and incest would ravage individual families; mothers and daughters would be in constant conflict; envy, jealousy, and covetousness would be everywhere; Jews and other minorities would be scapegoated; economic classes would be in conflict; and nations would be continually at war. It is understandable, in light of the general barbarity of modern Europe and specifically the surge in anti-Semitic violence and oppression during the turn of the century and then again in the post–World War I era, that Freud and his early followers were mostly Jews. For the cosmopolitan, urban Jew of the twentieth century, the social world was an increasingly dangerous arena. The world of the interior, even with all its attendant drives and conflicts, must have seemed a welcome respite from European politics, and Freud's ideas about the reasonable control of the drives, the only hope for humankind. Would that pre–World War II Europe could have taken Freud's cure.

CHAPTER FIVE

Healing through Self-Liberation

MESMERISM AND THE ENCHANTED AMERICAN INTERIOR OF THE NINETEENTH CENTURY

*This is Daddy's bedtime secret
for today: Man is born broken.
He lives by mending. The grace
of God is glue!*
　　　　—EUGENE O'NEILL
　　　　GREAT GOD BROWN

In 1836, Charles Poyen, a follower of the infamous Anton Mesmer, brought Mesmer's strange combination of Enlightenment science, hypnotism, romanticism, and spirituality to the United States. With it came the seeds of a liberationist ideology that would mix with the native abundance of the New World and grow into a whole new type of healing technology, one uniquely adapted to the optimism and material promise of the American cultural terrain.

In the nineteenth century, the United States was caught in a vise created by the potential material profit offered by the "virgin" continent, on the one hand, and the psychological wounds occasioned by immigration, racism, gender prescriptions, unregulated capitalism, and the weakening of tradition and community, on the other. This juxtaposition of seemingly unlimited abundance with severe confusion and suffering created a paradox, the effects of which could be seen in the strange psychosomatic symptoms that affected the new urban populations of the East and Midwest. The paradox posed a question, and mesmerism, an unlikely hero, provided an answer. Herein lies a strange and very American tale, one that describes the creation of a new and un-European

concept of the human being. Simply put, the human interior was conceived of as neither dangerous, secular, nor controlled by external events,
as Europeans believed; instead it was inherently good, potentially saturated in spirituality, and capable of controlling the external world: it was
an *enchanted* interior, a fitting partner for the enchanted geographical
"interior" that spread westward to the Pacific. It follows that whereas in
Europe the path to wellness was through *control* of one's interior, in
America wellness was to be found in *liberation* of one's interior.

Mesmer had been a charismatic figure among the upper classes in Vienna
and later in prerevolutionary France. He developed a cure for the rich,
bored, alienated, and troubled that seemed to be equal parts medicine,
spiritualism, and hypnotism. He assembled his afflicted patients around a
tub of water in which electrical wires and magnets had been inserted. As
the patients held the wires, Mesmer danced around the tub, dressed in a
lilac robe and armed with a special wand. He would sing, chant, and talk
to his patients, and at a propitious moment touch them with the wand.
Immediately they would fall into a deep, curative trance, during which
they might attain ecstatic spiritual heights, gain the gift of clairvoyance,
or experience a deep sense of well-being, and it was said, be relieved of
their troublesome, usually psychosomatic, symptoms.

Mesmer proclaimed, "There is only one illness and one cure." The
one, universal illness was the lack of connection to the great electrical-
mystical ground of being. An invisible spiritual fluid that was alive in the
world connected all living beings with a force greater and more sublime
than anything one could imagine. Mesmer called the substance "animal
magnetism"; it was thought to connect and rejuvenate people by bringing
into play the laws and processes of the natural world, the dynamic truth
still hidden from modern science. When one's electrical balance was
corrected, the substance would flow through the body, enriching and
"enlarging" the spirit. The cure that Mesmer claimed to produce would
lead, ultimately, to a spiritual society of harmony and brotherhood. For
this reason, historian Robert Darnton, in *Mesmerism and the End of the
Enlightenment in France*, thought that European mesmerism was a reflection of and an influence on the larger historical forces which featured
fraternity as an important ideal.[1]

Although at first Poyen faithfully followed Mesmer when conducting treatments in America, his practices soon took on a characteristic
American cast, emphasizing optimism and pragmatism. As the years
passed, mesmerism evolved and gave birth to new and ever more American offshoots, which foreshadowed the immense cultural changes at the
turn of the century. These changes were responsible for what Rieff has

called the "triumph of the therapeutic," the ascendance of a new cultural frame of reference in America. Today it is this psychological therapeutic, embodied in diverse social practices such as advertising and psychotherapy, that stands as *the* healer of the American self.

Animal magnetism, Poyen and the new breed of American mesmerists preached, could be recharged within the human body through a combination of arm and hand motions, the manipulation of special magnets and batteries, hypnotic trance, mental "daguerreotyping," quiet lecturing, and various forms of intellectual instruction. When the body's electricity was properly balanced, the mind was progressively brought in touch with the spiritual world of divinity and thus opened to new human potentialities. This is what mesmerists called the "wider," "freer" world of true reality. Patients exhibited spiritual gifts while in trance, and after contact with the source of spiritual energy, patients felt invigorated, renewed, transformed, their interpersonal skills improved and economic successes multiplied. Mesmerism and its heirs experimented with exotic alternative states of consciousness while embodying American naivete and optimism and a secular, anti-intellectual spiritualism. Mesmerism was first and foremost an ideology of personal, *inner* liberation. It emphasized the inherent goodness of the inner self and led to the development of practices that were designed to expand, revitalize, and finally liberate the natural spirituality—the enchanted interior—of the nineteenth-century middle-class American self.

THE UNITED STATES IN THE EARLY NINETEENTH CENTURY

"Europe," historian Robert Fuller noted in his study of American mesmerism, "lacked a crisis for which animal magnetism was a suitable cure;"[2] but the mid-nineteenth-century American middle class was moving toward a crisis tailor-made for Poyen's product.[3] The result was a whirlwind popularity for mesmerism and its heirs that lasted well into the twentieth century. In certain ways, mesmerism was the first secular psychotherapy in America, a way of ministering psychologically to the great American unchurched. It was an ambitious attempt to combine religion with psychotherapy, and it spawned ideologies such as mind-cure philosophy, the New Thought movement, Christian Science, and American spiritualism. It also anticipated aspects of current cognitive and object relations theories as well as certain practices prevalent in mass-marathon psychology trainings and restrictive religious cults, and certain aspects of twelve-step self-help groups, all of which will be discussed in later chapters. Mesmerism marked an important historical moment in the American curing of souls, and its influence is still discernible in contemporary popular psychology.

Although mesmerism might not have been suitable for handling the crisis confronting Europe, it was, with a few major adjustments, a good fit for the United States. When Poyen arrived, the optimism and expansiveness of the Jacksonian era was in full swing, and Americans were in the grip of a spiritual revival movement referred to as the Second Great Awakening. But by the 1850s the country was showing signs of the strains and confusions that would ultimately lead to important political and psychological upheavals. Political unrest related to racism and class conflict, the Civil War, the disillusionment and betrayal of Reconstruction, and the cultural crisis of the turn of the century all loomed just over the horizon.

Industrialization, urbanization, massive European immigration, and an increasing secularization were major features of the mid- and late nineteenth century in the United States. Industrialism and urbanization in particular started later but developed more rapidly than in Europe. Many small rural and mostly religious communities of the seventeenth and eighteenth centuries were gradually swallowed up by cities as were the communal self, the ethos of self-sacrifice, and the hope for divine salvation. Industrialism was breaking up rural communities and relocating individual families and family members in large factories and impersonal cities. The larger urban centers began to attract rural Americans with dreams of individual entrepreneurial success, the poor and destitute, and immigrants from non–Anglo Saxon Protestant cultures. By 1890 the Northeast seaboard cities had tripled in size. Immigration was introducing Central, Eastern, and Southern European peoples, with strange customs and incomprehensible languages. By 1890, 40 million new immigrants had arrived, and most had located in the cities. The Colonial Protestant abhorrence of putting the ascent of the self before that of the soul and individualism before communalism was swept off the cultural stage. The requirements of city living called for skills and tolerance that traditional rural customs could not provide. The monotonous work of the factory laborer, the isolating and boring work of the new white-collar clerks and administrators, and the increasingly restricted life of the bourgeois woman, consigned to the maintenance of the home as "a haven in the heartless world"[4] of the capitalist marketplace—all of these possible places within the mid-nineteenth-century cultural landscape were relatively new. The jobs or roles were sometimes so new that the old ways simply didn't apply; or the old ways were hostile to the new roles and the new ways of being that urban life required, and thus were rejected because they were inconvenient; or the old ways were simply never learned, because old rural communities were being destroyed, families displaced, or customs dismissed.

The sectional conflict between entrepreneurial industrialism and ruthless plantation agrarianism combined with the moral crisis over slavery to create the wrenching fratricide of the Civil War, perhaps the first of the modern wars of mass destruction. Moral crisis, grief, and political despair hung over the nation during and after the war. The industrialization and urban values of the North (including white racism) eventually prevailed, further fueling the impetus for individualism and an economy of acquisitiveness. The prewar abolitionist-feminist alliance, never on the most solid of footing, came apart when the abolitionists did not fully support women's suffrage. The abolitionists' progressive program, needless to say, was lost in the rush of mainstream political parties capturing the new Negro vote, stealing and exploiting the western frontier, and further transforming the nation into a modern, scientific industrial state.

So the first half of the nineteenth century found America poised on the edge of a new world, a world that could not yet be imagined, but could be sensed. The frontier beckoned those who dreamed of a pure world far from the corruption of the city, and near-destitute immigrants who dreamed of survival. It also beckoned those who dreamed of great riches, and those who were already wealthy but wanted more. Thus the homesteaders, the miners, and the railroads poured into the frontier. This was a time when Americans thought that a God-given Manifest Destiny authorized them to take and transform the entire continent, including the Great Plains, the West Coast, Canada, and Mexico.

It was a time of excitement and paradox. At the same time that Jacksonian democracy was the ideology of the day, the U.S. government was stealing Indian land, returning runaway Negro slaves, and refusing women the right to vote. At the same time that a Second Great Awakening was occurring, during which white Protestants were encouraged to reaffirm their direct experience of the indwelling spirit and the primacy of the community, religion was trying desperately to accommodate a radically different conception of the individual, one that was based on selfishness and acquisitiveness. It is from this accommodation to individualism and capitalism that a whole new approach to the self and its healing would grow.

The dislocations of the rural and European immigrants, the dismemberment of customs and cultures, and the disorientation of a rapidly changing industrial world all contributed to the conflicts, confusion, and lostness of American life after mid-century. There was a degree of alienation and loneliness in the cities rarely experienced in the United States. What had once been the Puritans' unified spiritual-communal mission to the New World was on the way to becoming a fragmented, multicultural, secular supercompetitive battleground.

THE EMERGENCE OF A NEW SELF WITH NEW ILLS

There are times in which sociohistorical changes come so rapidly, and the remedies available in the cultural clearing so ineffectual, that it seems as though the social institutions responsible for healing are helpless in the face of the suffering. It might appear that healers are groping for solutions, struggling to develop the words to describe the suffering and the concepts to explain it, or that they are almost randomly inventing remedies. Also in some eras oppressive political arrangements are so fundamental to the overall cultural clearing that certain insightful ideas about what is causing the suffering are simply too subversive to the entire sociopolitical system to be tolerated. Because they are too subversive, they are unspeakable. The second half of the nineteenth century was one of those times.

The changing social conditions clashed with the old configuration of the self, causing new illnesses to show up in the mid- and late nineteenth century, illnesses that could only be healed by a shifted configuration of the self, new understandings of illness, a different group of healers, and a new healing technology. These new illnesses were shaped in certain ways owing to the placement of the cultural horizon: What was available within the clearing that could express certain feelings, conflicts, aspirations, certain new ideas, distinctions, and relationships? In the case of the nineteenth century, especially in the experience of middle-class women, what could be used to express their restrictions, frustrations, confusion, and grief? As in Europe, the body was available.

Political complaints and rebellions often came to be embodied rather than articulated. The suffering came to be "written" on the bodies of people of the middle class, especially women—in listlessness, flushedness, fevers, vertigo, rageful "fits," convulsions, physical weakness and collapse, fugue states. What was it that was so unspeakable in the mid-nineteenth century? Well, to be un-Victorian. This could mean displaying characteristics such as a lack of personal ambition, entrepreneurial initiative, and dogged competitiveness. Middle-class men and women who exhibited such traits would be accused of laziness, cowardice, and hopelessness. They would be accused of possessing a weak character, perhaps caused by excessive pride, sexual appetites, and communal sympathies, or by an unwillingness to practice the kind of self-discipline and will-power that would postpone gratification of the animal instincts and allow for the accumulation of capital and the achievement of personal successes.

Chief among the personal successes of American bourgeois women at this time were marriage, the production and management of children, and the creation and maintenance of a proper bourgeois home.[5] Women were to dedicate themselves to modesty, passivity, and the supportive, enabling role, that of nurturing and submissiveness. They were not permitted an active, powerful role in the social world outside of the home, nor to explicit disputation or contention with their husband except in extreme and limited circumstances. Whereas Victorian men were expected to have sexual and aggressive impulses that should be controlled and limited to specific settings, middle-class Victorian women were not even permitted to *possess* aggressive or sexual impulses. In particular, women were prohibited from rebelling against the severe social restrictions based on gender. Disagreeing with or explicitly resisting the accepted role of women—or even worse, openly protesting against the unilateral behavioral prohibitions by voting, running for office, or politically organizing to bring about the abolition of slavery or the political enfranchisement of women—were considered abhorrent acts.

The pressure on American women in this severely restrictive society was intense: they had to be competent, strong, and intelligent, while not being openly so. They were often well educated, especially in moral reasoning, religion, and the humanities, yet they were not permitted to use their considerable talents and moral commitments to take political action or engage in professional careers; careers in the ministry, the world of business, medicine, and higher education were usually closed to them. At a time when the modern sciences and industrialization had greatly expanded the Western world's knowledge of the planet and the opportunities to travel and have adventures, middle-class women remained restricted and controlled, just when their vision and their appetites were growing. This tension led to a frustration, confusion, and anger.

MESMERISM AND ITS LEGACY

In whatever bodily form the unspeakable was spoken, it seemed as though Charles Poyen and the cast of American mesmerists, mind curists, and positive thinkers had a cure for it. Mesmerism, adapted to the

American landscape by successive generations of practitioners, seemed to speak directly and effectively to the emotional ills of the surprising number of middle-class Americans afflicted with psychosomatic ills. In East Coast cities such as New York and Boston, mesmerists were welcomed and celebrated as the news of their abilities spread. They lectured about and demonstrated the mesmeric experience in small group meetings, church assemblies, and lecture halls. Under their influence, mesmerism featured such practices as hypnotism, telekinesis, spiritual advice, instructions in religious texts, psychological counseling, and small group experiences. It became a type of popular, unchurched religious psychotherapy. Adherents, some of them middle- and upper-class doctors, scientists, and teachers, conducted experiments and undertook innumerable surveys. They were convinced that they had objectively and scientifically proven mesmerism's effectiveness, and they took to the streets with an evangelical fervor.

One of the newly converted was Phineas Quimby, who was later to initiate Mary Baker Eddy, the founder of Christian Science. He had learned from Poyen and then modified and further developed the practice. His major contribution, and it was an important one, was to relocate the primary cause of emotional distress: mesmerism's theoretical emphasis on unbalanced magnetic fluids was replaced with an emphasis on outmoded or incorrect (negative) ideas about life. This was a small revolution in mesmerist circles. Quimby's new focus would eventually lead mesmerism and its heirs to go beyond mesmerism's early task of symptom relief and to create instead an overall philosophy of life. Quimby's revolution was also part of the beginning of a new intellectual movement that would spawn one of the most influential theories in late twentieth-century psychotherapy: cognitive psychology.

Increasingly, Quimby came to focus on the process of correcting the patient's "mistaken" ideas, a process he referred to as teaching and establishing the universal, spiritual truth. One of the most important truths that he imparted was the concept that the single most common cause of illness was the incorrect belief that the material conditions of the world controlled individual lives and that the opinions of others, such as the moral standards of a community or the rules of a religion, should determine or even influence individual behavior. When one identified with "outer" conditions, one couldn't experience the magnetic forces of the divine order that resided within. Belief, to Quimby, was likened to a control valve that allocated the flow of the "vital fluids" of animal magnetism. When belief was correct, the valve was open and the conscious mind was exposed to the influence of the unconscious wisdom and well-being of the supreme force. This openness to the influence of the spiritual fluids naturally led to health and success. Through the guidance of mesmerism, the "lower" mind, preoccupied with the demands and standards of the material world, thus became overtaken by the "higher" mind of animal magnetism. The individual came to realize that the only realm to be concerned with was the realm of the interior: "All good things," Quimby lectured, "are found within."

In mesmerism the dichotomy between higher and lower, it is important to remember, was a distinction based on a secular spirituality. Believing in God, Thomas Lake Harris preached, is believing that "the spirit which we feel flowing into ourselves flows from an Infinite Existing Source."[6] A larger, freer self would be available for believers . . . who learned to control the material conditions of their lives through the thoughts and wishes of their conscious mind. Quimby's followers called this "mind cure." Fuller suggested that Quimby's innovation interiorized and psychologized the American Protestant ethic.[7] Before mind cure, the believer was accountable to an *external* God who had proclaimed an *external* standard of belief and behavior. With mind cure, the believer was accountable to an *interior* standard dictated by one's own, *individual* spiritual wisdom.

When Quimby died in 1866, he took the last practice of the old-style mesmerism with him,[8] but Mary Baker Eddy and a new group of mind-cure, New Thought practitioners took over the movement, emphasizing philosophy as much as symptom cure, and elevating the ideology of mind over matter above all other tenets. A husband-and-wife team, the Dressers, began the institutionalization of mind cure by offering a certification program that would entitle the practitioner to charge the going rate, $5 for each session.[9] Healing became conceptualized as helping people make an adjustment to the *spiritual*, rather than the material, world. As "the tides of psychic energy flowed freely" and were made ever more available to the conscious mind, mind curists argued that individuals could harness the spiritual power within themselves to achieve control over the material world.

It was at this time, during mesmerism's second stage of development, that women became more numerous as practitioners as well as patients. In the Dressers' certification program, 95 percent of the student-practitioners lived in large cities, most were middle-class, and women outnumbered men by two to one. Mind cure offered women an unusual opportunity. Middle-class women during the second half of the nineteenth century had been given good educations, usually emphasizing humanitarian values, and yet were not generally allowed to work outside of the home; mainstream religious and business institutions in particular were closed to them. They had the motivation to help humankind and the time to study and intern. Mind cure was also a relatively new field, so when women began studying, they quickly became knowledgeable and were able to move into positions of leadership. It is ironic that the same healing technology that fed on the political oppressions of middle-class women was also the profession that offered them many opportunities for employment and advancement.

Mind curists, in an attempt to lend legitimacy to their theory, argued that their techniques were derived from ancient spiritual practices that had made past eras great and guided adherents throughout human history. Mind curists believed that their ideology revealed the secrets of the spiritual universe, once lost but now regained, as well as the "true" spiritual identity of adherents. Practitioners lectured that the dual anatomical nature of the brain demonstrated the correctness of mind cure's ideology: one hemisphere of the brain embodied the intellectual and the willful functions; the other hemisphere was the resting place for God's spiritual connection, the vital fluids. If individuals identified with the worldly, material pressures of life, they would be cut off from the spiritual hemisphere and were then at risk for all sorts of misbeliefs and illnesses. If they gained contact with the spiritual message alive in the second hemisphere, they became influenced by the magnetic divine core, the immortal Self, and eventually they would even transcend the original dividedness of the brain. As mind curist Warren Felt Evans put it, "The Summit of our being which is the real and divine man, is never contaminated by evil, nor invaded by disease."[10]

Once in spiritual contact with the cosmos, the mesmerists believed, one could also *influence* the cosmos. Quimby had referred to this as "daguerreotyping" one's spiritual thoughts onto the material world; that is, one could imprint upon the material world one's innermost hopes and dreams as material images are imprinted on a photographic plate. Evans called this process "the law of thought transference." Regardless of what they called the theory, mind curists were sure they could control the world, thus garnering for themselves wealth and success, the realization of their fondest desires.

In these ideas one can see the beginnings of the third stage of mesmerism, the development of positive thinking or New Thought in the late 1880s. This movement deemphasized the spiritual renewal aspect of mind cure and focused instead on the *uses* of the spirit in the material world. "Adequacy for everyday life here and now," Ralph Waldo Trine preached, "must be the test of all true religion."[11] By plugging into the spiritual power of the vital force, the New Thoughters believed they could command uncontested power and wealth. For Emile Cady, God was an "unlimited supply of bounty." Certain conditions of mind are so connected with certain results that the two are inseparable.[12] By praying, the practitioners of positive thinking simply claimed an unlimited share of the universe's unlimited abundance.

The consequence of New Thought's theory about abundance and acquisition was to reduce moral striving to an exercise in narcissistic self-absorption. Henry Wood's book, *Ideal Suggestions Through Mental Photography*,[13] taught readers how to use mental pictures to bring what they want to life. According to the New Thoughters, Fuller noted, "God wants nothing more of us than developing the ability to make the outer world a perfect mirror of our own minds."[14] By contacting the spiritual force and utilizing its power, practitioners could dominate and control the material world as a means of satisfying their own acquisitive desires. The good had been eclipsed by the good life. The titles of popular books, such as those that composed Frank Haddock's multivolume "Power Book Library," illustrate the major thrust of the abundance theory approach: Haddock wrote *How to Get What You Want, The Personal Atmosphere*, and *Power for Success*;[15] Orestes Swett Marden was editor of *Success Magazine* and published *Every Man a King*; William Walker Atkinson, under the name Yogi Ramacharaka, wrote *The Secret of Success*; and in the twentieth century, Napoleon Hill wrote *The Law of Success* and *Think and Grow Rich*.[16] An amazing change had occurred in the spiritual practices of middle-class Americans. "Personal desire," Fuller noted, "not communal duty," became the primary motivating force in the lives of followers trying "to live in accordance with the divine."[17]

Mesmerism was the first psychological healing technology to popularize and develop a treatment regime that featured the expansion and liberation of the self. Mesmerism's subject was the interior, enchanted, potentially expansive self, a self so clearly syntonic with the American terrain and the power relations and forms of control that were a part of that terrain. Of course, mesmerism not only reflected this nineteenth-century American self; it also helped construct it. Central to its ideology were four major theoretical concepts. Each of these concepts has been successively elaborated upon by twentieth-century mainstream schools of psychotherapy. By studying mesmerism and the political functions it served, we can better understand aspects of current therapy practices that carry on aspects of mesmerism's ideology.

Apolitical Interiority

Mesmerism responded to the emotional suffering caused by the economic oppression, political upheavals, and cultural confusion of its era by
entirely *ignoring* the sociopolitical realm. Mesmerism explained the suffering of members of the middle class by blaming it on the victim,
specifically on the internal functions of the mind. Apolitical interiority
involved turning inward, away from the material, outer world and into
the spiritual, interior realm, where God, health, and undreamed-of
power resided. "[A]ll development," Horatio Dresser preached, "is from
an inner center or seed. . . . the only cure comes through self-help, and
the only freedom through self-knowledge."[18] Working together to effect
political change on agreed-upon goals was a solution never considered by
mesmerist doctrine. This tendency appears to have reinforced self-
contained individualism at a time when the proper configuration of the
self was being reshaped.

Cognitivism

The second concept in mesmerism's arsenal was an early form of what we
now call cognitive psychology, a school that believes specific principles of
thinking, located inside the individual's brain, determine what individuals
think and especially how they behave. The cause of his patients' symptoms, Quimby argued, was their outmoded ideas about human nature.
"Disease," therefore, "is what follows an opinion."[19] The cure, therefore,
was to open oneself to the magnetic fluid by identifying with inner rather
than external conditions made up of noxious stimuli.[20] The worst, most
destructive idea of all, Quimby taught, was to believe that the external
world affects one's life, rather than believing that one's ideas can influence
the world. Positive thinking and abundance theory, of course, were illustrative of this early form of cognitivism. The proper, positive thought,
Napoleon Hill instructed his readers, would bring success and riches; the
improper, negative thought would bring failure and poverty. Trine argued
that "thoughts are forces." "Within yourself," he continued, "lies the cause
of whatever enters your life. To come into the full realization of your
awakened interior powers, is to be able to condition your life in exact
accord with what you would have it. . . . The realm of the unseen is the
realm of causes—the realm of the seen is the realm of effects. . . . This is
the secret of all success.[21] By thinking properly, mesmerists argued, the
individual could literally, concretely, change the world. Again, the apolitical, individualist nature of mesmerist ideology, and its effect on the self,
seems obvious.

The True Self–False Self Dichotomy

The third concept mesmerism developed undoubtedly grew out of the first two. By attending to and identifying with one's interior spirituality, and by controlling and shaping the "positive" nature of one's thoughts, the patient could attain what mesmerists called a "transformation of identity." "The spirit where like the high priest we may commune with God," wrote Evans, is in "the inmost region of our being, and our real self."[22] By penetrating beneath roles and identities to find the divine core of being, Fuller noted, "mental cure was by now synonymous with discovering the true self."[23] By following the universal, inherent psychological truths that mesmerism had uncovered, practitioners could get patients in touch with their true spiritual identity. The true self is, of course, a moral belief dressed up in scientific clothing. What is true is a concept determined by the moral tradition of the era. In the case of mid- and late nineteenth-century America, the true and the good had to do with qualities such as ambition, productivity, optimism, accumulation of wealth and possessions, expansion of economic holdings and capital wealth. Therefore, the true self reflected those values. Mesmerism's concern with the self, and its privileging of the true self has been adopted by post–World War II psychotherapy theories such as certain humanistic psychology and object relations theory. The configuration of the self in the late twentieth century is somewhat different from that of the nineteenth century, but the true self–false self distinction currently seems every bit as salient as it was then. It may serve somewhat different political and economic functions today, but the overall schema—the emphasis on interior, insular cognitive processes, the focus on the well-being of the self, and the foundational American belief in the liberation of the enchanted interior—is as vibrant and important today as it was then.

From Cure to Abundance

Mesmerism's fourth concept was that mesmeric cure led to economic, material abundance. God had an "unlimited supply" of wealth, Cady argued,[24] and if one was properly attuned to the interior spirit, one could use the spirit to attain great wealth. Abundance was there for the taking; just as the resources of the frontier wilderness were available, so too were the spoils of the financial wilderness of everyday life available to the right-thinking citizen. Spiritual abundance led to material abundance. Just as Americans had a geographical manifest destiny, so too they had a financial manifest destiny. The abundant riches of the New World were there, ripe for the plucking. Here we see mesmerism's most prominent characteristic: its apolitical vision. The process of accumulating personal wealth, in the mesmerist vision, has nothing to do with socioeconomic arrangements such as class or gender, political or physical coercion, luck, dishonesty, or aggression. Wealth is found or "delivered," mesmerists argued, once the spiritualized thoughts were imprinted, "daguerreotyped," onto the material world. In mesmerism's world there was no exploitation of the workers, no stealing of land from Native Americans, no destruction of African Americans through slavery or sharecropping. Fuller found that "it was no longer the quality of one's care or conduct toward others that made a person deserving of natural reward; now it was the strength of one's thoughts about oneself."[25] Mesmerist ideology pertaining to abundance seems to be helpful in understanding the shift from a cultural frame that favored saving and self sacrifice to a frame that was obsessed with spending and immediate gratification—the enormous shift from a Victorian to a twentieth century consumer society.

Even today, abundance theory is alive and well in many religious cults and especially in restrictive psychotherapy trainings such as est. Unfortunately, it can also be implicit in many late twentieth-century mainstream psychotherapy theories, owing to the unexamined class bias common in psychotherapy, and its overall decontextualized, apolitical nature. One of the most telling criticisms of mesmerism—that it did not develop a historical perspective on its own practices and ground itself in moral concerns about relating to and caring for others—is equally applicable to some current psychotherapy theories. By psychologizing political problems, by interiorizing human being, by valorizing an isolated individualism, by privileging cognitive process above the material conditions of everyday life, by covertly providing a compensatory solution for a political problem instead of encouraging patients to explore the sociopolitical arrangements that caused the problem, current forms of psychotherapy also run the risk of contributing to the status quo in ways they would never consciously consent to. "It was the genius of mind cure," historian Donald Meyer observed, "to discover how the weak might feel strong while remaining weak."[26]

Mesmerism started out as a healing technology for psychosomatic symptoms, evolved into a spiritual mind-cure philosophy, and finally degenerated into a financially oriented and consumer-driven abundance theory. The religious commitment to community and proper living that had been at the heart of the mission of the early American colonists was subsumed by a preoccupation with personal acquisition and an obsession with the reified laws of an encapsulated mind. Mesmerism was a colorful and powerful movement, but then, by the early twentieth century, it was over. Eclipsed by the mental hygiene movement and psychoanalysis (see chapter six), mesmerism faded from view, although several of its concepts live on in current psychotherapy theories.

SOCIAL CONTROL THROUGH SELF-LIBERATION

In the mid- to late nineteenth century, the new problems facing the expanding nation were nearly overwhelming. Members of the middle class in particular were suffering from a lack of groundedness and certainty, from a disorientation and alienation from the everyday material world and from one another. The "glue" that held society together, Fuller noted, had "evaporated."[27]

Into this cultural void stepped mesmerism, with an ideology that provided a new adhesive, a *spiritual* glue that the mesmerists thought circulated through all people and had its source in God and the natural laws of the universe. "Every bit of us," wrote the noted American psychologist William James, "at every moment is part and parcel of a wider self."[28]

One way that mesmerism fit the era was precisely in the *covert* and compensatory political solution it provided for the moral and socio-economic problems of the time. Its discourse and practices were a response to the emotional and social consequences of a political system—industrial capitalism—that was gaining preeminence and creating a great deal of human wreckage in its wake. Mesmerism's task was to soothe and offer hope to individuals suffering from some of the more damaging psychological consequences of the economic system, further construct and guide the self most in synch with that system, and at the same time to explain psychological damage in such a way as to divert blame from the system. It accomplished this delicate task by psychologizing moral and political problems: It blamed the victim. In doing so, mesmerism could address the problems in code, symbolically. This code allowed mesmerism to deliver moral education and enact political solutions or compensate for politically caused damage without appearing to do so. Mesmerism provided a new community, established practices that offered new paths to human connectedness, moral guidance, spiritual certainty, and developed ways of temporarily easing or compensating for the alienation caused by capitalism. Thus mesmerism accomplished all this without overthrowing, or even upsetting, the social and political structures that caused the suffering.

Mesmerism was able to accomplish this grand tightrope walk in part because of the failure of institutional religion and other American institutions to adapt to changing times. A vacuum had been created that mesmerism filled. How could mesmerism heal without being subversive? It accomplished this feat by creating a way of controlling the populace through an ideology of self-liberation. The expanding American economy combined with traditional American character traits such as optimism, individualism, religious mission, and personal ambition to create a type of population that required a style of political control different from the European style of self-domination. Nineteenth-century Americans progressively grew to move away from overt self-domination techniques and repressive ideology in favor of an ideology that was directed at the well-being of the self; their preferred ideology stressed the expansion and growth of the self, which, it was thought, would inevitably lead to personal "power," achievement, and wealth. Unlike the European self with the secret, dangerous interior, the late nineteenth-century middle-class American self was shaped in part by mesmerism to be a self with a miraculous interior filled with divine powers, so that the self was a conduit to or an embodiment of the very source of creation and vitality. It was an enchanted interior, one that had only to be liberated, fully experienced, and followed in order to heal and achieve wealth. The American God, it appeared, was indeed a God of abundance: He had given His blessing to Americans through the abundant wilderness, and was in constant, intimate connection with them through the vital fluids and forces of spiritual magnetism. His greatest wish, it seemed, was for them to *take*. "Everything," Wood explained, "is already perfect and . . . we only need conformity. . . . [Prayer] is simply a conscious taking of what already is provided."[29] God wanted them to take. And they did.

Mesmerism's concept of the liberation of the expansive, ambitious, and potentially powerful middle-class self constructed a cultural frame of reference that, paradoxically, controlled the members of the late nineteenth-century middle class even as it appeared to set them free. A unique combination of psychology, religion, and political collusion made mesmerism into a powerful and effective force that unwittingly aided the state in controlling the population. Power is often exercised in uncountable, unseen ways—in this case by the ability to set the frame of reference for an entire country.

In the United States, the state had to develop compliance with its laws, participation in the market economy, geographical emigration to the west, cooperation with taxation, military conscription, and a cohesive family structure. In order to create and maintain shared understandings and social continuity, the cultural rules regarding everyday issues such as public laws, personal hygiene, verbal interaction, and economic agreements and contracts also had to be guaranteed. Given that individual freedom from institutional coercion was such a central value in the United States, it was necessary for the body politic to develop ways of creating voluntary compliance with the customs and laws of society. For members of the middle class, physical coercion was an unacceptable remnant of the feudal era, and self-domination as a metaphor for the set of practices that had guaranteed social compliance in the Old World was an increasingly problematic alternative. More and more, the kind of control practices that fit the middle-class American clearing were those that were framed in terms of individual freedom and that promised success, notoriety, and the personal accumulation of goods and capital. Compliance had to be framed as enhancing the pursuit of "life, liberty, and the pursuit of happiness."

Mesmerism was one of a number of practices that created and elaborated on the cultural frame of reference of the self-contained individual who was free from the coercions of the state, who had a personal, unmediated relationship with the sacred, who was most moral when liberated to pursue his or her own self-interest in disregard of the self-interest of others, who was naturally ambitious, acquisitive, and powerful. Before mesmerism, nineteenth-century pastoral counseling shifted in this direction, and after mesmerism, some twentieth-century forms of psychotherapy, New Age ideology, religious cults, and restrictive psychological training programs have continued the tradition.

EUROPEAN HYSTERIA VERSUS AMERICAN NEURASTHENIA

Of course, it was not only popular healing movements like mesmerism that responded to the new symptoms emerging at mid-century. At the same time that mesmerism's heirs were becoming popular, the part of the medical profession interested in "nervous disorders" was branching out of the asylums and beginning to treat the new nineteenth-century ills. Their work reflected the same trend we saw articulated in mesmerism: the shift from a European-oriented theory—healing through self-domination—to an American theory—healing through self-liberation. It followed, of course, that just as American theories of cure differed from European ones, so too did American theories of illness.

George Beard was a New York neurologist who became fascinated with the set of related symptoms he called "neurasthenia," or nervous exhaustion.[30] It was Beard, as much as any nineteenth-century physician, who popularized neurasthenia. He saw a pattern in the plethora of symptoms in which members of the middle class were awash, he could talk about the pattern in a way that patients and other doctors could understand, and he devised healing techniques that were believable and inspired hope.

By contrasting Beard's theory of neurasthenia with Freud's theory of hysteria, we can see important differences between the two societies in the mid- and late nineteenth century. Freud's conceptualization of hysteria unintentionally reflected the need of the state to control a population long traumatized by centuries of war, dislocation, and social upheaval, yet less restrained by custom, law, and compliance; whereas Beard's neurasthenia unintentionally reflected the need of the state in America to settle the continent, develop an industrial economy, and build a nation. In Europe, illness was uncontrolled sex or aggression; whereas in the United States it was the absence of initiative, the inability to work, that was considered sickness.

Beard developed his theory of neurasthenia in response to seeing symptoms similar to those that Freud saw: fatigue, incapacity, headache, insomnia, fits, convulsions, depression, dyspepsia, hypersensitivity, sexual disinterest or impotence, and obsessive, fixed ideas. But Beard, unlike Freud, did not interpret these manifestations as the eruptions of or conflicts over sex and aggression. Instead, he saw them as an indication that the patient was suffering from a loss of energy; the symptoms were a product of "nervous exhaustion," which caused the patient to be unable to work and be productive. He believed his patients were manifesting the same symptoms that a light bulb does when it "browns out" owing to an insufficient flow of electricity. He argued that the difficulty in storing and maintaining the proper amount of nervous energy was attributable to (1) an inherited weakness in one's nervous storage capacity; (2) a generalized weakened condition owing to the particular responsibilities and stresses of one's current social and working life; (3) a generalized weakened condition throughout the nation owing to the tremendous competitive, intellectual demands of life in white-collar middle- and upper-class urban settings; and (4) a recent shock or debility that had significantly depleted one's energy capacity.

Beard, and most physicians of his time who took up the neurasthenic diagnosis, thought that neurasthenia was an illness primarily of middle- and upper-class businessmen, those "refined" persons who did "brainwork." Males were made exhausted by their demanding white-collar jobs, and some females were also affected, owing to the demands of their social and parenting schedules (and owing to their natural sensitivities and nervous weaknesses, originating as disturbances of their reproductive systems). As time went on, Beard and his colleagues noticed that the patient rolls were filled with women and blue-collar workers in numbers equalling middle-class males.[31] In response, they revised their hypothesis to include three types of neurasthenia: spinal neurasthenia (caused by physical labor or women's work), cerebrasthetic neurasthenia (caused by mental activity), and lithemic neurasthenia or autointoxication (caused by overindulgence). Symptoms were initially so vague and all-inclusive that later theorists developed a system for determining whether symptoms were active in the digestive, vascular, motor, sexual, mental, or sensory systems.[32] The theory rested in part upon the belief that individuals *inherit* a certain storage capacity for nervous energy. This emphasis on inheritance was initially troubling to Americans and was softened in part by the belief that with caution, willpower, and by saving energy, individuals (even those who were themselves the offspring of nervously exhausted parents) could increase their inherited physiological capacities and pass on new and improved traits to their children.

But the diagnosis of neurasthenia brought with it its own forms of punitive treatments for female patients. Weir Mitchell's rest cure, for instance, incapacitated female patients: they were forcibly restrained if necessary, confined to their beds, force-fed liquids and sometimes a surfeit of heavy foods, and prohibited to read and write. It is not difficult to notice how this treatment replicated the sociopolitical environment in which the symptoms showed up in the first place, generally making female patients feel unconfident, physically weak, bored, deprived, useless, and deadened—all in the name of revitalizing them.[33]

Some tenets of neurasthenic theory were predicated on the American Victorian values taken from the world of business: work hard, be ambitious, and save what you have earned. "The patient," Dr. J. S. Greene explained, "may be likened to a bank, whose specie reserve has been dangerously reduced, and which must contract its business until its reserve is made good; or to a spendthrift, who has squandered his inheritance; or to a merchant, who has expanded his business beyond what his capital justifies, until he comes to the verge of bankruptcy."[34] This metaphor struck a resounding chord with nineteenth-century Americans.

Beard often prescribed a regime of what he called "electrotherapy," rest mixed with cautious exercise, a healthy but moderate diet, appropriate medications, and "chats" that delivered medical education, personal encouragement, and moral exhortation. The treatment Beard made famous, electrotherapy, involved administering carefully monitored low-voltage electricity directly to the body of the patient. His conceptualization of neurasthenia, and especially the practice of electrotherapy, was undoubtedly influenced by his close friendship with the American inventor Thomas Edison.

In a typical case, Beard described a clergyman suffering from cerebrasthenia:

> A gentleman of middle life, a clergyman by profession, had been engaged in labors of his calling in charge of a church under circumstances that drew severely on his patience and tact; about the same time he was prostrated by exposure to excessive heat, and the sequelae of this prostration were of a character quite frequently observed, namely a multitudinous array of nervous symptoms which annoyed him for a long time. These two factors together, acting on an inherited nervous diathesis, brought on a cerebrasthenia which, when I first saw the patient, had been present for a number of years, and had compelled him to change his ministerial position for that of teaching. He complained, first of all, of cerebral attacks, analogous to sick headache. . . . Other symptoms were indigestion, depression and at certain seasons, more or less diminution of sexual power. . . . All his symptoms pointed to the brain, especially these nervous attacks which, when they were upon him, unfitted him for any labor or enjoyment. They were excited by pulpit work, and, indeed by any form of mental annoyance, or by a feeling of responsibility; even the slight task of leading an evening prayer meeting or attending a funeral, was sufficient to induce an attack. . . . Iron alone was of little, if of any service, whereas he was certainly benefited by various electrical and medical treatment [sic] directed to the nervous system.[35]

This case presentation is typical of Beard: the many symptoms combined into one diagnosis, the focus on work, the medicalization of the patient's problems, the location of the cause of the problems in "the brain," and the therapeutic administration of electrotherapy. At a later point in the case he also describes devising a program to enhance the patient's mental "attitudes." It obviously did not occur to Beard, as it might to a late twentieth-century psychotherapist, that the clergyman suffered because he disliked his job. One may or may not be able to change one's job in the late twentieth century, but there is room in our current terrain for that issue to come into play. Apparently there wasn't much room for that question in the terrain of 1879. It was just taken for granted that if he could not work, it was because he was medically incapacitated. Beard appeared to assume that individuals, at least middle-class males, would always be ambitious, would always want to work, and would want to work in the ways that they were expected to work.

In other words, in late nineteenth-century Victorian America, conflicts about work, the inability to be productive, ambitious, and competitive were considered to be a psychiatric illness. The clergyman was diagnosed as ill because he could not be a proper bourgeois male. He could not put into words what was bothering him; he could only "put it" into his body: his dissatisfaction with his profession, or his confusion about Christianity, or his disgust with what bourgeois manners required of him, or perhaps simply his wish not to work in a white-collar job could only show up as a cerebral attack, a headache, or nervous prostration. If he was a recently emancipated slave, perhaps his problem with work might have shown up and thus be explained away as a form of "laziness"; there was room for that in the cultural clearing. If he was a recently defeated Sioux warrior, perhaps his problem with work might have shown up and thus be explained away as a heathen backsliding into the "uncivilized" lifestyle of the renegade members of his tribe who refused to live in white society or on the reservation; there was room in the clearing for that. Since those options were not open to white middle-class clergymen, the only explanation available was that he must be ill, and the only solution was the healing technology of the nerve doctors, a technology that would return him to a productive bourgeois profession.

To Freud, the clergyman's fits, headaches, and incapacities would probably have meant something quite different. They might have been interpreted as hysterical symptoms expressing repressed urges in disguised ways. For instance, Freud might have suspected that a disguised Oedipal fear of his father was at the heart of the clergyman's lack of competitive ambition. Perhaps a secret sexual fantasy regarding the figure of the Virgin Mary, first developed during childhood as a means of displacing an incestuous wish for his mother, might have haunted the clergyman whenever he approached the altar, causing him to be sick and thereby allowing him to avoid confronting the statue, and thus his secret wishes.

Where Freud saw dangerous, dark secrets and sexual or aggressive wishes, Beard saw lethargy and exhaustion; an absence of energy, enthusiasm, and resolve; an incapacity to enact the proper bourgeois role. Where Freud saw the necessity of restraining and controlling the self (albeit in the least harmful and most rational and conscious manner), Beard saw the need to energize and invigorate the self, to liberate and expand it, to set the self free to work. This difference in medical discourse reflected significant differences in the two societies. In Europe, one of the main tasks of the state was to *control* the modern populace, to ensure order and the continuity of the modern state and the capitalist economy in an area of limited resources. Thus the European bourgeois self was configured as a private, secretive self with a dark, dangerous, unconscious interior that was full of sexual and aggressive drives. The interior drives, Freud thought, must be controlled in an aware and rational manner so that society could continue and the individual could survive and be successful. Individuals, therefore, had to develop the capacity to exercise self-domination over or sublimation of their "primitive" instincts. Physicians before Freud, such as Jacques Joseph Moreau, Max Nordau, and Cesare Lombruso, had also warned against the violent, destructive, and criminal consequences of the degenerate traits and dangerous instincts that were inherent in the self.[36] European illness, then, was either the expression of too much violent or sexual instinct, or conversely, the effects of too much repression. We could say that the problem with the European self was that there was *too much* inside.

But whereas in Europe the solution was to *dominate* the citizenry, in the United States one of the main tasks of the state was to *mobilize* the citizenry, to encourage them to work, take risks, settle the frontier, tolerate the noise, filth, loneliness, and crime of the large cities, compete, achieve, and save, all in order to ensure growth and the ongoing health of the capitalist economy. Thus the American bourgeois self was configured as a private, staunchly independent self with an ambitious, optimistic, hardworking, pragmatic interior that was a potential, but flawed, container for nervous and spiritual energy.

In America the interior had to be continually repaired, expanded, and especially replenished so that society could continue and the individual could survive and be successful. The problem with the self, then, was that there was *too little* inside; this inadequacy led to a subsequent lack of energy, ambition, will, achievement.

The European cure was to control through the practices of *self-domination*; the American cure, in contrast, was to control through expanding and revitalizing the self through the practices of *self-liberation*. To cure the patient, the European healer had to get him or her to reveal dangerous secrets and devise ways to more consciously, rationally, and creatively control and express the instincts. The American healer, in contrast, had to cure by building the patient's naturally good self, expanding and strengthening it, replenishing and revitalizing its natural energy, ambition, will, and competitiveness, and then helping the patient express, and liberate those inner qualities.

The two cultural landscapes developed medical discourses that conceived of the self, psychological illness, and psychological healing in ways that revealed their different political and economic configurations. But both medical theories about the self described the populations of the two cultures in ways that ultimately justified the state's particular means of control. The European strategy of control described a landscape of inherent human badness, limited resources, potential violence, and the imperative to dominate the self; the American strategy, a landscape of inherent human goodness, undreamed of abundance, potential contact with the divine, and the imperative to liberate the self. But both were strategies of political control. It seems instructive that the liberation story developed in America, while more optimistic and hopeful than the European story, has produced forms of racism, gender oppression, and even genocide that, in destructiveness and depravity, have rivaled the European story in many ways. Ideologies of control, be they couched in dominationist or liberationist language, have a dirty job to do, even if they are dressed up to appear as though they are healing, inspiring, hopeful, and spiritual.

One of the major consequences of self-liberation theory was the stifling of political activity, especially group action. Nowhere can this be more clearly seen than in the effects of the ideology on women. Mesmerism actively recruited females and, unlike American mainstream medicine and religion, gave them an opportunity to move from the role of patient-parishioner to the role of practitioner. But women paid the price by being indoctrinated into an ultrainterior, hyperindividualistic, apolitical vision. Because mesmerism developed healing practices that blamed the victim, promoted a form of extreme cognitivism, and featured the supplying and rebuilding of a true self, it restricted the organized activities of the movement's female members to activities unrelated to political and economic restructuring. We can thus interpret mesmerism as a healing practice that unknowingly co-opted and misused the psychological suffering of women which was of a political origin, exploited it for financial gain and notoriety, and diverted the political dissatisfaction of women away from more direct political resistance. Given the current influx of women professionals into the field of psychotherapy, and the current apolitical emphasis on the supplying and building of the individual's true self, one wonders if a similar dynamic might not be at work today.

CHAPTER SIX

Strange Bedfellows

THE AMERICANIZATION OF PSYCHOANALYSIS IN THE EARLY TWENTIETH CENTURY

Analysis suits Americans as a
white shirt suits a raven.
　　　—SIGMUND FREUD
　　　　IN A LETTER TO OTTO RANK
　　　　MAY 23, 1924

One of the defining moments in American cultural history—one that embodied the interaction between European dominationist theory and American liberationist culture—was Freud's now famous 1909 lecture series at Clark University in Worcester, Massachusetts.[1] Neither psychoanalysis nor the United States has been the same since.

FREUD, THE MOVIE

Imagine Freud's visit to America as a bad Hollywood movie. It is 1909, and Basil Rathbone, playing Freud, is at the bow of a great ocean liner crossing the Atlantic. The wind is howling, the rain is beating against him; his cape, held by his forearm, is drawn up around his face, shielding him against the elements. He stares, brooding and morose, into the darkness; ominous, romantic music swells in anticipation. Freud, the great psychological explorer, is bringing with him to America the secrets of the human unconscious. He is about to set them at the foot of a shallow, crass American public that he is repulsed by and secretly despises. Why has he consented to do this? If his ideas are met with scorn and derision in his native, sophisticated Europe, how can he hope for success in the land of cowboys and Indians? What will become of him during this American adventure? How could this naive, unsophisticated rabble possibly respond to his dark, pessimistic vision? And yet, perhaps the old professor knows something no one else knows. Perhaps there lurks in the heart of America an unknown depth and intelligence, a heretofore undemonstrated ability to recognize and implement the truth.

Okay, that's unlikely. Perhaps "fate" has stepped in and moved Freud to accept the speaking invitation from Clark. Yes, that's it. He did not actually know why he agreed to speak in America, and he was uneasy throughout the journey. It turned out to be a brilliant move, a mythic moment in the history of psychotherapy, but Freud could not have explained how or why. Something was brewing in America that no one, not King George III or Thomas Jefferson, not Teddy Roosevelt, not even Freud himself, could have foreseen. Something was stirring; something was about to happen.

We pick up the movie again. In America, Frank Sinatra as A. A. Brill, Gene Kelly as William James, and Oscar Levant as G. Stanley Hall, unable to contain their excitement about Freud's impending visit, sing and dance their way through the streets of New York. Freud arrives, the three young American psychologists show him around New York and teach him several new show tunes. They travel to Massachusetts and are greeted enthusiastically by an assembly of psychologists and interested intellectuals at Clark. Slowly, Freud's Victorian brooding melts under the enthusiasm and innocent friendliness of the young Americans. In response, he modifies his presentations, making them simpler, less pessimistic, less focused on sexuality, and thus less upsetting to his audience. The response to his five lectures is a public respect and support heretofore unknown by Freud. In the audience two obscure but congenial young mesmerists, played by Ronald Reagan and George Murphy, smile and applaud enthusiastically. They hold a press conference to announce a new gimmick for their snake-oil act: "Dr. Freud's new psychic discoveries and abundant healing." In the back of the room a muckraking American reporter, played by Sam Donaldson, jumps to his feet and calls out: "What about these rumors, Dr. Freud, regarding you and your sister-in-law, Minna Bernays?" Despite these characteristically American disruptions, which momentarily shake Freud's aplomb, the talks resume. Over the course of the ensuing days, Freud's metamorphosis becomes complete as Rathbone exits and is replaced by the fatherly Robert Young, who provides inspiration from afar for the mental hygienist Thomas Salmon, the advertising executive J. Walter Thompson (played by Jack Nicholson), and the intelligence tester cum personnel management expert Robert M. Yerkes.

In the final scene, Freud bids a fond farewell to America and returns to his European homeland. In the course of his brief trip to America,

Freud has unknowingly started something that will transform psycho-therapy, influence the shape of popular culture, revolutionize advertising theory and personnel management, and eventually even contribute to saving capitalism from a second devastating depression. Ironically, the journey to America will also eventually transform psychoanalysis. As Brill, Hall, and James, the mesmerists, the hygienists, and the entire advertising profession stand on the shore and solemnly wave good-bye to their European guest, we wonder if they have any idea of what will come of this visit. They will tell endless stories to their grandchildren about how Freud changed them, but the story they will *not* tell is how they changed Freud. They will lecture their students about how psycho-analysis changed American psychotherapy, but the story they will not tell is how American capitalism used Freud's concept of the unconscious to shift the nature of the American economy and its cultural-political landscape. These are stories not well known to any of us, but they are well worth telling.

THE STORY BEHIND THE MOVIE

Because Freud was disgusted by and deeply suspicious of certain aspects of American culture, he was initially taken by surprise by the invitation to lecture at Clark University, and he deliberated at length before decid-ing to accept. He asked Carl Jung and Sandor Ferenczi, two devoted followers and friends, to accompany him, to furnish intellectual compan-ionship and moral support during his stay in America. To everyone's surprise, the lectures were enthusiastically received by Americans, whose ranks included prominent psychologists William James, A. A. Brill, and G. Stanley Hall. James, perhaps the most famous and respected American psychologist of his time, greeted Freud by exclaiming, "Yours is the psychology of the future."[2] Freud was surprised and touched by the gesture.

Indeed, James was right. Within only six years of the Clark lectures, psychoanalysis had become the most discussed theory in the nation's bustling magazine trade. Over the course of the new century, psycho-therapy would become one of the most influential social practices in Western society. Although Freud could not have conceived of it at the time, during those surprising five days, his troubled, lifelong search for a successor had ended. The heir to the leadership of the psychoanalytic movement was not Jung, nor Ferenczi, not even a he, or a she. Freud's successor was not an individual, but a country—the United States.

Freud's lecture series, in fact, can be seen as an element in the economic hegemony of the United States in the second half of the twentieth century. In the first decade of the new century, the United States sat poised on the brink of an unknown future. The political and economic events since the Civil War seemed to be leading the country into a radically new era, one of machines, scientific discoveries, and a life of potentially unlimited (and unimaginable) abundance. But the country appeared not quite ready, or able, to realize its potential, to take the leap into a new way of life. A crucial element was still missing. In 1909 Freud transported the missing ingredient across the Atlantic to America: it was the bourgeois Victorian unconscious. The unconscious was a concept that, after some serious tinkering, would someday be used by the captains of industry and advertising to help catapult the nation into the role of the leading superpower of the post–World War II era. It was a concept that would turn an energetic but naive American cultural terrain into a sophisticated, psychological, highly effective social influence machine. In the hands of American capitalism, the unconscious became a vehicle for the single most important cultural dynamic of the twentieth century: the consumerization of American life. Freud, of course, would have been apalled had he known how his concept would be used by American business and distorted by the very forces he dispised. The introduction of the bourgeois Victorian unconscious caused only a small historical ripple at the time, but now, in retrospect, we can see that from that moment forward, America was not, could not, be the same.

1909

The America in which Freud landed was poised on the brink of a new age. At the approximate midpoint between the end of the Civil War and the beginning of the fifties, 1909 is also midway between the rural America that barely escaped civil fratricide and the urban, corporate America that created and perfected the consumer economy. After 1865 America had finished its immigrant push to the West Coast, its cultural war and nearly complete genocide of Native Americans, and its consolidation into one industrial nation, North and South. It had also abandoned its halfhearted concerns for recently emancipated ex-slaves and forgotten its pre–Civil War interest in woman suffrage. The second half of the nineteenth century had consisted of a collection of dismal occurrences involving governmental corruption, political violence, racial exploitation, and social confusion. It was also a time of increased industrial productivity and power, enlarged corporations, the birth of national advertising campaigns, and the glimmerings of a consumer economy.

Increased industrialization and urbanization, larger corporations, the building of the advertising industry, and the beginnings of consumerism, in the years after World War II, would become the most powerful economic, political, and cultural influences of the era. But in 1909 the country did not have much of a sense about what lay ahead, because things were changing so rapidly and unpredictably. One engine of change was the new influx of immigrants. In the short space of thirteen years, between 1901 and 1914, the country absorbed its last unregulated wave of Central and Eastern European immigrants: 4 million Slaves, 3 million Italians, and 1.5 million Jews. Urbanization was another agent of change. In 1790 only 3.3 percent of the population lived in towns of 8,000 or more inhabitants; by 1900, 33 percent of the people were urban dwellers.[3] The shape of individual households was also changing dramatically. Whereas in 1790, 36 percent of American households had seven or more persons living under one roof, by 1900 the percentage had declined to 20.4 percent.[4] Industrialization and increased mechanization was a third engine for change: in 1909 less than half a million automobiles were on the road, but by 1917, 5 million would be in use.[5]

The nation was changing, metamorphosing into something new, but there was no national consensus as to what America would, or should, be like. The United States was on its way to becoming a diverse, multicultural nation of large urban centers, giant business corporations, with a government run by a massive bureaucracy and dependent on scientific experts. But it would take the nation forty years and more to realize it. In 1909 Americans still thought of themselves as God-fearing small-town, honest, hardworking farmers and small entrepreneurs who were, of course, white Anglo-Saxon Protestants. The disparity between what America and the American self were becoming, and how Americans saw themselves was probably one of the reasons the population was vulnerable to the corruptions and oppressions that characterized the turn-of-the-century "Guilded Age."

The reform movement known as Progressivism flourished in the first two decades of the new century because it appeared to address the disparities between image and reality. It was a middleclass movement that, on the surface, was anchored in the values of liberal economics, compassion, and fair play. But the Progressive agenda, typified by the reforms of Teddy Roosevelt's presidency, should more accurately be seen as an attempt to face up to the evolving shape of the American economy, and to forge a new alliance between government and big business that would be more in keeping with the emerging needs of the new twentieth-century corporations. The alliance, we can now see, was necessary for the development of a new world of giant corporations and a fledgling consumerism.[6]

Although the corporations fought against the new reform laws pertaining to child labor laws, some minimal rights of labor, and new antitrust sanctions, in the long run the new legislation actually worked to the advantage of the corporations. It is true that the reforms restricted corporate management by placing limits on its behavior and by protecting labor, but the limits and protections were minimal; workers were only protected enough to ensure that they could live and toil the next day. Progressivism was a movement founded on the values and concerns of the Euro-American bourgeoisie; the values, concerns, and needs of other cultures and classes were puzzling, if not anathema, to them. Most important, the reforms positioned the federal government as a significant player in the new twentieth-century economic landscape. The alliance between government and corporate management, which would come to be a distinguishing characteristic of the century, was made possible by these reforms. Without the reforms, corporations would have continued their nineteenth-century coerce-and-destroy strategy, and class warfare would have intensified. Progressive reforms ultimately opened up a new, infinitely more effective way of controlling labor and manufacturing customers, one that fit much better with the emerging twentieth-century therapeutic ethos. Once raw physical violence was considered unacceptable, corporations had to turn to various means of psychological manipulation as a means of controlling the population.

One of the prominent characteristics of the twentieth century has been the slow but growing ability of corporations to psychologize the management of labor and to plant a vast field of consumer desire and reap the ongoing harvest. Neither of these psychological manipulations would have been possible had it not been for Freud's articulation of the unconscious and the new, virgin territory, the "stretch of new country"[7] it presented.

If the United States was constructing a self that was a container for eager, ambitious spirituality and optimistic, acquisitive capitalist energy, and if the populace was controlled by self-liberation practices, then where did Freud fit in, with his Old World ways, with its Victorian character and self-domination practices? If the nation was moving toward a corporate, consumer-oriented, urban way of life, yet was confused by and reluctant to face that change, then how did Freud unknowingly assist America in coming to grips with its changing structure and in adapting to the requirements of a new economic and cultural landscape?

EARLY PSYCHOANALYSIS IN EUROPE

To understand the meeting between self-domination and self-liberation, and to understand how Freud's theory helped the United States catapult itself into a position of world leadership, we must briefly turn to the early years of psychoanalysis. In the first two decades after the turn of the century, Freud had begun what would become an intellectual revolution in Europe. Slowly his ideas regarding infantile sexuality, the Oedipus complex, and the unconscious began to be regarded with more interest. The small band of loyal followers who had initially gathered around him had grown and was becoming more confident. Each Wednesday night the group would meet to discuss cases and argue theory. Out of this mix would come Freud's increasingly sophisticated theoretical formulations. During the forty years Freud was alive during the twentieth century, his theory would undergo changes in emphasis and his practices would evolve through many structural shifts. What was originally a highly didactic and rational theory became over time a sophisticated explication of the unconscious and an emotional "working through" of transference. What was once a kind of daylong walking-tour psychoanalysis with Gustav Mahler around the town of Leiden[8] became over time the fixed fifty-minute hour. In the end, Freud's theory was a most remarkable and creative achievement.

But all was hardly sweetness and light in the inner circle; there was conflict, anger, and accusation. Several historians have characterized Freud as an authoritarian leader who was completely committed to his theory and would tolerate little disagreement. Also it began to appear that sometime in the near future psychotherapy would become a road to wealth, fame, and perhaps power. The battle over who held the truth of psychoanalysis, and thus who would lead the movement when Freud was gone, was soon joined, and several members of the inner circle, most notably Alfred Adler, Carl Jung, Otto Rank, and Wilhelm Reich, would resign or be cast out.[9] The case of Alfred Adler, the first apostate, is a sad and curious chapter in early psychoanalysis. Freud attacked Adler's orientation to social interaction and banished him from the circle because he thought it was a significant deviation from his own, more correct focus on sexuality and the unconscious. This seems to be somewhat true, but what Freud left unsaid was his opinion about Adler's public socialism and Jewishness, which some researchers suggest were threatening to Freud. Freud was above all concerned that the European medical establishment and the general population as a whole would come to accept psychoanalysis as a legitimate psychiatric practice. European anti-Semitism being what it was, perhaps he thought it unwise for a Jewish Marxist to be his second in command and ultimate successor.

This brings us to Carl Jung, Freud's great white hope. Jung was a Swiss psychiatrist working in Zurich when he first learned about Freud. Here was a forceful, charismatic non-Jew who was intelligent and creative and very much in sympathy with Freud's ideas. Although he and Freud had a warm, rich, collaborative friendship for several years, they grew apart and rejected one another on the basis of several theoretical disputes. Over time, Jung shifted the focus of his theory away from sex and aggression and onto concepts such as the collective unconscious, archetypes, and personality types. One is immediately struck by Jung's spiritual orientation and his creative style, but what is most apparent about his theory, especially in contrast to Freud's, is that he described a world that was less dangerous, less conflictual than Freud's. In Jung's theory, most everything "fit" into patterns. There were guiding principles, Kantian-like structures that were literally built into the psyche and were readily accessible through dreams and myths. Jung's world was more mystical, optimistic, and organic. The cultural differences between Freud's vibrant, passionate, conflicted, dangerous, diverse Vienna and Jung's more stable, homogeneous Zurich may have been reflected in their two theories.[10] In addition, several aspects of Jung's theory, such as his interest in personality typology, his belief in the genetic "givenness" of archetypes, and, of course, his emphasis on the "individuation process" as the sine qua non of human maturation, were expressions of a liberationist ideology. Little wonder that the two men became disenchanted with one another: they were working on two different theories, which were situated in somewhat different worlds, and they described two different selves, which suffered from different illnesses—thus they had devised two somewhat different healing technologies.

Regardless of what one thinks about the theoretical disputes of the two men, for some Jung's connection with the events surrounding World War II Germany justified Freud's rejection of Jung for a future leadership role. Jung collaborated with the Nazis when they took control of Europe and accepted leadership of a new psychoanalytic establishment created and used by the Nazis. He denounced Freudian psychoanalysis as the "Jewish science" and proclaimed that it was unfit to minister to the Aryan soul. To his credit, Jung was willing to disagree publicly with and denounce Nazi ideology after the war (unlike several intellectuals such as literary figures T. S. Eliot and Ezra Pound, and philosophers Martin Heidegger and Paul de Man). But damage had been done by his collaboration.[11]

Curiously, although the battle has continued over who will be Freud's successor, none has ever been crowned. However, in a certain, somewhat troubling way, it was indeed the United States that came forward as successor. Slowly, over the course of the early decades of the twentieth century, American culture began to appropriate and change psychoanalysis to suit its own needs, subtly but firmly putting a conformist, liberationist spin on Freud's subversive, dominationist theory. It was a way of being, rather than any one individual, that over time began to lead the world community of analysts. The optimistic, pragmatic, liberationist, business-oriented mind-set of the United States latched onto psychoanalysis and has yet to let go.

AMERICA'S UNCONSCIOUS: THE LAST FRONTIER

Freud's theories have been influential in the United States, both in psychotherapy practice and in popular culture. Yet the spirit of America has also infused psychoanalysis with an optimistic and pragmatic spirit that has in many ways transformed it; at the same time psychotherapy has been used to achieve capitalist purposes in ways Freud never would have dreamed of. Historian John Demos explored the irony of the United States, which Freud so much despised, granting Freud a great deal of respect and success. Demos suggests that this ironic outcome was the product of "the main line of historical change in the 19th century . . . [creating] a situation in which Oedipal issues became highly charged for many people. And among all the Western countries, this situation was most fully elaborated in the United States."[12]

Demos has cited several historical reasons for this unlikely fit between the New World and the Old World, between what I have referred to as self-domination and self-liberation practices. He emphasized especially the American concern for instilling in male children the conflicting qualities of independence and guilt, and developing in them a characteristic sense of autonomous, internal self-government. According to Demos, these dynamics produced "a massive intensification of the parent-child bond."[13] Yet Demos has pointed out that at the same time, the culture defined male success as the surpassing of the father, owing to the country's economic ideology and its experiences with geographical immigration. So a unique type of culturally syntonic competition was injected into the father-son relationship that fit nicely with Freudian theory.

Psychoanalysis was also well received in the United States owing in part to the state of American psychiatry in the first decade of the twentieth century. American psychiatry was still grounded in the physiological model of illness and cure, whereas psychoanalysis presented an approach that was both psychological and scientific. Psychoanalysis appeared to be more proper and civilized than mind cure, more scientific than mesmerism's heirs such as Christian Science. Because it carried the imprimatur of science, psychotherapy also appealed to those who were cut off from religion but were still searching for certainty and transcendence.

But most important, psychoanalysis took American thought into a new realm of cultural experience. Or perhaps we should say psychoanalysis named a phenomenon that had been emerging but was not yet acknowledged or recognized. Unbeknownst to Freud, Americans began to shape their own interpretation of psychoanalysis, which paved the way for a new cultural terrain encouraging personal improvement and productivity. The realm of the private interior, the unconscious, was at the center of the American modification of psychoanalysis. With the new American slant, analysis provided Americans something that was beyond the grasp of both neurology and positive thinking: a new, virgin territory, an interior frontier. Soon after the western frontier had been declared officially "closed" by historian Frederick Jackson Turner[14] in 1893, the last possible frontier, a new, internal psychological frontier, "opened" up.

The American concept of the unconscious provided several productive economic possibilities unimagined (and unintended) by the early Freudians. It provided new territory for psychological exploration and excavation by psychiatrists, psychologists, and psychoanalysts. This would ultimately prove to be a great financial boon to the profession of psychotherapy. It also gave expanded meanings and possibilities to the late nineteenth-century concept of "the therapeutic." The transformations that twentieth-century life in the United States demanded or would soon demand of its citizens (for example, continuing development of the personality, economic successes, geographical mobility, creative use of leisure time, independence-isolation from others, the capacity to tolerate high levels of personal debt, and adaptability to new places and new roles) now took on a "deeper" and more medicalized meaning with the discovery of the unconscious. Through the concept of the Freudian unconscious, therapeutic transformation became at once more explicit and more mysterious; it was placed under the control of a trained group of medical experts using a new, complex, but highly scientific technology. Because it provided a potential territory that contained unlimited emotional and mental resources that could be mined and exploited for profit by growing corporations, the concept of the unconscious opened up countless opportunities for profit making in industries such as advertising, entertainment, and politics. For example, unconscious sexual desire could be used to sell products unrelated to sex, such as cigarettes in the 1920s or cars in the 1950s. Jealousy, envy, or oral cravings could be used to conceptualize and justify manipulating consumers into buying what was not actually needed or even desired. Competitiveness or rage against the Oedipal rival could be exploited as a means of swaying voters toward one candidate or against another. All of these desires and feelings were situated by Freud in the dark, secret, but increasingly accessible unconscious. By naming these dynamics, Freud made a place for them to show up in the culture. By situating them in the unconscious, a territory that could be "entered" through psychoanalysis, Freud unknowingly made these dynamics available or accessible to other technologies, such as advertising and personnel management, that claimed to operate within the psychological interior. The urges and drives of the unconscious were thus more easily used in service of a soon to be developed twentieth-century corporate strategy for psychologizing labor conflicts and consumerizing the economy.

Thus, psychoanalysis unknowingly brought to America a crucial piece of the twentieth-century capitalist puzzle: a description of the unconscious. But did the unconscious frighten and threaten American capitalists and small entrepreneurs as it did the European bourgeoisie? Not at all. Just as the American wilderness had to be settled and conquered, so too did one's internal wilderness. Because of the tradition of the *enchanted* American interior, both geographic and psychological interiors, Americans tended to be less frightened and were more likely to be curious about the unconscious, and more apt to want to explore (and exploit) it than to dominate it. After all, enchantment was a potential gift from God, something to be "taken," to use Emile Cady's abundance theory term (see chapter five). Thus Freud was utilized but not surrendered to. Through Freud, "the therapeutic" in the United States took on a "deeper," more interior meaning than it had with mesmerism or positive thinking theory—and what was deeper, for the corporation or entrepreneur, was simply more territory to be exploited. Thus what in Europe had been a socially threatening theory of sexuality and aggression became in the United States a tamer improvement theory that was significantly altered over time by American optimism and pragmatism and shaped to suit the nation's economic purposes.

PSYCHOANALYSIS, MENTAL HYGIENE, AND THE AMERICAN MARKETPLACE

Long after Freud's initial modifications in the 1909 lectures, there were powerful forces at work in America that continued to influence and dilute the more severe and pessimistic elements of Freud's theory, especially elements that reflected the ethos of European self-domination. There was first and foremost the overall atmosphere of the United States, the cultural framework that was predicated on optimism, pragmatism, abundance, expansion, an ideology of limitless spiritual and commercial possibilities. And then there was the increasing trend toward self-liberation practices as opposed to self-domination practices, begun in the early nineteenth century, that would later be used by corporate capitalism in order to increase its power in the twentieth century. On a more mundane level, American psychiatrists, psychotherapists, and healers of the mind-cure ilk, like practical-minded practitioners everywhere, tended to accept and use those aspects of the 1909 version of psychoanalysis that they agreed with or that furthered their business and to "forget" or ignore concepts with which they disagreed. And let us not forget the pressures Freud placed on himself during the Clark talks in an effort to encourage new recruits. He later admitted he left out certain aspects of his theory and emphasized others, especially highlighting the ameliorative, pragmatic qualities of health and good functioning.

But the overall cultural landscape had the most important influence on psychoanalysis. This type of subtle influence can be seen in the activities of the mental hygiene movement and its effect on early psychoanalytic practices in the United States. The movement was begun in 1908 as a reform movement in the general spirit of the Progressive era and was greatly influenced by the philosophy of pragmatism. Started by a former psychiatric hospital inmate, Clifford Beers,[15] the mental hygiene movement was at first an attempt to reform the American asylum, which had by most accounts degenerated once again into a most gruesome institution.[16] The movement was in its early years funded by private donations, and over time it helped ease the needless suffering of inmates in American psychiatric institutions. By 1912 famous psychologists and physicians such as Adolf Meyer, William James, and Thomas Salmon (of the U.S. Public Health Service) had joined and taken control of the movement; it was then in a position to accomplish much more than Beers could have imagined. Once Salmon arranged for federal funding, the mental hygiene movement became an influential force not only in hospital reform but especially in preventive education for the general public. Mental hygiene

introduced and framed fundamental social parameters regarding the definition of psychiatric "health" and "illness," the meaning and function of
psychiatric intervention, and the activities associated with "normal,"
"proper" mental functioning. At this time mental and emotional difficulties and disruptive public behavior became forever located in the
purview of medical science.

Mental hygiene's major concept was typically American: if individuals could be made "ill" by the pathogenic interactions they had with
others, especially with members of their immediate families, mental
problems could be prevented by participating in healthy interactions.
The movement applied the bourgeois values of quantification, objectification, and cleanliness to the realm of emotional and psychological
complaints. In this conception of the intrapsychic, the realm of the mind
is a concrete, reified thing upon which the practices of scientific, medical
cleansing could be exercised. As psychiatrist Joel Kovel[17] has noted, the
concept of mental hygiene implies an overly concrete, reified view of
psychological processes and a bourgeois concern for sanitation and cleanliness. These two aspects of the term *mental hygiene* had a significant
impact on how psychotherapy was conceptualized by psychotherapists,
how it was viewed by the general public, and how it was integrated into
the capitalist marketplace.

Kovel has argued that mental hygiene neutralized and co-opted
Freud's more radical European posture by conceptualizing the unconscious as a container for psychological uncleanliness. The proper middle-
class solution to an unclean unconscious was to sanitize it periodically,
and thanks to Freud, the unconscious came automatically stocked with a
wealth of psychological "dirt" that would never be completely eradi-
cated.[18] According to Kovel, mental hygiene reduced the ruthless honesty of Freud's focus on sex and aggression to mental hygiene's more
mechanical, technological "dredging" of a sanitized unconscious. He
therefore accused mental hygiene of banalizing psychoanalysis. The
movement's optimism regarding the possibility of "reforming" the unconscious undoubtedly grew in part out of the American mesmerist
belief in the potentially sacred interior. Freudian "dirt" afforded little
challenge when confronted with the power of interior enchantment.[19]

The mental hygiene movement also contributed to and profited by
the modern historical trend in the West away from religious judgments
about social deviance and the tack toward replacing them with scientific
opinions. Deviants were no longer considered to be "undesirable, bad,
mad, or possessed: they . . . [were] *sick*, and need[ed] the ministrations of
a mental hygienist."[20] The unseating of religion as the dominant arbiter
of deviance, historians such as T. J. Lears and Warren Susman have

argued,[21] was indispensable to capitalism's growing hegemony, because the moral codes of traditional religion were hostile to the obsessive consumption of modern commodities. In contrast, early modern philosophers such as Locke and Hume, and thereby modern empirical sciences such as psychology, held that pursuit of pleasure rather than compliance with moral codes was the foundational human motivator.

Most important, the movement led to the medicalization and objectification of emotions because it conceived of emotional problems as being in the same category as physical illnesses (that is, in need of hygienic practices). By reifying the mental and by being overly optimistic about the accessibility of the unconscious, the movement came to objectify emotional conditions and thereby allow "for an *exchange-value* to be placed on states of mind."[22] In other words, once mental health and illness could be objectified and quantified, expenditures of time and money could be calculated for treatments of disorders, thereby facilitating and justifying psychotherapy's new role within the twentieth-century capitalist marketplace. Psychotherapy was well on its way to becoming a "medical profession."

It was after Thomas Salmon joined the hygienist movement in 1912 that a connection was established between the government and the psychiatric profession that continues to this day. With the advent of World War I there were a host of twentieth-century problems and opportunities that attracted psychologists to the war effort. Psychologist Robert Yerkes and his associates argued that through psychological testing, the state could evaluate the mental and emotional fitness of soldiers on a scale and with a scientific precision never before attempted.[23] At the same time, the technology of modern warfare created a new kind of casualty, the psychiatric casualty, and the Veterans' Administration, therefore, had a new type of psychiatric "illness" to treat, and an unusually compelling need for psychiatrists and psychologists. The government responded by funding projects under the auspices of the newly created National Committee for Mental Hygiene and by expanding training programs in universities and campaigns of public education.[24] It was the combination of the mental hygiene movement, psychoanalysis, and World War I that greatly increased the banalization and therefore the popularity of American psychoanalysis during its first decades. The government was just beginning to get a glimmer of how psychology, and psychotherapy in particular, could be utilized as a means of governing. For instance, early intelligence testing was developed for use in the U.S. Army during World War I and promoted by its inventors as an objective, scientific measure of innate intelligence. More recently, the original tests have been examined and found to be so culture-based and racist that they are now considered worthless as a measure of intelligence,[25] but at the time they were being used they had a scientific stamp of approval that made them a powerful political agent. The test results were used by the eugenics movement to justify racist claims and aid in the passage of the 1924 Immigration Act, one of the more infamous laws in U.S. history.

BEHAVIORISM, ADVERTISING, AND BIG BUSINESS

Another important trend in psychological theory that appeared before and grew in strength after World War I was the successful attempt by experimental psychologists' to conceptualize psychology as an empirical science capable of discovering natural laws in a manner similar to that of the physical sciences.[26] This view of psychology was quite efficacious for positioning psychology as an academic discipline in the late nineteenth century,[27] and for producing business applications for psychology's newly found expertise. For instance, John B. Watson, a Johns Hopkins professor, defined psychology as "a purely objective experimental branch of natural science. Its theoretical goal is the prediction and control of *behavior*."[28] By this Watson meant to encourage colleagues to work in the fields of advertising and what we would today call market research and personnel management. In 1915 Watson was elected president of the American Psychological Association (APA). Five years later, he began working in an advertising agency, and by 1924 he had achieved the position of vice president of a prominent advertising firm. On this path he had the company of A. A. Brill, a prominent psychologist and follower of Freud, and many amateur psychologists and public relations men such as Edward Bernays, Freud's nephew. Brill used his psychological expertise to develop advertising programs; among his achievements was a campaign that encouraged women to smoke.

Large corporations used psychology to ensure that consumption kept pace with production, a polite way to say that psychology helped business manipulate the public into desiring what they might not buy otherwise. Bernays advised advertising executives to conceive of advertising as the practice of "making customers"; this goal is accomplished, Bernays taught, by understanding "the personality . . . of a potentially universal public."[29] Here we see Bernays attempting to justify the presence of psychology in the corporate world by relying on the unquestioned assumption that there exists or potentially exists a scientific body of psychological knowledge about the personality of the universal human. The use of psychology in advertising was a development of major economic and cultural importance. It reflected a trend that had begun with mesmerism, had grown stronger with positive thinking and abundance theory, and shifted and finally co-opted psychoanalysis: the combination of liberation theory and the psychoanalytic unconscious, used in service of corporate interests such as the management of labor and the manipulation of the consumer.

Walter Scott, who referred to himself as an industrial psychologist, was elected president of the APA in 1919. Scott played an important historical role by encouraging corporate managers to use psychological technologies to predict and control the behavior of their workers. He suggested that psychology could develop testing devices that could determine the type of worker that would best fit a particular job. Historian John Reisman summarized Scott's argument by saying that the task and the worker are "a unity, [involved in] a biological kind of relationship . . . [in which] the man [would profit] from his labor, not only materially, but intellectually and emotionally."[30] Here again we notice psychologists turning to the physical science paradigm and the claims of a universal scientific technology to justify their practices. But a new strategy was also beginning to emerge. Scott implied a new conceptualization of mental "health," one that conceived of work—that is, the proper match between task and worker—as an important component of emotional health. This strategy became more prominent in the 1930s[31] and then, of course, in the post–World War II era, as management's psychological manipulation of labor became an unquestioned, accepted practice. The uses of psychology by management in the second half of the century were tolerated because nearly all aspects of middle-class life, especially "career choice," became thought of as opportunities for expressing one's core self and enhancing one's life. Psychology had thus become the scientific advisor to two quintessentially twentieth-century middle-class forms of the therapeutic: advertising and personnel management.

Part of the genius of early twentieth-century advertising was that it used techniques that combined behaviorism with the concept of the Freudian unconscious. Early cigarette campaigns were a good example of that curious but effective combination. Smoking was one of those twentieth-century leisure-time activities aimed at the middle class and justified in advertising campaigns through the appeal of "scientific" expertise. For instance, smoking was advertised as a relaxing activity that promoted health. It was also justified in popular culture with the argument that since the scientific expert Freud considered it harmful to deny oneself sensual gratification, it would be risking a neurosis if one denied the "desire" to smoke. In a further pop culture extension of the use of psychoanalysis, it was argued that "sucking" on a cigarette could be interpreted as a sublimation of another, more socially unacceptable desire, such as an infantile urge for the maternal breast. Seen in this light, smoking was thought to be an acceptable and perhaps creative solution to the pressures of modern civilization. Smoking was only one of a number of supposedly "natural" desires that advertising first created and then justified so as to encourage the consumption of leisure commodities.

CONSTRUCTING AND ENTERING THE INTERIOR

The activities of entering and influencing the realm of the private interior are central aspects of the everyday practices of the field of psychology. Psychotherapy, market research, political polling, diagnostic testing, career interest assessment, and advertising are all practices that collect information about an individual's private life and attempt to use that information to influence and/or control the individual's behavior, usually by promising to enhance his or her ability to carry out what are thought of as self-liberation practices, such as expanding, experiencing, controlling, attracting, acquiring, and consuming. It is difficult to identify many of the activities and especially the political consequences of psychology practices that enter and influence the private interior of the twentieth-century self-contained individual because they are so integral to our everyday way of life.

As we have seen in earlier chapters, the loss of community, tradition, and certainty was key to the construction of a self available for and even actively seeking inner revitalization and guidance. By the first three decades of the twentieth century, parents appeared openly confused about which social norms, values, and skills to impart to their children. Children were even less secure about the value of what their parents could offer. The world had become increasingly complicated, and sources of communal and religious guidance were losing their authority. As a result, scientific findings and professional expertise began to take on a new importance. The growing popularity of child-rearing advice manuals in the early years of the twentieth century (see chapter three) demonstrates an increasing willingness on the part of members of the middle-class to turn to and rely on scientific and professional guidance. Individuals were experiencing a lack of emotional resources and personal conviction caused by a loss of authoritative tradition and community. It was into this absence, increasingly conceptualized as an *interior* void, that the processes of advertising and psychotherapy inserted themselves. They were welcomed with open arms, open hearts, open stomachs.

As we have also seen in previous chapters, another significant force constructing the wish to be psychologically entered is the ideology of self-liberation, which has functioned as a subtle control on the late modern and also late twentieth-century populace. One cannot develop the practices leading to self-liberation unless one "opens" oneself to a psychotherapist, a trusted teacher, a spiritual master, a mass-marathon psychology trainer, a touching television commercial, a powerful politician. Because we locate the self in the individual's interior, and because we conceive of the healing process as one in which good things such as the ideas or the power of a charismatic leader are "taken in" and "internalized," desperation and charisma are important motives in the learning of self-liberation practices. This will be discussed in detail in chapter eight. It is shocking to realize how much of everyday twentieth-century life is taken up by our willing attempts to liberate ourselves by expanding, attracting, acquiring, and consuming. We learn how to enact these practices because we hold self-liberation to be a core moral value.

Did early twentieth-century psychotherapy contribute to setting this frame of reference? I think so. The individual's feelings and thoughts, because they were located by psychotherapy *inside* the bounded, masterful self, were considered to be products of intrapsychic processes, and not the products of culture, history, or interpersonal interactions. Psychological problems have been interpreted as illnesses that are conceptualized as residing within the person and caused by intrapsychic conflicts or malfunctions. By conceiving of mental ills in this way, interpretations of deviant behavior such as alienation, depression, and, in the post–world War II era, narcissism, were depoliticized. Because psychotherapy denied the central influence of history and culture, symptoms reflecting the frame of reference of the modern Western world—such as loneliness and alienation, extreme competitiveness, and a desire for nonessential commodities—had to be considered natural and unavoidable. As a result, individuals have been constructed to strive tirelessly to consume and expand, and at the same time to believe that the search is simply an aspect of universal human nature. If symptoms were considered natural and unavoidable, they were located outside of the realm of politics and history and thus could not be changed through political action: the status quo prevailed.

The only way corporate capitalism and the state could influence and control the population was by making their control *invisible*; that is, by making it appear as though various feelings and opinions originate solely from within the individual. Psychological science was presented as objective, scientific truth rather than as just another external or traditional authority. In a society in which science is the unchallenged truth, psychology was thus positioned to be highly influential and powerful. In time, psychology became the "paramount criteria of what is socially desirable or deviant."[32] Psychology's new position is in part what is behind the inability of psychotherapy theories to describe the individual as a historically situated social being who is a member of various socioeconomic classes, ethnic and religious groups, and neighborhood communities. Psychological control of the populace has been hidden from view, unintentionally, by an unknowing psychology.

Freud most assuredly did not set out to construct a straightforward political theory; in fact, throughout his life he tried to keep politics out of psychoanalysis and remain relatively unpolitical in his personal life. However, even Freud would have been upset by what American capitalism did to his theory, and to what purposes it was used.

CHAPTER SEVEN

The Road Not Taken

HARRY STACK SULLIVAN, MELANIE KLEIN, AND THE LOCATION OF THE SOCIAL

*"One will be with the forces of reaction
and human exploitation,
or one will be actively against them."*
—*HARRY STACK SULLIVAN
PSYCHIATRY, 1946*

In the twenties, thirties, and forties psychotherapists were confronted with two theoretical pathways, two ways of conceiving of the social world. One road led therapists to power, influence, and financial success, the other to political marginality and a less lucrative economic future. This chapter is about the two roads: their originators, ideas, historical contexts, and political consequences. There was, in truth, no direct theoretical battle, no specific confrontation, no one moment of choice between the American theory of Harry Stack Sullivan and the European innovations of psychoanalyst Melanie Klein. The leaders of the two paths never openly debated; probably they never met. In fact, the history books have not conceived of the between-the-wars era as a battle between Sullivan and Klein, or even less between two ways of discussing the social world. The battle is brought to light here only as a metaphor, not as an actual occurrence, because I believe that social interaction—its recognition, meaning, and location—is a central issue in psychotherapy. There was no direct, concrete confrontation between the two theories, but I would argue that there was an ongoing struggle over the nature, activities, and functions of American psychotherapy, and as the post–World War II era developed, one orientation emerged victorious.

The road that was taken, represented by Melanie Klein's object relations theory, prepared the way for psychotherapy's influence on the consumerism of the era to come. In this sense the spirit of her theory carried the day. Although during her lifetime few outside the rarefied world of European psychoanalysis had ever heard of her, she started a revolution in psychoanalytic thought. Klein argued that individuals, even infants, contain inherent, built-in psychic structures that determine their emotional reactions to others. The structures are a combination of expectations and emotions, forming what Klein called "internal objects." These representations of others interact with one another during intrapsychic fantasy, producing various emotional dramas. In other words, her theory locates social interaction *within* the self-contained individual. Klein's theories have been used by her successors, especially in America, in ways that unintentionally justified and further constructed the kind of self that is compatible with, and in fact drives the post–World War II consumer economy.

The road not taken, Harry Stack Sullivan's interpersonal psychiatry, was potentially as critical, intellectually difficult, and politically opinionated as its originator was. Unlike Klein, Sullivan situated social interaction in the space *between* people. He argued against self-contained individualism and believed that the study and remediation of racism, economic injustice, and nuclear war were proper subjects for psychology. He focused on the interpersonal causes and effects of anxiety, consciousness, and identity. The self in Sullivan's theory was a process, or system. Further, Sullivan did not conceptualize what he called the self system as something that should be strengthened; he saw it as an impediment to accurate perception and normal functioning. The primary goal of psychotherapy was thus not to build or repair the self but to deconstruct the self system. The profession's choice for Klein and against Sullivan turned out to be politically prudent and an economic windfall for psychotherapy. But was it the right choice?

During the years constituting the second quarter of the century fundamental changes in psychotherapeutic theory prepared the way for "the therapeutic" to extend what Philip Rieff has called its turn-of-the-century cultural "triumph" into nearly every aspect of post–World War II American life. By the boom years of the sixties, psychology had become an increasingly visible social science. Through the activities of what was called "applied psychology," psychology would be the social science perhaps most responsible for the continued dominance of self-contained individualism and the resurgence of capitalism. But first, before psychology could ascend to its post–World War II position of authority, psychotherapists, as psychology's official healers, had two major theoretical problems to solve.

First, psychotherapists had to become attuned to one of the major trends of the twenties, thirties, and forties: an increasing interest in the realm of the social. The decades between the two world wars became focused on social life: social interaction, personal relationships, and the processes of loving, relating, influencing, and controling. Twentieth-century scientific discoveries caused a communications revolution throughout the United States. The use of electronic technology swept the country, increasing the effectiveness of industrial labor, linking the coasts and shortening the distance between all national regions, multiplying the speed by which news, information, and advertising were disseminated, creating a national radio audience, and homogenizing the preferences of moviegoers and consumers throughout the nation. These changes brought other social changes: corporations were faced with the necessity of psychologically influencing, rather than physically dominating, labor; advertising was occupied with manipulating consumer desire; the entertainment industry was fabricating celebrity; the national press was manufacturing the news; the communications industries, such as AT&T, were selling the wonders of communicating; and transportation moguls, such as the automobile manufacturers, were convincing the public to move and travel. All of these activities required a new type of psychological approach that emphasized social interaction, dyadic relationships, and often romance and sex. One of the ironies of the era is that at the same time that attention was focused on social interaction, the dismantling of communities and traditions was continuing at an ever faster pace.

Accordingly, psychotherapy theorists began to address themselves to the realm of the social. They made declarations about the nature, causes, motivations, manifestations, developmental stages, and psychological meanings of social interaction. Most important, Sullivan with his interpersonal psychiatry and Klein with her object relations theory independently sought to properly *locate* social interaction in order to describe it and then to restore it to health. In the process, each would lay claim to its ownership.

The second theoretical problem psychotherapy theorists faced was developing new concepts that would allow for the description, explanation, and treatment of a whole new set of psychological puzzles, problems, and illnesses that were increasingly "showing up" in the cultural terrain. Individuals, it seemed, were becoming increasingly complex, so treatment plans needed to become increasingly sophisticated and technological. Under the scrutiny of mid-century science, and under the pressure of the new lens of social interaction and social influence, individuals began to appear to be richly interiorized and psychologically troubled in unlikely and unfamiliar ways.

The most prominent psychotherapy traditions in the United States, such as mesmerism and Freudian psychoanalysis, had to be radically modified to meet these two new challenges. The combination of Freud and mental hygiene, discussed in the previous chapter, had sufficed but for a short time. The European Victorian frame articulated by some Freudians depicted people as machinelike mechanisms dependent on Newton's hydraulic model of energy conservation.[1] This framework was increasingly out of sync with the new world of electronic technology and social relatedness. The same could be said for the American concept of the enchanted inner world of mind-cure philosophy, mesmerism's heir, which had degenerated into both spiritualism and sales technique. A new vision was needed, one that was attuned to the emphasis on the social, scientific, and technological, and sufficiently complex that it could allow for radically new descriptions, explanations, and treatment practices suitable to the anxieties, emotional upheavals, and exigencies that were now thought to be "natural" human ills.

Both interpersonal psychiatrists and object relations theorists tried to respond to the two issues that faced psychology. Ultimately, object relations theory triumphed; although it was roundly attacked by the psychoanalytic establishment for many years, it came to establish the overall theoretical framework for post–World War II psychodynamic psychotherapy as we know it.

THE WAR, THE ECONOMY, AND PROSPERITY

On the surface, the two decades sandwiched between World War I and World War II were as different as night and day. The twenties were filled with optimism, good times, and an expanding economy. The thirties were times of desperation, hopelessness, and an economy that floated dead in the water. One decade was often symbolized by gaiety, glittering lights, and the tinkle of champagne; the other by cold, bitter, grey days and the sight of bread lines winding through the streets. One decade was excited by a blossoming technological and communications revolution; the other stood by in horror as that same technology offered no help in the face of the depression and later played an important part in the Nazi's "final solution" to the "Jewish question."

However, scratch the surface of the two decades and they become more similar. Beneath the reckless abandon of the twenties was an anxiety that was difficult to name or explain. But when on October 24, 1929, the stock market fell, suddenly the country knew what to name its dread. Beneath the ostentatious display of wealth and conspicuous consumption were bitter class warfare (for example, the 1914 Ludlow massacre)[2], racial hatred (for instance, the 1919 Chicago race riot),[3] a blatant disregard of the Bill of Rights (for example, the 1918 Sedition Act),[4] and economic power held in the hands of a wealthy few, whose short-sightedness and greed would ultimately bring the country to its knees. Beneath the veneer of world peace was a rock-bottom terror that could be momentarily avoided or denied, but from which, finally, there could be no escape. Throughout the 1930s, with Hitler's rise in Europe, the United States, torn by the conflicting internal forces of activism and isolationism and weakened by the depression and its own racism and anti-Semitism, had done little to stem the tide of fascism.

Against this backdrop, it is easier to understand the shape of psycho-therapy in the three decades that preceded mid-century. There was throughout these years a strong tendency to avoid the political and ethical in favor of the technological, to avoid the humanistic in favor of the scientific, to avoid the humanitarian in favor of the expedient, to avoid the needs of labor in favor of the interests of capital. Psycho-therapy, being a child of its era, reflected those tendencies. It seemed to be a unified, scientific enterprise. But beneath the surface there were subjective jealousies, contentiousness, and outright intellectual warfare (like the conflict between Anna Freud and Melanie Klein).[5] Theorists were preoccupied with developing an explanation and a treatment ap-proach for an ahistorical, universal anxiety. At the same time that the communications revolution (the massive use of telegraph and radio) began to dominate big business, a faith in scientific technology became widespread.[6] As a reflection of the age, several schools of psychotherapy focused on scientific technicism and moved into a brave new world of industrial organization and personnel management.

World War I, the Great War, the War to End All Wars began the death knell of the modern European era, epitomized by the Victorian sensibility. That war, historians such as Modris Eksteins argued, called into serious question the belief structure of Victorian bourgeois society, a process culminating in the emergence of what is now called the post-modern era.[7] It ended an unquestioned, total acceptance of the value of personal restraint; the exercise of logic and reason; the natural efficiency of the upper classes to rule the nations; the commitment to hard work, gainful employment, and delay of gratification as ends in themselves; the "gentlemanly" patriarchal virtues of sportsmanship, fair play, and silent suffering; the particular type of constraints, deprivations, and oppres-sions visited upon women; white European society's natural intellectual and moral superiority to, domination over, and exploitation of non-European peoples; the bourgeois conception of a vaguely benevolent but unemotional God; and the natural superiority of laissez-faire capitalism as an economic system and its necessary partner, self-contained individualism, as a configuration of the self. All of these values and many more were shaken—perhaps even obliterated—by the senseless horror, waste, and devastation of the war.

However, the collapse of the moral underpinnings of the modern era did not appear to be felt as strongly in the United States. This was no doubt partly because of the geographical distance between the United States and the war: The devastation of the countryside, the suffering of civilian populations, the destruction of small industries, and the freezing of national economies were unknown in the United States, and the number of war deaths (and awareness about the deaths) of young men was significantly less in the United States than in Europe owing to the limited years of American participation. Americans didn't have to witness first-hand the horrors of modern warfare—the terror of endless trench warfare, the creeping fog of the deadly gas, the destructiveness of new bombs, grenades, and automatic weapons, the use of air raids and new techniques in combat, and the new psychiatric illnesses such as "shell shock."

The trauma of war seemed to escape the United States, or rather, the traumas were more easily denied by Americans. The war was portrayed by the press and the government as an unfortunate fix that the Europeans had once again gotten themselves into, which the Americans had to help them out of. "The Yanks are coming," the song went, and they wouldn't return home until they had saved the day and ended the war, until "its over over there." It was the patriotic duty of each young man to enlist, and in no time at all he'd be back home again. Serving in the armed forces was publicized as a kind of lark, an adventure. Of course, the sad truth was brought home to many families, but, in good individualist fashion, the country as a whole remained isolated, and thus silent, about the horror of it all.

But at what price, this silence? In order to deny the truth of the war, what psychological/perceptual resources were depleted? Where did the fear of death, and the enemy, go? The awareness of the devastation of the European countryside, the disorder wreaked on European national economies, the destruction of bourgeois values such as what Bertolt Brecht depicted in *Mother Courage,* the class inequities such as those depicted in Dalton Trumbo's *Johnny Got His Gun;* in other words, the crumbling of Western society as they knew it; how did this affect Americans? What effects did the shocks and fears caused by these events have on the American public? It was hard to tell, because the denial was so great.

In retrospect, the United States denied the trauma of World War I at its own peril. During the twenties Americans embraced a decade-long postwar prosperity built on a foundation of oppression, indulgence, and reckless speculation. The nameless fears and anxieties that hounded the twenties, chased disaffected bohemians to Europe, and drove the upper classes to drink and distraction, found their realization in the grinding poverty of the Great Depression and the horror that was Buchenwald, Auschwitz, Guadalcanal, the Bataan death march and the use of the first atomic weapons. There was, it turned out, a great deal more to worry about than it at first appeared.

The social and political gains of the Progressives, so solidly part of the mainstream of thought before World War I, were ignored, rolled back, repealed in the years after the war. The moderate majority voice, so clearly in evidence earlier, was nowhere to be found. Public sentiment was suddenly against the unions and for management: Antitrust laws were ignored, child labor winked at, and violent union-busting a common practice. Some of the more pernicious curtailments of civil rights during the war, such as the Sedition Act of 1918 that imprisoned Eugene Debs, were used during and especially after the war by the government to attack the unions. For instance, on January 1, 1920, Attorney General A. Mitchell Palmer arrested 3,000 strikers and protesters because they were "alien radicals." Friends and supporters who inquired about them were also arrested. Subsequently 556 were deported for radical activity. Violence against African Americans was steeply on the rise, with no help in sight from law enforcement or the courts. The Ku Klux Klan, revived in 1915 from its post-Reconstruction slumber, was suddenly riding a wave of public support. Legal as well as vigilante violence against recent non-WASP immigrants, leftists, and union members was common, as the trial and subsequent executions of Nicola Sacco and Bartolomeo Vanzetti demonstrated.[8]

The country had turned a deaf ear to the workers, the poor, immigrants, ethnic and racial minorities, leftist activists. In 1920 the Republican ticket of Warren Harding and Calvin Coolidge, solidly pro-business, swept the presidential election. And for the next several years the country as a whole seemed to enjoy increasing economic prosperity. Business profits were up, the unions were controlled, Prohibition encouraged a thriving, wealthy underworld, and the use of the new, applied science promoted the belief that success and money were on a never-ending curve up. Political scandals such as Teapot Dome, which originated in the White House, were considered inevitable and hardly cause for alarm; it didn't shake Harding's popularity or his administration's standing with the public. The country was on a spend-and-enjoy binge, a kind of denial high that was rarely questioned or examined. Entrepreneurs, high rollers, and risk-taking gamblers were admired, the cult of the film celebrity was in high gear, and Americans took it for granted that a certain amount of corruption and illegality were natural, inevitable products of a vibrant economy.

The nation was momentarily safe from the dangers of European militarism, business was booming, and twentieth-century science was producing new discoveries faster than big business could adapt them to the marketplace and exploit them for profit. Automobiles were everywhere: in 1917 there were fewer than 5 million cars on the road and fewer than one out of six farm families owned a car; by 1930 there were 23 million cars and 26 million households, and two thirds of America's farm families owned cars. In 1919 it was illegal to privately use a radio; by 1930 there was a radio in twelve million homes, or 40 percent of all households in America. The number of homes with electricity doubled between 1920 and 1930. Along with the discoveries in the natural sciences there were enormous advances in the communications industry.

There was a new sense of social activity in the air: people were more aware of one another through the inventions of the telegraph and radio, through the popularization of the car, the phone, and the beginnings of air travel. These advances were all being applied to the world of business, which encouraged the public's optimism about continuing, unending progress and success. The Nineteenth Amendment, which established the right of women to vote, was ratified in 1920, and in many areas of life it was thought to be more acceptable for women to be public, vibrant, independent. Cigarette smoking and public dancing by women, especially expressive dancing in which couples embraced, were increasingly common and accepted, as were women attending college, developing professional careers, and becoming involved in political activism.[9]

But the apparent economic prosperity and shift in gender roles was much more tenuous and temporary than it at first appeared. Although one could not tell by reading the popular press, studying advertisements, or enjoying radio programs, poverty, low wages, and exploitative working conditions certainly did exist, lurking just out of sight. Racism and ethnic group discrimination caused violence and hatred. The fear that Communism would be imported by radical Eastern European immigrants and would "infect" law-abiding Americans fed the nativism, Red-baiting, and consistent attacks on the civil rights of American citizens. It was also used to explain and justify the violent union busting characteristic of this era. The enormous profits brought about in part by the control of labor and in part by the increased effectiveness of advertising and marketing techniques were not being productively used by ownership: Profits were not safely invested, used to improve office machinery, or spent on research and development to secure future growth. All too often money was spent conspicuously on luxury items or invested in risky financial speculation. Far too much of the nation's wealth was concentrated in the hands of a few and spent irresponsibly. Many farms, especially those dedicated to wheat and cotton, were suffering from heavy debts and declining markets.

Insecurity, fear, anxiety were in the air. They were denied, they were ignored, but they must have been sensed. Perhaps the unacknowledged terrors of the war, denied but ultimately unavoidable, surfaced in the attacks perpetrated on non-WASP immigrants, labor, people of color, and Catholics. Perhaps the dynamics of denial were also responsible for Americans' inability to see the dangers inherent in the wasteful, dangerous economic practices in which the upper classes were indulging. Perhaps a sense of confusion and disorientation, produced in part by the moral bankruptcy of European bourgeois ideals that had been revealed by World War I, drove the middle and upper classes to overindulgence, a sense of entitlement, self-absorption, and conspicuous consumption. All of this and much more contributed to the stock market crash of 1929, the collapse of banks, and the relatively quick slide into a decade of severe economic depression. The world of the twenties, so pro-business, self-satisfied, and smug, so racist and full of fear and hate, fell. It crashed and broke. The brokenness spread throughout the world, and for a long time there was no fixing it.

Surely, somehow, the understanding that it could happen, or that it was going to happen and no one was doing anything about it, was available within the cultural terrain. For a long time the awareness of impending catastrophe hadn't shown up—there was no place for it. But occasionally, some visionaries caught a glimmer of the future. The unconscious awareness of danger would appear wherever it could find the room: in jokes, stories, myths, fantasies, and dreams. The causes and alleviation of anxiety were at the core of both Sullivan's and Klein's theories; we might interpret the centrality of anxiety in both their theories as another indication of the disguised awareness of danger.

It took a lot of pain, and a lot of desperation, for the country to realize that the beautiful, reassuring pattern of 1920s prosperity had, in fact, simply masked a grave danger. It was not easy for a nation that had been tricked, bribed, and seduced into believing in the accessibility of easy money and the unending spiral of progress and personal wealth to face the hard truth. It was not easy to realize that the philosophy of laissez-faire capitalism and its major accomplice, self-contained individualism, had ultimately worked against the best interests of almost all economic classes. But the country did, partially, come to see what had been hidden. During the thirties, year after year of crushing poverty, fear, and hopelessness helped the nation to see more than it had been able to see. In 1932 the country, in its desperation, turned to Franklin Roosevelt and what he called "the New Deal," an eclectic program that tried to save capitalism by controling some of its worst abuses and muting some of its lesser excesses. Instead of using its power to further the class interests of big business, the federal government under Roosevelt attempted to use some of its power to further the survival and the security of the working and middle classes.

The economic crash and the hard times that followed were finally enough to stir the nation, to move it to search for structural solutions to the unavoidable problems of unregulated capitalism. Roosevelt did this in an imperfect and limited way, but he was able to at least do that much because the everyday conditions of life had broken through the denials and fairy tales. In the 1920s the nation acted as though the country existed for the sake of the wealthy. But during the depression another voice could be heard, faint but resolute. A skinny drifter from Okema, Oklahoma, Woody Guthrie, transformed the frustration and despair of millions of Americans into music. He sang "This land is your land, this land is my land" to the poor and the dispossessed on street corners, in soup kitchens, and around Hooverville campfires. He went wherever the freight trains would carry him, and wherever he went, folks listened. When he sang it, it rang true.

THE TECHNOLOGY OF HUMAN INTERACTION

The crash and subsequent depression were ever present, undeniable, intrusive realities back then. But one would not get a strong sense of that by reading the psychotherapy theories of the time, or even, unfortunately, by reading current histories of those theories. But this should not be surprising. Psychologists had been trying to establish their field as an academic discipline, trying to find a scientific justification for their practices.

Psychology, if it was to become a player in that era, would have to present itself as a science and develop techniques that would further the progress of human interaction in personal life and in the world of business. In other words, it would have to develop itself as a *technology* of human interaction. Indeed, this was accomplished by psychology in many ways, some of which were discussed in the previous chapter. Psychologists presented the field as an Enlightenment-era type of discipline, claiming that they objectively studied the universal individual in order to discover universal laws of human being, so that they could treat the universal illnesses of a universal human psyche. Once this duty was accepted, psychologists could then take their place as the sole legitimate "experts" on human nature.

Psychology offered its expertise to business in the areas of advertising, marketing, public relations, and personnel management. Various scientific practices, such as personality assessment, intelligence testing, behavioral management, social influence techniques, and career counseling began to appear and were used by business in order to manipulate the consumer and control labor. The emphasis was on the scientific, technical use of social interaction in the pursuit of business goals.

Of course, psychotherapy theory was not as explicitly economic, but the same imperatives that influenced psychology's move into the world of business were also affecting psychotherapy. These influences can be seen in the mental hygiene movement (see chapter six). The movement's emphasis on a systematic, scientific, preventive psychotherapy technique reflected the tenor of the times, and its optimistic, pragmatic, and adaptivist tone stamped it as a characteristic American enterprise.

It should not be surprising that psychotherapy theorists and historians of psychotherapy do not study the sociohistorical context in which theories have been developed. Therefore to understand Sullivan, Klein, and the struggle over the location of the social, we will have to read between the lines to get a sense of what was happening in the world of the theorists, therapists, and patients that populate the textbooks.

There were three major revisions of psychotherapy during the twenties, thirties, and forties that had a major impact on American practices: Sullivan's interpersonal psychiatry, psychoanalytic ego psychology, and Klein's beginning work in object relations theory. All three were reflections of the time; all three attempted to address the practical needs of the field as it grew and tried to establish itself as an independent academic discipline, and all three developed complex theories that attempted to explain human experience.

SULLIVAN, HIS ERA, AND HIS DREAM

Harry Stack Sullivan was a strange figure of a man, and he remains to this day a strange figure in the history of psychotherapy.[10] He was stiff, formal, odd, secretive, abrasive, prickly, and sarcastic. He was driven, narcissistic, and on occasion humiliated his friends and colleagues, yet to his friends he was also loyal, respectful, caring, sometimes even loving. He was most certainly brilliant, inquiring, and incisive.

Sullivan's strange and abrasive behavior can be explained, no doubt, in part by confusing and alienating childhood experiences with his family and community (a community in which he suffered discrimination because of his Irish Catholic heritage), in part by the poverty of his childhood and early adulthood, in part by his unusual schooling, and in part by the contrast between his intense and deeply felt identification with his patients and the cavalier and sometimes contemptuous attitudes of his fellow physicians. Another reason for his oddness and eccentricity might be found in his understandable difficulty in sensing and trying to articulate an understanding of human being that was decades ahead of his field theoretically, and light years ahead of what most of his colleagues could tolerate politically. It is likely that Sullivan was often frustrated and impatient, both with the limitations of his colleagues as well as his own. He was trying to accomplish a difficult intellectual task in a guild atmosphere that was indifferent or disagreeable, if not downright hostile, to his project. Such an environment isn't conducive to maintaining a pleasant disposition, even for the most jolly of souls, and Sullivan was most certainly not jolly.

So what exactly was Sullivan's project? That is difficult to say because he was such a difficult writer. But I believe a key to his message can be found in the world in which he lived. Sullivan grew up in an indifferent, sometimes hostile world, one that was dangerous to him in several ways. His childhood had been permeated with poverty, isolation, and persecution. It appears that in adolescence he experienced a psychotic episode of undetermined severity and was hospitalized, although no records have ever been found to verify this. His mother appears to have been seriously depressed, his father distant and cold. He was an only child, and had little interaction with other children until his schooling began, and then only within the confines of the classroom. Sullivan's mother was a deeply disturbed woman who seemed to have suffered a psychotic depression when her son was very young. He was then taken care of by his maternal grandmother, who exercised a great deal of authority over him. After a time his mother returned, and in the years to come he related more to his female elders than to his father. He must have had to become exquisitely attuned to their moods and to what they required of him. His family's poverty, Irish ancestry, Old World ways, and Catholic faith made him an easy target for the ethnic group prejudice and discrimination that was rampant in upstate New York at that time. Themes important during his formative years, including the impact of social and economic influences such as prejudice, poverty, and rural culture and the impact of a parent's anxiety upon the child's self-esteem, are found in Sullivan's psychiatric theories.

Sullivan came of age when the country was just beginning to flex its muscles and develop an identity adequate to its immense resources and potential. He only made it through one semester of undergraduate studies at Cornell; he appears to have lost his academic scholarship and fled out of humiliation and poverty. He later returned to school, but to a tenth-rate medical school, where he survived in an undistinguished manner. He never attended any courses in psychiatry, nor did he have the luxury of a psychiatric internship (or, it appears, much of any internship at all). He happened upon a job at St. Elizabeths Hospital and was befriended by William Alanson White, the head of St. Elizabeths and a well-known psychiatrist. It was White who helped him find a position at Shepard and Enoch Pratt Hospital in Baltimore, where Sullivan stayed for several years and developed the clinical ideas and techniques that distinguished his career. He began his medical career in earnest as the decade of the 1920s unfolded. All this combined to create an atmosphere in which technology, especially human management technique, was highly prized. These trends were not lost on Sullivan, who developed a theory saturated in social interaction, mutual influence, and the technical expertise of the therapist.

Adolf Meyer, a Swiss-born psychiatrist, who was instrumental in the success of mental hygiene, was an important influence on Sullivan in Sullivan's early years at Sheppard. Meyer attempted to develop an alternative to Freud's psychoanalysis, and his interest in social interaction and political issues such as ethnic group and racial prejudice were similar to Sullivan's. However, mental hygiene had little to say about schizophrenia, a strong interest of Sullivan's, and in general the movement's theory was simply too thin and narrow for him—so he kept searching.

Sullivan's experiences with prejudice and economic injustice increased his awareness of the psychological consequences of socioeconomic forces in ways unusual for a psychotherapist. As a result he became increasingly curious about history and anthropology, and the integration of these fields with psychological study became his intellectual passion. In 1926 he met Edward Sapir, an anthropologist associated with what is now referred to as the Chicago School of Sociology. They met in the morning for an informal conversation, but their meeting lasted all day and well into the night.[11] The subject matter of their talk covered anthropology and politics, language and psychology, culture and personality, social rituals and psychotherapy technique. When that meeting ended Sullivan was on his way to becoming a different kind of theorist. It was an education for both men, but for Sullivan it was a seminal meeting: He was to frame his life's work in the themes of that conversation. Through Sapir he would become acquainted with teachers, a language, a set of concepts, in fact a way of thinking that would help him give voice to the self-taught ideas and school-of-hard-knocks learning that he had improvised but had been hard pressed to articulate adequately. Through Sapir, Chicago School notables such as Charles Cooley, George Herbert Mead, and William I. Thomas[12] became known to Sullivan, and through them he began to think in more explicitly cultural and historical ways. In all likelihood, Sullivan's meeting with Sapir radicalized Sullivan (as, undoubtedly, it did Sapir). Sullivan's critique of individualism was one of the achievements of his vision, matured and honed by many years of study, reflection, and practice:

> [I]t makes no sense to think of ourselves as "individual," "separate," capable of anything like definitive description in isolation. . . . No great progress in this field of study can be made until it is realized that the field of observation is what people do with each other, what they can communicate to each other about what they do with each other. When that is done, no such thing as the durable, unique, individual personality is ever clearly justified.[13]

Sullivan's characterization of romantic, unique individualism as an "illusion" was a product of his growing ability to historically situate the social practices of psychotherapy. He came to believe that theories that unquestioningly valorized, and in fact justified, individualism were philosophically incorrect and reflected the culture of their time, and thus unknowingly contributed to the political status quo.

Sullivan maintained that personal individuality is an illusion for two reasons. First, individuals are not isolated, discrete monads; they constantly interact and influence one another and their social surround. Thoughts, feelings, impressions, relational patterns, concepts, theories, and beliefs are not the products of a removed, singular, intrapsychic process; they are a consensual effort, aspects of the never ending mutual influence and shared understandings of the social world. As such Sullivan thought these psychological phenomena should be properly located in the social realm, not conceptualized as reified structures located in the sealed interior of a putatively isolated, self-contained individual. Second, Sullivan saw personal individuality as an illusion because he came to realize that the construct of the masterful, bounded, unique twentieth-century self is a cultural artifact.

In fact, Sullivan developed a new vision not only about the individual but also about the discipline of psychotherapy as a whole. His vision was an interdisciplinary one, informed by cultural studies and committed to an ongoing program of political research.[14] He began to think of his ideas as sketching out aspects of a new theory, which he referred to as "interpersonal psychiatry." To further his vision, Sullivan became the moving force behind many professional conferences and much intra-disciplinary political intrigue, the creation of the Washington School of Psychiatry and the William Alanson White Institute, and finally a new journal, *Psychiatry*. He created an interdisciplinary research team, includ-ing him, political scientist Harold Lasswell, and anthropologist Edward Sapir, in an attempt to further what he called "the fusion of psychiatry and social science." He used the journal to demonstrate how psychiatry could address various psychological, political, and cultural issues. Studies about personality and lifespan development, he wrote in the first issue of *Psychiatry*, "in culture[s] . . . widely divergent from our own . . . will show the limitations of many of our current formulations and point accurately to advantageous fields of investigation."[15] In the first volume, the journal showcased articles on "cultural conditioning," what we would today call the social construction of gender, differences between Freud and Marx, and also included a review of a 1937 book titled *The Folklore of Capitalism*. In the fourth issue of the first volume, the journal inaugurated a new feature, a literary/political analysis of a piece of contemporary propa-ganda.

Sullivan's critique of self-contained individualism was simply one of many radical clinical ideas that flowed from his vision of the self as seated in an interpersonal context. According to his idea about "the self system," the system is not an entity that psychotherapy was in charge of properly "building," but rather something that the discipline should be dedicated to deconstructing. Finally, although he certainly did have his technological and positivist moments (for example, his concept of the therapist as a communications "expert," and his certainty about what constituted "reality" and "distortion"), his overall theory about technique seems to have flown in the face of mid-century American trends toward a technicized and highly professionalized psychotherapeutic process. For instance, he refused to use interiorized concepts such as inner *structure* and focused instead upon interactional *process*. "The term dynamism," he explained in the first issue of *Psychiatry*, "is to be preferred to 'mental mechanism,' 'psychic system,' 'conative tendency,' and the like, because it . . . [doesn't imply] some fanciful substantial engines, regional organi-zations, or peculiar more or less psychological apparatus about which our present knowledge is nill."[16]

Toward the end of his life, Sullivan's views led him to dedicate all of his energies to overtly political issues such as the dangers of nuclear weapons and the amelioration of poverty, hunger, racism, and other causes of dictatorships and international conflict. This activity was but a continuation of his political positions of the thirties. Weighed down by the spectre of racism and militant fascism in Europe, Sullivan fought back with the weapons at his disposal. "Psychiatry," he argued, "has a basic role in making sense of human affairs, individual and collective."[17] He had evidently hoped to move the discipline along slowly, educating colleagues at a pace they could tolerate, from what he called an understanding of "the psychiatry of private living" to "a psychiatry of politics." However, with the advent of World War II in Europe, his old timetable appeared a luxury the world could no longer afford: "The course of [world] events forbids . . . [a] quiet progression. A psychiatry of the state is demanded. . . . The publication committee [of *Psychiatry*] therefore inaugurates a department of political psychiatry . . . [the primary activity of which will be to analyze] influential political symbols with special reference to their use in propaganda."[18]

In 1946, after many years of political activity, Sullivan called for "a cultural revolution to end war,"[19] to be led by psychotherapists and social science researchers. Sadly, but predictably, his direct political activity (and his insistence that racism and economic injustice were proper subjects for psychological study) increased his isolation within psychiatry. His vision, conflicted and self-contradictory though it was, potentially threatened psychotherapists' dreams of ever increasing apolitical technological breakthroughs and heightened social status, wealth, and power within American capitalism. "[I]f psychiatry hopes to make sense in the world today," Sullivan wrote in the same editorial, "some of its practitioners must raise their eyes from a goal of passing in moderate respectability from their professional birth to the obituary notice."[20] Needless to say, this challenge did not elicit a positive response.

Sullivan has been characterized as the quintessential American therapist, always focused on the pragmatic and the practical, ever optimistic about the efficacy of scientific technique as practiced by therapist or researcher, hopeful about therapeutic cure, insisting upon preserving the doctor's respect for the patient, and active in organizing professional groups and planning projects to improve the future through the associations to which he belonged. And indeed he was all of the above. But he was more than that. He was tormented in the way a few individuals are tormented when they have seen, "darkly," some great vision. These people often struggle throughout their lives to describe the vision to others, others who are usually uninterested or who only occasionally, and imperfectly, understand its meaning. Sullivan's torment lifted him beyond his American fascination with technology and expertise, above his American optimism about the scientific amelioration of individual suffering and the pragmatics of psychological cure. He never lost these inclinations, of course; one can see traces of them in all his work. But sometimes in his inarticulate struggles one can see flashes of a larger, more encompassing, less compromised vision.

The development of what we would today call these hermeneutic, social constructionist ideas no doubt helped Sullivan understand more about his own interests and intellectual proclivities. It led him to a fuller understanding of why his ideas about psychology had always been centered on interpersonal interaction, why parental anxiety had been a cornerstone of his theory, why he was never satisfied with orthodox Freudian psychoanalysis, and why he insisted that an examination of the socioeconomic status of the patient and the effects of class, ethnic, and racial oppression upon the patient were quite properly *psychological* issues, indispensable to psychotherapeutic treatment. These proto-constructionist ideas led him to an interest in the interactional dyad and to group processes. They have helped current interpersonalists better appreciate the therapist's use of his or her experience in a more direct way in the therapy hour. They also help explain why in the last years of his life Sullivan spent more time organizing for educational reform and against the atom bomb and less time treating individual patients. But although he became better at understanding his own particular views, he was then faced with a far greater problem: how to get others to understand his ideas.

The basic problem was this: Sullivan's interpersonal vision, taken to its philosophical conclusion, was not a comforting one.[21] It would have called attention to the fact that what we think of as reality is socially constructed, that we live on the surface of a tiny speck of dust in the vastness of eternity. It opens up the existential abyss. The social constructionism and hermeneutics lurking just below the surface of Sullivan's ideas are especially threatening to practitioners of a profession such as psychotherapy, because they make us aware that there are no universal, objective healing practices. All healing practices are social artifacts, products (and reproducers) of their cultural landscape, and as such are embedded in an inescapable web of moral agreements and political activities. Healing practices only exist in particular moral frameworks and inevitably serve particular socioeconomic functions. To mainstream American psychiatrists of the 1930s and 1940s, this would not have been pleasant news, nor would they have taken kindly to the messenger. To take up Sullivan's interpersonal challenge fully, to situate psychotherapy within the history of its era and to consider psychotherapy as an indigenous healing practice of a specific cultural group, would have meant a fundamental rethinking and restructuring of psychotherapy. It would have also meant that psychotherapy would be actively involved in the critique and restructuring of the larger sociopolitical structures of society. I'm not at all sure that Sullivan could have or would have articulated his vision in exactly this way, but I suspect that his colleagues sensed the fundamental threat his vision would eventually pose to their practices, their livelihoods, and ultimately their socioeconomic standing.

If indeed Sullivan's colleagues did intuitively understand the ultimate political implications of his vision, it would help to explain the vociferousness and hostility with which they attacked him and his partners in crime (the dread "Cultural School" of psychoanalysis),[22] Karen Horney and Eric Fromm. It was because of the cooperative efforts of these three that an interpersonal vision of psychoanalysis was built. Horney and Fromm were both former Europeans who had studied with Freud and eventually developed differences with him. Horney presented the most direct challenge to Freud's views on female sexuality. Unlike Sabina Spielrein, who seemed to allow Freud and Jung to either co-opt or silence her ideas,[23] Horney assertively put forth her disagreements with Freud in a way that caused her great disfavor within psychoanalytic circles. Among the most creative ideas of Horney's prolific career were her insights on relatedness, culture, and psychiatric epidemiology. She believed that neurosis is caused by disturbances in interpersonal relationships as well as intrapsychic conflict. Included in the interpersonal realm are history and culture. Horney developed one of the first straightforward cultural critiques of the United States by a psychoanalyst. Although Horney's cultural critique was a target of psychoanalytic derision in the 1930s, her ideas appear surprisingly contemporary, almost commonsensical, today.[24]

Fromm also developed ideas that took him away from Freud; he was more interested than Freud in political and cultural issues and their impact on individual personality. He developed a psychoanalytic-Marxist-interpersonal-existentialist synthesis that was the basis for a productive literary career.[25] He also did something few psychoanalysts have done: he wrote openly and knowledgeably about his Jewishness and how it significantly informed and shaped his psychological theory.[26] In his emphasis on the effects of culture he was joined by Horney, and they both found Sullivan in the rich New York intellectual life of the 1930s. It was never an easy, simple alliance among these three; they had their theoretical differences and, no doubt, their personal disagreements. Fromm, for instance, despairing over Sullivan's emphasis on normality and his tendency to discuss only the *conscious* identity, accused Sullivan of "selling out to Mammon."[27] Sullivan, no doubt, thought Fromm too imprecise and too enamored of individualism. Horney, on the other hand, was probably too Freudian for either of her two colleagues. However, the relatively short period of time that they worked together provided psychotherapy with an alternative theoretical frame that has been rare, indeed, in the history of the field.

Sullivan's Basic Ideas

Sullivan's major disagreement with Freud stemmed from different conceptions of human being and the self. Freud's drive theory presupposed a Victorian self that contains interior, instinctual drives that had to be controlled and dominated by the rational mechanism, the ego, so that the individual could gain social acceptance and so that civilization could survive. Sullivan's concept was that the self is located in and derived from the interpersonal field, which includes both dyadic (two-person) interactions and the larger sociohistorical sphere of cultural values and beliefs. Freud's self is dependent upon a mechanistic, hydraulic theory of energy conservation and discharge; the self is constantly trying to discharge energy in an effort to reach equilibrium. Sullivan's concept of the self is based on an interactive, mutual influencing process in which the individual is constantly adapting to the environment, learning by attending to the linguistic and bodily cues delivered by others. The self is motivated by "security" needs, attempting to create and maintain interactions that do not produce anxiety or rejection in others. Freud's concept of the self is a deep, intrapsychic, conflicted self that contains secret, dangerous drives that must be dominated so that a balance among psychic forces can be achieved. Sullivan's concept of the self is an interactive, vulnerable self immersed in the social surround, a self that contains a natural drive for health. For Freud the danger lies within; for Sullivan it is without.[28]

Sullivan thought that anxiety, not everyday worries and concerns, but debilitating, fragmenting, paralyzing anxiety, is interpersonal and contagious.[29] When a parent experiences this type of anxiety, the children are affected and seriously disrupted by it. Children therefore would become acutely aware of the parent's experience of anxiety, would learn to anticipate and defuse it, or at least muffle or, as a final alternative, avoid it. They would avoid their parent's, and, by extension, their own anxiety and fragmentation by "selective inattention," dissociation, or "parataxic distortion," all degrees of perceptual distortion. It is the child's learned response to the anxiety of others, the ability to attend to behavioral cues, anticipate reactions, and then act to prevent, assuage, or avoid the other's anxiety, that causes most problematic behavior in adults. The primary tool of the child's strategies of prevention, amelioration, and avoidance is "the self system," the subconscious emotional and behavior patterns of attunement and anticipation that each individual develops in order to adapt to the particular interpersonal environment in which they are originally "thrown."

Children learn the rules of the particular environment in which they are embedded through a process Sullivan called "consensual validation," the interpersonal communications that are exchanged through language, touch, inference, feeling tone, body language, costume, and so on. In the early years of life parents, older adults, and older peers teach the child what is acceptable and proper, but this is a process that is constantly influencing and shaping people, no matter what their age, status, or position. The process Sullivan called "reciprocal emotions" is a crucial aspect of the consensual validation process (explained below). Emotions, especially intense emotions such as anger, fear, and anxiety, are thought to be important indicators in the interpersonal field, markers that instruct participants to notice, attend to, or ignore specific events in the moment.

According to Sullivan, individuals are constantly monitoring their interpersonal environment seeking clues about how to behave. The process of consensual validation is continually in use, as people attend to one another's emotional states and exchange coded information regarding what is proper and improper, anxiety provoking or soothing. This naturally happens in the psychotherapy office as well as everywhere else. The process of therapy consists of monitoring the emotional and behavioral fluctuations in the room, noticing when the patient's anxiety is rising, or when the patient is selectively not noticing various present events. This process is meant to assist the patient in learning what causes inattention and how inattention is produced. It was Sullivan's belief that if patients can come to understand how and why they selectively ignore or dissociate, they will be able to notice their present environment and be better able to respond to it and to the new consensual validations that can be developed between therapist and patient, and perhaps also, by extension, those that can happen between the patient and others in the world outside the therapy office. Emotional problems, Sullivan thought, are caused because patients are restrained from using the perceptual talents naturally at their command. When, through therapy, the obstacles to accurately perceiving others and oneself are removed, the innate motive for health will take over, and the patient, in cooperation with the therapist, will naturally develop new patterns of behavior that more accurately reflect the social clues being sent by others.

Therapists can assist the patient in this process by being aware of when the therapist is selectively inattentive during a session, or when the therapist experiences a rise in anxiety. Through his or her increased awareness, the therapist can guide the patient to explore what is being avoided. Therapist and patient can then trace those appearances to their interactive cause (the patient's behavior), and thus guide the patient in exploring what happened in that moment, why the patient got anxious, and what he or she did to avoid the feelings. An important technique

Sullivanians use to uncover the various inaccurate or ineffective perceptual patterns in the patient's life is the detailed inquiry. In this process the therapist carefully follows the patient through the patient's life story, or through a description of a recent life event or a problematic pattern in the patient's life, asking for precise details about the event in question. In this way the therapist leads the patient into a fuller awareness of the feelings that led to a particular dissociative experience.[30] In time this will help the patient better understand how selective inattention is caused, and for what purpose. When the patient stops ignoring or dissociating, that is when the patient sees himself or herself in the way others see him or her, the therapy is concluded. Successful therapy returns the patient to a state of "normal" perception and behavior, which is, Sullivan believed, an absence of inattention, distortion, and dissociation.[31]

Sullivan thought the therapist should be a "participant-observer" in the therapy process. This means the therapist is free to be more active than an orthodox analyst, lending his scientific "expertise" to the interaction, noticing (silently) when anxiety is provoked in the therapist, and then inquiring, shaping, and leading. He considered the therapist an expert in interpersonal interactions, not a transference object, as in psychoanalysis; therefore the patient was not encouraged to develop a regressive transference (a momentary reliving of the parent-child relationship) to the therapist. The therapist, together with the patient, would develop hypotheses about the patient's past, and about the patient's present behavior, and then set about to "test" them to determine their accuracy. Sullivan strongly believed that certain accepted therapeutic practices such as the delivery of interpretations that call attention to the supposed internal, unconscious motives of the patient or the direct confrontation of psychotic "dread," should be avoided because that process is hierarchical and disrespectful and it could intensify the patient's anxiety to intolerable levels. Theoretical statements that presuppose the existence and value of an isolated, unique individualism toward which the patient should strive should be avoided because that model of human being is simply a historical artifact that is philosophically incorrect and politically harmful.

For Sullivan the social realm, including psychotherapy, is an interpersonal, interactive field that is socially constructed. This theoretical vision reinforced several of his long-held personal beliefs, such as his emphasis on mutual respect in the therapy office. For example, he continually insisted that "we are all more simply human than otherwise," by which he seemed to mean that the supposed qualitative difference between therapist and patient is a hierarchical fiction in which the therapist should not indulge. Some have suggested that

Sullivan's embrace of the therapist as "expert" conflicted with his disavowal of the therapist-patient hierarchy; this paradox seemed to have escaped him. Probably the theoretical concept most representative of Sullivan was that personal individuality is an "illusion."[32] This concept finds Sullivan at his best: as social constructionist, as therapist, as social theorist, as activist for social change. Through this idea he integrates the sociohistorical and the therapeutic in one grand (and immensely unpolitic) moment. By realizing that self-contained individualism is a social artifact, and thereby not the accurate reflection of an absolute external reality, Sullivan was able to disengage himself from the principle ideology of his time, and thus from the power relations that created and maintained it. In a profession that embraced self-contained individualism—and thus solidified its expertise in the mid-twentieth-century capitalist marketplace—Sullivan stood alone, resisting that trend. Even the semi-Marxist Fromm waxed eloquent about individualism; it was Sullivan who stood his ground and uttered the unspeakable. After his 1944 manuscript "The Illusion of Personal Individuality" was published in 1950 in his journal, *Psychiatry*, it was not seen again until it appeared in a collection of his posthumous papers in 1964. It was simply too subversive to be tolerated by the field.[33]

Yet as obvious as it is that Sullivan was a social constructionist, it should also be noted that he was also an ambivalent, sometimes reluctant constructionist. For instance, ideas such as consensual validation and reciprocal emotions were clearly constructionist ideas; his attack on personal individuality could only have been developed by a historical consciousness; and the concept of therapist as participant-observer appeared to be an attempt to articulate an understanding of the mutuality of interpersonal interaction. However, Sullivan's ambivalence was revealed when he would talk about "reality" as if it were one pure, reified thing out there in an external world, and "truth" as if it were the accurate correspondence to some one true thing. He had an unswerving belief in a kind of objective empiricism, the scientific method, and the therapist's status as "expert." He accepted without question the notion that there is such a thing as "normal," that most people have attained it, and that it could be achieved by his patients if only they would have a successful therapy. And, for all his talk about interaction, mutuality, and therapist-as-participant, he could not bring himself to take a final step into what in the years since his death has become a more direct, emotional interpersonalism, complete with a franker conception of countertransference (that is, the therapist's reactions to the patient) and its inevitable and potentially helpful nature.[34] In this view, the therapist's actions, feelings, and thoughts are regarded as resources, not dangerous distortions best hid-

den away from the patient. In this view the therapist's emotional responses to the therapeutic moment, even surprising actions, are thought
to be resources, unconscious responses to and communications with the
patient, part of the pattern of mutual interaction that can be analyzed and
learned from. Recently, Levenson[35] has suggested that Sullivan could not
take this last step because he was avoiding activating his own anxiety,
which would inevitably have appeared if he were to bring more of
himself into the therapeutic moment. It was not, Levenson suggested,
the patient's anxiety that Sullivan was trying to avoid stirring up; it was
his own. The failure to examine the therapist's part in the transference-
countertransference enactment was thus owing to Sullivan's *own* security
needs, not his patient's.

Sullivan was, all things considered, extremely complex and contradictory. It was his contradictions that no doubt drove Fromm to distraction, Horney to anger, and the rest of us away from his dense,
idiosyncratic writing. But most of all, his contradictions must have driven
him to frustration and impatience. He was struggling with extremely
difficult and insightful concepts; others didn't understand and appreciate
his ideas, and sometimes, neither did he.

The Dream

It is not easy to get a good look into Sullivan's head—he often kept it, and
his heart, carefully hidden. We know very little about Sullivan's private
life, but we do have one dream, which he discussed once when lecturing.
It has been cherished by interpersonalists, handed down from supervisor
to supervisee, and no doubt interpreted by one and all. This dream can
conjure up a feeling for what was Sullivan's brilliant, but contradictory
vision and a sense of the sociohistorical, political nature of his vision, and
how it fit with the era in which he lived. It is a dream reported by his
biographer, Helen Swick Perry, and later interpreted by Edgar Levenson
in an article entitled "The Web and the Spider."[36] Here is the dream as
reported in its entirety by Perry:

> You all recall the geometric designs that spiders weave on
> grass, and that show up in the country when the dew's on the
> ground. My dream started with a great series of these beautiful
> geometric patterns, each strand being very nicely midway be-
> tween the one in front of it and the one behind it, and so on—
> quite a remarkable textile, and incidentally I am noticeably
> interested in textiles. Then the textile pattern became a tunnel
> reaching backward after the fashion of the tunnel-web spiders,

and then the spider began to approach. And as the spider approached, it grew and grew into truly stupendous and utterly horrendous proportions. And I awakened extremely shaken and was unable to obliterate the spider, which continued to be a dark spot on the sheet which I knew perfectly well would re-expand into the spider if I tried to go to sleep. So instead, I got up and smoked a cigarette and looked out the window and one thing and another, and came back and inspected the sheet, and the spot was gone. So I concluded it was safe to go back to bed.[37]

Perry recounted the dream to illustrate Sullivan's perspective on hallucinations and his hatred of pat interpretations that do not take the particular patient into consideration (for example, spiders are the universal symbol for the bad, devouring mother). Relating the symbol of the spider to an incident in Sullivan's childhood, Levenson interpreted the dream to suggest that Sullivan, because he was about to work in a schizophrenic ward, was terrified that the ward would somehow reactivate the acute psychotic episode that he probably had experienced years earlier.[38] But the dream can also help us understand Sullivan and his theories, because it can help us understand the world in which he lived. Let us remember Louis Sass's point that studying humans is not like reading a text, but more like standing behind them and reading over their shoulder the cultural text from which they themselves are reading.[39] Sullivan's dream can be seen as a reflection of a larger text: post–World War I America.

It is important to remember that Sullivan was personally acquainted with the grinding destructiveness of ethnic-group hatred, racism, and economic injustice. The loneliness, confusion, and crushing sense of inadequacy from which he suffered when he first moved to an urban setting at nineteen years of age would have undoubtedly been psychologized and, he thought, thereby misunderstood and improperly pathologized by the psychiatric establishment had he sought professional help.

Sullivan became convinced that his personal experiences with what he sarcastically called "the industrial revolution" played a crucial role in the development of his therapeutic practices and in his success rate at Sheppard. At the same time, Sullivan was a psychiatrist, not a community organizer; he was dedicated to helping individual patients, and his professional standing was determined by his acceptance of this orientation. Thus he was caught between his wish to help individuals and his understanding (more fully articulated several years after the dream) that many of the emotional ills of his time were caused not by intrapsychic structures but by sociohistorical structures. This is a bind in which psychotherapists are still caught. We are maneuvered by culture, training, and an absence of alternative practices into conveying, in Joel Kovel's words, "the myth of individual psychology and cure in the midst of a diseased society."[40]

This psychotherapeutic dilemma is one aspect of what was being illustrated in Sullivan's dream, some three or four years before Sullivan's intellectual development could put it into words. Readers by now have thought of several initial formulations about the dream, no doubt, depending on their theoretical orientation. One that occurs to me, which I will not discuss at length, is how much the dream appears to be about fear, anxiety, and real-life danger, the foundational concepts of Sullivan's theory, and how even the beauty of an intricate structure (the self system?) is not a timeless protection against the beast (the family system?), but is, instead, part of the trap the beast has woven. Each of our interpretations, to the degree that it is coherent and does not violate the text of the dream or Sullivan's personal history, is of potential value in helping us to understand this most remarkable and complex man. I do not believe that the text holds only one meaning.

The aspect of the dream that I would like to offer for consideration is its political-historical-cultural meaning. The dream is a dream of things that become more dangerous than they at first appear. The web is beautiful in its design and precision, but then it becomes an enclosed path, which draws the dreamer into its depths, and then a trap. At its heart lies a spider, which grows to gigantic proportions and becomes increasingly threatening and dangerous. And then, the greatest danger of all is revealed: The spider does not disappear when the dream ends and the dreamer awakens. A remnant of it lives on in the waking world and remains ready to leap to life again, as soon as the dreamer gets in touch with that which is disavowed or disowned. The dreamer becomes aware of the presence of danger or dread in the everyday world—it cannot be denied.

What in Sullivan's life had such a beautiful pattern and yet became increasingly dangerous as he continued to observe it? What started out looking as natural and pure as a piece of beautifully woven cloth, a geometric aspect of nature, but revealed itself as having a beast at its core? Readers will have their own answers, as Sullivan had his. I have my own: America. Or more accurately, the experience of living in post-World War I America.

Search as Sullivan might for psychologized formulations and mechanical technologies, and try as he might to fit into polite American society and a prestigious psychiatric profession, Sullivan's dream told him what he knew at night but could not yet articulate when awake. At the heart of U.S. society in the 1920s, with its vibrant economy, optimism, confidence, triumph in World War I, its seeming orderliness, belief in scientific progress, and avowed commitment to democracy and equality, lurked a beast. And the longer one studied this beast, the more powerful and dangerous it became. Once one realized the hideousness of the beast, its spectre could not be avoided or dismissed, because it was a constant, everpresent aspect of everyday American life.

The outward "natural" pattern of reason and middle-class decency is attractive and comforting, like a textile that becomes a soothing blanket. But Sullivan's geometric weave does not become a blanket, it becomes a trap from which he cannot escape. In his life he experienced firsthand the pain and destructiveness of prejudice and economic injustice. He lived with the disorientation of cultural differences and the consequences of an uncompromising individualism in an urban setting that was inhospitable and isolating. He suffered from lifelong fears about his inadequate personal finances. Perhaps all this sensitized him to the inequalities of laissez-faire capitalism and the shaky foundations upon which it stood in the early 1920s. Some seven years after the dream the stock market collapsed and the United States was plunged into a depression that almost destroyed the nation. The "war to end all wars" had ended only three years before the time of the dream. Yet within his lifetime the world would be engulfed in the most devastating and hideous war in human history. Could Sullivan have intuited the beast lurking below the comforting pattern of middle- and upper-class prosperity, the triumphs of modern science, and the Treaty of Versailles?

There is more to this interpretation. It was not just domestic politics and the precarious state of the world that came to life in the spectre of the spider. Sullivan was distressed by the racial oppression and economic injustice that were endemic to the United States, but he was also haunted by psychotherapy's *collusion* with those arrangements.

At the same time, Sullivan was a psychiatrist, not a community organizer; he was dedicated to helping individual patients, and his professional standing was determined by his willingness to accept this orientation. Thus he was caught between his wish to help individual patients and his understanding (more fully articulated several years after the dream) that emotional ills were caused not by intrapsychic structures, which "are by no means inborn, relatively immutable, aspects of the person,"[41] but by sociohistorial structures.

Sullivan was profoundly troubled by the inadequacies and implications of an overpsychologized, ahistorical psychotherapy. Yet in the early years of his career he did not have the intellectual tools or the supportive colleagues to help him develop the words to name the fundamental problem and the weapons to fight it. When he did begin to understand the nature of the beast, and psychotherapy's unknowing collusion through its ahistoricism, attachment to individualism, and unanalyzed class bias, he devoted the rest of his life to researching the collusion and developing an alternative to it. "One will be with the forces of reaction and human exploitation," Sullivan thundered, "or one will be actively against them."[42] He urged his colleagues to lead the cultural revolution against war by using their professional skills to identify and ameliorate the "root causes" of poverty, racism, and charismatic authoritarianism.[43] While doing so Sullivan exercised his characteristic sarcasm: "The petit bourgeois ideal is all right for the psychiatrists who are correctly defined as doctors who have failed in the practice of medicine. They have found for themselves a useful function in sheltering society from those whom it has destroyed."[44]

Try as he might, his own personal, intellectual radicalization was rarely acknowledged beyond his circle of friends and colleagues. As Havens and Frank, and more recently Gerson and Greenberg and Mitchell have noted,[45] although Sullivan's thinking appears to have influenced or anticipated many current theories, he is rarely given the credit he deserves. His ideas were not popularly acclaimed or acknowledged in mainstream psychology, in part, it must be said, because his style was so ponderous. But of course it was much more than his writing style that led to him becoming unmentionable or at least marginalized in mainstream therapy circles. His historical perspective, his comprehensive interactionism (to use Gadlin and Rubin's idea, cited earlier) challenged the comfortable position psychotherapy was carving out for itself. While trying to institute his agenda of interdisciplinary, politically oriented research, Sullivan argued that the discipline "is no longer the art of observing and perhaps influencing people who are suffering grave mental disorders. . . . It has passed through the phase of panacea and cure-all, of fad and foolishness. It is becoming a science that is fundamental . . . to research into almost any aspect of people and interpersonal relations, broadly conceived."[46] Ultimately, most normative histories of psychoanalysis have ignored his more political pronouncements, downplayed his clinical insights, and portrayed Sullivan as being near the periphery of the discipline; whereas first ego psychology and then Melanie Klein's object relations were located at the center of activity and were thought to be the theories that would eventually carry the day.

EGO PSYCHOLOGY'S DEPOLITICIZED VISION

Ego psychology was an outgrowth of psychoanalysis and has generally been seen as the most conservative of the mid-century adaptations of Freudian drive theory. Ego psychologists focused on the synthetic processes of the ego, insisting that they were crucial to normal functioning. They attempted to stay within the confines of orthodox psychoanalysis while updating and widening the theory to include explanations for twentieth-century issues such as child development, adult social adaptive processes, adult cognitive development, and new psychological problems that would in the postwar era come to be referred to as character disorders. Anna Freud, Freud's daughter, was thought by most to be the unofficial leader of ego psychology; she studied children and the normal processes of development within the orthodox framework of drive and defense. She, Franz Alexander, and Heinz Hartmann (and later John Bowlby, Erik Erikson, and Margaret Mahler), anxious to move psychoanalysis beyond the confines of the strict conflict model, which involved regulating id drives and modifying a too harsh superego, argued that there were many tasks and skills that adults needed to master that were not wholly determined by the tripartite power struggles of id, ego, and superego. They maintained that there was a "conflict-free" zone in which ego functions such as separation-individuation, autonomy, and reality testing naturally developed. The ego, as adult regulator, reality tester, identity formulator, logical compromiser, reasonable negotiator, was no longer conceptualized as being ancillary to the id; it was given an origin (and a territory) all its own. Ego psychologists were more involved with the task of expanding the scope of psychoanalytic explanation, and thus making the case for its acceptance as a full-fledged science, than they were with responding to the growing society-wide interest in social interaction, although they did address the psychological functions that had to do with social competence and adaptive behavior.

Ego psychology wasn't quite interactional, in the way Sullivan's and Klein's theories were, but it was a move in that direction, and it did advance psychoanalysis by developing a series of theoretical explanations for complex twentieth-century adult functions and concerns. The major reason for the popularity of ego psychology, and of course, the major flaw of the movement as far as constructionsts are concerned, is that its proponents uncritically accepted the "given" social world without significant question or resistence. The theory proceeded by assuming that it is proper to adapt and conform to cultural norms and social expectations. Because the social world was considered apolitical, and its requirements and demands universal, ego psychology was free, under the banner of objective science, to develop a rationale for social conformity and political compliance that would be quite convenient for those in power. The thought that the linguistic distinctions, social categories, and material conditions of everyday life—such as gender roles, lifestyle decisions, and the means of production—are socially constructed and therefore complicit in the local arrangements of wealth and power never seemed to occur to or at least was not mentioned by them. Therefore American psychoanalysis, under the influence of ego psychology, did not offer a strong resistance or effective alternative to conformity and compliance. The banality of corporate life, and the taken-for-granted oppression of people because of their race, gender, or class were thought to be separate from the interests and intellectual range of psychoanalysis. In that lay both ego psychology's popularity and its weakness.

Ego Psychology and Freud

Although several analysts[47] have developed a historical narrative about ego psychology's Freudian lineage, these arguments seem more an attempt by ego psychologists to legitimize their vision by wrapping their theory in the "flag" of the founder than an attempt to develop a convincing historical argument. Far more plausible, I believe, is the critical cultural history view that Freud—unlike midcentury ego psychologists—lived in a Victorian and early twentieth-century world tormented by the conflict between overpowering emotions and the restrictiveness of social rules and traditions. Contrastingly, ego psychologists grew powerful in mid-century America, a society characteristically focused on the value of success in the capitalistic marketplace, influenced by a technological frame of reference, confused by the discrediting of religion and community traditions, and yet paradoxically preoccupied with the individual's task of achieving social acceptance. Ego psychology's emphasis on adaptation and the insistence that there is one basic developmental pathway and one set of universal adaptive ego processes seems to have been driven more by the needs of postwar, particularly American, society than by philosophical realizations or revelations wrought from new clinical data. The ego psychologists' emphasis on adaptation, the independence and importance of the ego, and the realm of conflict-free psychic functions seems politically right at home in America, but less in sync with Freud's Viennese world and the vision that grew out of it.

One idea about the function of Freudian theory in Victorian Europe suggests that Freud's theory was simply a reflection of the larger "repressive" zeitgeist—and thereby unwittingly involved with capitalism and the modern state.[48] However, there are other kinds of cultural history interpretations of Freudian theory. One alternative suggests that Freud's theory was centered on conflict, the conflict between sexual desire and social tradition, because Freud was struggling to make a crucial political point. According to this view, in his early theory Freud was unknowingly attempting to describe the human condition by conceptualizing a human essence beyond the reach of the various sociopolitical influences of the modern state. He was searching for a kind of bedrock (and because of his training as a physician, a physiological bedrock) that could stand as a fortress against the prejudices, oppressions, and irrational violence perpetrated upon the public by the state. He thought he had found that bedrock, universal and uncontaminated, in the sexual and aggressive drives.

In other words, Freud's insistence on intrapsychic conflict as the bedrock of human psychology, and the Oedipus complex as the bedrock of conflict, was not solely a reflection of late Victorian, fin de siècle bourgeois patriarchy; it was also an attempt to develop a critical political discourse, to resist the all-encompassing, coercive power of the state by appealing to a "higher," more natural source: the id. The drives, in this view, as origins of subjectivity, give individuals a platform on which they can stand, a place from which they can resist the influence of bigoted culture and the power of the state. In the last twenty years, this strategy has come to be regarded as problematic by constructionists. Contemporary writers have argued that the body is not at all a pure, natural force undisturbed by the cultural and political forces of the era but is instead socially constructed. That means that Freud's hope of discovering a source of uncontaminated desire, or at least of privileged subjectivity, has become less credible. But his motivation, according to this reading, was moral and political. Freud was searching for essential human qualities that could endure both the coercive violence of the modern "civilizing" process and the consequences of accommodation. The unconscious, in this view, is seen as the repository for that which is disavowed and disapproved of by and thus must be kept hidden from the state and from one's consciousness.

Freud's mature theory, especially his development of the tripartite theory of id, ego, and superego, was more complex and sophisticated than his earlier theories. In it we see that the privileging of biology has been supplanted by his growing embrace of a more interactive, dialectical vision. He conceptualized psychological life as being in a constant state of flux and change, wherein subjectivity (id) is continually in conflict with cultural prescriptions (superego) and the necessity of accommodating and complying (ego). These three psychic forces conflict in ways that are continually shaping affective experience and social behavior. One's sense of self at any one time is determined by the influence that has the upper hand, which in turn determines the voices that are momentarily speaking through the individual. Polymorphously perverse urges are influenced by cultural rules, which are all mediated by the necessity to conform. If any one voice breaks free and consistently determines behavior, all is lost: if, once and for all, id wins, civilization is destroyed and all is violence and perversity; if superego wins, restriction and repression are the only possible responses to life; if ego wins, accommodation and conformity are the only future.

The Oedipal narrative, then, becomes a metaphor for socialization.[49] This argument suggests that Freud's tripartite theory was not simply, or even primarily, an attempt to develop a more efficient, technicist, therapeutic technique. Instead it was an expression of his wish to address larger philosophical and political concerns, reflected in the writings of his last decade such as *The Future of an Illusion* (1927), *Civilization and its Discontents* (1930), *Why War?* (1933), and *Moses and Monotheism* (1939). By privileging flux and disavowal, and by highlighting Oedipal conflict, Freud was depriviledging and thus resisting the state.

Ego Psychology and the Cultural Terrain at Mid-Century

What are we then to make of ego psychology, which privileged adaptive processes such as consistency, coherence, and compromise? If the hidden function of Freud's Oedipal move was an attempt to resist the state, what was the function of ego psychology's move that focused on the intrapsychic motive to adapt, fit in, and get along in a contentless, unparticular society? By historically situating ego psychology, we can make some tentative suggestions. The United States, in the two decades surrounding mid-century, was a terrified, traumatized country. It had been savaged by the Great Depression and deadened by World War II. Fear of another depression, fear of the USSR, racial prejudice, social uncertainty regarding gender, the overall trauma of the war, never ending holocaust and atrocity revelations (including the West's complicity with Nazi policies), and the uncertain reintegration of American soldiers into peacetime U.S. society were some of the tensions the country faced. The United States craved stability and feared the unknown, the different, the unusual, the extreme, the destabilizing, the "other."

Given this social terrain, it is not difficult to develop an explanation of why ego psychology diverged from Freud's emphasis on conflict and Sullivan's political vision. Americans had never been drawn to a cultural framework that featured conflict. Their fledgling eighteenth-century government had a society to organize, a frontier to conquer, and a continent to settle—expansion and success were always America's mother tongue. Middle-class Americans, especially in the nineteenth and twentieth centuries, have characteristically been focused on pragmatically adapting, fitting in, and succeeding economically.

Several prominent ego psychologists were European analysts, Jews recently escaped from Nazi Germany. They had stared into the heart of European anti-Semitism and class conflict. They were displaced, disoriented; they had to learn a new language, become familiar with new social customs, and earn new professional credentials, all in an era of uncertainty and instability. In this terrain, it is not surprising that these analysts cast around for the reliable, the familiar, the stable. It is not surprising that they looked for general organizing principles that stressed adaptation, social survival, and economic cooperation.[50]

The analysts who developed ego psychology gravitated toward the intrapsychic processes that fit their personal interests and preoccupations. However, given the state of the U.S. economy, ego psychologists also took account of the profession's interests, especially its economic interests. American technology, or rather the central control of American technology, had been a crucial element in the Allied triumph. By mid-century, it had become obvious that the scientific discoveries that had been developed by Western science, and their applications to capitalist industry, had set the frame for the future and that technology was a dominant feature of the new postwar zeitgeist. Psychoanalysis, if it was to carve out a significant piece of the postwar pie, had to position itself as a scientific technology. The medicalization of psychotherapy that took place in the first quarter of the century under the label "mental hygiene"[51] took a slightly different, and more complex, turn at mid-century. Psychoanalysis needed to position itself as a medical technology; to do this, it had to position mental processes as a proper object of scientific study and operation; it had to reify the ego, make it into a "thing," something concrete, real, describable, consistent, understandable, and fixable. All of this was accomplished by the innovations of the ego psychologists, who proclaimed the ego to be independent of the instincts (the id) and the culture (the superego); the ego was considered a worthy object of study in its own right, the key to proper mental functioning and mental illness, and in fact the most important element of the internal world of the self-contained individual.

The elevation of the ego helped make psychoanalysis a more serious player in the mid-century cultural terrain. Now psychotherapists had a "thing" to work on in a scientific, technicized way, they had an improved, medicalized language to describe and justify their work, and they had a way to discuss not only neurosis but also "normal" mental functioning, and thus a justification for their profession's involvement in many aspects of everyday life, such as human development, family relations, schools, and the workplace.

The ego psychologists took off in a direction opposite that of Sullivan. Sullivan had emphasized the processes of mental life; ego psychologists reified them. Sullivan noticed the political nature of psychiatric practices; ego psychologists insisted that rationality and adaptive processes are independent of the body and cultural traditions. Sullivan argued that psychology should only study and make statements about what can be seen, observed, and measured; ego psychologists developed concepts about mental processes that cannot be reliably verified by any observable phenomena. Sullivan insisted on conceptualizing psychiatry as a social practice, and the psychotherapist as a kind of social activist; ego psychologists furthered the medicalizing and scientizing of the field. Perhaps most importantly, Sullivan lectured the field on the importance of culture as the determining factor in human being. This stance, when developed in a comprehensive manner, leads to the philosophical hermeneutic position that humans are cultural beings reflecting local truths and moral understandings, not universal beings preconstructed from a biochemical blueprint and adapting to a contentless society. In contrast, ego psychologists developed the idea that the ego is structured in an ahistorical, universal, acultural, and apolitical manner.

Freud had universalized and privileged the instincts in order to resist the coercive power of the state, whereas ego psychology moved to create and privilege a universal ego objectively managing the psyche in a contentless, neutral society. To accomplish this transformation of the ego, ego psychology defined, explained, and claimed ownership to new realms of psychological study, such as cognitive operations, child and adult development, ego defenses, internal object relations structures, and typologies related to character structure, all of which were thought to be universal, acultural, and apolitical. Although these claims currently appear unsupportable, given the culturally specific nature of the processes of the ego,[52] the claims were extremely effective in their era. The ego psychologists' theories and practices greatly increased their realm of expertise and thus their professional reach. But most important, their vision of the self unknowingly facilitated the state's ability to control the populace because it endorsed automatic compliance to the cultural frame of reference. The strategy of universalizing and privileging the ego delivered a good deal of power and influence to psychoanalysis, psychotherapy, and psychology in general, but by doing so the field moved further away from the social paradigm Sullivan had labored to bring into view. Over time, Sullivan's testy, politically critical vision lost out to ego psychology's adaptive, politically quiescent position. Sullivan and his followers were ignored, marginalized, and sometimes rejected in public by mainstream psychoanalysis and normative psychotherapy. The profession, under the leadership of ego psychology, did very well into the early postwar years, carving out a comfortable economic and social niche in the boom years of the fifties and early sixties. In the short run, Sullivan's loss was the profession's gain. But in the long run the field had turned its back on a challenge that still will not go away.

Sullivan's theory was one attempt to change psychoanalytic drive theory and bring psychotherapy more in line with the intellectual spirit of the era between the wars. Drive theory was too mechanistic and limited for many analysts, and some, like the ego psychologists, tried to shift its emphasis and correct Freud's "errors" without appearing to explicity criticize or challenge him. Sullivan's directness was something of an exception to this pattern; Melanie Klein and the growing school of object relations theory was not.

MELANIE KLEIN AND THE BEGINNING OF OBJECT RELATIONS THEORY

Melanie Klein was one of the most colorful, outspoken, and creative psychotherapists of the twentieth century. Her theories shocked the psychoanalytic community of her time, and even to this day they are too radical to be embraced by most therapists. However, her work began to develop a new path, one that allowed psychoanalysis to develop complex theories, explain involved interpersonal dynamics, conform to the social trends of mid-century, and treat new patient populations such as children and those suffering from severe character disorders. Most important, her theory paved the way for her followers to develop the successful new post–World War II therapeutic ethos, an ethos infused with the most powerful ideology of the era: consumerism. It is for this reason that, despite her battles with Anna Freud and the orthodox Freudians, despite the criticisms she had to endure, Klein set the agenda, the direction, for psychotherapy in the second half of the twentieth century. Hers was *the road taken.*

Klein was born in Vienna in 1882 to a Jewish family, the product of her older father's marriage (his second) to a much younger woman.[53] Melanie was the last of four children, two of whom died early in life. Her father, an intellectual and a physician, was quite old when Melanie was born, and he seems to have had little to do with her, his favorite being the older daughter. Melanie's mother, however, was very attached to her, leaned on her emotionally, and consciously used her as a mother-substitute. Klein's brother Emanuel was an intellectual, poetic young man who encouraged Melanie's intellectual aspirations; his death, when she was twenty, was an emotional blow. At an early age Melanie married a friend of her brother's, an engineer named Arthur Klein; his work forced them to live in several small towns throughout Eastern Europe. Her dream to become a physician like her father was buried in the provincial villages and gender-related responsibilities of a young wife and mother. It was in Budapest that she again became intellectually active and first became fascinated by psychoanalysis. She was analyzed by Sandor Ferenczi and encouraged by him to begin treating children. Although she had attained no degrees, she was a bright, enthusiastic disciple, and in due time she was admitted to the Budapest Psychoanalytic Society. Anti-Semitism was a significant problem in Hungary, and partly in response to that threat and partly to escape from an unhappy marriage, Melanie and her youngest son, Erich, moved to Berlin; her older son, Hans, and her daughter, Melitta, were sent to boarding schools and later the university. In Berlin Melanie studied under and was analyzed by Karl Abraham, one of Freud's foremost early followers. Life was difficult for her, both emotionally and financially, because of the separation and then the divorce. Her ideas were not well received in Berlin, and in 1926 she wangled an invitation to speak in London. Soon after that engagement she arranged to live and work there, with the blessing of Ernest Jones, a founder and leader of the British Psychoanalytic Society.

Klein's presence in England turned the Society upside down. Her ideas about infant development and child analysis extended (some thought distorted) Freud's theories in troubling and radical ways. The English analysts listened, disagreed, and were finally won over by her. There followed several years during which she made brilliant innovations, took part in creative partnerships, and received public acknowledgments of her pioneering work. But then, in the mid- to late 1930s, the troubles started. Melanie's daughter Melitta, in concert with her analyst, Edward Glover, began to disagree and then personally attack Klein. Many of the analysts from the continent who were steeped in Freudian orthodoxy and were fleeing Hitler's reach and seeking asylum in England, Israel, and the United States were cool if not hostile to Klein's ideas. Those who landed in England were already aware of the growing rift between Melanie and Freud's daughter, Anna, the other prominent child analyst of the movement, and naturally they sided with Anna. This group joined with the previous English discontents to form a formidable opposition to the newly evolving Kleinian theory and the clique that was loyal to it.

When Freud and his daughter Anna arrived in England in 1938, one step ahead of the Gestapo, they found a full-fledged dispute about to happen. The dispute was fueled in part by animosities within the Society and in part by the theoretical disagreements between Klein and Anna Freud that had begun years before. The intellectual arguments devolved into a series of personal attacks and power grabs: Freud's legacy, control over analyst-trainees, and in fact the future of the psychoanalytic movement in England (and probably all of Europe), hung in the balance. In an attempt to resolve the bitter struggle, the Society held a series of dialogue-debates in 1942 and 1943.[54] These were referred to, in typical British understatement, as the "Controversial Discussions." Out of these meetings came a compromise over ideology and training programs that finally made coexistence between the two groups possible. Klein and her followers had won: instead of being banned, like Adler and Jung had been, Klein stood up to the Freuds and yet retained the right to practice, teach, and train future analysts within the society.

The Kleinians' main strategy was to be more royal than the Queen. Klein argued that, far from deviating from Freud, she was *more Freudian* than his own daughter: it was Klein who took the "death instinct" seriously, who extended and refined the concept of introjection that Freud had first used to explain the formation of the superego, and who was not frightened by the aggression, envy, and negative transference that lurked in the darkest "depths" of the psyche. For all of these reasons Klein claimed to be the true bearer of the psychoanalytic mantle.

Klein's Theory

Klein argued that the data collected in her child analyses proved that several of the ideas that Freud either tentatively suggested, mentioned in passing, or developed late in life, such as those about the processes of introjection and projection, the importance of object relations, and the power of the death instinct, were correct and in fact indispensable to psychoanalytic theory. Her interpretation of psychoanalytic theory, in brief, went like this: infants are born with a set of psychic structures, similar to the perceptual-moral structures Kant imagined, that set the infant's interpretive framework and thus determine some of the infant's emotional reactions from its earliest days of consciousness. The self is composed of the psychic structures, the inborn functions, and the fragmented parts of the ego; these are the "objects" that interact. Klein's part-objects are the products of inherited, intrapsychic structures, and the distorted, partial glimpses of a few caretakers; they are not based on the real individuals—shaped by culture, history, and social interaction—with whom the individual interacts. These psychic structures of the individual form a kind of inherent readiness, a preconceptual framework, that is fed solely by the two inherent instincts, the life instinct and the death instinct. The individual's characteristic personality style is from the beginning of life shaped by the relative proportion of the two instincts. If an infant girl, for example, possesses more life instinct, she will be predisposed to being loving, attached, joyful. If the death instinct is stronger in her, hostility, envy, hatred, and destructiveness will predominate. The combination of the two forces causes her to yearn for and love her mother and her mother's breast yet hate, fear, and envy them, long before the mother's gratifying or depriving the child consistently impacts the child.

To escape from the anxiety generated from her inherent hostile aggressiveness toward others or toward herself, an infant instinctively "spits out" (that is, projects) her destructiveness "into" the mother. The infant also projects the libido into the mother, in order to develop an ideal figure, which the infant will, at times, "consume" (that is, introject). Unable to conceive of her mother as a person who does good and bad, or herself as a being who can experience conflicting emotions simultaneously, the infant is genetically programmed to fragment and "split" the psychic image/experience/expectation of the breast, the first object, into a good breast and a bad breast. These objects are then projected "into" the mother. The splitting off and projecting of the bad object—called the part-object—is done for several reasons, for instance to protect the infant from the bad breast image, which is imagined as dangerous and persecutory, by removing it to a distance; or to separate the internal experience of the bad breast from the experience of the good breast, so that the bad won't spoil or contaminate the good. The good breast image is also at times projected into the mother, so as to begin the development of an ideal object, someone to depend on and believe in. Sometimes the bad object is projected "into" the mother, combined with the infant's "real" experiences of the mother when the mother is acting bad, and later consumed (that is, introjected) by the infant; this projection, of course, negatively affects the infant's overall self-image. The good image is also occasionally mixed with real life experiences of the mother when she is acting good and introjected back into the infant.

It is important to remember that the imaginings of the infant, when under the influence of the inherited psychic structures, are at first not at all or only minimally affected by the social interactions between infant and mother. These structures are *intrapsychic*; under the influence of the life or death instincts, they generate experiences such as fear, envy, love, gratitude. Klein referred to these experiences as "phantasy." Contemporary Kleinians, such as Thomas Ogden, use this spelling when referring to the emotional experiences generated when the infant is fantasizing and experiencing under the influence of the psychic structures.

The inherited fantasies consist in part of the infant wanting to bite, eat, consume, and destroy the part-object good breast because of envy and hatred of the good things inside the good breast, and the more generalized destructive wish to destroy everything in its path. Other fantasy, driven by the good object expectations, pictures the infant warm, gratified, and safe. Fantasy related to the bad-object expectations also consists of paranoid experiences. The infant will experience great anxiety, both in response to what his own destructiveness will do to him and what it will do to others. In an attempt to avoid or modify his anxiety, the infant will project his aggressiveness outward, onto those who inhabited his limited social environment. The destructiveness will be "split off" from and disidentified with the infant's fragile, fragmented ego, and "located" in the other (the mother). However, the infant will then be terrified of the danger, the threat, from without. The infant will fantasize that the bad mother object (that is, the bad breast) is coming to get it, coming to persecute and attack it. This will provoke in the infant unbearable terror and helplessness. These fragmented part-objects Klein called "persecuting others"; Klein thought that the infant experiences the part-objects as stalking figures, and that the infant reacts by psychologically fleeing and physically striking out against these figures. For instance, when the infant suffers from colic, Klein imagined that the infant is fantasizing that the persecuting figures are attacking its digestive system. Similarly, when the infant suffers from hunger, the persecuting figures were fantasized as attacking the stomach; when the infant suffers a headache, the figures were imagined to be attacking the head. Klein argued that evidence from child analyses proved that children imagine the good part-object to be filled with milk, love, warmth, soothing, and the good, reparative penis of the father. The bad part-object is imagined to be filled with feces and urine, the persecuting others, and the bad, punishing penis of the father. The infant will also identify with the bad part-object and at times try to "introject" it, incorporate it within itself once again. When this is accomplished, there is no way the infant can escape the persecution, because the attack comes from within.

As her theory became more sophisticated, Klein de-emphasized Freud's developmental stages. Instead she argued that there are two basic *modes* of experience, the paranoid-schizoid mode, and the depressive mode. These modes were not conceptualized as discrete developmental *stages* that are experienced, worked through, and then never experienced again unless regression occurred. Instead they were thought of as modes of being that are to varying degrees of intensity available to individuals throughout their lifetimes. The paranoid-schizoid position is experienced first in the early months of life.[55] Klein used the term *schizoid* to indicate the centrality of the mechanism of splitting, and the term *paranoid* to emphasize the fears generated by the fantasized attacks and introjection of the bad object.

As Klein conceptualized it, the depressive mode is a more psychologically complex state of being. It is characterized by the capacity to simultaneously acknowledge and tolerate the good and bad qualities in others and in oneself. Klein named this the depressive mode because it is characterized by the awareness that the hatred felt against the bad object is, unavoidably, also directed at the good object, because the two part-objects are, in actuality, one person. Thus the child becomes sad, frightened, grieving, and is able to experience guilt at the damage or potential damage he has inflicted on his mother. At the same time the child also becomes aware that not only is the mother a whole person, but he also is whole, not all good or all bad. With this awareness comes the understanding that, just as the whole mother is vulnerable to the child's attacks, so the whole child is vulnerable to the mother's feelings. Further, with the understanding of wholeness comes the awareness of psychological separateness. This in turn forces the child to face his dependence on the mother and his vulnerability to loneliness and loss. These awarenesses are frightening and depressing to the young child.

Even more upsetting for the child is the awareness that he has a rival for the mother's attention: the father. As the parents become whole persons in the child's eyes, the child notices that the parents sometimes prefer one another rather than the child. The child also notices that either one of the parents may compete with him for the other parent's attention or affection, and that the child is quite vulnerable to either parent's disapproval or attack. Love, envy, rage, fear are all experienced in the depressive position, as they are in the paranoid-schizoid position, but more fully and with more awareness. In a move that shocked the analytic community, Klein dated the beginning of the depressive position, and thus the Oedipus complex (which she claimed developed in the depressive position), at nine months to one year of age.

Klein believed that, in time, the depressive mode develops in the child a keen sense that the mother has been wounded by his or her envious, rageful attacks or insatiable desires. This is because of the child's growing awareness of the mother as a whole person. The child then attempts to make "reparation" to the wounded mother, to repair the damage that has been done, through love, apology, allowing her the father's reparative penis, caretaking, and attending to the mother. This is a more mature exercise of the life instinct than was seen in the paranoid-schizoid position. It allows the child to reach out to others, develop compassion and charity, and live and carry on in a world too complex to be automatically safe or magically benign.

Both the paranoid-schizoid mode and the depressive mode were considered by Klein to be positive achievements. The splitting and projection/introjection of the paranoid-schizoid position allows the infant to survive the overwhelming terrors and rages of the early months of life while still developing emotional attachments to the "real" people in his environment. The depressive position is an achievement in that it allows for a full relationship between two whole, complex, psychologically separated individuals. It opens the way to more comprehensive feeling states and psychological conflicts, such as those engendered by the Oedipal triangle.

Klein was quite serious about the date of the onset of Oedipal conflicts. She believed that children have knowledge of genital intercourse by means of the inherited psychic structures. Although small children do not understand sex in the way that adults do, Klein thought that children do indeed symbolize being emotionally gratified, envious of, or frustrated by the parents' various organs and orifices during fantasy. Although the envy and desire at these early ages are more related to psychological safety, emotional acquisitiveness, and physiological gratification than to anything explicitly sexual in the adult genital sense, the triangle, with all its attendant desires, rivalries, and repressions, is Oedipal all the same, or so the Kleinians argued.[56]

Perhaps the Kleinian concept most instrumental for post–World War II object relations theory has been the concept of projective identification. This is a brilliant idea that makes use of some of Klein's most sophisticated theoretical ideas. Projective identification is the process by which the infant is thought to project certain split-off fragments of herself into the mother with such intensity that the child actually identifies the mother with the split-off and projected quality, and treats the mother as though the projected feeling is a natural, and inherent, aspect of the mother's subjective state. In various ways the mother is maneuvered into experiencing the projected feelings as if they are actually her "real" thoughts and feelings, or to behaving in ways consistent with the projected feelings. Although Klein developed this concept from her child analyses, Kleinians use it to understand and treat adult patients, especially borderline and narcissistic personality disorders. Projective identification differs from the basic process of projection in that the patient's intense experience of the projection influences others to experience themselves as actually feeling and/or behaving as the patient imagines. In other words, projective identification functions to cause others as well as the patient to identify with the feeling state that has been projected.[57]

In practice, projective identification helps account for the intensity of certain psychotherapeutic transference-countertransference interactions in which the patient is certain the therapist hates, envies, is using him in ways identical to how others in the patient's life have hated or used him. The therapist is equally certain that this is untrue but is baffled to notice that she is actually acting in accord with the patient's accusation. Klein explained this phenomenon in two ways. In one scenario the patient projects a hostile, destructive impulse into the therapist, so as to disown the impulse. The patient will then unconsciously act in ways that will provoke the therapist to have feelings toward the patient that are consistent with the patient's projected feeling. In the second scenario the patient will treat the therapist in ways consistent with how he himself has been treated, in order to invoke in the therapist the experience of being persecuted or hated that the patient cannot consciously tolerate. The patient, in other words, will force the therapist to experience what it was like to be humiliated and/or hated like the patient was.

This complex phenomenon, Klein argued, is an important event in therapy, because it brings feelings into the session that the patient usually only reports or intellectualizes about. When the therapist is able to tolerate the feelings of hatred, envy, and destructiveness and not project them back onto the patient, the patient can have the opportunity to face and work through those feelings. Klein thought that projective identification is important because it can lead the patient to the depressive mode and the capacity to make reparation to the wounded parent. This, according to Klein, is the way to analytic cure.

Klein's contributions to analytic theory were filled with both possibilities and dangers. The main criticisms of her ideas were that she ignored or minimized the influence of the father on the child, dismissed or at least de-emphasized the Oedipus complex in favor of the infant-mother relationship as the central conflict of human development, shifted the focus of psychological life from the clash between individual and society to the clash between various internal objects, placed the age at which complex feeling states and Oedipal conflicts occur at an impossibly early stage, and distorted the process of the development of the superego in order to justify her emphasis on object relations. She was also accused of being authoritarian, controling, paranoid, and manipulative. Her enemies accused her of trying to build a psychoanalytic empire instead of an open intellectual process, unethically psychoanalyzing her three children, coercing her analysands and supervisees, and in general bullying and intimidating others. Even her friends sensed her sometimes dark charisma: as Virginia Woolf wrote, Klein was "a woman of character & force some submerged—how shall I say?—not craft, but subtlety; something working underground. A pull, a twist, like an undertow: menacing. A bluff grey haired lady, with large bright imaginative eyes."[58]

Klein's Theory and Post–World War II Psychotherapy

Psychoanalysis owes some of its post–World War II success to Klein's early object relations theory. Klein opened up psychoanalysis to the study of the dark complexities of human interaction and claimed these areas as the sole property of psychotherapy. Her emphasis on the structural nature of object relations made it possible for psychotherapists to delve deeply into some of the most negative of human interactions—into greed, envy, hatred, rage, destructiveness—and to consider them the proper subjects of psychoanalysis. Klein conceived of the self as containing these inherent emotions and internal structures from the first months of life. These ideas would have been difficult for nineteenth-century psychoanalysis to accomplish given Freud's hydraulic theory based on energy vectors, or for ego psychology, given its tamer adaptionist approach. Klein's emphasis on the "internal" interaction of various object relations structures was instrumental in helping psychoanalysis join the twentieth century's interest in social interaction, which eventually encouraged more thought about the influence and manipulation of individuals, which in turn inadvertently fit well with the managerial needs of mid- and late twentieth-century capitalism. The study of group process, for instance, has been influenced by Klein's students, most notably Wilfred Bion. Her focus on the mother-child dyad and what are today referred to as the preoedipal years came to be used by others to draw attention to the minute social interactions that build a self, instead of the broader moral demands to control an already built self, which were discussed by Freud. The interest in building rather than controlling the self, barely evident in Klein's work, was robustly taken up by several post–World War II object relations theorists, including D. W. Winnicott in England. Through Klein's pioneering efforts, later theorists were able to help psychotherapy drop the issues of the nineteenth century and address the mid-twentieth-century world and its unique problems. Without this change in focus, psychotherapy could not have moved into the position of power and influence it enjoys today.

Klein developed a theory that brought psychotherapy into sync with the twentieth-century interest in social interaction, yet she ignored the political world that sensitized Sullivan to racism and economic injustice, and thus made him a pariah. She accomplished this difficult balancing act by *locating* the social in the individual's interior. This is what I have referred to as her "geographical strategy." Her strategy allowed her to plumb the depths of the individual twentieth-century soul yet never face the fuller historical and political meanings to which interactive theory calls us. In Klein's theory there is a great deal of interaction, but much is thought to take place *inside* the self-contained individual. She insisted that the objects and part-objects were not produced by the sociohistorical. In this way she was able to create and maintain a safe distance from the overt political discourse that would have challenged psychoanalysis' unquestioned acceptance of self-contained individualism and its implicit involvement with the modern capitalist state. I doubt that she was aware of the consequences of her ideas. I'm sure her geographical strategy was not a conscious strategy—but one remarkably effective nonetheless.

Klein's analysis of her son Erich provides an example of her unwillingness to acknowledge the social realm of history and culture. She began Erich's analysis in Budapest when he was a young boy of five and continued it in 1920 when she separated from her husband and brought Erich to live with her in Berlin. When she later wrote up the case she disguised the fact that "Fritz" was in fact her son Erich.[59] Klein wrote to Ferenczi that she was distressed because the analysis was not going well; over time the boy's anxiety had increased rather than decreased, and she vowed to be more explicit in her interpretations when they resumed his treatment. Erich suffered from a relapse in Berlin, however, including a "phobia" about venturing outside. Karl Abraham, Klein's Berlin analyst and teacher, knew that she was analyzing Erich and encouraged her to be persistent in interpreting the repressed (Oedipal) material, and indeed she was. She explained to Erich that the cause of his anxieties was his fantasy about having coitus with his mother. She often interpreted his play and his symptoms in this way.

For instance, in response to his phobia about venturing outside, she asked him to describe a street that was particularly frightening to him. He answered that the street was one that was filled with young toughs who tormented him. Klein ignored this fact and realized that the street was lined with large trees. She interpreted the trees as phalluses and explained to Erich that this meant that he was desiring his mother, and his anxiety was no doubt caused by the castration anxiety that inevitably followed this desire. It was only many years later that Erich's brother Hans (a reluctant adolescent analysand of his mother) explained this scene and many others to Erich. Hans told Erich that the bullies were an anti-Semitic gang that routinely attacked Jewish children. Erich, in fact, was never told by his mother that he was Jewish; he discovered it accidentally when he was ten.[60] As was the practice among some middle-class Jews in Central and Eastern Europe, the Kleins had their children baptized in an attempt to escape their Jewish fate.[61] But Klein's avoidance of the issue and her apparent ethnic-group self-hatred appear intense even for those difficult times. The extreme asocial nature of her theory might be, in part, a reflection of her deep ambivilance about her Jewish identity.

There appear to be many reasons for Erich's anxiety that can be traced to his experiences in the social realm.[62] He was an unwanted child, and because of Klein's marital difficulties and the recent loss of her mother, she suffered from a relatively severe agitated depression during Erich's early years; Erich's father, Arthur, was often absent during the first few years of Erich's life, owing to the war and the marital separation. Erich was upset by anti-Semitic attacks, although he didn't recognize them as such until years later. Upon arriving in Germany, he and his mother moved each year for five years. Melanie and Arthur tried one more time to repair the marriage, but it failed again after a year; this time mother and son moved out, never to return. This was, obviously, an excruciating time in Klein's life. Soon Erich was sent to a boarding school, and then to Frankfurt to be analyzed by Clara Happel. There he lived in a foster arrangement with a teacher and his family. As Grosskurth writes, "It is little wonder that the child was disturbed, but Melanie Klein takes none of these external factors into consideration."[63]

It is difficult to know what is more remarkable in this incident with Erich: Klein's dismissal of, her almost phobic denial of, the influence of the "external" social realm, or her remarkable self-centeredness. As one reads about Erich's and Hans's analyses one gets the distinct impression that Klein repeatedly placed herself in the center of her sons' psychological lives. She relentlessly explained to them that their interests, fears, preoccupations, and desires were focused on her. It seems problematic for the analyst repeatedly to refer to *herself* as the analysand's main object of desire. One is moved to wonder to what degree her conflicts over her Jewish identity, her extreme denial of real-life sociopolitical events such as anti-Semitism, and her apparent self-centeredness and denial of responsibility affected her theoretical concepts.

The effect of Klein's life on her intellectual discourse becomes even more apparent when we note her view that the child's desire, envy, and hatred for the mother are not initially caused by the actual behavior of the mother but by the inherent psychic structures within the child. Although she consistently placed herself as mother at the center of Erich's libidinal world, she attributed his anxieties, anger, and envy to his inherent psychic structures and the unavoidable conflicts and dramas constantly being played out by his competing internal part-objects. Given that several people who knew her at the time, including Erich himself, have commented that she appeared to be a rather cold, ungiving, sometimes preoccupied mother, it seems convenient for her to be so certain that the real-life social interactions between mother and son would not be the most significant factor in the child's emotional life.

The issue of Klein's personal struggles and inadequacies with regard to her children and the effect of these on the development of her theory is even more salient when we consider the case of her daughter, Melitta Schmideberg. Evidently Klein analyzed Melitta when she was seventeen; in the text Melitta was referred to as "Lisa."[64] Klein's discussion of the envy an infant daughter feels for the good breast, and the resultant unprovoked attacks by the infant in an attempt to devour, destroy, and possess the good breast, rings somewhat hollow when one considers that the breast offered the baby Melitta does not sound particularly "good," and when one considers the ongoing theoretical disagreements and personal accusations Melitta later delivered during the "Controversial Discussions." In particular, Melitta, herself a physician and practicing analyst, claimed that her mother's therapeutic practices were often a kind of "brainwashing." She argued that Klein forced her patients and supervisees into a subservient, dependent position, manipulated them into a kind of coercive helplessness, and developed a true believer/charismatic leader dynamic with her followers. Melitta used as examples Klein's relationships with Joan Riviere and Paula Heimann, both devoted followers who came to disagree with some of Klein's ideas and were subsequently cast out of the inner circle by Klein. Interestingly, it was during and after Melitta's public criticisms that Klein fully developed her concepts about the *unprovoked* envy and hatred of the infant for the mother.

I am not criticizing Klein's theory because she might have been a bad parent. Indeed, many famous intellectuals have been bad parents—the constant study, work, and high intellectual productivity often does not allow for the time and focused attention that good parenting requires. We almost never accuse male analysts of practing parenting that was not equal to their theoretical prescriptions. We do not expect it of them because of the prescriptions of the male gender role. But unfortunately we often expect female theoreticians to be perfect mothers—this double standard in Klein's case, or in any case, is unacceptable. In truth, the vicissitudes of gender undoubtedly caused Klein great frustration during her young married life and made her envy those who were professionally trained at what she had longed to accomplish. She had wanted to be a physician, she was obviously a brilliant thinker, yet because of the demands of child rearing and housekeeping she was unable to pursue her

career; meanwhile Arthur pursued his career, free of parenting responsibilities.

I am, however, suggesting that Klein's personal struggles with intellectual frustrations and envy, and her struggles with her children, perhaps
caused by the emotional absences during which she battled depression,
her unhappy marriage, and her narcissism, did influence her theory. In
particular, her formulations concerning the unavoidable rage and envy of
the child toward the good mother and the unprovoked nature of the
infant's attacks upon the mother functioned in her theory not simply to
solidify her approval within the close world of orthodox psychoanalysis
but also to explain away her responsibility for her children's emotional
disturbances (especially her daughter's accusations) and to amelioriate
her guilt over her neglect of them and her use of them as a means of
advancing her career.

In any event, it does not seem unethical for a theorist to use her own
life experiences and the understandings developed from her own soul-
searching and self-analysis to inform her theory. It is probably inevitable
that psychotherapists would do so, and in fact it would seem useful to do
so. Of course, Klein was certainly not the only analyst whose personal
life influenced the development of theory. Freud's "discovery" of the
unconscious appears to have been motivated in part by his unwillingness
to face the prevalence of child abuse by upstanding bourgeois fathers.
Aspects of Anna Freud's theory—especially her difficulty in addressing
the dark side of parent-child interactions—might have been influenced
by her relationship with *her* father, who had also been her *analyst*. One
might argue that great theorists such as Socrates, Darwin, and Freud
were able to have such an enormous impact on history specifically
because they were able to organize and articulate what was in the hearts
of others by developing a creative understanding of their own personal
lives. It is probably this talent that makes a theory popular: it is not that a
specific theory captures the one universal truth of humankind, but rather
that a specific theory articulates the local truth of a specific set of people
in a specific moment in history.

KLEIN, THE LOSS OF COMMUNITY, AND THE BULIMIC SELF

What are the taken-for-granted assumptions that are embedded within
Klein's theory? What is the shape of the world that is implicitly described
by her theory? And how does her theory reflect and reproduce those
assumptions and that world? Instead of studying Klein's theory as the

gathering of pure, ahistorical scientific data, or as an isolated reflection of Klein herself as a "text," we need to stand behind her and read over her shoulder the cultural text from which she herself was (unknowingly) reading.

The world that Melanie Klein described, the landscape in which she, her patients, and her theory lived and functioned, was one in which destructiveness, hatred, envy, greed, and acquisitiveness were taken-for-granted features. The psychological terrain that she described was populated with enraged infants, inherited destructiveness, unavoidable envy. Because of the infant's internal structures, if the mother behaves badly her behavior reinforces the infant's predisposition to be frightened and to attack and withdraw; if the mother behaves well her behavior opens up the infant's envy of the mother's "goodness," which then triggers the infant's predisposition to devour and destroy the good. There is no way out: the infant is predetermined to rip and tear.

Similarly, the infant is forced by his nature to have an overriding experience of paranoia and terror. Because the infant fantasizes that the "persecutory others"—the fragmented representations of the infant's split-off destructiveness—are inside of the infant and again coming to terrorize and attack, there is absolutely no way of self-protection and no place to hide, since the attack is coming from within.

Therefore, Klein described a world in which there is an unquestioned backdrop of violence, hatred, scapegoating, persecution, envy, and acquisitiveness. The infant cannot win, cannot feel safe and secure for long; the mother, likewise, cannot succeed in developing a loving, safe environment for the infant that would endure over time, nor an effective way of giving and getting love and gratification. This picture seems to reflect the social world in which Klein lived and worked. Her frame of reference was the Europe between the two world wars; it was a time of political hatred, violence, and danger. Ethnic divisions, anti-Semitism, and class conflict were constant sources of tension in Europe, despite the lighter style of the twenties. "Persecution," to use Klein's term, was everywhere.

A second aspect of the world that Klein's theory unknowingly described was the unquestioned acceptance of self-contained individualism. It seems ironic that her vision, which was in ways more aware than drive theory of social interaction and more involved with the ways in which interaction affected the individual, also dismissed social interaction. She placed the interactive microdramas of the part-objects solely within the self-contained individual, maintained that these dramas are predetermined by the gene pool of the human species, and argued that psychoanalysis holds the key to the translation of the predetermined interactions. By doing all this, Klein dismissed (or greatly diminished) the meaning of social interaction at the very moment it appeared as though she embraced it and opened it up for study. It is this unconscious theoretical maneuver that I refer to as Klein's "geographical strategy." Her no doubt unwitting strategy gives social interaction a kind of intellectual tokenism that appealed to the popular social trends of the time, and it seemed to claim a new realm of study for the field of psychology, yet at the same time Klein's theory artificially limits and thus neutralizes the fuller, more historical and political meanings of the social realm. By locating the social *within* the individual, and by arguing that the social, either in the form of person-to-person interaction or political structures, has little or no impact on the inexorable workings of the inherent psychic structures, Klein effectively delegitimizes social interaction as a major determinant of psychological life. Kleinian theory thus failed to develop a historical perspective on self-contained individualism, the political and economic functions of psychotherapy, and the connections between the two. Klein, by neglecting to fully study the social, was fated to reify social interaction as internal object relations and limit the richness and complexities of human being to the insular, individual dramas characteristic of bourgeois life under twentieth-century capitalism. By so doing, Klein developed a psychotherapy that would be popular (because it could deal with and exploit the realm of the social) yet politically uncontroversial (because it did not explore fully the ramifications of the social). Limited by her social context, Klein was not able to fully extend what she had begun. Her journey into social interaction could not be finished, at least by her.

Perhaps the best example of how Klein's theory both reflected and limited the description and study of social interaction is her exploration of the psychological processes of introjection and projection. Klein's patients are forever described as either "spitting out" split-off aspects of their internal objects, such as their hostility or envy, or "taking in" the split-off aspects of the others in their environment. Klein and her followers thought that the spitting out and taking in processes are the major psychic processes by which the self is protected, controlled, and finally developed. We might wonder if the self Klein described could whimsically be characterized as a "bulimic self." After all, it is a self whose defining characteristics are the processes of consuming and regurgitating.

I do not mean to propose that Klein's theory is important because it anticipated the prevalence of eating disorders that U.S. society is experiencing today. It is true that anorexia and bulimia have become important features in the psychopathology of our time, but I am not suggesting that Klein invented them, discovered them, or was the first therapist to treat them. Rather Klein and her theory were part of the larger cultural landscape of the era, as were eating habits, psychological symptoms, and gender prescriptions pertaining to cosmetic standards of the body. In other words, the forces at work on young late twentieth-century women that moved them to disordered eating practices such as bingeing and purging were the same forces that moved Klein to conceptualize the psychological processes of infant development in terms of taking in and spitting out. It is not that one caused the other; they are both reflections of a larger cultural frame of reference.

The larger frame of reference is, of course, consumerism, one of the most powerful political/economic forces of the post–World War II era. As we have seen, various historical forces and events, such as the loss of a sense of community and the needs of post–World War II capitalist economies to stave off another worldwide depression, combined to create in the United States and Western Europe an economy based on the continual consumption of nonessential and quickly obsolete consumer items. Consumerism is an overall way of being that is the result of the era's economic strategy. The predominant self in the post–World War II era needed to be configured in such a way as to adapt to, and in fact promote, consumerism. The consumer society was achieved through the constructing of a self that was empty, a self that feels naturally and irresistibly driven to consume in order to fill up the emptiness.

The self described in Melanie Klein's theory, while not yet a totally empty self, has certainly moved in that direction. It is a self that is continually bingeing and purging; it must feel empty in order to consume the way it does; it must feel hungry and covetous of what is "outside" itself. By examining Klein's ideas in their historical context, especially those ideas that diverged from Freud's, we can learn how and why her description of the self and her version of psychoanalysis became more salient to psychoanalysis and to the post–World War II era. When a cultural frame of reference is strong and monolithic, such as in the Victorian era, it is understandable that psychological struggles will be conceived of as the products of conflict between broad cultural norms and personal individual wishes. But as Victorian culture fragmented, and tradition and community lost authority, personal and especially dyadic relationships (conceived of as being separate from the social realm) became increasingly important. When personal relationships become thought of as the only means for creating meaning, developing a sense of personal integrity, and imparting cultural norms to one's offspring, it is understandable that a psychological theory that emphasizes dyadic (especially parent-child) relationships as the primary building blocks of mental health would become prominent.

When dyadic relationships became the vehicle for personal meaning and the transmission of cultural values, it makes sense that psychological theories emphasized (1) the importance of the mother, who is associated in the West with nurturing, family, and child rearing, rather than the Freudian father, who is associated in the West with disciplining, the marketplace, and cultural norms; (2) preoedipal issues in psychoanalysis, which are related to emotional nurturing, the building of the self, and the mothering role, rather than Freud's Oedipal issues, which are thought to be related to developing ethical character, controlling the self, and the fathering role; (3) social interaction, social influence, and manipulation of children, workers, and consumers, rather than the Freudian energy shifts and the conflicts related to broad moral truths colliding with biological drives; and (4) psychological technologies designed to promote emotional nourishment and guidance in order to *build* an unformed self, rather than conflict resolution technologies designed to *control* an already developed Victorian-like self.

Klein's theory emphasized or led to each of the above points: it emphasized the importance of the mother over the father, preoedipal issues over Oedipal conflicts, and social interaction and object relatedness over mechanical energy vectors. Her theory also eventually resulted in the creation of a school of psychotherapy that emphasized the development and subsequent liberation of the self rather than the domination of the self. It therefore makes perfect sense that Klein would have diverged from Freud on the above points, points that eventually made her the pioneer who set off on a new road that led to a brave new world.

Klein helped psychotherapy address the characteristic twentieth-century interest in social interaction while at the same time avoiding the philosophical/political pit into which Sullivan's interpersonal vision had disappeared. Paying too much attention to the social realm, studying too carefully how culture, in Merleau-Ponty's famous phrase, is sedimented in the body, learning too well how communal traditions and linguistic forms constitute reality, developing a sense of how intellectual discourse and social practices reproduce the status quo—all these would inevitably lead to realizing that social science discourse and practice are disguised moral discourse. Although therapy often presents itself as neutral, objective science, it not only reflects but also reproduces power relationships, cultural values, and the current configuration of the self. When this conclusion is reached, the epistemological privilege that psychotherapy claims is destroyed, its pretense to a universal, apolitical truth is undone, and its economic position is threatened. A full study of the social would thus lead psychotherapists to consider history and politics as appropriate subjects of study, to conduct research on the moral messages implicit in psychotherapy theories, and develop interpretations about psychotherapy's political and economic functions within U.S. society. Sullivan, albeit haltingly, walked down this road. For Klein the possibility never existed.

The job of raising children and passing on the broad cultural frame of reference to the next generation fell in the post–World War II era to a precious few relatives. At the same time the economy became increasingly dependent on an alienated consuming. As a result, the process of the transmission of cultural norms and values became conceived of as the process of consuming a few significant others during the course of a few relatively short intimate relationships. To justify the professional practice of psychotherapy as a science, enculturation (previously a social, religious, and moral activity) became reconceptualized as the psychological development of the child. In the post–World War II era, the subfield of child development and the putative universal laws that it was to discover and codify were used by psychotherapists to explain and justify the configuration of the post–World War II empty self without having to use politically dangerous explanations derived from historical and cultural analyses. As child development began to unknowingly utilize the metaphor of consuming to describe the process of enculturation, psychology became more understandable and popular. Psychotherapy ideology further shaped and reinforced consumerism by arguing that the processes of coveting, envying, and consuming are natural, universal human traits. Psychological theories, primarily object relations theory, made it scientifically legitimate to conceive of the process of growing up as a type of consuming and the goal of human life as the constant filling up of the empty self. It was Melanie Klein who began to walk this theoretical road and persuaded others to follow. It has been an extremely advantageous road for psychotherapy, rich in influence, status, and money.

But in the process of making the field respected and powerful, this road has led to a philosophically indefensible dismissal of the social realm and thereby an unknowing collusion with capitalism and the arrangements of post–World War II consumerism. The road we have chosen, it turns out, is the web in Sullivan's nightmare, the road that pulls us, inexorably, into the lair of the beast. However, unlike Sullivan, we are much better at suppressing an awareness of the beast, at banishing it from our consciousness, when we awaken. Sullivan's nightmare, it seems, has become our everyday reality.

CHAPTER EIGHT

Self-Liberation through Consumerism

POST–WORLD WAR II OBJECT RELATIONS THEORY, SELF PSYCHOLOGY, AND THE EMPTY SELF

Where's the rest of me?
—*RONALD REAGAN*
TITLE OF HIS AUTOBIOGRAPHY

Out of the rubble of World War II a new era arose, one of undreamed of affluence, television shows, credit cards, the Pepsi generation, and Dinah Shore belting out "See the U.S.A. in your Chevrolet." This new era, colorful and full of promise, was a radical departure from the deprivations of the thirties and the terror and hatred of the forties. The era began a few years after the end of World War II; it started in confusion and fear, had a brief middle period of protest and rebellion, and then a quarter century of increasing complacency, bigotry, and greed. Where did this new era come from? How did it get formed? What is its predominant configuration of the self? What political and economic interests does it serve?

The postwar era has been deeply influenced by psychology, oriented toward youth, focused on liberation, and obsessed with consuming. It has been driven by the culmination of two quintessentially American trends: the promise of individual salvation through the liberation of the self and a twentieth-century strategy based on the avoidance of economic stagnation (and thus a second depression) through the manipulation of consumption. The two trends joined forces to create a new dynamic, a striving for self-liberation through the compulsive purchase and consumption of goods, experiences, and celebrities. The partnership between unbridled consumption and the promise of individual salvation, facilitated by the American ideology of inner liberation, has become known as consumerism. It has been the single most important political innovation of the era, the driving force of the second half of the century. The predominant self of the era, the empty self, is the engine that makes it all run.

PSYCHOTHERAPY COMES OF AGE

Psychology, and psychotherapy in particular, were influential in the emerging era. D. W. Winnicott's post–World War II reworking of Melanie Klein's object relations theory in England,[1] and Heinz Kohut's creative transformation of orthodox Freudian theory in the 1970s in the United States[2] both reflected and, in the way of all social practices, had a hand in reproducing key psychological features of the new era. The American interest in Winnicott and the shift in preference from Freud to Kohut were part of a vast shift in the cultural terrain of the new postwar world. Both Winnicott and Kohut placed the self—a masterful and bounded, emotionally expressive, attention-seeking, entitled, self-centered way of being—at the center of social life. That self, emerging out of the postwar terrain, became the fulcrum from which a new generational cohort (the postwar baby boomers) and, in fact, the entire nation, was moved and manipulated.

Heinz Kohut was a remarkably gifted psychoanalyst, writer, innovator, and theoretician.[3] In 1940, as a young Viennese medical student, he emigrated from Germany and later settled in the United States. He rose to be a successful analyst, a president of the American Psychoanalytic Association, and later still the innovator of a new revolutionary theory of psychoanalysis. He died in 1981, four days after speaking at a conference celebrating self psychology, the psychoanalytic movement he had painstakingly created and nurtured.

Kohut's theory concentrated on the development and cohesion of the self and focused on aspects of relating that fit perfectly with post–World War II American culture. Psychodynamic psychotherapy, by utilizing self psychology's principles, was made accessible to individuals suffering from borderline, schizoid, and narcissistic personality disorders, which the psychoanalytic establishment had previously considered untreatable. These disorders—referred to as disorders of the self—are now considered to be among the most numerous of our era. Kohut had developed a theory and a set of therapeutic practices that made it possible to treat the illnesses emblematic of our time.

Kohut liked to tell a certain story about himself and Freud.[4] The story captures in metaphor the psychological features of the sea change taking place in postwar America and Kohut's sense of his place in that era. It was 1938, and Europe had become a giant oven for the Jews. In Austria the Nazis were in the process of rounding up the Jewish population and transporting them to the death camps of the Third Reich. Freud, like many Central European Jews, had difficulty facing the awful truth; as a result, he delayed too long in preparing for his escape from Vienna. If it had not been for the intervention of others, Freud and his family would have been rounded up and slaughtered. As the window of opportunity was closing, Freud's friends finally convinced him that he had to escape, and a compromise was negotiated with the Nazis by which he and his family were allowed to flee to England. The old Professor and his entourage of family, friends, colleagues, and patients clambered onboard the Orient Express, heading west to Paris and then London.

Kohut, personally unacquainted with Freud but fascinated with his theories, was at that time a young medical student from a highly assimilated middle class Jewish family. When he heard of Freud's potential escape, he rushed to the station to take in the scene. Off to one side, Kohut was a silent witness as the train started up and slowly moved away. Freud stared out the window, unbelievingly, no doubt trying to memorize the moment, the familiar scenes, his beloved Vienna. As the train passed the platform where Kohut stood, the men's eyes met. Kohut tipped his hat to Freud, and Freud returned the gesture. By this time Freud was old, sick with cancer, and grieving. His city, his country, the entire continent of Europe was aflame. Kohut, on the other hand, was young, ambitious, and hopeful. Not long after Freud's escape, both Kohut and his mother fled Austria. Kohut landed in England and two years later immigrated and settled in the United States. Unlike Freud, Kohut concealed his Jewishness throughout his new life in his adopted country.[5] He did so in artful and occasionally deceitful ways. While at the train station Freud was bidding farewell to a world often hostile and finally openly violent to his people. The message was evidently not lost on Kohut: when he tipped his hat in recognition and farewell, perhaps he was saying goodbye as much to his identity as a Jew as to the Viennese world of his youth, both aptly personified by Freud.

Being the student of history that he was, Kohut cherished this fleeting moment with the great man, and implicitly seemed to attribute to it great import. In truth, Freud and Kohut had connected at a departure point in both their lives. Perhaps Kohut felt that the moment illustrated his chosenness, his destiny to carry on and extend Freud's work, his leadership, his mission. Perhaps, in that one moment of acknowledgment, Kohut felt as though the torch had been passed. Perhaps, in a way, it had been.

The self that Kohut "found" in America in the 1950s and 1960s was remarkably similar to the self enshrined by humanistic psychology and the Winnicottian self object relations theorists imported from England in the 1970s and 1980s. Not surprisingly, psychotherapy theories from the 1960s through the 1980s described a self similar in most ways to the self displayed in television commercials, magazine ads, and the blockbuster sixties musical *Hair*. This was a self that was exhibitionistic, self-involved, thoroughly acquisitive; it valued emotional expressiveness, a lifting of political and personal constraints, and immediate gratification; surprisingly, it also valued political idealism, generosity, and communal living. This self displayed a thoroughly contradictory way of being, chaotic, paradoxical, yet occasionally ennobling—in short, narcissistic. It was a self fundamentally at odds with the self-reliant, self-sacrificing self of the Victorian American frontier, a new self that had its beginnings in turn-of-the-century "personality" and the irreverent 1920s flappers. How had the self been reconfigured in such a short period of time? Why did it take such a shape? Who (or what) profited by it?

By the early fifties, a new world was forming. Out of the confluence of the economic needs of corporate America, the power of the fledgling electronic media, and the business and pop cultural uses of psychological theory, a mid-twentieth-century consumerism arose that would radically transform Western society. To conform with and promote the new consumerism, a complementary configuration of the self had also begun to emerge, shaped by new social practices. In the fifties and sixties, Winnicott's true self–false self dichotomy and Kohut's ideas about the centrality and essential naturalness of narcissism and the cohesion of the self were moving about in the minds of their inventors. In later postwar decades these ideas would be fleshed out into extended theories by Winnicott's followers and Kohut's later writings and come to both reflect and influence the preoccupations of the era in startlingly accurate and effective ways. These new ideas described the aftermath of early postwar changes and became part of a trendy new psychologized language. In the process the theories of Winnicott and Kohut and their successors would change psychoanalytic thinking, making it more understandable and accessible to the lay audience and especially to the thousands of new nonanalytic therapists whose numbers and enthusiasms were to be one of the hallmarks of the late postwar era. In turn, Winnicott's and Kohut's new self theories would help set the overall psychological frame for the last decades of the century, by articulating the configuration of the self, inventing many new therapeutic practices, encouraging and utilizing academic interest in the field of human development, and by unknowingly supporting a socioeconomic trend that the theorists would probably have abhorred: the growing consumerization of American life.

Therefore, in tandem with liberationist ideology and the strategy of excessive consumption, the object relations framework that Melanie Klein had created and Winnicott expanded, and upon the passing of the Freudian torch to Kohut, the overall cultural scene was set. Society stood ready to receive the seedlings of the postwar era. Or perhaps a better way to conceptualize the moment is to use the saying Dizzy Dean made famous during the fifties on the Baseball Game of the Week: "The ducks," he would chuckle knowingly, "are on the pond." One thing, however, was clear: a change was brewing. By 1971 Carole King could sing "I feel the earth move, under my feet," and a whole generation knew that the "tremblin' " was caused by more than just the proximity of her lover. The cultural terrain was shifting.

The United States stood poised on the brink of a new historical era, one characterized by military might, widespread political paranoia, and economic affluence.[6] The emerging era would, in the future, be characterized by some as "Pax Americana," the era controlled by a new superpower, the international youngster, the United States. Winnicott's object relations theory and Kohut's self psychology reflected the major psychological trends of the era: a preoccupation with the adventures and vicissitudes of the self, a focus on personal liberation and one-on-one relationships, a taken-for-granted belief in psychological interiority, coherence, and mastery, and an unknowing immersion in the ideology and practices of consumerism. The hallmarks of the new psychotherapy theories were their focus on the fundamental importance of a cohesive, core self; the building of that self by consuming psychological "objects" and liberating the unique "trueness" of each individual; and the justification of that self through a reliance on the growing scientific status of developmental psychology. These social, intellectual, and psychoanalytic trends reflected and later helped reproduce the postwar configuration of the self, which I have earlier referred to as the empty self (see chapter three for a fuller discussion). This self made possible the triumph of consumerism and the credit economy. Without the empty self and its characteristic interior emptiness and yearning, the economic and cultural shape of the postwar era, including its youthful bravado, escalating inflation, and unquenchable consumer desire, would have been unthinkable.

THE IMMEDIATE POSTWAR YEARS

As the first years after World War II passed, Europe and Japan undertook massive cleanup and reconstruction, financed and supervised by the United States. The Yanks returned home and the country began to integrate them back into its social fabric, to make new plans, envision new dreams, build new cities and suburbs, tell new stories. Upon returning they found that the country was still haunted by memories of the depression, yet they and their loved ones were tempted by implied promises of material abundance in the new postwar world: the cars, houses, refrigerators, electronic gadgets, and leisure activities. So they all stood, entitled, ready to receive. The world had survived the most horrific war in the history of humankind, and before that an economic depression that was the most serious challenge to capitalism that the modern era had yet produced.

The movie *The Best Years of Our Lives*, released in 1946,[7] illustrated the cornerstone of the emerging era. In this movie, several war buddies return home and begin life again after their ordeal. They all have a difficult time of it, suffering and failing; they are confused, angry, and defeated. The protagonist, quite by accident, stumbles one day on a fleet of discarded war planes, just like the beloved plane he and his buddies flew in the war. The old planes have been cast aside. They are ignored and laughed at by the new postwar world that the hero can neither understand nor accommodate himself to. He eventually lands a menial job with a company that redeems the planes from a wasteful, ignominious destruction by disassembling them and selling the metal to construction firms. These new companies, of course, are those that fanned out across the country, exploiting the postwar push for low-income suburban starter homes for the new families created by the returning young soldiers. Out of the ashes of the dead war arose the fuel for a new America, the ingredients of new suburban communities. The secret of the postwar boom years was thus symbolically revealed: consume the war, metabolize it, transform it into a new America—one that is clean, antiseptic, hopeful, ambitious, affluent, and suburban (see chapter three).

Two great lessons of the war were illustrated by the movie's primary metaphor. The first lesson was that the depression had been transcended because the war provided a solution to the problems of how to liquidate surplus goods and justify the central management of the economy. The war also had provided a ready-made, never satiated appetite for manufactured items (for weapons and ammunition) and an obvious rationale for centralized management. Somehow the country would have to reproduce that dynamic during peacetime if the nation was to avoid another depression. The second lesson of the war was that fear of an external enemy, combined with an exorbitant military budget, supplements a peacetime economy in many ways, by providing jobs, an interest in consumer items based on a military theme (such as war toys and movies with themes related to war, spying, and violence), and a popular rationale for a federal funding program for weapons and munitions manufacturers, an international spy network, and a domestic secret police. There was a link, the movie appeared to suggest, between the presence of an enemy, the active manufacture of the weapons of war, and the creation of never ending consumer desire.

Perhaps hating an enemy is not only the product of emptiness, but also a way of *constructing* emptiness. Perhaps hating and fearing is itself an activity that depletes one's individual resources and shrinks the horizons of one's psychological terrain to such a point that one experiences oneself as empty. Defining oneself through what one is not (for example, a Communist conspirator) is a strategy that might inevitably lead to a sense of personal absence. The Communist of the fifties was used in ways similar to the African American of the minstrel stage and the Native American of the Plains Indian Wars, as "the other," an example of what the proper American is not (see chapter three).

The two lessons of World War II were both brought to fruition in the decades after the war by the development of a new configuration of the self, the empty self. Citizens with a deep, gnawing sense of personal emptiness will always want to purchase new gadgets, no matter how innane or unnecessary; consume unneeded foods; identify with charismatic celebrities; and hate and fear the evil "enemy" in foreign lands, or even worse, in their own backyard.

The history of the first fifteen years after the war seemed to bear out the movie's lessons. It is astonishing to look back to that time, to look through the veneer of vapid situation comedies, the growing economy, the unquestioned gender roles, the self-confident preeminence of big business, the presumption of military superiority, and see the fear just below the surface. For the seemingly endless years of World War II, the country had been engaged in a terrifying war, battling some of the most evil forces in the history of humankind. Although Americans did not suffer as immeasurably and acutely as Europeans, they had confronted fear, deprivation, loss, and mourning. They knew how close the world had come to being taken over by the Nazis, and that knowledge profoundly affected them.

One is also struck by the subtle but omnipresent confusion of the time. The great leader of the West, Franklin D. Roosevelt, had died. In his place a frightened, self-deprecating Harry Truman struggled to gather information and bring himself up to speed. The USSR rapidly began to flex its newfound international muscles. Europe had to be rebuilt, and Japan and Germany had to be rehabilitated. American industry had to be converted to a peacetime footing; but no one seemed to know how to do it without sliding down the slippery slope to another devastating depression. Civilian corruption and the power of organized crime began to be publicized, especially after the televising of the Kefauver hearings in the Senate. The spectre of domestic Communism, and its self-appointed nemesis Senator Joseph McCarthy, dominated the American people, focusing their terror, exacerbating their uncertainty, and offering a consoling panacea for other uncertainties.[8]

But above all one is struck by the immense irony of those early postwar years. America had vanquished a powerful alliance founded on racism, authoritarianism, and imperialism. The victory was costly but necessary, since the enemy was so undeniably evil. However, in the isolated moments when the postwar denial lifted, Americans were confronted by profoundly discomforting realities: the racial segregation of the U.S. Armed Forces, Jim Crow laws in the South, white mob violence against Negroes in the North and Latinos in California, the oppression of women, anti-Semitism, severe economic injustice, and vigilantism remained taken-for-granted aspects of its social framework. The Nazi death camps, the surprise attack on Pearl Harbor, and the Japanese mistreatment of POWs in Asia were despicable acts that had justified the Allied cause, but could one overlook the violence and destructiveness of institutional racism throughout the United States, the Allied firebombings of German cities and their civilian populations, the unnecessary use of the atom bomb on Hiroshima and Nagasaki, the internment camps for Japanese-American citizens, domestic poverty and economic injustice? There were some disquieting parallels between the barbarism of the Axis powers and some of the less extreme but nonetheless despicable, and perhaps fundamental, wrongs being committed at home in America.

If the war was not fought to defeat racism, barbaric violence, or imperialism, what had it been fought for? That question was the engine that drove the first ten years of postwar American confusion and floundering. The country, first under Harry Truman and then Dwight

Eisenhower, groped toward a coherent answer. It was not long after V-J Day that Truman began to realize that the prewar New Deal agenda could not simply be reimposed onto the postwar world. He faced an enormous task: to consolidate the social gains of the Progressive and New Deal eras while simultaneously avoiding the horror of a new depression. It became obvious that Truman didn't really know how to accomplish this, nor did anyone else. To focus on social justice meant he would suffer the slings and arrows of the Right; to focus on ensuring the health and prosperity of postwar corporate capitalism meant he would be attacked by labor, the intelligentsia, and the Left. The Truman presidency was marked by these oppositions.

Eisenhower came to office on a wave of enormous popularity. But soon he fell prey to paradoxes and divisions similar to those that had plagued Truman. The country drifted, ill at ease and dangerously vulnerable to demagoguery, nuclear confrontation, and racial hatred. As the Korean War ended, McCarthy self-destructed, and the USSR, under Premier Nikita Khrushchev, made a few unaccustomed friendly noises. The anxiety seemed to subside. The country even survived a potential early Richard Nixon presidency, when in 1955 Eisenhower suffered a heart attack and the vice president stood ready to assume command.

Racial strife intensified as the 1954 Supreme Court determined that the segregation of public schools was illegal, it must be stopped, and implementation should proceed with "all deliberate speed." Eisenhower, ambivalently, emphasized the word *deliberate*. However, not even the subtle sabotage of the White House could indefinitely stem the tide of civil rights activism and Southern white resistance and violence. Negro communities, civil rights organizations, and the federal courts were putting pressure on schools throughout the South to desegregate, and the white South resisted and stonewalled with every weapon at its command. By 1956 only 350 out of 6,300 Southern school districts had experienced even token desegregation, and all were in the border states, none in the Deep South.[9] In 1957 white opposition to the federal law on school desegregation led by "White Citizen's Councils," became openly violent. The state of Arkansas took a stand that was so brazenly unconstitutional that even the "deliberate" Eisenhower was compelled to take action to protect black children and enforce the Supreme Court ruling: he called out the U.S. Army. Governor Orville Faubus of Arkansas used state troops to prevent black children from entering previously all-white schools, and Ike had to counter Faubus's actions. The sight of federal troops enforcing federal desegregation law was a new sight on national television, but by the early 1960s it would become standard fare. In 1956, after a year of boycotting the municipal bus system, the Negro community of Montgomery, Alabama, under the leadership of Martin Luther King, Jr. won the right of free access. Violent reactions to sit-ins and demonstrations in segregated public facilities exposed racial oppression in ways the country could no longer ignore. In 1957 Congress passed the first civil rights act since Reconstruction. It was pitifully weak, but it was a beginning. The fight for the nation's soul, eerily repeating the mid-century battle over the abolition of slavery one hundred years earlier, was again underway.

Although there were many international hot spots during the 1950s, in the last years of Eisenhower's second term the two superpowers seemed to be moving toward accommodation and a lessening of tensions. The policy of "containment," first broached by foreign policy specialist George Kennan during the Truman administration, had rained down a firestorm of hatred, contempt, and criticism on Truman. The Right had cried treason for even contemplating a policy that stopped short of complete victory over Communism. But by the end of Eisenhower's reign, containment had given way to an even more accommodating policy: "coexistence." Some thought that only the old four-star General Eisenhower and his cold-warrior Secretary of State John Foster Dulles could have carried out such a "cowardly," un-American policy and escaped without a right-wing lynching. But in truth the times were changing. The Russians had shaken America's sense of nuclear invulnerability with a chain of successes in space, starting on October 4, 1957, with the launching of *Sputnik*, the first and most famous satellite in history. The United States was forced to reevaluate its presumed military superiority, and to cast a stern look at its educational system and, in fact, its population's overall "fitness." It was a sobering turn of affairs. The United States was probably still "ahead" of the USSR in terms of nuclear weaponry, but being "ahead" no longer meant much if all that could be accomplished was mutual destruction.

In general, Americans had become complacent, soft, and obsessed with things. Television, empty calories, summer vacations, and leisure activities, and new Detroit gas-guzzlers with big tail fins and lots of chrome increasingly occupied the thoughts of middle-class Americans. They could regroup, but they would have to sacrifice and work hard to regain a sense of superiority or at least a semblance of equality with the Russians.

But the country had settled into acceptance of a grudging, uneasy coexistence with its fellow nuclear superpower. Even the twin bullies Nixon and Khrushchev, in a 1959 face-to-face shouting match in Moscow, eventually controlled themselves and ended their discussion in relative harmony. Obviously, something in the country had changed. A certain pressure had eased; the hard, McCarthy-like edge had softened a bit. Why? Probably the single most important element of the growing tolerance was a new economic prosperity. By the late fifties American business was booming. The economic lessons of World War II had been learned, the economy had been retooled for peacetime (albeit a military peacetime), television was transforming the cultural terrain, and there was abroad in the land a kind of individual permissiveness and acquisitiveness unlike anything that had been seen before. The country, historian Eric Goldman explained, "ambled down its middle road, worried now and then, even having its frenetic moments, but usually happily absorbed in private affairs. . . . The great waves of prosperity kept rolling in, overwhelming any concerns about the world."[10]

By the late fifties, the country was resembling the commercial, overcommodified world of today. A few details assembled by John Blum et al., Stephanie Coontz, Carl Degler et al., and Eric Goldman help illustrate this point. In the fifteen years after World War II, the money spent on advertising increased by 400 percent, showing growth greater than that of the gross national product.[11] In 1954 only 10 percent of the public could even imagine investing in the stock market; by 1957 one in nine actually owned stock. In the summer of 1957 over half of the population could afford to enjoy a traveling vacation. Instant credit had been discovered! Diners Club was suddenly a multimillion dollar business. A Duluth, Minnesota, businessman had his picture taken exhibiting a wallet with a foldout device that accommodated fifty-eight credit cards. Approximately one in three women could afford to get her hair tinted at a beauty shop—this in a country where, during wartime, its young women pretended to wear expensive nylon stockings by drawing a black seam up the back of their legs. Cars became a symbol of the new consumer era. In Detroit, sales were booming. Even foreign cars were selling: in 1955 a mere 56,000 foreign cars were imported and sold; only two years later the figure had jumped to 200,000.[12] By 1960, 90 percent of American households owned at least one television set.[13] Between 1940 and 1960 the gross national product (GNP) rose 114 percent, although population had only grown at 36 percent. In the next ten years GNP would double, going from $500 billion in 1960 to $1 trillion by 1971. In 1940 less than 44 percent of American families owned their own homes; by 1960 the figure was 62 percent. The wages of manufacturing workers rose 16 percent between 1947 and 1957, and they went up another 17 percent between 1960 and 1969.[14] Although income distribution remained unequal and relatively constant, the appearance of prosperity and upward mobility carried the day.

THE EMERGING NEW POSTWAR SELF

But more than business was booming. There was a new zeitgeist in the air, something operating in many spheres of life, but it had not yet become visible. It would be alluded to by John F. Kennedy in the sixties and later exploited by advertising; by the seventies and eighties it would be used to co-opt the civil rights and antiwar movements and to privatize, isolate, depoliticize, and subvert the earlier youth rebellion. That old standby, the enchanted American interior, with its desperate wish to be liberated, was showing up again (see chapter five).

As we have seen in earlier chapters, one of the prominent American traditions is a belief in the existence of the spiritual and moral "goodness" of the individual's interior, and the imperative of helping the inner self to grow, prosper, and be liberated by becoming more emotionally expressive and more valued in the individual's everyday decision-making process. Although the influence of this romantic idea has waxed and waned in the cultural landscape, it has on the whole been an influential idea, especially in the last 150 years. In the thirties and forties it was relatively quiescent, but with peacetime and prosperity, it again gathered momentum.

Youthfulness, expressiveness, personal entitlement, self-centeredness, acquisitiveness, self-confidence, optimism are some of the qualities that describe the new developing spirit of the postwar era. The new teenage subculture in the postwar years, depicted in *Gasoline Alley* (1949) and briefly discussed in chapter three, had blossomed into a countrywide phenomenon by the late fifties. Americans of all ages seemed more expressive, enthusiastic, hungry for experiences, less inhibited. Most of all, middle-class white Americans were characterized by a sense of unconditional entitlement; they felt entitled to money, commodities, experiences, food, special treatment, respect (sometimes deference), speaking their mind, expressing their feelings, getting their way. It became easy to stereotype Americans and categorize them into a recognizable "type." If there was a choice between purchases, experiences, or celebrities, they were thought to prefer the one that was the biggest, most expensive, and most flamboyant. They presumed that white was the natural skin color, English the natural language, and that God was an American. In a room full of citizens from various nations, it was thought one could usually discern who the Americans were: they were louder, more emotional, less tradition bound, more interested in "relating." There was a good side to this, but also a downside, captured by the title of William Lederer's best-selling 1958 book *The Ugly American*. As the U.S. economy continued to boom, Americans seemed to act as though anything worth having could be bought, and some went out and tried to do just that.

Somewhere after the end of World War II, and after the first lackluster stage of Eisenhower's administration, a new dynamic had come of age. Consumerism, and its complementary configuration of self, was gathering momentum. This new configuration is nowhere more clearly illustrated than in the following anecdote about an interaction between the respective bully-boys of the twin superpowers. In 1959 Vice President Nixon, positioning himself for the 1960 Presidential campaign, traveled to Moscow and found himself cheek by jowl with Khrushchev in a model kitchen in the U.S. National Exhibit.[15] They began to argue and bully one another, and while so occupied they arrived at a moment that summed up the economic framework of the new dynamic. Khrushchev baited Nixon by saying, in effect, "You think your kitchen gadgets are so good? Ours are as good as yours." Nixon retorted by saying, in effect, "Oh yeah? Our country is better than yours, not only because we have better gadgets, but also because our housewives can *choose* which gadgets to buy. But the choices of your housewives are limited and controlled by your government! The greatness of America lies in its freedom of consumer choice!" They went on to accuse one another of threatening the peace, and to warn one another not to deliver missile-rattling ultimatums. Then Nixon intoned: "Is it not far better to be talking about washing machines than machines of war, like rockets? Isn't this the kind of competition you want?"[16]

Right there, in a fake 1950s kitchen, the U.S. perspective on the ground rules of the cold war for the next thirty years were laid out for all to see. What were we fighting for? The right to choose among many brands and models of washing machines. What was freedom? Not political freedom, nor freedom from want, but the freedom to choose which consumer products to purchase on credit. The entire political vocabulary of a nation was becoming transformed. Consumer choice had become an ultimate measure of the good.

An important aspect of the great battle in which the United States and the USSR were locked, complete with ICBMs equipped with nuclear warheads, was thus revealed: it was a battle that focused on the wallet of the consumer. Many times over the course of the next thirty years, U.S. politicians tried to situate the battles of the cold war in the department stores. There, the country was told, was where the real battles were waged. The searing question of the moment, Nixon implied, was not whether or to what extent the political structure of the United States guaranteed inalienable social rights or citizen participation in government; not whether or to what extent the political structure of the USSR guaranteed meaningful employment in an egalitarian society; not whether the two nations would engage in a nuclear war that would destroy the planet. Instead, the battle between the two superpowers turned on which economy was more effective in producing and consuming the most consumer goods. In fact, the political-military contest in which the two countries also engaged, that is, which country could develop the most powerful military weapons or win over the richest or most strategic Third World countries, could also be interpreted as a contest over which country could produce and consume the most. The United States used the cold war in part as a vehicle for encouraging unlimited production and consumption of commodities. One way to sell more products is to produce more surplus products, and one way to justify the production and consumption of surplus is to elevate consumer choice to the highest of patriotic values, with each purchase signifying a blow against the enemy.

In other words, the discourse of war had been reframed: in the new terrain, war was "cold," the battlefield was located in the department store, the soldier was configured as the shopper, the weapons of war were retooled as advertising campaigns, efficiency reports, marketing surveys, and arrangements of personal credit. As was discussed in chapter two, different cultures have located the seat of emotions in various parts of the body. In the modern era in the West, the indigenous psychology often located the mind in the head, and the emotions in the heart. Now, tongue in cheek, we can imagine that a further shift in location was taking place. Now, the hearts and minds of the people, that ultimate cold war prize, were located in an organ recently brought to prominence: the wallet. Or, more precisely, the credit card, which resided in the wallet.

Why did the terrain get configured in this way? The phenomenon is an example of Foucault's concept of "positivity" (as discussed in chapter two), the exercise of control through setting the cultural frame of reference. With the Nixon-Khrushchev fake kitchen debate we see language reflecting and producing a change in the meaning of central political concepts. *Freedom*, for instance, was once a word with a rich, complex set of political meanings. It pertained to issues such as inalienable rights, participatory democracy, and the absence of constraints on individual belief and privacy. But in the consumer society of the late fifties, freedom was sometimes reduced to the opportunity to choose between brands of toothpaste.

By the late fifties the purchase of goods was at times elevated to an act of political or moral virtue.[17] Both the United States and the USSR co-opted certain emotions left over from World War II, mainly fear and paranoia, and built up their economic and military competition in an effort to solve internal political and economic issues. This competition was preferable to battles fought with bullets and bombs, but it was immensely costly to individual consumers and wasteful of the natural resources, energy, time, and creativity of the nation as a whole. Among other things, the policies employed in the United States necessitated the development of universal credit and an easy to acquire personal debt, since the consumption of unnecessary, expensive, planned obsolescence, and often harmful commodities was beyond the means of most Americans. These consequences have proven to be destructive to the nation in several ways—untold hours of labor, and billions of dollars of natural resources and consumer credit have been spent to produce and purchase nonessential and quickly obsolete products—but these policies did accomplish an economic boom that has lasted the better part of four decades.

The boom has had a lasting effect not only on the national deficit but also on the American psyche. Prosperity and the continued building of a consumer society also required that the government provide an environment friendly to big business, so as to encourage the growth of industry, the creation of jobs, and an increase in the production of goods. Whereas Truman had blustered (and waffled) about the struggles between big business and big unions, Eisenhower's cabinet had contained men like Secretary of Defense Charles Wilson, the former president of General Motors; and Secretary of the Treasury George Humphrey, the former president of another giant conglomerate; and M. A. Hanna who stood four-square for business and made no bones about it, but they were also flexible and oriented to a pragmatic managerial ethos. It was Wilson who made the famous statement "What's good for General Motors is good for the country." He invoked the "escalator clause" in labor negotiations, which linked wage increases to increases in the cost of living index. Humphrey shaped an agreement between U.S. Steel and the coal workers that was surprisingly pro-union. The old-line business community howled about betrayal, but the administration remained unperturbed.[18] These were "practical men," anxious to see big business take off without "unnecessary" ideological impediments such as the need to fight labor every step of the way. The country caught on to this style and ran with it. Business learned to roll with the punches; whatever labor gained, management passed on to the public in the form of escalating prices. Inflation began to rear its ugly head, and by the late sixties it was taken for granted as an aspect of the economy. But in the fifties business was booming, the public was consuming at an ever increasing rate, and all was right with the world. Consuming had become the face of human being.

To be young, white, and middle-class in the fifties and early sixties was to live a life of quiet privilege. The deprivations of the depression, the horrors of World War II, and the alienating confusion of Korea were all unknown to the early baby boomers. Their parents wanted them to be spared the terrors they had faced. The economy was on a continuing upswing, democratic capitalism was depicted as a meritocracy built on fair play, and God was on America's side. There was good and there was bad, and it was easy to tell which was which. And the shock of encountering the racism, greed, and betrayal that lurked in the underside of America was still off in the future. The baby boomers grew up in a sheltered landscape that was unrealistic, idealistic, and somewhat banal. For the moment, baby boomers had only to play, consume, and look forward to college, love and marriage, and then the suburbs.

There was a toll to be exacted, however, for the banality, conformity, political avoidance, and psychological accommodations of the fifties. It was not readily apparent—it would show up in subtle cultural signs such as clinical depression, vague middle-class unrest, outbreaks of paranoid hatred against Negroes or accused communists, surprisingly rigid prescriptions on gender roles, puzzling and undirected adolescent rebellion. Something was wrong, but what? People, especially the young, were suffering from an unease, but why? In the greatest country on earth, what could be wrong? It was not exactly a thing, it was more like—a nothing. Like an absence.

A Big Four summit meeting was scheduled for May 1960, and hopes were high that if even the dueling bulldogs Nixon and Khrushchev could have a civil conversation, perhaps the two nations could come to an understanding regarding problems such as Berlin and Cuba, and the nuclear standoff that threatened the future of the entire planet could be eased a bit. Then disaster hit: an American U-2 reconnaissance plane, flown by Airman Gary Powers, was shot down over Russia; in a series of ill-advised bumblings, the administration, trying to manage the disaster, stumbled from one exposed lie and contradictory statement to the next. At first Ike insisted that the plane did not violate Russian airspace, that it was collecting weather information, and finally that the flights would continue. Soon each statement was reversed by the administration or proven incorrect by the press. At the last possible moment, in mock fury, Khrushchev called off the summit. For the moment, an important opportunity had been lost. Tensions remained high, but the twin problems of Berlin and Cuba would have to be taken up after the presidential election, by the next, as of yet faceless, administration. Ike, the beloved World

War II warrior, was retiring at the height of his popularity, his approval rating an unheard of 68 percent. The illusion of stability and safety he had brought to the nation was being withdrawn at a pivotal moment.

THE SIXTIES

Then John Fitzgerald Kennedy stepped forward. But he did not step as much as bound. And we all bounded with him. He was the quintessence of the new era: hopeful, cocky, bright, intelligent, funny, handsome, urbane, a bit too rich, a bit too smart for his own good, a bit (perhaps a lot) out of control. He inspired the nation, called upon us to lift ourselves up to new heights. He asked us to sacrifice, to be dedicated, to be idealistic; and his words were music to the ears of the new postwar generation. In fact, the music was already in the air, but the nation didn't hear it until he came along.

The Republican Nixon, bedfellow of the toxic McCarthy, lurched, lumbered, and slouched his way toward the election. Jack stood tall and slim, he smirked, he was tough, he was us. The vote in 1960 was the closest in history: only 113,000 votes out of 73 million separated the two candidates.[19] For the new generation of baby boomers, about to come of age during the decade that had just begun, he was everything they wanted to be. Unfortunately, there was also something about him that would come to trouble them, something they couldn't put into words or admit to themselves yet: he was too rich, too privileged, too politically moderate to be what the nation needed him to be. He was good—he was much better than what opposed him—but he had his limitations.

Kennedy's limitations showed up right away. He wavered in his early days, tripping over the Bay of Pigs, failing to grasp the momentous historical meanings at stake in the civil rights battles,[20] and his attempts to get his legislative package through an entrenched, fifties-oriented Congress were roundly defeated. He recouped in foreign policy with his confrontation with Khrushchev in the Cuban Missile Crisis, never blinking, and that seemed to help him in future negotiations, such as in his initiation of and success with the limited nuclear test ban treaty. And although he played an imperialist game in Vietnam, it was a relatively small game; at least he did not jump in feetfirst.

But it was in the South that the nation needed more from JFK, and from Robert Kennedy, his attorney general and brother, than it got. It was a tall order, to stand up against the powerful Southerners in his own party, to rally the country against racism, to use the power at his disposal to crush the traditions of segregation and violence—tall orders

SELF-LIBERATION THROUGH CONSUMERISM 227

indeed. But Kennedy wasn't able to do it. Probably he was playing a waiting game, trying to play his cards just right, trying not to overextend himself, not to get too far out on a limb. Perhaps he thought he couldn't challenge the South too much, at least not until after the 1964 election, when he could extend his moral reach, when he would be safe. Of course, he was limited by the boundaries of his own birth and privilege, and he might have sensed that the inch-by-inch battles of the civil rights movement would reach out in ever larger (and more Northerly) circles. Perhaps he sensed that someday the movement's reach would threaten the corporate structure of liberal America in ways that hit much too close to home, to *his* home.

Race is such a fundamental issue in the United States that any amount of change is potentially threatening to those in positions of power, and any amount of change can lead to more extensive change. Kennedy was a rather moderate liberal. He could tolerate, even welcome token moves, but the indications are that he was unprepared for (and even uncomfortable with) the momentous moral challenges about to confront him and the nation as a result of the intensified efforts of the civil rights movement. This appears to be a generic limitation of liberal politicians in the United States: they have the money and political clout to make it into office, but because of their wealth and power they cannot risk a wide-ranging political restructuring because they have too much to lose.

Of course, there was to be no second term, there was to be no safety—not for him, and, finally, not for us. How Kennedy might have grown in office, how he might have changed, how he might have led—these are all things we will never know. His assassination on November 22, 1963, began a series of catastrophes that first wounded and finally destroyed the promise of the baby boom generation. His murder was the first of four political murders in the sixties that have marked our era like a wound that won't heal or a bridge destroyed by war and never repaired. He was the first to go, and in some way something in the post–World War II generation began dying at that moment. Perhaps the continuing resolve and moral force that would have been necessary to withstand the seductions of wealth and accommodation began to bleed out of the baby boomers as first one and then another of their leaders was gunned down in public view.

Vice President Lyndon Johnson assumed the office after Kennedy's death, accomplishing much more in the domestic legislative agenda than Kennedy had, and adding much to it, making it his own. He called his legislative program "The Great Society," and for a while it had promise. It suffered from certain limitations commonly associated with moderate liberalism, but it had promise. During the early years of the Johnson presidency, bills were passed that finally had some teeth in them: there were civil rights bills, such as the 1964 bill that prohibited racial, religious, or gender discrimination in public places; the Voting Act of 1965, which gave federal officers the power to step in under certain conditions and register black voters; and the 1967 bill that ended discrimination in housing. He passed legislation on economic opportunity, Headstart, Medicare, and welfare reform. His early presidency was marked by spectacular legislative successes.

During the mid- and late sixties several factors, such as the effects of prosperity and peace, the remarkable growth of television and its psychological impact on children, the growing consumerism of the postwar era, "up-to-date" parenting techniques, the threat of nuclear war, the excitement engendered by Kennedy's charisma and the optimism nurtured by Johnson's early victories—all combined to develop in the early postwar generation a particular way of being. The various elements of this phenomenon were referred to in the mainstream media as youth culture, the New Left, the hippie lifestyle, the psychedelic subculture, the human potential movement, the peace and love generation, the counterculture. What was common among many of these unlikely bedfellows was a belief in various kinds of liberation and a rejection of many aspects of mainstream middle-class American life. Some of these groups or movements believed in political liberation, some in a lifting of psychological or sexual constraints; some in spiritual transformation, and some in direct political power; some in moderate, peaceful evolution, and some in radical, violent revolution. But all held some form of liberation and transformation to be an ultimate value.

This youthful liberationist perspective was reflected in the clothes people wore, the music they favored, the drugs and food they consumed, the living arrangements they chose, the books they studied, and the ideas they espoused. They were colorful, egalitarian, and expressive; they valued experience, gratification, and naturalness; they favored topsoil over freeways, personal freedom over constraint, communalism over competitive individualism, and the artist-hero over the corporate drudge. Theirs was a highly idiosyncratic and contradictory vision. In part, it was informed by the romantic tradition of expressive individualism, in which truth is located in the private interior of each individual and grows organically, producing a kind of heroic creativity. The tradition of the political Left, split and embattled though it was, also contributed to their vision, as did escapist, anti-intellectual, antirational, mob-inclined traditions of the West, which psychologist Nathan Adler has referred to as the "antinomian" tradition, a tradition that has appeared throughout West-

ern history in the form of the occult, the gnostic, the ecstatic, the yearning for oceanic merging, the alienated wish to be "filled with gods."[21] The
naive idealism of youth, made more insistent and unrealistic by the
affluence, permissiveness, drugs, and passive television viewing characteristic of the postwar years, was another influence. Paradox abounded:
the sixties perspective was life-affirming, liberationist, yet conformist
and consumerist.

It is problematic to speak in unqualified generalities about these
baby boomers as if they were a monolithic group, as if they were *the*
youth culture. Not all postwar baby boomers held these values and
practiced this lifestyle. There were many parts of the country in which
this particular sociopolitical constellation was never very popular. There
were, even among those who were white, middle-class, and college-
going, many different degrees of allegiance, with many differing meanings imputed to it. Other socioeconomic and ethnic groups, such as the
white upper class, the black middle class, and the white non-Anglo
working classes accepted, rejected, and reshaped some of the characteristics of this group to better fit their circumstances and values. There were
also numbers of youth who supported the war, didn't believe that the
country suffered from *institutional* racism, and were in step with their
parents, the government, and the economic status quo. Many of these
people would vote for Nixon in 1972 and Reagan in 1980 and 1984, would
come to favor themes of "law and order" and "peace with honor," and
thought "welfare queens," if not commies, were lurking around every
corner. Yet with that disclaimer in mind, there was, indeed, a middle-
class youth zeitgeist emerging, one that affected a significant proportion
of the postwar generation, and the country as a whole.

During the mid-sixties, the Beatles had left behind the sappy fifties-
style of "I Want to Hold Your Hand" and moved through the more poetic
and bohemian "Norwegian Wood." They were becoming more skilled
and developing a distinctive voice: offbeat, artistic, yet political in a
peculiar, characteristically sixties style. Then, in 1967, they came out
with the album that quickly became an emblem of the generation: *Sgt.
Pepper's Lonely Hearts Club Band*. "Lucy in the Sky with Diamonds"
captured in one lyrical, psychedelic moment the delicious disorientation,
the glorious, life-affirming liberation, the engulfing wonder of being
young, hopeful, and confused. There was in this song a sense of the
magic of liberation, the dreamlike state of wonderment, imagination,
and drugs, the confusion and disorientation of the emerging new perspective of the young generation, beginning to flex its creative muscles.

The Beatles would make many contributions to the generation's
identity. For instance, the free speech-civil rights-antiwar movement at

UC Berkeley, its members standing defiantly together in front of the administration building, about to embark on actions that would shock the entire nation, suddenly found themselves singing "We all live in a yellow submarine" in one grand, unplanned moment of communal understanding. But few albums galvanized the generation the way *Sgt. Pepper's* did. It captured the youthfulness and hope ("Sgt. Pepper"), the communal solidarity ("A Little Help from My Friends"), the liberation of poetry, drugs, love, sex, and imagination ("Lucy in the Sky with Diamonds," "Getting Better," "Fixing a Hole"), generational conflicts and alienation ("She's Leaving Home"), the lostness and the boundary confusion ("Within You Without You"), the fears engendered by love, conformity, and old age ("When I'm Sixty-Four"), and a sense of the sorrow and tragedy that lurked just below the surface ("Good Morning, Good Morning," "A Day in the Life"). These were all songs of our time. There was something in each of these songs, and with how they all fit together, that reflected the generation, that held up a mirror to its face, that caught the moment and catapulted it forward.

There was a youthful vitality, a hopefulness, a new perspective in the air; if the boomers could expand their minds, the thinking went, if *all* of them could open themselves to the wonders and potentialities of life, then anything would be possible. For a short time, the forces of hope, moral fervor, and youthful play brought forth in some a political dedication that was not self-serving, a spirituality that was less escapist than activist, an interest in dialogue, a joyful curiosity, and an abandon that was not solely an expression of consumerism. (Although it did help if you had a good stereo and the right style of bellbottom jeans.) This combination of idealism, dedication, and concern held together, for short moments, the contradictory forces that comprised the generation. These were hopeful, glorious moments, moments that held out the possibility of a better, more humane future. But soon opposition among the forces would shatter the togetherness, scattering elements of various causes to extreme poles. Political dedication became more calculating, concrete, and less psychologically insightful, and in locations such as Berkeley, where resistance had been at a fever pitch for years, demonstrations were vulnerable to rage and the mob. Spiritual interests became more escapist, otherworldly, and passive, easy prey for drug dealers or the authoritarianism, simple solutions, and anesthesia found in cults like the Moonies, Hare Krishnas, or Children of God. Youthful curiosity and joy became increasingly disconnected from the moral purposes that earlier informed the movement and vulnerable to the materialism and sybaritic gratifications offered by an expanded, highly skilled advertising industry. It was easy, given the predispositions of the generation, for advertising to use symbols such as liberation and transformation to reintroduce its members to the consumer ethos. For instance, there was a Coca-Cola ad that featured a song that began "I'd like to teach the world to sing, in perfect harmony." It was not easy to remember, once in the grip of emotion, that the song was about selling caffeinated sugar-water—not spreading harmony and love—to the four corners of the planet.

Baby Boomer Uniqueness

In the mind of the nation, those born after the war were symbolic of the new era, just as Clovia was in *Gasoline Alley*.[22] They were bright, fresh, optimistic, energetic, innocent of, and unmarked by, the ravages of the depression and World War II—the embodiment of everything the country had fought for. Like Clovia, they were above all lucky: born into peacetime and a booming economy. Their parents vowed that this generation would not suffer as they had suffered. And so a mystique grew up around them.

They were given too much, overprotected, told a bit too often they were a generation apart. The sense of being different from one's parents was, historically, something that had been brewing in the United States from the late nineteenth century.[23] A generation gap was noticeable as farm children moved into the expanding cities and as the children of immigrants grew up to be American citizens, more Americanized in language and custom than their parents would ever be. But that trend reached its zenith in the post–World War II generation.

The differentness of the baby boomers was spawned partly by historical events, partly by the nation's self-deceptions, and partly it was encouraged for commercial motives. Indeed, it is true that the affluence, safety, and scientific advances of the postwar years created social conditions unknown to the baby boomers' parents. As a result, a distinction, sometimes an alienation, began to separate generations. The parents, unable to anticipate their children's problems or apply their own experiences to understanding them, sometimes felt helpless and inadequate, and the children unhelped and perhaps alone.

Second, the nation wanted desperately for the events of the previous decades—the despair of the depression and the terror of the war—to amount to something. It would have been too threatening for citizens, especially the parents of new children, to face their fears about another depression and all that would mean politically. And it was vitally important for them to view their victory over fascism as a triumph of good over evil. This outlook contributed to their difficulties in confronting the Allies' anti-Semitic–tinged isolationism, which implicitly rewarded Nazi aggression and atrocities, and then the domestic institutional racism (and sexism) that pointed to similarities between fascist and American socio-political systems. These young parents could concentrate their hopes (and avoid their fears) by idealizing the nation, indulging and over-protecting their children, and at the same time denying the hard political facts—the racism, economic stratification, and violence against women—that simmered below the surface of the post–World War II era. This mix of avoidance, indulgence, and idealization combined to add justification to the baby boomers' experience of themselves as a genera-tion apart. They thought that few outside of their cohort could under-stand them, and thus no one could lead them. The baby boom generation embodied the affluent, brash innocence of postwar America—the good and the bad of it.

As it turned out, the good and the bad of it was used by corporate America to sell products as never before. Advertisers appealed to the baby boomers' sense of uniqueness and specialness at the same time that they re-created and shaped it. They learned to sell to the generation by evoking its sense of specialness. This was a market brought up on electronic ads, always with more naivete and money—and less cynicism and suspicion—than any other segment of the population. The shaping and exploiting of the baby boomers' generational identity was one of the central and most effective advertising strategies of the postwar era, continuing even into the present. From jeans to vacations, cars to insur-ance plans, soft drinks to careers, the generational identity of the baby boomers continues to be high profile. They have been, and will always be, the original members of "The Pepsi Generation."

Finally, there was something about the postwar cultural terrain that made "transformation" appear an everyday, relatively expected, magical process. Perhaps there was something about how easily life was pre-sented to them, the simplicity of the good-versus-evil cold war stories their early lives were saturated with, how truly magical the flashing electronic stories in television and the movies were. The passive, voy-euristic experience of "watching" episodes and lives unfold made emo-tion and change easy to come by. Sacrifice, hard work, tolerating the passage of time, accepting the randomness of events—these virtues were all somewhat foreign. The baby boomers were used to simple answers and easy solutions—things happening quickly, for the right reasons, and without great personal sacrifice. They were used to consuming, not producing; gratification, not frustration; immediacy, not long-term plan-ning. Perhaps it is not surprising that their change in perspective came by way of drugs, spiritual change through radical, guru-forced sudden trans-formation, and political activity in the form of colorful, dramatic confrontations and mass celebrations. This worked fine for a while, when the problem—the war—was obvious and the enemy—the "masters of war"—so easily demonized. But later, after the war, when the work of effecting political change required years of study, sacrifice, and ongoing determination, the cohort could not cope.

The War at Home

With all the jaunty youthfulness and joy of the Beatles' *Sgt. Pepper* album, there was also a note of sadness. Behind the colorful bravado, beneath the bounce and brass of rebellion and contrariness, lay alienation and the foreshadowing of despair. For a few years, it was unclear why Sgt. Pepper was so sad and "lonely." As the era unfolded, as the struggles continued and then were lost, as many despaired, were lost to drugs, emptiness, and the war, the generation learned why Sgt. Pepper was so upset.

Although Lyndon Johnson's early presidency was a spectacular legislative success, the late sixties brought an increasing grief and pessimism. There were things that Johnson could not control, like the rebellions in the inner cities in the mid- to late sixties, which were a response to the centuries of abuse, degradation, and death that had been inflicted on the black community. Johnson did not do all he could to respond, undoubtedly he could not really understand the rebellions, but at the same time he also did not use the entire arsenal of police-state tactics that he had at his command. Johnson also could do nothing about the assassinations of Malcolm X in 1965, of Dr. King in March 1968, and then of Robert Kennedy in June of the same year, on the night of his triumph in the California primary, which, taken together, crushed the nation as no foreign enemy could.

Yet the inner-city rebellions were not the nadir of Johnson's reign; neither were the assassinations. Something far worse caused his downfall—all the worse because it was something he *did* have control over, something he could have stopped, something he never should have allowed to escalate: Vietnam. That is the word that sounded the plague-bell of the postwar cohort and crushed whatever they could have been. The war was unnecessary, stupid, cynical, hypocritical. It turns out that the whole long episode was a political lie from first to last, from Johnson's Bay of Tonkin "incident" to Nixon and Kissinger's cynical "Peace with Honor" slogan. For the generation that grew up white and middle-class, privileged, indulged, sheltered, and above all idealistic, it was the worst of all wars.

The baby boomers were raised with a sanitized view of U.S. history and an idealized view of their own place within that history. They were raised to believe that all countries should be motivated by benevolent and charitable motives and that their country more than any other acted in good faith around the world. The electronic magic of film and television, comic books and adventure stories, everyday experiences for this generation, carried on this fiction, as did their public school history classes. The adventures of Spin & Marty, Davey Crockett, and Beaver Cleaver hardly inspired critical thinking or a realistic appraisal of life in the real world of competitive capitalism, either domestically or in foreign affairs. Reactions to cold war hysteria, comic books, and television shows did not prepare baby boomers for their inevitable confrontation with perspectives other than those presented by Disney and General Motors. The young cohort was sent to college to become financially successful. Instead it learned to think, to study history, to spot a lie. Vietnam was the worst of wars because it was the kind of lie that the cohort was taught to see through and resist.

The baby boomers lost their innocence during the mid- to late sixties, in voter registration lines, protest marches, the sting of tear gas, the 1968 summer streets of Chicago, the stench of napalm. The world as it really was forced its way into the consciousness of the cohort; as youngsters in the fifties, they had watched the nightly news, disoriented and unbelieving, and saw the Montgomery, Alabama, bus boycott, the state troopers and their dogs attack protesters in Birmingham and threaten elementary school children in Little Rock. But it wasn't until they left home, went to college, and struggled with lessons about northern racism and their own draft boards, that they were shaken out of their complacency. They saw what U.S. soldiers did to that small country in their name and what was done to those soldiers because the nation forced them to go. The youth fought, they resisted; some were carted away to be terrorized and die in the war, some were jailed, some fled to other countries, some cheated and lied to escape the draft board, but none were untouched. And as the years went by, their sense of outrage grew along with their sense of betrayal. As the political battles intensified and the stakes increased, the social terrain became polarized. Families split apart, as sons fought with parents, parents (siding with their children) fought with grandparents, and factions within one generation fought amongst themselves.

Most of all, it was nearly impossible for the baby boom generation to locate a place to stand in order to give voice to their understandings, disagreements, outrages, and dreams. It was difficult for them to know where they stood because at that moment in time they didn't have much solid ground on which to stand. It is true that they were raised on a kind of moderately liberal idealism, but it was an idealism that often depended on a sanitized version of American history, denial of the everyday lives of people of color, women, the poor, and a denial of the intellectual and emotional poverty in white middle-class communities as well. The post–World War II generation was the product of the enormous sociohistorical forces that shaped the modern era in the West: industrialization, urbanization, secularization. In the process of immigrating from Europe, adapting to a new society, being exploited and exploiting the labor of others, conquering the indigenous peoples and taking their land, surviving the depression and World War II—in the process of all this, communities had been forever destroyed, traditions broken and discredited. In the place of family, community, and tradition, baby boomers were offered the anonymity of the suburbs, the banality of a watered-down, uncreative mainstream religion, the morals of Saturday morning cartoon shows, cultural messages embedded in countless thousands of thirty second television commercials.

The postwar generation was privileged, naive, and vaguely well-meaning, but on the whole shockingly unprepared for a sudden confrontation with the facts of late twentieth-century life. Made to deal with a complex, probably unsolvable series of moral challenges, they were overwhelmed. Confused, betrayed, and sometimes disillusioned, they felt they had nowhere acceptable to stand, except in places that they could construct by themselves. Out of the denial, one-dimensional idealism, and consumerism of mainstream postwar culture, they had to develop a new perspective. They tried to supplement their experience with more critical political and religious traditions from their own society and from others, but ultimately the patchwork effort fell short.

Slowly, the verve, creativity, and resolve of the baby boom generation broke under the strain. Nixon was reelected, even in the face of Watergate, the secret bombing raids throughout Southeast Asia, and various repellant domestic policies. The frustration grew to rage, the confusion led to despair, the wish for spiritual experiences flowed to easy drugs or an isolated, escapist, out-of-touch mysticism. The coalition of civil rights-antiwar-spiritual activists known as "the movement" collapsed under the weight of bickering factions, jealousies, confusion, rage, despair. It died of its own unfocused confusion and a task far, far too great.

The postwar generation had too much to fight against and not enough to fight *with*. For a few years the drafting of bright, college-educated sons of the white middle class forced average Americans to face long-standing political issues that in earlier times had been followed only by disaffected intellectual minorities (such as the Beatniks and before them the expatriate writers in Paris) or the powerless minorities (people of color and the underclass). Middle-class whites experienced directly and personally the brutality, inequalities, and hypocrisies of the system. They were, for a moment, without the insulation of the privileges of class and race. They had to face the issues because they had no choice. It is rare for the middle class to have nothing to lose—and therefore it is rare for it to be radicalized, but this was one of those moments. The experience was over fairly quickly, because soon there came first the lottery and then the declaration of "peace." But those who lived through this time developed an increased sensitivity, understanding, and a motivation to study and sacrifice for radical political change.

But the moment ended. Without the draft, middle-class Americans again had too much to lose by advocating change, and without the war they were again confronted with political issues too complex for them to solve or even easily understand. Relieved of the desperation brought about by the war and its easily-understood problems, complete with an easily demonized enemy, the movement lost its broad middle-class support. Without that base, its ranks became vulnerable to the seductions of advertising, affluence, and the fears of economic insecurity. The movement split apart, became increasingly marginalized, and finally ceased to be a viable political force.

For those baby boomers crushed by years of frustration and sacrifice, consumerism offered the promise of material luxury; for those hounded and fearful, there was the promise of safety and peace. For those inclined toward the spiritual, there was the promise of unimagined highs through drugs or the exotic techniques and psycho-religious technologies of encounter groups and the human potential movement. For those confused and floundering, there was the promise of pure truth and perfect certainty through complete surrender to an authoritarian, charismatic guru. For those lacking in self-confidence and self-esteem, there was the promise of happiness, popularity, and sex appeal through the purchase of the proper commercial products. For those who had given up on the possibility of common goals and cooperative political action, there was the promise of personal achievement and the accumulation of wealth. For those despairing of the morality of public life and the efficacy of political activity, there was the promise of turning inward to mysticism, self-actualization, or individual psychotherapy. These were all expensive choices that required the sacrifice of money, time, dedication, critical thinking, or long-held political hopes and dreams. But the options were seductive and alluring.

Baby boomers bought them, in part, because it was what they were trained to do from their first breath: it was in their bones; it was them. And because there was no alternative.

The years passed, presidents paraded by, the causes came and went. Their despair and confusion was converted into new, more practical graduate schools, more realistic career choices, worries about life insurance "protection" and childcare, a preoccupation with real estate prices, and occasional abuses of credit cards.

In 1980, the cruelest joke of all was played on the baby boom generation: Ronald Reagan, the California governor who cut his political teeth on misunderstanding and brutally suppressing the Berkeley antiwar movement, came to power. For many in the cohort Reagan's election as president was unthinkable, unimaginable, beyond comprehension—yet it happened. In fact, it happened in part because a sizeable number of baby boomers voted for him, especially for his second term. Reagan's handlers, playing on the country's greed, depending on its political despair and exhaustion, using the media as an extension of their own public relations department, defeated the incumbent Jimmy Carter and installed Reagan as the fortieth president of the United States. Although Reagan's presidency has been portrayed by some as a time of safety and prosperity, others such as Donald Bartlett and James Steele, Kathleen Jamieson, and Michael Rogin have argued that his policies undermined the middle-class, blamed the poor for their problems, and lined the coffers of the rich.[24] As president, Reagan instituted a regime of insult and oppression at home and combined that with untruths and terror abroad. If the number of arrests and indictments and the amount of lost taxpayer money are used as a yardstick, his administration was the most corrupt and illegal in American history, surpassing even Warren Harding's with its Teapot Dome scandal and Nixon's with its Watergate cover-up. As the nineties progress, continuing revelations surface regarding details of the Iran arms-for-hostage deal, the funding and cover-ups of the death squads of the Salvadoran military, Oliver North's uncontrolled Lone Ranger activities, and the savings and loan debacle.

Ironically, although the Reagan administration will go down in history as one of the most dishonest and cynical in history, it will also be remembered as one of the most popular. This paradox can only be understood as part of the larger dynamic that characterizes the postwar era in general and the last twenty years in particular: consumerism, and the origin and functions of the configuration of the predominant self of the postwar era, the self that makes consumerism possible, the empty self.

THE SELF AND ITS PSYCHOLOGICAL "POTENTIAL"

The liberationist, transformational ideology of the era was reflected in the discipline of psychology as well as in music and politics. Several new theories about human interaction, illness, and cure emerged in the postwar years. Jungian ideas about myth, dreams, and the unconscious appealed to and were readily adopted by the youthful counterculture. Although never occupying a dominant position in the psychotherapy landscape, Jung's theories about personality types, the dialectic between dominant and disowned traits, the power of the archetypes (especially in reference to gender), the psychological importance of spirituality, the attraction of ritual, and the timeless journey of psychic transformation were ideas well suited to baby boomers of an esoteric bent, of which there were many. Writers such as Joseph Campbell popularized some of Jung's ideas, such as the hero's journey, and parlayed them into near-celebrity status. Unfortunately, some of Jung's most popular ideas—such as the timelessness of the archetypes—fall prey to the philosophical problems occasioned by all structuralist theories. That is, because structuralism is by definition ahistorical, it tends to unknowingly reify the current historical moment, thus justifying the current configuration of the self and in turn justifying and supporting the larger sociopolitical arrangements of the day. This criticism seems particularly apt in reference to popularized Jungian concepts such as "the Self" and the supreme value of individuation. These two concepts make it possible for some Jungians to join forces with aspects of object relations theory, creating an evocative but also problematic mix.[25] However, it should also be noted that with the usual passel of problems with structuralism comes one of its positive traits as well: Jungian archetypes—thought to be inherent and thus always available—do not appear to constitute an empty self in the same way that object relations theory and self psychology do.

In this way Jungian theory is less a good fit for the post–World War II cultural clearing than it at first appears. Although Jungian thinking about culture often appears to be just another kind of disappointing tokenism, James Hillman has developed a forceful critique of postwar psychotherapy practices that draws from cultural and political arguments and at times appears to border on the hermeneutic.[26] Hillman features an appeal to a romantic, premodern world of mythical beings and envisions a type of enlivened counter-Enlightenment "pantheism" as an alternative to the late modern era's emphasis on the unified, expressivist, deeply unique humanism inherent in most forms of psychodynamic psychotherapy. His jeremiad about the problematics of therapy has been a contribution to the current confrontation the profession is having with itself.

A second innovative creation of the postwar era has been family therapy.[27] A true child of the communications revolution of the last century, family therapy started out with a grounding in sociology, a focus on interactional processes, and a concern with social context and the force of interactive systems.

Family therapy actually has a relatively old lineage in the United States, its predecessors reaching back to the settlement houses, social workers, child-guidance clinics, and educators working with speech and developmental disabilities. But it required the *chutzpah* of the postwar years for therapy to take the innovative leap into a new treatment modality. As befits a brash young upstart, family therapy revels in a particularly iconoclastic "origin myth," first revealed by John Elderkin Bell.[28] In a 1951 conversation, Bell heard that "a Dr. Bowlby" was experimenting with "group therapy with families." Bell was intrigued and decided to give the new form a try, and the rest is history. Several years later Bell discovered, much to his surprise, that Bowlby meant something quite different from what Bell thought he meant. Bowlby met only very occasionally with the whole family, and then for only specific reasons. Bell's misunderstanding launched a whole movement. In America, psychological inventions even take their inventors by surprise! Ever since that moment, family therapists have been using metaphor and paradox to describe and bring about change.

From that humble beginning, family therapy has matured into an important and respected treatment modality. Currently family therapy is comfortable with videotaping therapy sessions, one-way mirrors, consulting teams that actively intervene in the therapeutic hour, and postmodern concepts such as narrative and constructivism. Because family therapy is commonly thought by professionals and lay people alike to be a practice responsible for the intervention and treatment of in-the-moment emergencies such as family violence and sexual abuse, drug addiction, and divorce and custody issues, it is commonly focused on practical issues and utilizes interventions that are often more behavioral and directive than those in individual modalities. Family therapy has also been prominent in struggling with one of the most crucial current and future treatment issues: the impact of race and ethnicity within the therapy hour. In all of these issues one can see the salience of post–World War II era values such as a concern for the disempowered (such as children and the working class), concerns regarding the cost and effectiveness of therapy (resulting in brief therapy practices), and the importance of personal vitality and expressiveness as signs of health (resulting in a revisioning of the role of the therapist and a redefinition of the goals of therapy).

It is also a testament to the power of self-contained individualism that even a modality such as family therapy—one seemingly dedicated to the study and uses of social interaction—has a continuing difficulty developing a historically situated perspective on its practices. It is thus often unable to conceive of social interaction and the salience of cultural influence beyond the rather isolated interactions contained within the couples dyad or the nuclear or at most extended family unit. As a result, family therapy has not been immune from the effects of individualism, the construction of the empty self, various ideological pop psychology bandwagons, or the seductive possibilities promised in the uses of systems theory in the corporate workplace.

A preoccupation with "the self," its natural qualities, its growth, its "potential," abstracted out of and removed from the sociopolitical, became increasingly prominent in the post-war years. The changes that had begun immediately after the war, such as those chronicled in *Gasoline Alley* (discussed in chapter three) had been enlarged upon and intensified by the late sixties. Individualism in the postwar era, less and less leavened by communal commitments and moral traditions, was endlessly promoted by the advertising industry and implicitly elevated to an unquestioned social value. The public was increasingly driven by escalating wishes for personal recognition and sensual gratification and tantalized by the prizes of an economic boom and the promise of possible electronic fame.

Humanistic psychology started as a rebellion against what it characterized as both the mechanistic, formalized, elitist psychoanalytic establishment and an overly scientistic, removed, fragmenting behaviorism. In 1964 a group of humanists met in Old Saybrook, Connecticut, to discuss a "Third Force" in the discipline of psychology that would be neither Freudian nor experimentalist. Out of that meeting came the movement called humanistic psychology. It sought to change the entire focus of psychology. With its roots in the values of existentialism, humanism, and the sixties liberation movements, the Association for Humanistic Psychology (AHP) developed a philosophical platform based on

1. a centering of attention on the experiencing *person*, and thus a focus on experience as the primary phenomenon in the study of man;

2. an emphasis on such distinctively human qualities as choice, valuation, and self-realization;

3. an allegiance to meaningfulness in the selection of problems for study and of research procedures;

4. an ultimate concern with and valuing of the dignity and worth of man and an interest in the development of the potential human inherent in every person.[29]

Humanistic psychology quickly grew in numbers and hopefulness. By 1966 psychologist James Bugental announced that

> a major breakthrough is occurring at the present time in psychology. Like man's other major changes—the introduction of the steam engine, the decline of feudalism, the beginnings of the laboratory method in psychology—its presence and potentialities are difficult to recognize for those of us who are so deep in daily concerns. Yet, I am convinced that the parallels I cite are not vainglorious. I think we are on the verge of a new era in man's concern about man which may—if allowed to run its course—produce as profound changes in the human condition as those we have seen the physical sciences bring about in the last century.[30]

Bugental described humanistic psychology as "a tremendously exciting development in our field of psychology. . . . [We are] getting back to what psychology seemed to most of us to mean when we first entered the field. We are returning to what psychology still seems to mean to the average, intelligent layman, that is, the functioning and experience of a whole human being."[31]

Humanistic psychology was part of a larger cultural trend within the Western intelligentsia that was affected by various Soviet atrocities and military and police-state adventures such as the 1939 German-Soviet pact, the 1956 Hungarian Revolution, the Korean War, Khrushchev's revelations regarding Stalin's abuses of power, and the Sino-Soviet split. The intelligentsia and the Left were disillusioned by the string of atrocities perpetrated by the Soviets. As a result, many European and American intellectuals shied away from direct political activity and withdrew into an isolated, subjective, alienated world described by philosophers Jean-Paul Sartre and Albert Camus in their earlier works such as *Nausea* and *The Stranger*. The post–World War II splits, fragmentations, and internecine battles within the Left can be traced in part to this disillusionment and the inward turn that it brought on. The turn inward also influenced aspects of humanistic psychology. Although after the war

Sartre became more political, the publication of his English translations lagged far behind the original European publications. His earlier, more apolitical pre-1946 works, such as *Nausea, Being and Nothingness*, and *The Flies*, were the only ones available in English to most Americans in the sixties. Unfortunately, his subsequent, more political work, was difficult to find in English—especially in America—and philosophers that attacked apolitical existentialism, such as Heidegger and Gadamer, were not translated and/or available until much later.[32] Sartre's *Critique of Dialectical Reason*, for instance, was translated in 1976, most of Heidegger in the seventies and eighties (for instance *Basic Problems in Phenomenology* in 1975), and Gadamer's *Truth and Method* in 1975. As a result, humanist alternatives to orthodox psychoanalysis and academic psychology in the sixties were informed by a European existentialism that was not current, decidedly apolitical, and thus sometimes thrown off stride and then used by postwar capitalism and its emerging consumerist ethos.

But many humanistic psychologists weren't aware of this discrepancy and had no reason to wonder about it, because their critique of mainstream psychology fit so well with the zeitgeist of the new era. Humanistic psychology's liberationist, transcendental, expressivist tendencies, combined with an optimistic, pragmatic stance, moved it in a direction often compatible with the energetic, flamboyant, on-the-make, sometimes nihilistic, always consumer-oriented postwar landscape.

Bugental's enthusiasm and hopefulness captured the flavor of the times and the excitement of the innovators. Humanistic psychologists felt as if they were riding the wave of a new force, about to usher in a new way of being. The future, they felt certain, was theirs. Small retreat/training centers, such as Esalen Institute in Big Sur, California, sprouted up. Esalen came to embody the glories and the contradictions of the movement. Every new form of creative philosophy, psychotherapy, or educational technology could be found at Esalen. Overlooking the beautiful Big Sur coastline, it became famous for encounter groups, movement and dance therapy, human potential workshops, bodywork, massage, and nude hot tubbing—experiential learning of every kind. The activities engaged in at Esalen would seem to require an amount of leisure time and expendable income unavailable (and cultural interests distasteful) to the working class and underclass. It started by bringing in the likes of Aldous Huxley, Paul Tillich, Norman O. Brown, and Arnold Toynbee, and then attracted psychology media stars such as Abraham Maslow, Carl Rogers, Will Schutz, Bernard Gunther, Virginia Satir, Gideon Schwarz, Jack Downing, Barry Stevens, George Leonard, and Rollo May. However, the brightest star in the firmament was the guru of gestalt therapy, Fritz Pearls; he became the resident celebrity of Esalen, alternately dazzling and disgusting the participants of his public therapy workshops. Michael Murphy, one of the cofounders of Esalen, called Pearls

> the greatest turner-oner of them all!! Though he would some-times humiliate people, they would gladly participate in his dream workshops which were fantastic! It was the damnedest thing! There was often a lot of learning, and usually a lot of humor, but it was certainly show biz. One time we decided to have a "Being" laboratory where everybody would get to-gether and talk the "Being" language. It was a disaster! It ended with Fritz crawling across the floor. . . . At the height of all this, Abe Maslow leans over to me and he says, "This begins to look like sickness."[33]

In both the AHP platform and in Murphy's description of Fritz Pearls we can see the good and the bad of the postwar ethos: the rebellion against mechanistic formalism, a valorization of freedom and individual worth, a striving for personal responsibility and improvement, yet at the same time a blindness to the problems inherent in vague categories such as "experience," a lack of historical perspective on the construction of the self and the ethnocentrism and classism inherent in the values of a hypertrophied individualism, a self-righteous devaluation of opposing points of view, a difficulty in opposing the advance of nihilism, and a blind acceptance of the romantic vision of the inner truth, inherent potential, and personal liberation of the true self. Above all, what stands out in the AHP's ethos is its unquestioned embrace of the post–World War II configuration of the self: the self of humanistic psychology was subjective, often antitraditional, ahistorical, and preoccupied with indi-vidualist concerns such as personal choice, self-realization, and the apo-litical development of personal potential. By 1978 the movement had become so enthralled with subjective individualism that Bugental could argue, "The dream of being God is the dream of being most truly what we are. . . . Human beings must certainly recognize at last that each is the center of a subjective universe. We are God. . . . We may yet preserve the possibilities which are latent in our very being. . . . We are not the crea-tures we imagined. We can become the creators of what will be."[34]

In a way, these values are rooted in a strain of American individual-ism and liberationist theory that is historically important and may have a certain utility in everyday twentieth-century life. But in psychological theory these values are rarely grounded in a historical perspective, they float like isolated beliefs, unattached to communal practices and a body of traditions and shared meanings. Unfortunately, the more these values became separated from the historical situation in which they were embedded, the more they were used by elements of the society to manipulate the population for commercial and political purposes. Commercials using the implicit meanings of self-enhancement, actualization, and unending gratification have become commonplace, whether the product is toothpaste, an automobile, a weekend workshop on releasing anger, schooling for a career change, or a divorce attorney. At its best humanistic psychology displayed an alternative, creative, critical voice; it appeared ambivalent about but ultimately still supported an extreme individualism and an interest in the liberation (that is, "self-actualization") of an apolitical self. At its worst, it spawned authoritarian organizations selling prepackaged, nihilistic "transformational" technologies damaging to participants and dangerous to the body politic.

Floating in decontextualized, isolated space, some late twentieth-century outgrowths of the human potential movement have produced more than their share of bizarre theories, exploitative practices, and authoritarian, sadistic charismatic leaders. Particularly problematic applications of these practices have shown up in spiritual-therapeutic cults, such as the Rajneesh cult, Polarity Fellowship, or mass-marathon psychology trainings.[35] Researchers and ex-members have reported that some mass-marathon trainings are deceitful, coercive, manipulative, focused on controlling participants, and financially exploitive. The training program organizations usually orchestrate large weekend "educational" programs that claim to help participants get in touch with their "true, inner feelings." But many of these training sessions develop a highly structured, coercive process that is secretly designed to "prove" the group's specific ideology and produce a conversion experience. This ideology, presented in the guise of psychological truths and humanistic values such as individual choice, personal responsibility, and true feelings, coerces participants into an ever accelerating involvement with the program, including persuading them to give the organization their money and labor. Lawsuits regarding issues ranging from deceitful sales practices, to conducting psychotherapy without a license, to wrongful death have been numerous and are usually settled out of court and therefore sealed from public view. Some researchers have suggested that the psychological damage that is sometimes the consequence of these trainings has been greatly underreported and underestimated.

The power wielded by charismatic gurus, therapists, and group facilitators, and the abuse of that power, has been part of the underside of the postwar era. Ironically, some of the psychotherapeutic movements that most valued the liberationist motif and the romantic concept of the transformation of the individual self have been the most vulnerable to authoritarianism, to the loss of critical thinking and personal autonomy, and subsequently, to abuses of power. Of the many disillusionments suffered by the baby boom generation in its young adulthood, the betrayals perpetrated by the liberationist, romantic, human potential psychotherapies have been among the most puzzling and profound.

THE EMPTY SELF AND THE POST-WORLD WAR II ERA

The tradition of self-contained individualism has certainly been the predominant ideology of American middle-class life, with roots that go far back in Western history, reaching especially to the Enlightenment era in Europe. Mastery and boundedness have opened up capacities for individual agency and initiative, personal autonomy, and critical thinking that have been productive in Western society. Modern science, medicine, scholarship, capitalism, and industrialization were all made possible by this way of thinking about human being. But especially when competing human forces such as community and tradition have been discredited or destroyed, mastery and boundedness work against cooperating and sacrificing for the good of the group. By the late twentieth century, the combination of industrial capitalism, large-scale immigration, the loss of community and tradition, and the press of consumerism has resulted in a landscape in which relatedness usually shows up either as the result of a social profit-loss calculus, as the product of the isolated parent-child dyad (and later in life, the romantic dyad), or as part of the impression management and personnel manipulations of the workplace. This is indeed a bleak, unsafe landscape with only very limited space for social interaction. Isolation and dissatisfaction have become a taken-for-granted way of life.

As a result, individuals, especially middle-class individuals, have struggled with feelings of unreality, hopelessness, low self-esteem, and despair. Despite the openness, optimism, and expressive confidence that earlier twentieth-century Americans displayed, the emptiness that has evolved is now far too prevalent to be dismissed. It constitutes the underside of mastery and boundedness. The empty self has become the predominant configuration of our era.

Through the empty self concept I mean to convey the prevalence of the subjective experience of interior lack, absence, emptiness and despair, the desperate yearning to be loved, soothed, and made whole by filling up the emptiness. This is how the empty self works: the insatiable, gnawing sense of internal emptiness drives individuals to yearn to be filled up; to feel whole, solid, self-confident, in contact with others. Advertising preys on this yearning by linking it with images and slogans from liberationist ideology. In our society advertising functions as a "therapeutic," a way of healing the empty self of the viewer. Ads promise a personal transformation, implying that by purchasing and consuming the product, "taking it in," consuming it, becoming one with it, the consumer's self will be built and the consumer's identity will become magically transformed. This transformation process is particularly effective in television advertising, because the medium itself rests on a kind of perceptual, passive consuming of images. Advertisments promise that the transformational healing will come about when the consumer ingests the accoutrements of the model or celebrity featured in the ad, which will automatically liberate, set free, the core spiritual power that is hidden inside the consumer, and which will implant, build, or increase in power the secret, divine energy of the consumer's enchanted interior. I have referred to this advertising strategy as the "lifestyle solution" because the transformation comes about because the individual has consumed and metabolized the accoutrements, the lifestyle, of the celebrity in the ad.

This advertising strategy works in part because it is not only *material* commodities that the empty self craves. Given that in our commodified world almost everything "shows up" as a commodity, and given that individuals are painfully aware of their personal confusion, lack of self-confidence and self-assurance, it seems understandable that individuals want to emulate celebrities who demonstrate certainty, confidence, and assurance. We call these traits charisma. Charismatic leaders such as entertaining artists, sports heroes, and political leaders are used today as part of a lifestyle solution strategy to sell products, experiences, and to develop voter loyalty in political elections.

The election of Ronald Reagan as president is an excellent example of how the empty self dynamic was used to manipulate voters (consumers) to purchase (vote for) and consume (merge with) a candidate. It is unlikely that Reagan's political platform was the reason for his success; it was as simple in its rhetoric as a B movie. Reagan knew little about the actual issues of the day, about how little his proposals made sense, about how ultimately damaging his policies were and continue to be to the country. His vice presidential running mate, George Bush, once called Reagan's policies "voodoo economics." It is much more likely that Reagan was elected because he projected a persona of calmness, self-confidence, and absolute certainty. He made people feel that he knew exactly what he was doing, and that he was absolutely comfortable and assured about it. Reagan acted as though he felt the way individual citizens wished they could feel about themselves. Citizens, in an uncertain and difficult time, wanted to feel the way Reagan appeared to feel. President Carter, Reagan's 1980 opponent, had told the country that they were in a "malaise." Carter himself, some commentators noted, acted as if *he* was in a malaise. Voters didn't want to feel the way Carter felt. They wanted to be like Reagan, and bask in his self-assurance; they wanted to *feel* the way Reagan felt.

In other words, Reagan was sold the way all commercial products are sold. There is nothing new in this idea; commentators have been writing about the selling of the President since Joe McGinniss reported Nixon's advertising strategy in the presidential election of 1968.[36] It is the *way* Reagan was sold that is important. The dynamic between Reagan and the people was closer to that of a cult guru and his disciples than a statesman and his constituency. By identifying with, imitating, and finally voting for Reagan, the voter was implicitly promised an interior transformation. The "Morning in America" advertising theme of the 1980 election sold a feeling, an attitude about the country and its citizens. It wasn't about trickle-down economic theory (which exacerbated our now disastrous national debt), a refusal to be intimidated by the Iranian terrorists (the administration secretly tried to bribe them to free the hostages), or true conservative policies (Reagan operatives consistently ignored or violated the Constitution when it suited their purposes). The election (in fact Reagan's entire eight-year presidency) was designed to present the candidate as a transformational object, a celebrity who could be purchased and "ingested" in order to liberate consumers from their emptiness and despair. And the technique worked beautifully.

Of course, the empty self dynamic and the use of the lifestyle solution is not confined only to soft drink commercials and political campaigns. There seems little doubt that charismatic leaders of all types, such as religious gurus, cult leaders, the leaders of mass-marathon psychology training sessions, and even unethical psychotherapists use the society-wide despair and helplessness to force participants to spend money and subject themselves to techniques that subsequently manipulate and exploit them. The wish to idealize, "take in," and consume the charismatic figure, and thus a new identity, a new life, can be compelling, especially when the potential consumer is surrounded by others who have already purchased the product, merged with the leader, and are vocal about their new, cured self and their transformed life. Therapists who are hungry for adulation and power can easily create overidealization and submission (whether it be psychological, sexual, or political) within the therapy setting. The occurrence of sexual exploitation of the patient within the therapy setting, which appears to be more common than previously thought,[37] could be partially explained by this dynamic. Emotional and financial exploitation and psychological damage within restrictive cults, with religious, psychological, or political themes[38] and mass-marathon psychology training sessions,[39] can be similarly understood. But what about the voices of resistance to this dark, Orwellian vision? How have psychotherapists, those responsible for studying and healing the self in our society, resisted and/or been influenced by the empty self dynamic? Has the empty self dynamic also influenced their theories?

PSYCHOTHERAPY THEORY AND THE CONSTRUCTION OF THE EMPTY SELF

Probably many psychotherapists believe that their practices are an effective means of resisting consumerism's complete sociopolitical triumph. However, during the course of my struggles with the philosophical ideas and the historical perspective discussed in this book, I have come to a disquieting conclusion: psychotherapists have been slow to recognize the discipline's role in sustaining the empty self and contributing to the shape of the overarching twentieth-century frame of reference it serves. Several therapists have publically opposed various aspects of the status quo. Heinz Kohut, for instance, spoke to this issue when he disagreed with the positive emphasis ego psychology placed on adapting to one's social milieu.[40] But as a profession therapy seems uncomfortable with grappling with how therapy practices are *unintentionally* political and how they unknowingly reinforce the status quo. Therapists think that because they guard against valuing adaptation at all costs, or because they believe that the patient's mental "health" will automatically translate into a correct political position, they are not contributing to the status quo. But if they think these kinds of answers satisfy the above concerns, they are wrong.

Most therapists have not been trained in the kind of philosophical and political analysis that is required to understand the more subtle and complex ways that social practices *inevitably* reproduce the status quo. I'm sure there are exceptions to this statement, but these momentary shifts to a historical and cultural perspective are probably too confusing and threatening for most of us to maintain, and are soon avoided and then forgotten. Just because we "forget" these issues, however, doesn't mean that they disappear.

First and foremost, psychotherapists have not been able to develop a historically situated perspective on our discourse and practices. Our failure to think about our practices as part of our culture and history is owing in part to the intellectual traditions in which the field is rooted and to which the field is indebted. Each of the previous chapters has been an attempt to illustrate this. Our failure to think historically is also a result of our wish to earn a living, do well financially, be accepted in the social world in which we live. To take the intellectual plunge and situate our work historically would jeopardize that. We would have to face the fact that we treat local selves plagued by local illnesses, not the one universal self that suffers from a few timeless illnesses. If we admit that, we could not claim that these illnesses can be treated with a universal healing technology that we have scientifically proven to be the one, true healing technique.

In other words, if we begin down that slippery slope of history, we lose our grip on the powerful social status that is granted to scientific practices and theories. If we lose that, then we will be seen as philosophers, sociologists, humanists—not medical scientists. The position of privilege we enjoy, albeit tenuously, in our scientific, hierarchical society today would be challenged. This would reverse the intellectual battles the social sciences have waged for the last four hundred years, long before there was thought to be such a thing as social science, to carve out a place within the intellectual academy and the capitalist marketplace. It would reverse the discipline's hard-fought gains and reduce its practices to a kind of moral and literary discourse, a fate worse than death in a world that values "hard" science over "soft-headed" philosophy.

Furthermore, there is another problem in store for psychotherapists if they were to start thinking about their work sociohistorically. Developing a historical perspective about the discipline's practices would lead therapists to notice how some of the foundational philosophical elements of modern Western thought, such as the Cartesian split between matter and spirit, or the correspondence theory of objective truth, have led to the kind of political structures and moral dilemmas that the discipline faces today. In other words, if we were to undertake a serious study of how psychotherapy contributes to the construction of the empty self and consumerism, we would see that revolutionary changes would have to come about for there to be a shift out of the frame of reference of our current world. We would have to face great despair, continuingly fighting frustration and hopelessness. Who among us would voluntarily submit to that? We would, if we decided to go ahead with the project, have to rework the philosophical way we think and especially the way we speak. We would have to start trying to weed out the Cartesian concepts from our vocabulary, and we might start sounding like some of those abstruse philosophers such as Foucault, Derrida, Deleuze, and Lacan.

However, there is an even worse fate awaiting us if we start situating psychotherapy historically. We would come to see that even the most sophisticated and humane psychotherapy theorists, those who seem concerned with social interaction, the examined inner life, and loving, intimate relationships—like Winnicott and Kohut—even these, perhaps especially these, significantly although unknowingly, have contributed to the consumerism of the postwar era. This is a disturbing prospect because it reveals our personal confusion and inadequacy, and those of our leaders as well.

Why Winnicott and Kohut?

I do not feature Donald Winnicott and Heinz Kohut because I believe them to be the malevolent perpetrators of the consumerism of the postwar era, or of incompetent, exploitive, or abusive psychotherapy. They aren't responsible for any of the above. They were both highly ethical individuals who were dedicated to ameliorating the suffering of others. I feature them because they are *exemplars* of our time. Their theories and the commentaries of their followers wrestle with many of the major issues of our society. They have captured something central about our era's way of being human; they speak to us, in our joy and misery. They describe us, and because of that they have achieved respect in our society and among their peers.

Because their theories have been so popular of late, and have been translated into the social practices of psychotherapy, developmental theory, advice books, and parenting programs, it stands to reason that they have influenced and shaped the era more than most. However, when I suggest that Winnicott and Kohut have influenced the era, I mean something specific. I mean that object relations theory and self psychology have shaped the era the way *all* social practices shape an era— unknowingly, subtly, by contributing to setting the cultural frame of reference.

Social practices are not consciously planned, deceptive, or coercive; They further the status quo by, at first, reflecting the cultural landscape of an era. By reflecting the overall framework, by using a certain language and implicitly expecting certain behaviors and actions, social practices reinforce and then perpetuate the rules of the game. Rules are set by the thousands of unconscious microbehaviors that are the warp and woof, the Sullivan's web, of everyday life: the warm welcome of a hello, the contracting of joyful wrinkles around the eyes, a tilt of the head, the quick raising of the eyebrow, the quiet sound of surprise, the murmur of dissent, the step backward, the rapid loss of facial expression, the sentence that ends with a low, cold note, the body held in quiet disdain. Social practices set the frame not by forcing, abusing, and torturing, but by treating the established, implicit, unspoken rules of the game as the only proper way of human being.

All of this is done as subtext, between the lines of social dialogue. Social practices, especially intellectual discourse like psychotherapy, influence by being not the hammer that pounds, but the brush that paints. Scenes are brought into view through language, cultural metaphors, and habitual activities that set the parameters of what is possible; within a particular scene, certain things can then "show up," and others cannot. We could say that Winnicott and Kohut were, and in fact we all are, trapped by our language and rituals, but that would be inaccurate. Culture does not trap, it insinuates, it constitutes, it constructs. It is "sedimented" in the body. Just as culture frames life in such a way as to permit certain things to "show up" in a specific clearing, so too, inevitably, does it exclude other things from appearing. That is a type of power.

Winnicott and Kohut were attempting to offer constructive alternatives to certain elements of the status quo. I do not believe they were the evil twins of late twentieth-century capitalism. But they lived within a certain frame, were thus constituted by it, and in various ways perpetuated it.

DONALD WINNICOTT AND THE EMERGENCE OF THE SELF

As discussed in the previous chapter, Melanie Klein helped psychoanalysis take an important leap forward. Her ideas helped psychoanalysis become more complex and interior, join the social trend fascinated with social interaction, and develop a frame that gave us the capacity to discuss issues such as envy, hatred, and rage in ways more in step with mid-century Western culture. Most important, she discussed social interaction and avoided situating psychotherapy within history and culture, thus reproducing self-contained individualism and maintaining her good standing in mainstream psychoanalysis. There is no evidence available to us, of course, that indicates that Klein did any of this consciously or purposely. Her theory developed the way all intellectual achievements develop: they appear. And they appear because they fit with their era. She neutralized the potentially radical political effects of social theory by locating the rough and tumble of social interaction *inside* the self. Because Klein did not develop a comprehensive historical perspective on the practices of psychotherapy, her theory had the effect of relegating social interaction to a kind of theoretical tokenism. To Klein, object relations meant the interactions between and among inherent, internal psychic *structures*, which contained universal impulses/feelings/expectations, and not the dialogical call and response of one human to another. Although Klein insisted that her theory was not a deviation from Freud, in hindsight it seems obvious that her concept of internal objects, Kantian-like structures resembling Jung's archetypes almost as much as Freud's three-part model, was indeed a departure. Because Klein subsumed the process of enculturation into the study of developmental psychology, she unintentionally developed a new and politically significant metaphor about the process of enculturation. This was crucial because by doing so she could then discuss infant development as a "taking in" of the parent, for example, the eating or regurgitating of the parent, without it being apparent to her or her readership that she was formulating a theory of development that was based on a consumer model.[41]

Scotland's Ronald Fairbairn, of all of Klein's followers, was the one who took the most radical theoretical step with Klein's ideas by suggesting that the primary activity or nature of the libido is not pleasure seeking, but object seeking; that is, the strongest motive in human life is to seek relationships, not impersonal energy discharge. This was a direct challenge to orthodox psychoanalysis. He also disagreed with Klein about the nature of psychic structures, arguing that internal objects are not inherent, unavoidable psychic structures, but memory-fantasy structures caused by painful or confusing parenting. Individuals, he believed, form imaginary objects when the *real* parenting is inadequate or dangerous, in an attempt to avoid the pain caused by inadequate parent-child interaction, and to provide a substitute parent through imaginary interactions. Fairbairn, Harry Guntrip, and Donald Winnicott came out of the so-called "Middle School" of British psychoanalysis. It was so named because during the disputes over theory in the British Psychoanalytic Institute, a loose confederacy of analysts refused to favor either Klein or Anna Freud. Although the Middle School seemed to favor Klein over Anna Freud, it chose the politic strategy of denouncing neither of them, and was thus able to learn and borrow from both.

Fairbairn and Guntrip made important contributions to English object relations theory, but it was the affable Winnicott, the English pediatrician, as well as his American followers, who brought object relations theory into the postwar era. Just as the masterful, bounded, feeling self slowly emerged out of the inchoate communality of the medieval era, so too did it emerge in post–World War II psychotherapy theory, rising out of the babble of mesmerism, mental hygiene, and ego psychology. As the modern self emerged in the history of Western society, and as the post–World War II self emerged in the history of psychotherapy theorizing, so too did post–World War II theories begin to picture the self as developing out of the undifferentiated infant-mother dyad of the early months of life. No one represented this trend, no one described it (and prescribed it), as well as Winnicott did.

Winnicott's theory focused on human-to-human relating. Unlike Klein, when Winnicott looked at the infant he did not see a bundle of inherent, internal structures that would sometimes turn the child into a monster. Neither did he conceptualize the process of relating as the archetypal interactions of those internal structures. Winnicott was not burdened with having to toe the Freudian line nearly as strictly as Klein had been. Freud had died soon after arriving in England, Anna Freud and Klein were focused on one another, most of the orthodox Freudians had moved to the United States, and in any event Winnicott was more the accommodator and synthesizer than the fighter. He quietly walked down his own, idiosyncratic path, which was then brought to the United States by his followers and came to be quite influential to psychodynamic psychotherapy in the later postwar years.

Winnicott wrote a kind of psychotherapeutic poetry. His ideas were a hymn to the postwar years and to the predominant self of that era. At the center of his theory, in fact at the center of his universe, stood the self. His work was a kind of do-it-yourself parenting handbook on how to construct the postwar self. More than any other twentieth-century analyst before him, Winnicott delivered practical instructions about how to raise a child in the postwar era. His articles, books, and BBC radio lectures (one series entitled "The Ordinary Devoted Mother") helped parents cope with the enormous difficulties of raising a family in the disorienting years immediately following the war. He was devoted to children, respectful of the innate capacities of mothers, and intensely focused on the microinterchanges between the two. He was sure that the secrets of human being were contained in the intimate space between caretaker and infant in the early months and years of life. Demonstrating his allegiance with Klein, Winnicott devoted himself to the study of infancy with an emphasis on object relating; demonstrating his agreement with Anna Freud, he was optimistic and protective of the child patient in therapy and studiously avoided her father's last ideas regarding the death instinct. He was a radical environmentalist, arguing as no analyst had before him that the child and its developing sense of self were shaped by the caretaking style of the parents. He developed a theory that moved from Klein's tokenism to a more straightforward, but still ahistorical approach to the social realm. His theory, and especially his description of the self, should be immediately recognizable to most citizens of middle-class postwar Western society. More than any theorist who had predated him, Winnicott implicitly described the era.

It is often said that Winnicott's psychology is a psychology of the dyad. He is rightly credited as one of the analysts who described a "two-person" developmental theory; that is, a theory that features the mutual interaction between infant and caretaker. He argued that there is no infant without a caretaker, usually a mother, and no mother without an infant: together they form the "nursing couple." If the mother could provide a "holding" environment for the infant—that is, if the mother could adequately focus on her, interpret her needs and provide for them, contain and survive her rage—the infant would then experience a relatedness and a sense of psychological safety that would nourish her and propel her into life. Secure in the holding environment, the infant could begin to develop her own unique individuality; she could develop trust, spontaneity, creativity, autonomy, and a sense of psychological and physical boundaries that would sustain her throughout her life.

Winnicott thought the process worked like this: In the beginning of life the infant and the mother are one unit. "The baby is . . . all these parts . . . gathered together by the mother who is holding the child and in her hands they add up to one."[42] Through what Ogden called the "protective, postponing envelop of the maternal holding environment,"[43] the mother anticipates the infant's needs, provides nourishment, stimulation, and safety, and does not intrude on the infant's private moments. Winnicott believed that the infant, if adequately contained in the holding environment, would develop an indispensable tool of growth: the illusion of omnipotence. The infant would come to believe that he somehow magically produced the breast, for instance, just by wanting it. The infant, by virtue of the mother's artful anticipations and timely responses, is thus protected from the terrifying awareness of separateness from and vulnerability to the mother and the world at large. Slowly, through the microinteractions of moment-by-moment call and response, the infant/mother learn about one another, adrift on a sea of mutual need and interaction.

Winnicott called this "play space," the experience in which the infant was neither "me" nor "not-me," neither one nor the other. The two-that-are-one move and shift in a timeless dance that takes place in the illusional space between them. The mother's dedicated gaze "mirrors" the infant reflecting back a vision of the infant that will come to be the infant's vision of herself. It is often said in object relations circles that the infant, looking in the mother's eyes, sees herself in her mother's loving gaze. After a time, the infant learns to respond in kind. A dialecti-cal experience evolves, one that will in the future help the infant develop a sense of her own unique way of life, safe from the dangers involved in experiencing the terrors of separateness too soon. In this "potential space," the infant can be safe to be spontaneous, creative, true to her impulses and feelings. She can develop the capacity to be fluid and expressive, to be alone, to be self-directed, to have a solid sense of self.

Over time, as the infant's abilities grow, the mother begins to do less anticipating of needs, which allows the child to express himself more directly. The baby becomes more complex, his needs less transparent. As a result, the mother also begins to make mistakes in her caretaking. The baby begins to face the reality of psychological separation from an imperfect mother who resides in an imperfect world. Winnicott referred to this moment as the "insult of reality"; he called the process "disillusion-ment." At this stage the dialectic between what Jay Greenberg and Stephen Mitchell have called "contact and differentiation"[44] has heated up. If the mother's mistakes are small enough, and the requirements of the moment simple enough, the baby can tolerate the frustrations and face the truth of separation. If the mother can realize her mistakes and repair the damage, the child can take another crucial step toward an autonomous self: the child can learn that although the world is not perfect, through complaint, response, and repair, it is at least bearable. Love, to Winnicott, is "failure and mending."

Propelled in part by the everyday exigencies of the world and in part by the natural push toward psychological separateness that Winnicott thought is inherent in all babies, the infant begins to deal with the inevitable disappointments of life. Winnicott coined the term "the good-enough mother" to indicate that a mother does not require superhuman intelligence, nor a wealth of technical knowledge, to nurture an infant, but simply the natural intuition of motherhood and the well-intentionedness to perform parenting functions in an adequate manner. If the mother meets the challenges, the baby grows up with an increasingly solid, strong, autonomous self. But if the mother does not adequately mirror the infant, or if she impinges too much on the infant's unstruc-tured privacy, if she cannot herself bear to be separate from her child, or if she is herself insulted or threatened by the baby's limits or its separate needs, then the child cannot naturally grow and unfold. The infant's self will be inhibited and stunted, focused on the mother rather than on its own needs and experiences, unable to be alone, to be emotionally ex-pressive, or unable to initiate and act autonomously.

It follows, then, that in Winnicott's schema the psychological quali-ties that constitute a mentally healthy self are those of integration, spontaneity, autonomy, and authenticity. Psychopathology, in turn, he defined as the constriction of emotional expressiveness and the lack of wholeness and trueness. Winnicott explained psychological regression as an attempt to return to a time when the environmental container failed, in order to redo the old unsatisfactory scenes. Psychoanalysis could cure patients, according to Winnicott, by providing the parental nutrients that had been missing or were distorted in earlier parent-child experiences. If the care is properly provided, Winnicott thought that the the self would be able to break out of the regression and grow again in a natural, unimpeded way. Antisocial behavior, for instance, was thought of as an unconscious attempt on the part of the adolescent to force the world to offer the proper psychological boundaries, boundaries that unfortunately had been nonexistent in the earlier parent-child relationship.

Throughout Winnicott's writing it is easy to notice Melanie Klein's strong influence. Although he did not agree with Klein's more extreme ideas, he did make use of her overall theoretical framework regarding internal objects, the process of introjection, projective identification, the significance of the depressive position, and the importance of reparation. Winnicott seemed to believe that the infant possesses inherent expectancies (that is, Klein's internal objects), although he thought they are much less decisive or specific than did Klein. Internal objects receive their content, Winnicott thought, when the mother's failures in empathy are extreme, causing the infant intolerably intense emotional responses to a sudden awareness of separateness. To protect herself against these feelings, the infant would imagine a microworld, peopled by internal objects whose functions were identical to the infant's own psychic trait of omnipotence. The objects, which Ogden referred to as "unconscious omnipotent internal objects,"[45] are fantasized for defensive purposes; they are not inherent givens. These omnipotent internal objects possess traits similar in nature to Klein's in that they were thought to be unforgiving, critical, rageful, punitive, controlling, envious, and so on.

However, Winnicott did not stop there, as did Klein; he went on to study the more reality oriented interactions between baby and mother in the everyday world. Winnicott hypothesized that when the baby is ready to deal with the awareness of separateness from the mother, he destroys the omnipotent internal objects that he has earlier created. The child then depends upon the external, real mother to be there emotionally, to hold and understand, even though he has attempted to destroy the mother. If the real mother can be there emotionally for the child, he then begins, through the process of introjection, to develop an internalized image of the real mother, which Ogden has called "the external-object-mother."[46] Slowly the baby comes to take in and assimilate the nurturing features of the real, good-enough mother. Failure to develop this type of good internal object causes the baby to cling to the more primitive, magical, omnipotent object, to become more rigid and more immersed in a punitive, hateful dynamic.

With the newly developing external-object-mother exerting more influence, occasionally the child is able to create transitional objects. These are magical creations, neither all internal nor all external, that bridge the gap between the mother's absence and her presence. They help the child to hold herself, to nurture and soothe herself in the absence of the real mother, and thus to better tolerate the inevitable frustrations and psychological separations of life. This is the rudimentary beginning of the mode of experiencing Klein referred to as the depressive position, when the baby begins to experience herself as a whole, unified being, and when she begins also to imagine her mother as a whole, real person. This leads the child to the realization that she has an immediate impact upon the mother. The awareness of her impact on the mother terrifies the child, since up to this point she has conceived of her fantasized attacks as being directed only at the bad mother, the part-object. The realization that the mother is not a split-off bad-object-mother, or alternatively, the split-off good-object-mother, but one person who sometimes acts bad and sometimes acts good, brings with it the understanding that the child can hurt the mother. This, in turn, moves the child to reach out to the mother and give her "gifts," such as smiles and affectionate sounds, in an attempt to repair and apologize to the mother. If the mother can demonstrate that she can survive the attacks and if she warmly accepts the child's gifts, the child has the opportunity to internalize an increasingly warm and mutually interactive partner. The child is also better able to notice and come to understand that there is both an internal, psychic reality and an external reality in life. The child learns that it can experience the dual nature of reality and can in fact distinguish between the two forms of reality.

One of Winnicott's most original contributions to the field, and one that most clearly demonstrates the profound influence of romantic thought on his theory, was his idea about the nature of the self. He argued that one of the great dichotomies in human life is the difference between what he called the "true self" and what he called the "false self." He thought the determination about which self would be predominant in the overall shape of the child's individual way of being in the world was the most fundamental issue in the life of the individual. It is fragile, this true self, quite vulnerable to danger, and indispensable to the life of the individual. It is imperative that the true self be allowed to unfold without external restriction or impingement; the fear of exploitation of the true self is the child's greatest terror. The true self develops in the child who is the product of the proper holding environment. In the safety and reliability of the mother's attention and concern, and in the "potential space" of play, the infant experiences the freedom to be spontaneous, expressive, and creative. The core essence of this little being, whatever it is, is allowed to come out and be expressed and presented to the world, to grow naturally, according to its own timetable and with its own very personal qualities. The true self flows, naturally unfolds, intuitively grows toward the light.

If the child, in its vulnerable dependency, is being held by a mother who fails to adequately provide the various behaviors that make up good-enough mothering, the child's true self will become hidden from view. Instead a more adaptive, compliant self, the false self, will develop. The false self exists so that the child can adapt to the abandoning or engulfing mother; the child tries to please and comply to the mother so that the mother will stay involved with the child. The false self also exists in order to protect the true self by drawing attention away from it, so that the true self can hide, far away from the criticisms, disappointments, and intrusions of the inadequate holding environment. The false self will do anything in order to stay involved with the mother; it will lie, collude, or cause damage. The false self will offer itself to be used, or it will use others, all without question or complaint. The overall task of the false self is to protect the true self from having to develop along the lines of another person's agenda. For the true self to be forced to develop differently than it naturally would is experienced as an annihilation or violation of the core essence, the unique potential, that lies within. Therefore the true self must be hidden, at whatever costs, from the dangers of the inattentive or intrusive other. For Winnicott, the greatest imperative of human life, perhaps we could say the greatest moral good, was to live a life that permits a natural unfolding of the honesty, the core truth, that expresses one's unique individuality.

All good things flow from the true self, unrestricted by the influences of the external world. Morality, for instance, can only be a true, honest expression of the individual's conscience if the individual has developed a strong true self that can integrate the external world's standards of right and wrong. If the psychological boundaries of the individual have not been well set in childhood, morality will either be felt as a type of unwanted, manipulative intrusion, as in antisocial behavior, or as a rigid, authoritarian aspect of the false self. Second, Winnicott thought that a democracy could only function in a nation comprised of citizens with masterful, bounded, feeling selves. If citizens had boundary confusion, or a lack of psychological autonomy, the democratic process would be taken over by dictatorship. Winnicott had the tendency to reduce most things, including politics, to the realm of developmental psychology.

Winnicott's theory sounds so smooth, so simpatico, so much a reflection of the post–World War II world and the values it holds dear. It exudes the ethos of what is thought of as humane child rearing, the vision of the self that is accepted without question as the one universal, or at least most advanced, form of human being. It is so much all of the above that it is hard to discern the change in values, the subtle but significant shift in perspective that has occurred, the shift in England that Winnicott both reflected and contributed to. First and foremost, the self has become an unquestioned, concrete "thing," a recognizable entity. It is universally acknowledged to be a self with specific psychological boundaries, a deep, interior core of initiative and mastery, and a private life of subjective emotion. It is understood that this self lives in a world that is extremely dangerous; the self's autonomy and integrity are in constant jeopardy, but the self is also positioned in the center of the world. It is our world's most prized possession, and everything, including parents, morality, and public policy, revolve around it. The building and liberation of the true self, the development of its integration, its capacity for emotion, expressiveness, boundedness, mastery, differentiation, and internal structures are the most important achievements of the individual and, by inference, of the society. The future of individual citizens within the society, the very foundations of democracy and law and order, is predicated on the proper growth of this particular self. Winnicott, in a decidedly romantic voice, argued that there is a core truth in each individual that should be the ultimate arbiter of right and wrong; it is the product of a native, intuitive goodness that is located in the innermost center of each of us, and it should not be questioned or tampered with. It is simply to be held, delighted in, and allowed to evolve according to a natural, inherent plan.

In the shape of this self and the reverence in which it is held, there are several basic traits that stand out. One, Winnicott's self is indeed a form of the modern, Western self that is masterful, bounded, and emotional. Two, it is a self that is at first empty. Its interior, it is true, is populated by an obtrusive false self, several part-objects (such as the external-object-mother), and, of course, the colorful but timid, secretive, true self. But more prominent than the objects and selves is an absence; it is in the emptiness that objects float, interact, overlap, cover up, and collide. Without introjection, the process by which external "objects" are consumed and stored interiorly, and a kernel of the romantic true self, initially there would be little inside the individual. In Winnicott's theory, growing up and learning to become a contributing member of one's society has come to feature the taking in and consuming of the proper parental objects. I do not mean to imply that Winnicott believed that there is absolutely nothing inside the individual; I simply mean that emptiness—absence and lack—is an unintentional but essential aspect of his vision. Probably Winnicott did not intend to feature absence; in fact, his theory seems focused on ameliorating emptiness. But in this reading emptiness does become central.

Here we can see the language of consumerism shaping and influencing Winnicott's theory in ways we can be sure he neither noticed nor intended. In line with Klein's formulations, Winnicott described the development of the self as a process in which the infant introjects and internalizes parental objects; by properly doing so, the internal true self is strengthened and eventually liberated. Child development, in Winnicott's description, has in part become a process of consuming the proper commodity. If we situate Winnicott's theory historically, we notice that child development has been unknowingly recast as a kind of postwar consumer activity. For instance, the process of modeling oneself after and imitating parents was described by Winnicott as introjecting and internalizing parental objects, and being honest and truthful about one's feelings and opinions was described as liberating the true self. It seems as though the language and habitual behaviors of the postwar era have shaped the cultural frame of reference to the point that the essence of child development and psychotherapy have become, and still are, the consuming of the proper objects and the liberating of the enchanted interior, the two mainstays of postwar American advertising. Winnicott didn't notice this then, and current psychotherapists still don't notice it now, probably because it is all so in sync with our current way of being that it is difficult to see. As hermeneuticists say, it is impossible to see the eye that is seeing; that is, it is difficult to see the framework that permits the process of seeing.

Most troubling of all, Winnicott's vision of human being is one that is predicated on the maintenance of an illusion, the illusion of omnipotence. As Greenberg and Mitchell have pointed out, for Freud psychological maturity and the goal of psychoanalysis was to bring about freedom *from* illusion.[47] Paradoxically, for Winnicott proper human development and the curative psychoanalytic process was contingent upon the freedom to *create* illusion. We might wonder about the purpose, the function, of this illusion. According to Winnicott, the illusion functions to protect the child from a premature awareness of separation, and, with the proper parenting, the illusion will evolve over time into a healthy appreciation of personal limits and the reality and rights of others. But perhaps he was wrong. Perhaps the illusion of omnipotence appears not because it is an indispensable stage in the universal process of *child* development, but rather because it is an indispensable step in the construction of the particular local *adult* self of our time and place. Is it not an essential aspect of our current Western and particularly American ideology, that we can get anything we want if we work hard enough and are clever enough? Are we not told that today's woman can "have it all," and that an African-American child can be "anything" he wants to be when he grows up? Are we not shown in movie after movie that the successful individual figures out what he wants and gets it, no matter what the cost? Are we not encouraged to purchase whatever we desire, regardless of the cost and the size of our bank account, through the use of credit cards, second and third mortgages, and state-sponsored lotteries?

We could no doubt come up with dozens of straightforward examples of this kind of socially accepted grandiosity, this adult valorization of the illusion of omnipotence. We don't usually interpret these ideas in this way, because they are such an accepted part of our world they are difficult to see. But what if, by unknowingly inducing the illusion of omnipotence in our children, and including it in our theoretical concepts, by believing it to be a universal, positive aspect of infanthood, we are contributing to the ongoing construction of the very self that we do not approve of and would not want to perpetuate? What if the illusion of omnipotence that Winnicott values contributes to the construction of a self whose primary characteristics are an endless, sybaritic sense of entitlement and a manipulative, coercive need to control others? In other words, what if children do not grow out of the illusion? What if the illusion continues throughout one's life as an indispensable quality of the empty self? Then Winnicott would be encouraging parents to raise their children in ways that would create the very ills he was attempting to heal.

HEINZ KOHUT AND THE VALORIZATION OF NARCISSISM: THE SELF TAKES CENTER STAGE

Many of the concepts that Winnicott and the British Middle School developed were similar to those developed by Heinz Kohut. Kohut, more than any other psychotherapist, put the self on the postwar American cultural map. He consolidated contemporary thought and the popular experience of human life and codified it into a scientific theory of mind, development, psychopathology, and cure. He and his followers translated the theory for nonanalytic therapists and transformed it into a body of psychotherapeutic practices, a self technology, for the post–World

War II self. Kohut was one of those rare, charismatic geniuses so attuned to the age that they speak and the rest of us recognize ourselves in their words. What he spoke about reorganized, or perhaps revolutionized, psychotherapeutic thinking and practice in the last quarter of the century. He touched upon aspects of the cultural frame of reference as diverse as popular culture, political campaigns, fine literature, and religious cults. What he spoke about was the self. He located it at the center of psychological life and, in fact, at the center of the cultural stage.

At the beginning of the chapter, we left Kohut on the platform of the train station in Vienna in 1938, witnessing the Freud family's forced departure from Vienna, connecting from afar with his hero, and perhaps carrying in his heart a sense that he had inherited the Professor's mission and would accomplish great things. In 1942 Kohut traveled to the United States and settled in Chicago. Before long he accepted a prestigious residency in neurology at the University of Chicago and was soon considered the future chairman of the department. However, he also began working in psychiatry, and by 1947 he was entirely dedicated to psychoanalysis.

According to Charles Strozier's biographical account,[48] Kohut's brilliance and dedication were immediately noticed by the medical-academic community. He was also cosmopolitan, humorous, energetic, entertaining, artistic, and charismatic—a real man-about-town. In a perfect metaphorical move, he took up residency in the sixth floor of the Billings Hospital. This was not uncommon at the time, especially for recent professional (and usually economically struggling) immigrants and/or graduate students; for instance, Thomas Szaz was also a sixth-floor resident. But the symbolism is so inviting: Kohut lived and breathed his work. His dedication, his superb command of the humanities (including music and the arts), his ability to engage and enthrall others—all these qualities came together in his passionate focus on psychoanalysis. When he graduated from the Chicago Psychoanalytic Institute he was immediately given a position on the faculty, and in succeeding years he became increasingly involved with the American Psychoanalytic Association. His tireless committee work, teaching, and public speaking earned him the title "Mr. Psychoanalysis" among his peers. His early writing, what there was of it, was characterized by intelligence, insight, careful attention to detail, and obvious scholarship, but not at all by the boldness and creativity by which late twentieth-century psychotherapy has come to know him. By 1964, when he was voted president of the Association, he had come into his full power.

But very quietly, something was happening with Kohut's theorizing.

Slowly, and probably against his will, he was evolving ideas that opposed Freud's. This was undoubtedly a mixed blessing for the man who had dedicated himself to guarding, preserving, and protecting the canon. For a long time he avoided articulating his vision, and then for a longer time he avoided acknowledging its deviations from orthodoxy. His beginning writings on his new ideas were so distracted by the wish to fit into orthodox Freudian theory that they were difficult to read, let alone understand. But by 1971, with the publishing of *The Analysis of the Self*, the radical nature of his work was increasingly difficult to deny; by 1977, with the publishing of *The Restoration of the Self*, it was impossible. He had gone beyond the point of no return: he had disagreed with the Professor, he had challenged Freud, he had created a new theory.

At the heart of Kohut's theory, at the heart of his challenge to Freud, in fact, at the heart of his universe, was the self—masterful, bounded, and subjective. His theory was a theory of the self, even though he never really defined what he *meant* by the self. However, that has never stopped psychotherapists from knowing, deep within our collective soul, what he was talking about. We knew because he was describing us. Something in what he wrote moved us to feel as though he had his finger on the pulse of our nation. He named something that had to be acknowledged, something that was floating in our national consciousness but could not be fully appreciated until he came along. By naming it, of course, he brought it into being, shaped it, and perpetuated it.

The most significant way that Kohut's theory differs from orthodox psychoanalysis is in its emphasis on the nature, formation, functions, illnesses, and healings of a new theoretical entity in psychoanalysis: the self. Quite naturally, he named his theory self psychology. It is true that a few other twentieth-century psychotherapists, such as Sullivan, Winnicott, Otto Kernberg, and Edith Jacobson, had developed ideas about the self, but, with the exception of Winnicott, these theorists did not talk about the self either as an entity, or as an entity separate from the activity of the ego. Kohut, even more forcefully and in a more American manner than Winnicott, brought a new psychological entity into view, and the consequences were beyond measure. Kohut's bold stroke, forced out of its theoretical closet by 1977, was to claim that primary to the Freudian drives of sex and aggression, more central than psychic conflict, more integral than the Oedipal drama, and independent from the tripartite structures of id, ego, and superego, are the vicissitudes of the self. In particular, Kohut argued that attempts to develop, maintain, and enhance the cohesion, autonomy, esteem, and emotional vitality of the self are the most important psychological issues in the life of the individual. Through

Kohut (and Winnicott's followers, who were starting to be heard) the self became the most important psychological entity in the American psychotherapeutic terrain, and its health and illness became the most important clinical issue in diagnosis and treatment. Through Kohut, a new developmental "line" became articulated, which pertained solely to the development of the self. He called this the pattern of healthy narcissism; it consists of two aspects of development, the "mirroring pole" and the "idealizing pole." Even neurotic distress such as castration anxiety, deficits in ego functioning, or fears of annihilation have eventually been reinterpreted by Kohutians as the products of a fragmenting self. In other words, through Kohut, the self has taken over from earlier analytic concepts as *the* primary psychological concern. The self has taken center stage.

Briefly, Kohut came to believe that the self is formed in infancy, through the microinteractions between parents and child. In fact, he stated that the self begins at the point in time when "the baby's innate potentialities and the [parents'] expectations with regard to the baby converge."[49] In other words, when the parents attune to the infant, the self naturally begins to form. If the parents do their job, the child develops a "healthy narcisissm," which evolves into a healthy adult self. How do the parents attune? First and foremost, parents attune through the exercise of empathy—by noticing, paying attention to, focusing on, understanding what the infant feels, admiring, and adoring the infant, and by communicating these feelings directly to the infant. By acting empathically parents recognize the infant's need to be "mirrored." Slightly later in the child's development, parents also attune by allowing the infant to idealize them and intensely identify and psychologically merge with them. Kohut taught that the self of the infant, although innately possessing a unique psychological blueprint of its "nuclear self," has to be nourished into being. This natural, universal process of growth is accomplished through the slow psychological internalization of the qualities and functions of the parents, who function as "selfobjects" for the child. The term *selfobject* is one coined by Kohut to illustrate the unseparated, psychologically merged nature of the infant-parent relationship: when the parent functions in this way for the infant, the infant "takes in" the parent and actually feels at one with the parent; they are merged internally into a new unity, which erases the hyphen in *selfobject*. It is not possible for the infant to develop a self unless he lives in an adequate selfobject milieu. The selfobject performs for the infant the functions of a fully operating self, such as regulating tension, maintaining self-esteem, self-cohesion, and a sense of continuity over time. By mirroring the child's feelings and capabilities, and by allowing the child to exhibit in front of them, the parents help the child experience himself as the parents sees him: as cohesive, autonomous, continuous in time, and full of feelings; as beautiful, intelligent, powerful, interesting, attractive. By allowing the child to idealize and merge with them, the parents help the child feel powerful and self-sufficient.

When the parents are adequately attuned through empathy, they shape their behavior in order to best meet the needs of the child, including anticipating the child's needs for food, sleep, love, and attention, and tolerating the child's needs to merge with and idealize the parent. Accurate empathy allows the child to feel seen, admired, and powerful, and to be protected from the frightening and painful realities of the world, such as the child's relative powerlessness, vulnerability, and psychological separateness. However, no parent can be perfectly attuned to a child, and no parent can maintain adequate empathy indefinitely. Herein lies both the dangers and the opportunities of infant development. If parents can keep their empathic failures to a minimum, and if they are able to minimize the importance and intensity of the failures, the child will, with practice, be able to perform for herself the self-regulating function of which she was momentarily deprived when the parents failed. For instance, the child who is able to stop fussing and is able to quiet herself by babbling or singing to and rocking herself, and who finally manages to fall asleep, is a child who is beginning to develop autonomous self-regulatory functions. In the momentary absence of parental empathy, the child has the opportunity to develop the capacity to be empathic to herself. It is at these moments, Kohut believed, that self structure is actually built. He called this process "transmuting internalizations"; it is often likened to the process of taking in and metabolizing oxygen. Very slowly, bit by bit, supplies from the outside are consumed, the structure of the self is built, and the inherent pattern of the nuclear self is expressed. The internalizing process inherent in selfobject merging has succeeded by allowing the child to develop the capacity to take care of herself, to regulate tension and self-esteem, to become autonomous, cohesive, and masterful. In time and with the proper empathy, the self no longer requires the constant selfobject milieu in order to regulate tension and achieve cohesion and autonomy. The desperate reliance on the constant regulating and unifying functions of the selfobject can then be attenuated. The relationship between parent and child slowly evolves into one of increasing psychological separation and object relatedness. Kohut argued that as the self becomes stronger and more cohesive and autonomous, the urge to exhibit oneself evolves into healthy adult ambition, and the urge to idealize evolves into healthy adult ideals and values.

If the parents cannot act in an adequately empathic manner, that is, if they cannot accurately mirror the child and encourage him to exhibit and be proud, or allow the child to idealize and merge with them, certain consequences characteristically emerge. The child will begin to manifest symptoms that indicate that the self is not maintaining an adequate amount of cohesion, self-regulation, or self-esteem. For instance, the child's poorly formed self may cause the child to become fragmented, behave erratically, and feel debilitated by shame, unbearable emptiness, or self-hatred. As a result the child will manifest certain "disintegration products" such as anxiety, rage, or sexual preoccupations. The child will then begin to try to solve the problem by finding others to soothe him or by trying to soothe himself. The child might try to find someone to mirror him, by extravagantly showing off; he might blindly idealize someone and try to psychologically merge with their wisdom or strength; he might try to soothe himself by becoming grandiose, thereby convincing himself that he is all powerful and cannot be affected by others; he might try to revitalize himself by overstimulation, seeking some sort of sexual fetish or physical intensity.

If the failures in parental empathy continue and become characteristic of the child's milieu, the above attempts to restabilize the self and recover psychological equilibrium (that is, to recapture self-cohesion, tension regulation, and self-esteem) will become recurring, driven behavioral patterns, long-term adaptations to an inadequate environment. Attempts to evoke mirroring or merging behaviors in others, or personal displays of exhibitionism, obnoxious grandiosity, or perverse sexuality, Kohut believed, are indications of developmental deficits during the formative years of the self. They are desperate attempts to evoke a substitute or to compensate for a missing or inadequate selfobject milieu. Kohut categorized these behaviors as narcissistic traits, and considered them to be indications of a narcissistic personality disorder.

Until Kohut, psychoanalysis was thought to be ineffective in treating personality disorders such as narcissism. However, Kohut believed that narcissistic personality disorders could be effectively treated if instead of relying on drive-resistance theory and orthodox practice, psychoanalysis would attend to the needs of the self, by discovering and then filling in the developmental deficits caused by the continual and/or severe failures in parental empathy. The characteristic responses to the fragmentation of the self that adult patients expressed toward the therapist, such as the need to be mirrored and the wish to exhibit, or the need to idealize and the wish to merge, he referred to as "narcissistic transference reactions." He believed that these symptoms necessitate a treatment stance different from that appropriate for neurotic conflicts. He suggested that the analyst empathically respond by understanding (mir-roring) the patient, or by tolerating the patient's overidealization and merging behavior. If the analyst could accomplish this, slowly the patient could internalize the analyst's qualities and behaviors (the analyst's self-object functions). Then the earlier interrupted development of the self could begin again, and in time the natural growth of the self in the proper milieu would build self structure and actualize the patient's inherent blueprint, located in the nuclear self. Crucial to this process are the inevitable empathic mistakes of the analyst and the analyst's unavoid-able absences, owing to sickness and vacations. If the analyst can keep the significance and intensity of these failures to a minimum, the patient will be able to build the requisite amount of self structure, and thus develop the capacity to self-soothe.

Central to Kohut's vision of analytic practice was his belief that empathy is the primary activity that aids in the building of self structure, and his corresponding de-emphasis on intellectual interpretations as the means for bringing about a cure. For Kohut it is understanding, not confrontation, that cures; it is building and liberating the self, not de-stroying illusion, that is the central activity of psychoanalysis. Indications for the conclusion of analysis, in Kohut's theory, would be the reduction of overidealization of the analyst, personal grandiosity, the demand for mirroring, and the wish to merge. The growing ability of the patient to self-regulate tension, shame, and fragmentation, to act upon ideals and values, to liberate his or her healthy ambition, and to be creative and spontaneous were indications that the analysis was completed.

The influence Kohut exerted in the field of American psychotherapy is difficult to overstate. His ideas influenced psychoanalysis and psycho-dynamic psychotherapy, of course, but to this list we might do well to add humanistic psychology, the human potential movement, feminist therapy, relational therapy, some forms of family therapy, cognitive therapy, and even the practices of behavior modification. As Greenberg and Mitchell have argued, Kohut's "emphasis on the crucial importance of the cohesiveness, continuity, and integrity of the subjective experience of self has been original and extremely useful clinically."[50] His emphasis on working with the overall experience of the self of the patient, and his encouragement of the role of empathy and attunement in treating the patient have influenced nearly all American therapeutic modalities in the postwar era.

Among his many interests, Kohut held an abiding interest in history, and sometimes he used self psychology theories to explain group behav-ior or to understand a historical figure. He speculated that the concept of narcissistic transferences could be applied to the behavior of groups, and if this was done carefully we could understand a great deal about the charismatic leader–dependent follower dynamic, the process of revolutions, and the seemingly inexplicable atrocities and the toleration of atrocities in our society. For example, the euphoric grandiosity and over-idealizing prevalent in some group experiences can be seen as an indication of the lack of self-cohesion with the individual group members and/ or the group as a whole. In Kohut's view, the charismatic leader is used by the group members or the group itself to hold together a fragmented or disintegrating self. By understanding the wounds and aspirations of the group, and by encouraging the group to new heights of achievement through the force of his or her personality, the selfobject leader mirrors for and merges with the group and thereby soothes and contains the fragmenting group self.[51] These conditions generate group phenomena such as unquestioning loyalty to the leader and the official ideology, compliance with the leader's commands, a sense of belongingness and group unity that incite mass euphoria, and an unrealistic belief in the rightness and ultimate triumph of the group.

Kohut himself used self psychology to discuss historical figures such as Adoph Hitler, Winston Churchill, and their relationship with their followers.[52] In that same monograph he also applied self psychology to Freud's relationship to his early followers and the reverence with which later analysts have held Freud and his early theories. In doing so he tried to explain why Freud's more recent followers have had difficulty being flexible and creative within the overall frame of psychoanalysis. Two current historians, John Demos and Charles Strozier, studied at the Chicago Institute and applied self psychology to various historical issues; for example Demos has looked into the dynamics of the Salem Witch Trials, and Strozier has studied Abraham Lincoln.[53] I have also used self psychology to discuss the recruitment-indoctrination process in religious cults and psychotherapy groups, historiographic issues, and the post–World War II consumer society and its effect on psychotherapy theory. In fact, the empty self argument in this book uses self psychology as a point of departure. The suggestion that the postwar economy has contributed to an empty self that facilitates the purchase and consumption of unneeded and sometimes destructive commodities and experiences is, in part, a Kohutian argument.

I depart from most versions of self psychology, however, when I argue that self psychology has itself been influenced by the consumerism of our time and is not a timeless, universal healing technology. To take that step, we need to use constructionist, hermeneutic theory to historically situate all psychotherapy theories, self psychology included. Without taking that step, self psychology would be treated as a reified, transcendent truth; then we would never be able to critique self psychology as we have critiqued earlier theories. Without taking that step, our attempt to situate psychotherapy historically and our attempt to develop new theories that do not reproduce the consumerism of our time would be doomed to incompleteness and failure.

Kohut Interpreted

Several writers have, over the years, contributed incisive and helpful critiques of Kohut's theories. Among these are Morris Eagle, Lynne Layton, and Louis Sass.[54] Sass, for instance, has reminded us of the strong Cartesian and romantic influences on Kohut. He suggested that self psychology describes a self that is organicistic (it grows naturally and evolves properly in accord with an inherent developmental pattern if simply given the correct amount of nourishment), expressivistic (it thrives when it is allowed to be emotionally expressive, one of the primary values of the romantic era, and falls ill when forced to remain silent or become false to its true feelings), and universal (it is thought to transcend history and culture; it is the one true way of human being). Eagle, besides his detailed technical criticisms, has noted that Kohut favors the realm of values and ideals, the victories of ambition, and the development of self-esteem over intimate relationships. He argues that Kohut values triumphs that are the products of individual, isolated pursuits, not those that involve cooperative activities developed in adult relationships of mutual obligation, trust, and involvement. Like Sass, Eagle notes that Kohut's values seemed to be the product of romantic ideals that enshrine the singular artistic genius-hero. Other people are very much valued, but only so long as they are needed; they are to be used and then left, so that the principal figure, the expressive self, can go on to achieve great things, alone. The "developmental morality" that Kohut explicitly criticized, Eagle notes, ironically showed up in Kohut's work as well.

Lynne Layton has also noticed that Kohut favored the realm of values and ideals. However, she considers this stance more the product of patriarchal thinking than simply the romantic influence. In an examination of Kohut's case studies, Layton has argued that he distinguished between and valued work over love, the public realm over the private, individual ambition over cooperative sacrifice, ideals over intimacy. Although Kohut spoke continually about relationship, Layton noted that it was a particular kind of relating, selfobject relating, that drew his attention and his implicit criticism. Patients are considered cured when they have achieved relative independence from selfobject relating. Then they are free to go out on their own, to achieve and triumph in the male world of work. As Layton demonstrates, intimate adult relating in the lives of the patients is consistently ignored or at best diminished in Kohut's case studies.[55] She argues that failures in the processes of mirroring/exhibiting (implicitly assigned to the mother) were thought by Kohut to be compensated for by relative strengths in the processes of idealizing/merging (implicitly assigned to the father). This male bias, she argued, is responsible for Kohut's theoretical concept of the dual lines of development, one libidinal and one narcissistic, and his privileging of the narcissistic line, which is thought to produce the self. Layton's strongest point is her charge that Kohut's error "lies in his taking appearances as essences and theorizing the given as the healthy."[56] For instance, Kohut thought that the symptoms he saw in his patients were transhistorical, and the nature of the self he hypothesized was a universal, essential selfhood. Because of this, Layton argued, he universalized the male vision that he saw both in his patients and in the society as a whole.

This accusation, that Kohut mistook appearance for essence and called the given health, is at the heart of my contentions about the post–World War II empty self and psychotherapy's complicity in the construction of the empty self. But, unlike Layton, I argue not only that Kohut saw the appearance of patriarchy and called it essence, although I believe he did, but also that he saw the whole mid- to late twentieth-century clearing—the *appearance* of emptiness, confusion, isolation, the commodification of human life—and called it *essence*. By doing so he reified the given, gave it a scientific justification, and encouraged its continuation. Ultimately, this is the source of his limitation, and ours as well.

In looking at the self that Kohut described, there are several qualities that are obvious. One, the self is the primary and most important element of the person. Although this idea seems self-evident to those of us in late twentieth-century America, let us remember that it would be a foreign, counterintuitive idea to those who live in different cultures or earlier eras in the West. Two, Kohut's self is the masterful, bounded, feeling self of the late modern era in the West. He took this self to be the one, universal self. Three, he conceived the role of the therapist as being responsible for building, maintaining, and enhancing the patient's self. Four, Kohut added another essential quality to the self: its emptiness. As with Klein's and Winnicott's object relations theories, Kohut described an individual whose interior contains certain objects, like "the nuclear self" or the momentary presence of a selfobject, but they exist in an emptiness that the individual is responsible for filling up, someday, with expanded forms of these objects. Five, Kohut explained the existence of this particular self by claiming that he knew when it is produced: during the universal development of the child. Kohut thus unknowingly escaped the dangers of situating the self historically or culturally by claiming that there is an ahistorical, universal self that is provable by the scientific discipline of developmental psychology. By now this strategy should seem familiar; Klein and Winnicott used the same approach. Six, he argued that this particular Western self, formed in infancy, is the product of the interactions between parent and child, which are located in a historical, acultural arena. Therefore any untoward symptoms or behavioral deviations from the norm were caused by parental failures, not the requirements and consequences of political and economic structures. If parents perform properly, Kohut believed, the universal self unfolds naturally, according to its inner blueprint. It is certainly possible, Kohut yimplicitly argued, to raise healthy, well-adjusted, untroubled children in the postwar era. Seven, self structure is both built (through psychologically taking in and metabolizing the parent's qualities) and liberated (through the unfolding plan of the nuclear self). The consumer language in his formulation should be obvious. The two characteristic elements of twentieth-century American consumerism—individual salvation through the consuming of commodities and the liberation of the enchanted interior—are clearly evident. Eight, adult psychological symptoms such as emptiness, generalized acquisitiveness, anxiety, shame, perfectionism, competitiveness, fragmentation, rage, disorientation, powerful urges to consume, exhibit before, idealize or merge with others are all considered to be "disintegration products" of an unstable, poorly built self. Nine, Kohut argued that psychoanalytic cure is in general the same as healthy growing up: the natural, organicistic developmental process, which was interrupted in childhood, is thought to be reactivated in analysis. By internalizing the analyst's selfobject functions, the patient finishes the consuming, building, liberating process, and the self is properly completed.

Kohut's theory was developed at the time that American consumerism was a defining cultural force. To be human, Kohut seemed to be saying, is to be a psychological consumer. The self he described is an empty self that longs for the proper commodity, the empathic selfobject, in order to fill up the emptiness and liberate the enchanted interior. This universal self was unknowingly defined by Kohut as a consumer self; in fact, Kohut thought this was easily proven by the empirical data gleaned from psychoanalysis and the scientific study of infant development. In this way the masterful, bounded, feeling self of our era, the empty self, found scientific justification. Behavioral deviations from the norm of

middle-class behavior were medicalized by Kohut and effectively explained away by pathologizing them: loneliness (labeled as insufficient
psychological separation or abandonment anxiety), moral confusion
(disorientation), the inability to maintain constant, Western-style psychological boundedness (self-fragmentation), extreme forms of consumerism (the urge to take in and merge with a selfobject), and personal
entitlement (the demand for mirroring) were interpreted as "disintegration products," pathological symptoms of an unstable, fragmenting self,
caused by inadequate parenting in the early years of life. Kohut interpreted certain symptoms as pathological deviations from a realistic
norm. However, another way to interpret these symptoms is to consider
them unavoidable, understandable products of an attempt to live up to an
impossible ideal and to survive in a dangerous, alienating, consumerized
world. Perhaps the symptoms are the norm, a norm that is in part
constructed through the prescriptions of self psychology's ideas regarding the normative development of the self.

Kohut's theory, then, was framed in and defined by the language of
consumerism. Kohut described a world in which, ideally, children develop in part by using their parents—by consuming, metabolizing, and
then leaving them. Although in most of his writing Kohut thought that
when the self is properly developed, the individual would become independent of the selfobject functions of others, in his last years he revised
this opinion, arguing that to varying degrees healthy individuals use
others in this way throughout their lives. Thus, throughout one's life,
others "show up" as commodities; the individual is pictured as consuming others and metabolizing their good qualities, in order to accomplish
the building of the masterful, bounded, feeling self.

This is, of course, not all that there is to Kohut. In fact, interpreted in
a less political way, one can portray Kohut as trying to describe an
interactional field-theory approach to human development and psychotherapy. Had he used a less reified and commodified language, and had
he historically situated his theory, his work could have been a blow
against the political status quo rather than a reflection of and a contributor to it. But he did not develop a consistent voice that spoke of both
process and politics. As a result, for all its poetic, humanitarian, and
hopeful spirit, his work had limitations and problems.

How helpful is Kohut's vision? What effect does it have on the kind
of world in which we would like to live? Kohut is often praised because
he emphasized the crucial importance of human relating, in contrast to
Freud's putative vision of impersonal energy release. But does Kohut's
theory really feature human relating? Can the essence of relating be
reduced to consuming and metabolizing? Kohut is often praised because

he emphasized the crucial importance of empathy in therapy, as opposed to Freud's putative vision of intellectual interpretation and confrontation. Indeed, empathy has proven to be an important, perhaps indispensable component of postwar psychotherapy. But if the therapist *only* empathizes, if the therapist's sole function is to understand, how productive can that be? Is understanding alone what the patient and the society need, or is more required? Is it even *possible* to produce a decontextualized, amoral understanding of another person? If the therapist's job is to build and liberate the self, if it is to make up for poor parenting, if it is to replace, enable, help the patient to get along in, achieve, and conform to our current consumer society, are we justified in calling this a critical practice, or is it closer to compliance?

Kohut is often praised for his creative ideas regarding the importance of grandiosity and omnipotence in infant development. He regarded them as universal but temporary phases in the natural unfolding of the self. But how temporary are they? Are they temporary stages in the life of the infant, or are they learned ways of being, long-term patterns of adjustment that are indispensable to our consumer society? Where would our economy be today if Americans did not consider themselves entitled to every consumer item they can purchase or find credit for? Where would the celebrity, culinary, exercise, diet, and cosmetics industries be today if adults did not feel driven to be unique, to stand out from the crowd, to comply with the fashion industry's standard of beauty, to be noticed and powerful and famous. In other words, where would these industries be if adults were not exhibitionistic and grandiose, hungry for mirroring and merging with celebrities or politicians? Is it just a coincidence that the very qualities that Kohut described (and thus implicitly prescribed) as indispensable to healthy infant development do not appear to recede but instead become major motivators in the consumer activities of adults? Did Kohut mistake appearance for essence?

If psychotherapy theory accepts the empty self as the essential nature of human being, and if the emotional effects of our consumerized era are accepted as ahistorical illnesses, then we have no way of resisting consumerism. Psychotherapy then becomes just another voice implicitly encouraging compliance with the status quo. We are told by self psychology and object relations theory that the empty self is the *natural* configuration of human being, and its attendant problems, such as disunity and confusion, self-preoccupation, loneliness, acquisitiveness, and competitiveness, are caused primarily by parental failure; that the drivenness to fill up one's interior emptiness by consuming psychological objects is an essential, natural, healthy human activity; that the child naturally and normally experiences herself as the entitled, self-absorbed, omnipotent center of attention; that the essence of psychological growth is consumption, and that the natural way of relating is consuming, metabolizing, and then leaving the selfobject other. In other words, just as in other spheres of life, in the psychological realm the natural, proper process of human living is consuming and metabolizing. It seems impossible to imagine how these messages could *not* have the effect of reproducing the cultural terrain, and especially the consumerism, of our era.

As interested as Kohut was in history, he did not take the step of developing a consistent historical perspective on his own theory. Instead he had a tendency to reify the current self, universalize its configuration, scientize its origin by claiming a developmental progression, medicalize deviation from the normative characteristics of that self, and technologize its healing. Kohut looked at the post–World War II middle-class self and saw emptiness, hunger, confusion, fear. He saw in his patients and probably within the society as a whole an inability to live up to the normative configuration: the masterful, bounded, feeling self. But then, instead of trying to interpret that self by situating it within the history and culture of its time, he mistook appearance for essence: he thought that the emptiness he saw was an unavoidable, essential aspect of normal development. By doing so he unwittingly exonerated the political structures responsible for constructing the emptiness and failed to foresee that he was contributing to the perpetuation of this social arrangement.

With Kohut we lost an opportunity to develop an opposition to the consumerism of our time. But we can regain that opportunity now. We don't have to be constrained by a wish to be included in the accepted realm of psychoanalytic theory, by the Cartesian split, by Victorian values of mastery, boundedness, and domination, and by the American fantasy of inner liberation. Most of all, we don't have to be limited by a wish to be apolitical healers, physicians removed from the rough and tumble of village politics, administering an ahistorical healing to universal illnesses.

The self psychology Kohut founded, as Greenberg and Mitchell have noted,[57] had elements in common with the British Middle School, with ego psychology, with humanistic psychology, and even with Sullivan's self system approach, although Kohut thought them all antecedents or copies of his wider, deeper vision. But there were important differences as well. Sullivan, influenced by the greats of the Chicago School of Sociology such as Charles H. Cooley and George Herbert Mead, understood that the self is a process, a dynamic system, and not a thing. Kohut, so much under the influence of romantic thought, wrote as

though the self is concrete, real, and immensely salient; it is alive, growing, expressive, willful; it is the center of one's initiative, the embodiment
of one's self-conscious subjectivity, the container of one's genetic blueprint, the core of one's being. The self is properly built in a specific
manner, and if that process isn't followed, if the self is deprived of certain
types of "provisions," the self will suffer in various characteristic ways
that will lead to the absence, fragmentation, or rigidity of certain psychic
"structures" that Kohut thought are indispensable to the mature shape of
the self.

Why did Kohut reify the self? And why did we, therapists, patients,
and bystanders alike, often respond to his message as though it was the
one true vision? It must be because his vision both reflected our world
and brought something into being that our world desperately needed,
something that was so functional it became indispensable to our way of
life. Kohut articulated what had become the linchpin for the post–World
War II era in the United States: the official scientific description, origin
myth, and ahistorical healing technology for the self of our time, the
empty self. With Kohut's theory we now had new words to claim that
the current way of being was the one, universal way of being; to describe
how it "naturally" develops; to identify deviations from the norm as
universal "illnesses"; and to prescribe various scientific techniques in
order to heal those illnesses.

By making the self into a thing Kohut gave the country an understandable direction, and hope, in troubled times. By reifying the self
Kohut could describe enculturation and maturing as forms of consuming,
and thus speak our language. But beyond that, once Kohut made the self
into a thing it could be worked on, shaped, transfigured, retooled. Once
the self is a thing it can be brought into the economic marketplace. Once
the self is a thing Kohut could then apply specific scientific technologies
to "it," set scientific standards for "its" assessment and repair, scientifically study "its" growth and development, train future technicians in
the proper healing techniques for treating "it." In other words, once the
self is a thing in our late twentieth-century capitalist economy, it becomes an object that can be commodified—it can be brought into the
realm of capitalist relations. Thus certain illnesses and their attendant
healing practices can be divided and categorized according to certain
agreed upon standards. Kovel, speaking about the medicalization of the
unconscious in the early twentieth century, remarked that by objectifying the unconscious and the emotions, the alliance between the state and
the fledgling field of psychotherapy was able to determine "an exchange-
value" for "states of mind"[58] (this was discussed at length in chapter six).

Perhaps by making the self a thing, with a specific essence, a prescribed configuration, and a natural set of problems, psychotherapy has been able to bring it into the "general framework of capital relations."[59] The self, then, by being made into a thing, became a commodity like any other. Kohut's theory thus seems to have been seriously influenced by the same forces that are at work in other sectors of our society. Today we can see traces of the commodification of the self throughout the commercial world. For example, there is a magazine entitled "SELF"; a Clairol commercial ends with a voice-over that proclaims: "Thirty-nine shades. Find Yourself"; bodybuilding programs at coed gyms advertize the advantages of "self-shaping"; various volunteers and professionals identify themselves with what is referred to as the "self-help movement"; Virginia Satir, human potential guru par excellence, wrote "When . . . some parts . . . [of how I] look, sounded . . . thought and felt . . . turn out to be unfitting . . . I can discard that which is unfitting and keep [the rest,] and invent something new for that which I discarded. . . . I own me, and therefore I can engineer me."[60]

Object relations theory and self psychology, of course, have not been the only, or even the most intense, reflections of the consumer ideology of the postwar era. If anything, more popularized theories such as addiction theory, twelve-step self-help groups, and the pop psychology embrace of trauma theory as the sole cause of adult psychopathology are even more consumer-oriented than past psychoanalytic theories. For instance, addiction theories characteristically argue that the individual has been transformed into an "addict" through the continual ingestion of a drug, the bad commodity. Addicts are then thought to be powerless in the face of the commodity and in order to regain control over their lives their only hope is to completely abstain from consuming it. But they cannot achieve abstinence solely by their own efforts; they cannot withstand the siren call of the bad commodity until they appeal and in fact *surrender* to a "higher power." Only in this way, it is argued, will consumers regain control over their lives, because once the commodity is consumed it overpowers the consumer. In this view, the commodity is all-powerful (see chapter ten for further details).

Kohut told a story that our era needed to hear; he comforted us and made us understandable to ourselves; he brought compassion and care to the therapeutic moment. But he also universalized the configuration of self, instead of allowing it to be particular and local, and by so doing medicalized our political suffering, normalized the destructive consequences of our consumerized world, and mystified the constructed arrangements of power and privilege.

CONCLUSION

This chapter, to paraphrase Paul McCartney, has been a long, winding road through one of the most unusual, contradictory, and colorful eras in American history. The post–World War II era has been cautious, raucous, surprising, cynical, creative, destructive. It has been a youthful and especially psychological era. Its primary character, alone on the cultural stage, has been the self, the masterful, bounded, emotional, and now empty self. It is the self that has been the single-most important concern of the era. Its cohesion, stability, and trueness; its origin, development, and protection; its emotional "health," normality, and expressiveness have been nurtured and guarded at all costs. It is this American self that was the engine that helped capitalism escape a new postwar depression and thrive throughout the second half of the century.

The post–World War II self has had many faces, such as the early fifties face, cautious, somewhat confused, unsure of what would come next; the rebellious, unpredictable, colorful, naive sixties face; the increasingly frustrated, angry, bitterly disappointed face of the seventies; the sad, self-involved, acquisitive face of the eighties. But uniting each of these public presentations has been consumerism, the characteristic most commonly associated with the postwar era. The belief that one could find individual salvation through the liberation of one's core essence, and that one could liberate that essence by purchasing and consuming the proper product or merging with the perfect celebrity, in other words by filling up the empty self—that, in our time, is the face of everyone.

The face of everyone has been constructed out of the fears and machinations, the hopes and dreams of our postwar era. Consumerism saved us from an economic depression, but it brought us to the brink of nuclear destruction; it failed to heal the stratifications of gender, race, and privilege, and it may yet move us to the complete despoliation of our environment. Consumerism brought to members of the middle class an affluence and psychological-mindedness previously unheard of, but it also caused a commodification of human relating that has been degrading and self-defeating. Finally, it caused the United States to squander precious environmental, financial, and human resources in service of wasteful and ultimately destructive campaigns of paranoia, acquisition, and consumption.

Psychotherapy has not been immune from all this. Without psychotherapists realizing it, our theories have often reflected the post–World War II consumer landscape, normalized its necessary ingredients such as the empty self, and explained away its unavoidable consequences, such as emotional isolation, selfishness, drug addiction, and the nihilistic use of others. Psychotherapy theories consider these consequences to be anomalies, deviations from the healthy norm, and therefore we set out to heal them. If we were to historically situate our practices we might consider that these consequences are in fact not anomalies but the norm, and that when we medicalize and pathologize the norm, we ignore the dangers of the status quo and unknowingly perpetuate it. Ultimately, we have helped reproduce an aspect of the cultural landscape we abhor. By reifying the self, we have helped construct reified people. Reified people, in turn, require reified cures. "Thirty-nine Shades. Find Yourself."

CHAPTER NINE

Psychotherapy as Moral Discourse

A HERMENEUTIC ALTERNATIVE

The world is a bridge,
cross it
but build no house upon it.
—ACBAR

Throughout this book I have argued that social practices not only inevitably reflect the cultural clearing of their time and place but also unknowingly reproduce that landscape—the moral and political arrangements that frame and structure it. In the process of discussing various Western, and especially American eras, I have tried to show how psychotherapy has reflected and reproduced the frameworks of its respective eras. I hope in this process I have also conveyed how difficult I think psychotherapy's task is, how unintended are the political consequences of its practices, and how I respect the men and women of the field who have taken it upon themselves to try to ease the suffering of others. But intended or unintended, social practices have political consequences, intellectual discourse is inevitably involved with the exercise of power, and the self, unavoidably, is morally constituted.

THE THERAPIST'S FEAR OF THE MORAL AND THE POLITICAL

It is difficult for psychotherapists to examine their theories with an eye to the moral and political, because they do not like to think of their work in this way. Politics and morality are dirty words in our late twentieth-century world. Some therapists, especially those of the baby boom generation, having given up the hope of massive political change, chose psychotherapy as a profession for a number of humanitarian, altruistic, and personal reasons, including the hope that they could to do well (financially) without doing harm (politically). For many, that was the most that could be hoped for in the post-Vietnam world of their young adulthood. For these reasons and many more, not the least of which is the training and professional socialization to which therapists are exposed, they often think of psychotherapy as a private activity, most often involving the fewest number of people possible, preferably only two. Most therapists like to think that when they close the door, the "outside world" is excluded. Many like to think that what transpires between therapist and patient is based on a healing practice that is either (take your pick) scientific, objective, technological, and removed from the realm of the everyday, or else romantic, subjective, artistic, and removed from the realm of the everyday. They like to think that what they do as psychotherapists is less an influencing than a sorting out, less a persuading than an allowing, less an offering of opinion than a pointing out of obvious scientific truth.

I think it safe to say that psychotherapists like to think they stand against self-righteous moralizing (words that, in their minds, usually appear together) and against lecturing and arguing about politics (the only two ways most imagine political dialogue). The psychotherapist's belief that moral discourse is a kind of moralizing and political dialogue and adversarial coercion is attributable in unequal parts to the effects of cultural values, historical events, and personal proclivities. The proscription against morality and politics in the psychotherapeutic process is an unexamined legacy of the modern age and the Enlightenment era agenda that framed it. In that frame, freedom was thought to be produced by the *absence* of religious restrictions, folk superstitions, and governmental coercion. When that absence appears, it is thought that individuals can develop philosophical objectivity, employ the scientific method, and thus discover empirical truths that can be a reliable guide to everyday living. In this frame, community and tradition, in fact any "outside" influence on the individual, is thought to be a restriction on "freedom." Second, the political disillusionments suffered by the baby boom generation, including the assassinations of President John F. Kennedy, Malcolm X, Martin Luther King Jr., and Robert Kennedy, the debacle of Vietnam, and the Watergate revelations probably had an impact on those who chose therapy as a career by reinforcing a hopelessness and cynicism about political activity. Finally, adding to the weight of culture and history is a self selection that takes place as middle-class youths who are communally and politically inclined tend to move away from careers as psychotherapists because of the excessive individualism that saturates the discipline.

Of course, this book's reason for being is to disagree with the view that the office door can keep out the world, and to challenge the assumption that if we don't self-righteously moralize, or don't lecture or argue, we escape the moral and political. As I hope I have shown, the history of psychotherapy can be interpreted in such a way as to demonstrate that the field has always been, and will always be unavoidably—although unintentionally—a moral discourse with political consequences.

Because we continue to live in the shadow of racism, sexism, economic injustice, and the pervasive influence of consumerism, the suggestion that sometimes psychotherapy is complicit in the arrangements of our society is a supremely discomforting, in fact an infuriating idea. Most therapists are intelligent, well meaning, and well read—they know what it means to be accused of reproducing the sociopolitical status quo.

Of course, I do not mean it in a simple, concrete, or insulting way; most therapists would not describe themselves as being for the oppression of people of color, women, and the aged; the exploitation of the underclass; nuclear war; a revival of the House Un-American Activities Committee; or wars to advance imperialism. The status quo I have in mind is much more subtle, much more insidious, more complex, many sided, less one-dimensional and evil, much harder to locate. After all, there are aspects of the status quo that are positive and helpful. The status quo is the product of many traditions, some of which we may approve of and want to perpetuate. Still, with that said, there are also those subtle but negative aspects of the status quo that most psychotherapies perpetuate, aspects that are central and fundamental to our society and thus not immediately or easily visible.

There is also a morality implicit in the legacy and mainstream practices of psychotherapy that offers an *alternative* to the status quo. These practices have their roots in aspects of Western tradition that stand in *opposition* to the alienation and commodification of our time. In fact, the moral practices of psychotherapy both collude with and resist the status quo.

PSYCHOTHERAPY, THE STATUS QUO, AND TOKENISM

Foremost among the subtle aspects of psychotherapy's reproduction of the status quo, of course, is the configuration of the self of our time, the masterful, bounded, empty self. Psychotherapy is a social practice that is a technology of the self. Presumably, it helps people live better. Better, of course, is a qualitative and evaluative term. It is, if you will, a moral term.

What it means to help people live better always depends upon a people's understanding of what it means to be properly human—it depends on the definition of the self. If the therapist's idea about the proper configuration of the self is radically different from the patient's, chances are the therapy won't last long. So therapy is always a dialogue between the people involved over what is the proper way of being. It is an attempt to develop a set of shared understandings about what it is to be human. It may be a subtle, complex, implicit negotiation, but it is always in process. The configuration of the self is one of the most important moral and political issues in the cultural terrain; it is part of the foundational constituents of the frame of reference in any society. It is bedrock. So the practices that secure the social foundation—and psychotherapy is among them—are centrally important to a society's continuity.

I have attempted to show how our current psychotherapy theories and practices have unintentionally reproduced the empty self, and thus, inevitably, the illnesses to which the empty self is vulnerable. But there are other ways that psychotherapy reproduces the status quo. For instance, psychotherapy has, throughout its history, been unwilling to follow a comprehensive interactionist perspective—that is, a fully historical and cultural perspective regarding the social world. In a 1979 article, Gadlin and Rubin examine the long-standing argument in social psychology over which influence—endogenous personality traits or the impact of the immediate social situation—has the most predictive power.[1] Although for many years social psychologists have separated into two opposing camps regarding this issue, a third seemingly compromise position was developed, called interactionism. Proponents argued that rather than being forced to choose between one alternative or the other, it would be more accurate to conceive of the *interaction* between persons and in-the-moment social pressure as being responsible for behavioral outcomes. However, Gadlin and Rubin have argued that the limited compromise, a linear, superficial interactionism, was not an adequate solution to the controversy; indeed, they thought it was simply another form of business as usual. After all, the proponents still conceived of the social as an isolated, ahistorical, apolitical moment; by doing so they failed to consider the power inherent in the cultural frame of reference and rendered invisible those historical forces and socioeconomic factors that actively shape the frame of reference. In other words, the compromise was *intellectual tokenism*. Only a radical perspective, a historically situated, philosophical hermeneutic perspective can begin to embrace the complexity of the interrelationship of individual, society, and nature. Only a perspective that analyzes the larger sociocultural framework, such as the *distinctions* among individual, society, and nature can properly ask the hard questions about any psychological theory, questions related to the political functions and consequences of the theories themselves and the distinctions that the theories take for granted. A theory that uses a more comprehensive interactionist perspective must also be able to ask hard political questions about its *own* sociopolitical functions. Self-critical questions would indicate that such a perspective understands that not only does a psychological theory help "constitute sociopsychological reality, but [it] is itself constituted by social process and psychological reality."[2] In other words, a comprehensive interactionist approach would *expand* the concept of the "situation" in order to include the historical context in which the subject of study is embedded. Nothing less, Gadlin and Rubin have argued, would be acceptable. The hermeneutic alternative I offer in this book is an attempt to begin putting these commitments into practice.

A psychotherapy theory that situates its practices historically would be aware of psychotherapy's sociopolitical role in various historical eras, including its own. Today psychotherapists could historically situate their practices by studying how they contribute to self-contained individualism, the configuration of the empty self, and the smooth functioning of consumerism. By noticing how socially caused suffering has been medicalized and thus depoliticized, psychotherapists could better understand how the presentation of the discipline as a universal, intrapsychic healing technology has political and moral consequences. They could better understand how their practices disguise the exercise of power, the impact of economic forms of production, and the injustice caused by oppression owing to race, gender, and class. They could also understand how their practices contribute to the suppression of cooperative group action that might develop political and structural solutions to societal problems.

In previous chapters I have demonstrated that psychotherapy theory, instead of using a comprehensive interactionism, has developed just the kind of tokenism that Gadlin and Rubin have criticized. Throughout its history, therapy has acceded just enough to social critique to seem au courant and to deflect criticism—but never enough to fully acknowledge and critique the political functions and consequences, the "constructivist" processes, of its own practices. For instance, in chapter seven I suggested that Melanie Klein and her early object relations followers had difficulty extending their conception of the social realm beyond the relations of internal objects, or at most the interactions within the parent-child dyad. This location of the social in the private interior and the reduction of the social to the dramas of the intrapsychic is what I have called Klein's "geographical strategy." By studying the parent-child dyad, the romantic couple, or more recently, the transference-countertransference dynamic enacted in the psychotherapy hour, current object relations theory certainly has taken steps in the right direction, that is, into the social realm. But, by not taking into account the larger cultural and political world in which patients live and theory is promulgated, Klein, Winnicott, and the current generation of object relations and self psychology therapists have helped psychoanalysis ally with the era's increasing interest in social interaction without having to study and critique the era's power relations and political structures, or *psychoanalysis'* role in promoting those relations and structures. Object relations theory, self psychology, and what is called the relational model are examples of this partial interactionism. Irwin Z. Hoffman, through his use of social-constructivism, and Donnel B. Stern, who uses hermeneutics, have critiqued these theories and have come to similar conclusions.[3] Object relations theory has brought a great deal to the therapy hour. Its tokenism, while advancing psychotherapy's push for legitimacy, acceptance, and influence in the late twentieth century, has unfortunately also inhibited the discipline's ability to comprehensively study and resist the political status quo. Psychotherapy has thus defined its area of expertise in such a way as to exclude, for all practical purposes, most explicit discussions of moral and political topics. Hoffman's recent description of a political discussion in the therapeutic hour was notable for its uniqueness, and Lane Gerber has begun to explain how the thoughtful treatment of political issues can and should be considered appropriate topics in the therapy hour.[4]

This brings us to a third way in which mainstream psychotherapy has unintentionally reproduced the status quo. Psychotherapy theories that believe, for instance, in the romantic notion of the organicistic growth of the nuclear self, such as self psychology or the developmental theory of Daniel Stern,[5] argue that if the therapist or parent is properly attuned to the patient or infant and responds "properly," the self of the patient or infant will simply continue to grow and develop naturally and healthily. In self psychology's view, the masterful, bounded self of the modern era is a *natural* occurrence, emerging like any other event of nature; parenting (or therapy) is at its best an interactive attunement and a providing of emotional supplies. When the proper supplies are offered, the patient or infant unreflexedly consumes and metabolizes them and goes on with life, seemingly without skipping a beat. The building of the self in childhood or therapy, in this vision, is part of the unproblematic, organic world. Almost no thought is given to the political functions served by such a concept of the self: the consumer metaphor of development (the selfobject is consumed and metabolized in order to build self structure), the consumer-oriented view of psychopathology (interaction with an inadequate parent interferes with the taking in and building of self structure and/or promotes the ingestion of the bad object), or the cross-cultural problems involved in the taken-for-granted assumption that the Western self is the one universal self. Let us remember the hermeneutic concept that it is not possible to live in the social realm without affecting or being affected by it. It is simply not possible to be neutral, objective, uninvolved. As a human being and as a human being carrying out a healing practice, a therapist cannot *not* be involved. Yet, as I have pointed out previously, throughout their history, most psychotherapy theorists have claimed a privileged epistemological position, one that is outside of or removed from social influence. Therapists who take this position claim that they can be present without being influenced, and intercede without "bias" or political motive.

Thus the power involved in setting the frame of reference is not acknowledged—instead it is obscured or "disguised."[6] Ideology that is camouflaged is *particularly* dangerous, because those wielding the influence deny its power at the same time that they exercise it. Therefore, by refusing to extend its examination of the social, psychotherapy theories such as self psychology do more than simply *accommodate* the status quo. By *exercising* power while *disguising* power, psychotherapy is an unintentional but major player in sociohistorical processes, including the maintenance of a modern era, Panopticon-like self-surveillance, the concept of intrapsychic interiority, and the emphasis on internal emptiness— processes that reproduce the current configuration of the self and the political arrangements and moral agreements in which the self is embedded. In other words, the claim that psychotherapy is an apolitical, amoral practice is itself a political act. Once, the field could plead guilty because of ignorance. Now, with a number of social constructionist, hermeneutic ideas available, that defense is no longer tenable.

MORAL DISCOURSE, POLITICAL ACTS

Earlier chapters have touched on some of the dangers inherent in obscuring the moral framework, political ideology, and economic consequences of a social practice. By inventing a spiritual substance that connected each individual soul with every other and with the divine, mesmerism took a moral stand and committed a political act. The moral stand was to value the importance of community and human involvement. The political act was to keep that value *implicit*, by creating opportunities for community involvement without placing responsibility for its *absence* on the rapid industrialization and urbanization caused in large part by the requirements of nineteenth-century capitalism. Mesmerism claimed it was healing a universal, ahistorical, internal illness through the practice of a universal healing technology. By making that claim, by removing the causes and cures from the realm of the social—that is, by refusing to place responsibility on the economic system—mesmerism became a political player. Presumably, mesmerists didn't have a clue that they were doing all this, but they did it nonetheless. A case could be made that late twentieth-century Twelve-Step programs—which feature a nonpolitical (medical) model of addiction, rely on a taken-for-granted individualism, describe a nonsectarian, omnipresent spirituality, and prescribe a continual, ongoing immersion in a group process—use moral and political strategies similar to those exercised by mesmerism.[7]

The true self-false self distinction is an aspect of Winnicott's and James Masterson's healing technologies[8] that present themselves as effectively removed from the realm of moral considerations and the larger social world of history and politics. Yet they can be interpreted as being directly involved in morality, history, and politics. The morality of true and false and the economic utility of expressive, desiring subjects seem obvious. In our society, things that are true are good by definition, and those that are false are bad. Although object relations theory generally instructs the therapist to be neutral, the evaluative nature of the true-false distinction belies the instructions. The value placed on honesty, emotional expressiveness, and personal creativity is a *moral* judgment; therefore theories should not claim that they possess the objective scientific truth about a natural "thing." To maintain that the causes of the bad, false self are located either in the intrapsychic realm, or at most in the parent-child dyad, is a political act that ignores the history—and political functions—of such distinctions in modern history. By positioning the self as removed from or only minimally involved with the social realm, object relations theory unknowingly draws attention away from the socio-historical forces that shaped the masterful, bounded twentieth-century self, which is caught between isolation and engulfment, terrified of being unnoticed and yet determined to be independent.

In another example, by mistaking appearance for essence,[9] Kohut and Winnicott unintentionally *prescribed* the historically constructed child that they thought was natural. By encouraging parents to relate to their children in such a way as to treat the child's grandiosity, sense of entitlement, and acquisitiveness as natural and good, Kohut and Winnicott implicitly instructed parents in how to tolerate in the society and construct in their children some of the very narcissistic traits that self psychology and object relations theory are then responsible for healing.

By decontextualizing developmental stages and presenting them as ahistorical essences, theorists allow the sociohistorical causes of personality to go unnoticed and thus escape responsibility. Unfortunately, only a few developmentalists, such as Ben Bradley, William Kessen, and Stephen Seligman and Rebecca Shanok have resisted this approach.[10]

EMBRACING THE MORAL AND POLITICAL

I do not intend to criticize psychotherapy as being somehow "biased" or "nonobjective." As I have argued throughout the book, the problem is not that social practices like psychotherapy have *failed* at being objective; it is that they have *tried* to be objective, and that, even worse, they have claimed that they have adequately *accomplished* that end. This is dangerous because, in the West, when ideology masquerades as a physical science it becomes more valued and thus more politically effective. I understand that psychotherapy's stance is not conscious imposture. In a world in which healing shows up as either superstition, religion, or science, of course the field would choose to be considered a science. It is, no doubt, not conscious deceit: because culture is sedimented in the body of the healer, the language of science has naturally become the language of the psychotherapist. It is not a conscious deceit, but from a hermeneutic perspective, mainstream psychotherapists have avoided noticing that they strike moral stances and executed political strategies. Would it be too much to ask the psychological healers of today to develop a description of their practices that would be more directly expressive of what they are about?

For instance, it is possible to examine current forms of mainstream psychodynamic psychotherapy and interpret them in such a way as to draw some general conclusions about the morality implicit in their practices. Psychotherapy is in a contradictory position in late twentieth-century society. On the one hand it unknowingly reproduces the status quo by helping to construct the masterful, bounded, empty self, by valorizing the enchanted American interior, and by framing psychotherapy as a liberationist enterprise—three activities that have greased the wheels of late twentieth-century consumerism (see chapters three and eight). On the other hand, there is also a morality implicit in some psychotherapy practices that offers an alternative to the status quo. These practices have their roots in aspects of Western tradition that stand in opposition to current forces of alienation and commodification. For instance, mainstream practices often stipulate that patients must be treated with respect, listened to and understood, granted the privilege of confidentiality, and protected from a dual relationship with the therapist that would cause financial, ideological, or sexual exploitation. These practices demonstrate a morality contrary to that which is implicit in capitalism's unyielding allegiance to the profit motive and the era's omni-present commodification of relational life. Further, psychotherapy offers alternative values such as respect for the patient's experience and ideas, a belief in straightforward talk, and the importance of understanding and emotionally relating with others. It values self-examination, introspec-tion, and the striving for self-knowledge and psychological insight. It offers instruction in alternative social practices, such as the skills of listening to others, speaking honestly, and acting assertively. These atti-tudes, values, and social skills indicate that psychotherapy practices a morality that in certain ways opposes the dominant late twentieth-century consumer ethos.

Some schools of psychotherapy, especially psychoanalysis, also of-fer tools that can sometimes deconstruct the power relationship between patient and therapist within the therapy hour. Psychotherapy does this through the analysis of the transference-counterference dynamic—what patient and therapist think about, feel, and enact in the therapy hour regarding the therapist-patient relationship. By addressing the motives hidden within the ebb and flow of power in the therapy hour, psycho-therapy implicitly encourages the patient to demystify domination, nos-talgia, and regression, and instead to value insight, responsibility, and a confrontation with loss. It challenges patients to face the part they play when the therapy hour is composed of domination and compliance. Here we can see aspects of the implicit morality of psychoanalysis at work: the valuing of awareness over drivenness, of choice over prohibition, and of personal responsibility over the nostalgic wish to be dominated and used.

Psychotherapy, therefore, implicitly puts forward various moral ideas that often *conflict* with one another. Although the overall practice of psychotherapy is conducted within an individualist and consumerist moral frame, it also challenges, or at least undermines, that frame. But the alternative practices and values from nonmainstream ethnic traditions or alternative aspects of Western tradition, because they are not explicit, consistent, and are usually carried out under an individualist and con-sumerist banner, are inevitably inadequate to the task.

"The point," Foucault once said, ". . . is not that everything is bad but that everything is dangerous." All theories are immersed in and consti-tuted through the social—they are unavoidably moral and political. As a result, they are from the first subtly involved in the rough and tumble of local politics, which is unavoidably a threat to one faction or another. All theories, Foucault meant, are political—and the more their proponents deny it, the more political (that is, dangerous) the theories become.

Foucault's assertion, of course, applies as well to the ideas I employ. It should not be a surprise to anyone for me to "admit" that the way I have used philosophical hermeneutics to interpret the history of psychotherapy is decidedly unmainstream. There is no question in my mind (nor, probably, in the reader's) that I have shaped my argument in an attempt to persuade the reader to join me in a certain moral and political project. My prejudices and biases are the foundation of this book. I am sure that the way I have portrayed the history of psychotherapy—and the United States—is not the only way those histories can be described. Because of my ideas, interests, and commitments, I have found certain things of importance and other things unremarkable. Still others I consider important but not directly applicable to the argument I am making. In this book, Jungian theory, cognitive psychology, behaviorism, psychopharmacology, and family therapy in particular have not been given their due. They were not excluded because I thought them unworthy of discussing. Not at all. But I did not set out to write a textbook. Instead, I tried to present an interpretive cultural history—that is, an argument, a reasoned, illustrated, and I hope sound argument, but an argument nonetheless.[11]

The argument is based on certain concerns and values of mine. As a hermeneuticist I do not believe that I researched this book, nor that anyone researches any book, simply by "discovering" neutral facts, collecting them one by one, and then adding them up and reaching an inescapable scientific conclusion. Instead we do not so much find data as construct them; we do not objectively search—we seek out what we think is important. We think that particular things exist because of the frame of reference with which we see and think. I looked in certain places because I thought important information would be there, and because I thought it important for the reader to know what was there. I wanted to find this information to make a certain argument, and I wanted to make that argument in order to engage the reader in a certain way of thinking.

We value certain ideas and are committed to them because of the constellation of intersecting traditions that make up the framework of our lives. Because of the intersecting traditions of my life, I value certain moral concepts, and I want my work as a psychotherapist to reflect those concepts. I think that certain psychotherapy practices can help individuals, families, and communities develop or increase their mutual respect for one another, their ability to cooperate together more effectively, their interest in caring for one another, their ability to enjoy and cherish rather than threaten life, their ability to honor cultural differences and not threaten the integrity of the traditions of others while understanding, critiquing, and constantly modifying their own. I also hope that psychotherapy practices can assist patients in shaping a world in which more of us have less alienating work, an adequate amount of food, shelter, health, and safety, and perhaps even occasional moments of happiness. To work toward that vision, I expect that each of us will have to develop a better understanding of ourselves as individuals and as members of a group, and in doing so we will have to be better able to be honest and forthright in our own self-dialogue and in our dialogue with others. I also expect that we will have to develop a better understanding of our traditions, and through learning, wrestling with, and reshaping them, develop a better understanding of what we value, what we oppose, and what we are willing to fight for.

These values, which I think many therapists share, are not thought to be directly communicated by mainstream therapeutical practices. But I think psychotherapists have tried, surreptitiously of course, to influence patients to adopt some of these values. According to Foucault, this is what all social practices do. Owing to certain sociohistorical forces, especially those that move psychotherapy to present itself as an objective, scientific technique, these moral commitments have been forced out of the consciousness of both patient and practitioner. Also, because of the discipline's unquestioned embrace of self-contained individualism and its unknowing support of the consumer ethos, there are also moral understandings unknowingly communicated to patients that are contrary, perhaps antithetical, to the values listed in the previous paragraph.

I first began to apply hermeneutics and social constructionism to the practice of psychotherapy in an attempt to weed out practices that contributed to self-contained individualism, encouraged the consumer ethos, and helped construct the empty self. This continues to be a difficult task. Because the hermeneutic perspective is founded on the acknowledgment of the sociohistorical context and the interactive, interpenetrating nature of human life, the hermeneutic approach requires that therapists historically situate the patient, their professional role, and their healing practices; it also requires that psychotherapy theories acknowledge the intertwined, interpenetrating, interdependent nature of human relating. This then provides some safeguards against unknowingly colluding with negative aspects of the status quo through activities such as ignoring the psychological effects of current political structures (and thereby blaming the victim); unquestioningly accepting distinctions such as inner-outer, mind-body, and individual-society; employing psychotherapy theories that are based on a consumer metaphor (such as object relations theory); adhering to unquestioned gender or racial prescriptions; enacting unquestioned role prescriptions such as that between doctor and patient; and enforcing the power relations of class.

The act of historically situating the therapeutic setting does not necessarily rule out making use of roles, power relations, or authority hierarchies, such as the asymmetry of the therapist-patient relation. It simply helps the therapist to be more conscious of them and more mindful of their potential influences. The choices related to whether, how, and to what degree therapists will involve themselves in such roles, relations, or activities are the determining factors. But if therapists are conscious of these choices, and discuss and write about them, I presume the therapist, colleagues, and perhaps even some patients will know more about why a particular therapist makes the choices he or she makes and what are the broader consequences of those decisions.

For instance, some psychotherapists, such as Rachel Hare-Mustin, Jeanne Marecek, Lynne Hoffman, and Deborah Luepnitz,[12] by virtue of their feminist, constructionist perspective, have been able to expose various sexist practices in family therapy—practices that privilege the authority, point of view, and wishes of the husband/father/son to the detriment of the wife/mother/daughter. In a second example, that of the power relations between practitioner and patient, some constructionist and/or interpersonalist psychoanalysts, such as Merton Gill, Jay Greenberg and Stephen Mitchell, Irwin Hoffman, and Donnel Stern,[13] by virtue of their emphasis on the transference-countertransference dynamic, have upheld a moral commitment to the demystification of power within the therapy hour. Importantly, Hoffman has argued that a commitment to a constructionist perspective does not necessarily preclude an asymmetry in the analyst-analysand relationship. Drawing on these ideas, one could argue that asymmetry is unavoidably present owing to (a) the social expectations of the doctor and patient; (b) the nature of the capitalist marketplace; and (c) the accrued knowledge, skills, and wisdom of the therapist and the therapist's commitment to the moral understandings and behavioral constraints of the profession. In other words, the exercise of qualitative standards in arrangements regarding hierarchy, authority, and asymmetry are not necessarily bad, but they can be dangerous if not historically situated, politically understood, consciously decided upon, and repeatedly discussed.

Of course, no technique, ideology, or set of practices can guarantee complete safety from the abuse of power in the therapy setting. Indeed, abuses have been committed in all arenas and by therapists of all stripes. But therapists who believe themselves above the ethics of the field, think of themselves as immune from mistakes or countertransference, and are true believers, sure that their technique proscribes all mismanagement, are especially vulnerable to the misuse of power. When a healing practice will not allow for discussion of the in-the-moment power relations of an interaction, the patient is potentially at risk.

INTERSECTING TRADITIONS

Hermeneutics is particularly compatible with my concerns because of its emphasis on the embedded, socially constructed, interpenetrating nature of human being, the importance of historical and political influences in healing practices, and its awareness of the omnipresence of moral understandings and the necessity of everyday moral decisions. The use of hermeneutics in psychotherapy can help the practitioner be more aware of the unavoidable binds in which psychotherapy finds itself and the ubiquity of power relations within the therapy hour (such as the relations of class, gender, or the patient-doctor dyad). It can help the practitioner realize that the normative concerns and preoccupations of the white middle class, such as self-contained individualism and the consumer ethos, are not the only perspectives that exist for Americans. Sometimes those norms have negative consequences, and sometimes they don't— but they are not the only norms available. Hermeneutics can help lessen the practitioner's contribution to the construction of the empty self, the normalization of consumer activities such as acquisitiveness, competitiveness, and envy, and the medicalization of behavior caused by political structures.

Hermeneutics conceptualizes therapy as inevitably embedded in a values discourse. It calls on psychotherapists to be neither self-righteous moralists, nor to take to the streets in rebellion, but it does suggest that we put our own house in order. One way to engage in this reordering is by developing a kind of axiology, a study of values. We could work to delineate which values are embedded in which theories, and how those values are communicated and reproduced within the therapy setting. If, for instance, we refuse to continue naturalizing consumerism, or scientizing and reproducing the power relations of gender by elevating current gender prescriptions to universal essentialisms, our patients and society as a whole might be better able to develop new ways of living and relating.

But if culture is so foundational in our way of being, how do we think critically, oppose the status quo, and have independent thoughts? How is psychological change possible? How do people oppose the mainstream? For instance, how did the White Rose in Germany or the French

Resistance locate a perspective that freed them to rise up against the Nazis? A possible answer lies in the idea that, although we are socially constructed, and culture is "sedimented" in us, we are not influenced solely by a single, monolithic culture. Philosophical hermeneutics presumes that each of us lives at an *intersection* of traditions. Traditions sometimes conflict, are obscure and opaque, rely on justifications that do not convince us, and divide us as well as bring us together. We find ways of resisting community practices, governmental policies, the demands of charismatic leaders or authoritarian officials because we have alternative perspectives, traditions, or alternative aspects of a tradition to draw upon. The determination about what constitutes the good and what is true is a continuing, ongoing dialogic negotiation. Our ability to find other traditions or aspects of our indigenous tradition that help us understand what we disapprove of in our normative community frees us to resist the status quo and develop new alternatives.

For instance, some theories consider family rules such as what can be noticed and/or commented upon and what must remain unseen and/or unnamed to be products of a "dysfunctional" family system. But the functional-dysfunctional distinction contains several problems, such as the implicit meanings and implications of the word "functional" in late twentieth-century capitalist society. Should our highest goal be to be functional in a world such as ours? It is a distinction fraught with philosophical and political problems.[14]

A hermeneutic perspective might help us think of the reproduction of family patterns and the keeping of family secrets as commitments to a particular moral frame. Family roles and rules can be understood to be composed of the larger cultural frame of reference, smaller subcultural and community traditions, and finally the interactional rules of specific families. Within a family, there might be conflicting moral understandings and therefore conflicting behavioral responsibilities. For instance, a young woman might comply with a behavioral prescription dictated by an obligation to and an attachment with her dead father. Let us imagine that for various reasons the father alternately had ignored and was mean and humiliating to the young woman, and that other family members, including the mother, had been afraid of and dependent upon the father and therefore did not criticize his treatment of her. Let us also imagine that this family lives in what was once a relatively cohesive ethnic community that has been severely undermined by some mainstream American values. The values of mainstream American culture regarding the specific twentieth-century configuration of gender have made increasing inroads in and in ways were similar to the mainstream indigenous culture, but let us imagine that this particular indigenous culture contains a minor but important sect that discourages sexist practices and beliefs. Lately there has been a movement among women in the community, informed by an unlikely combination of American feminism and the ideals of the sect, a combination that values cooperation between the sexes and the worth of women as well as men. This movement is dedicated to fighting against certain intrusions by the dominant culture (and the mainstream indigenous culture), such as the violence against women that the youngsters see on TV, witness at school, and are exposed to in the neighborhood.

In order to get along in her family of origin, the young woman long ago learned and practiced the moral code of silence. To comply with the rule of silence, and to stay emotionally involved with her father and mother in the limited ways available to her, she unconsciously came to believe that it was natural and proper for *all* men to treat her as her father did. This was a taken-for-granted assumption of the psychological terrain of the world in which she had been born and raised and it was continually enacted through everyday social practices. Therefore a gender-role prescription she brought to her adult life was to *expect* all men to ignore or abuse her. But then, let us imagine that the woman has given birth to and is raising a male child. In the course of everyday life, the young woman begins to experience a conflict between honoring the obligation to and reproducing the moral terrain identified with her father, on the one hand, and on the other, her growing commitment to the combined moral understandings that the women of the community are developing. The second moral frame obligates her to relate to him with trust and mutual respect and to teach him to act the same way toward her. She will not be able to respect him or teach him to respect her, if she continually *anticipates* that he will—and should—act toward her as her father did.

Hermeneuticists argue that each of us, each day, engages in the continual process of unknowingly learning, constructing, and reconstructing the parameters of the social world in which we live. In order to live and survive in that world, we must be at work constantly producing, interpreting, anticipating, and influencing our social surround. By unconsciously constructing a world in which men *naturally* ignore and abuse her, the young woman in our example is unknowingly complying with a moral prescription to not notice other possibilities for male-female interaction. She will *refuse* to notice, through selective inattention or dissociation, the relations between males and females that are kinder and more respectful than her relation with her father and will *overemphasize* and perhaps unconsciously seek out the relations between males and females that are similar to her relations with her father. (This will not be difficult to do, since the dominant culture and her mainstream indigenous culture initially shaped the gender relations that produced her relationship with her father.) Therefore she is complying with a moral requirement that she "honor" her father and unknowingly reproducing her relationship with him instead of being open to other, less disappointing or hurtful relations, or perhaps even warm, helpful, and loving relations in the present. But her growing sense of being a member of the feminist-minority sect movement could influence her understanding of what constitutes her moral obligations to her son, her community, and her role as a mother. These influences might help her choose to leave what is now a fantasy relationship with a father located in the *past* in order to fulfill her moral obligations as individual, mother, and community member in the *present*. These responsibilities might even help her develop a shifted, reconfigured, more subversive understanding of what it means to "honor" her parents. But it will be difficult for her to shift her commitments, and how she thinks about herself in relation to her commitments, because cultural products such as a moral frame are sedimented in the body; that is, because they are experienced bodily as "me," change is difficult and new ways of being are at first experienced as "not me."

Similar to the influence exercised by the feminist group in the indigenous culture, we can conceptualize psychotherapy as a set of interactions that embody a competing and alternative moral frame that challenges the one to which patients have been previously committed. Patients will at first try to involve the therapist in interactions that enact the moral frame to which they have been previously committed, because that is all that is available to them. They will unquestioningly expect the world of the therapy office to be morally constructed similar to the world of their earlier life. It is the job of the psychotherapist to demonstrate the existence of a world constituted by different rules and to encourage patients to be aware of available moral traditions that oppose the moral frame by which they presently shape their lives. Through the interactions between therapist and patient, patients will have the opportunity to confront the implicit moral understandings enacted through their behaviors, expectations, and emotional responses. They will be able to sketch out a picture of the larger cultural terrain in which they were originally thrown. Finally, they will have the opportunity to experience how their commitment to the old terrain and its moral code has affected them, and to contrast that with the possibilities that are presented by the moral frame offered by the therapist and those alternative frames available but unacknowledged in their present life. By interacting with the therapist over time, patients may notice that new emotional and behavioral possibilities have emerged, and they may develop their own version of the morality offered by the therapist, combine it in various ways with other traditions in their lives, and choose to commit to a different, slightly shifted moral way of being.

If the woman in the above example came to therapy, the therapist could conceptualize family dynamics as an intersection of various and sometimes conflicting moral commitments embedded in moral traditions. By not treating the conflict solely in an asocial, intrapsychic manner, the therapist would not be supporting the dominant ideology of self-contained individualism. If the therapist did not characterize the parent-child dyad as an isolated, decontextualized universe, the historical and political forces of our era would be considered permissible subjects of the psychotherapy hour. Topics such as the way messages about gender roles are disseminated and how violence against women is encouraged in everyday social communication such as in jokes and stories, television sitcoms and commercials, magazines, comic strips, movies, and family traditions would then be available for psychological analysis, as would the topic of how gender is enacted *within* the therapy hour in the transference-countertransference dynamic. It would be more difficult to unconsciously reproduce the consumer ethos of our time if the therapist were to conceive of the growth of the child in interpersonal, social, and educational terms in which the child is enculturated into a particular world, rather than in current developmental language, according to which children must *ingest* parents in order to *build* a self. In the above example, if the therapist chose not to emphasize the building of the son's true self, the liberationist ideology of the enchanted American interior would not be reproduced, and thus another aspect of the consumer ethos of our time would not be encouraged. By framing this scene in terms of moral commitments, choice, and communal responsibility, the therapist would not view the woman as a passive victim of abuse or neglect, but as an *active* agent, constrained by her complicity with particular social practices in her world, but also potentially *empowered* by her embrace of alternative social arrangements and her use of the alternative arrangements in her resistance against the more common practices. Thus, by using a hermeneutic formulation, a crucial aspect of the gender prescriptions of our time—the passivity and helplessness of women—would not be perpetuated by the therapy. It is important to remember that the social arrangements of the young woman's world include the moral ideals that help her shift her terrain as well as those which constrain her. It is her active sifting through of various moral perspectives that allows her to shift her way of being.

If human being is conceptualized as a product of the cultural clearing, the interaction between various influences and an individual's adaptations to those influences becomes prominent. Behavior is not thought to be automatic or determined; it is thought to appear (or disappear) according to the specifics of the cultural context and the person's response to that context. In the above example, just as one tradition—the combination of the dominant culture and the family system—brings certain behaviors into view and prohibits others, so too would an alternative tradition—the combination of the minority sect within the indigenous culture and the beliefs of American feminism—evoke and encourage competing behaviors. If the young woman had come to a hermeneutically oriented therapy, the political aspects of her situation, for instance the conflicting rules regarding gender, would be allowed to emerge in the therapy hour, just as would issues and ideas with more of an individual or a family focus. Connections between the moral frame of her family of origin and the larger society's construction of gender would be explored, as would the connections between the ideals of the emerging feminist group and the minority beliefs of the indigenous tradition.

Hermeneutics calls upon us to develop ways of shifting our *perspective* about our lives, individually and collectively. It could help us develop ways of thinking more about *the world* we live in, not so that we diminish our own individual piece of it, but so that we can place our piece of it in a different perspective. For instance, those who do research on the social construction of emotions[15] argue that there is no such thing as a purely, unsocial, "true" feeling. This is a shocking thought for most of us, especially those of us, patients and practitioners alike, who work in therapy to discover and articulate just that type of pure feeling. Constructionist researchers suggest that feelings are constructed, not found. They are constructed from the cultural framework in which all individuals are immersed. It is not so much some isolated, inner, intrapsychic Truth that is experienced when one gets in touch with one's feelings, as the saying goes. It is more that as an undifferentiated mix of emotion becomes shaped and differentiated, as it is placed into a particular moral frame, the feeling emerges, becomes identifiable, understandable, and thus socially useable. The feeling becomes felt after it is categorized, framed in a particular way by the shared understandings of our cultural frame of reference, which have been embodied by us. Then, finally, we experience and *understand* the feeling, because we have *framed* what it is. Because we can put it in a moral context, it can appear and be recognized. It is then available to be used by us as proof of the correctness or incorrectness of a particular behavior: as punctuation, if you will, to everyday moral and political acts.

In the same way, I do not believe that in each of us lies some purely asocial, core, true self that we must learn to trust, express, and be guided by. Instead, our experience of individual, self-contained "trueness" is a product of the shape of the larger cultural clearing in which each of us is embedded. What some psychotherapists might call the true self is what hermeneuticists would call the way of being that best corresponds with our current configuration of the self and the moral concepts that have constituted that configuration. The true self, therefore, means the approved form of the self, the approved way of being, not some objective, scientific measure of universal selfhood. It might feel "true" because the cultural concept of proper being is sedimented in our bodies, and therefore when we act properly we "feel" as though we are proper. But that feeling is not a universal measure of ahistorical properness—it is just the opposite. It is the stirring of a highly contingent, socially constructed affective response that indicates to us that we are behaving properly within our given social context. When we act masterful and bounded, that is, when we experience ourselves as self-contained, autonomous, expressive, assertive, and powerful, when we desire certain commodities, activities, or individuals that have been culturally prescribed, we experience an emotional affirmation of our way of being—we *embody* the anticipated approval of our culture.

Further, by labeling certain behaviors and sensations as "true," therapists are making a political move. They are claiming that those behaviors and sensations are acknowledged to be correct in a way beyond dispute, by definition. Thus therapists who use the true self concept are claiming a privileged epistemological position, which, as explained at length in previous chapters, is philosophically problematic. This claim camouflages a moral stance and thereby obscures the therapist's ideology.

If our culture prescribed a way of being at variance with self-contained individualism, or if certain schools of psychotherapy attempted to develop a way of being that was more communal and less self-contained, a different way of being might someday come to be considered proper. To the degree that we could think of ourselves as essential parts of a living community, a community of persons with whom we share certain moral understandings, obligations, and responsibilities, the self could show up as being constituted by the qualities of consideration and cooperation. As a result, we could probably think more considerately and act more cooperatively, and in the process feel true, genuine, and that our behavior is justified.

If we can change our psychotherapy theories so that they are more historically situated, and our psychotherapy practices to make use of hermeneutics, we could put forth a different moral frame. Hermeneutics, psychologists Blaine Fowers and Frank Richardson repeatedly remind us, encourages us to "examine our moral frameworks and carefully sift them in order to recognize and rework those aspects that are found wanting."[16] For instance, by valuing the social world, by locating social interaction and human subjectivity within the space between people and within history and culture, by acknowledging the interweaving of the individual and the society, by recognizing and honoring the ongoing relatedness and involvement of human life, by valuing the polyvocality of our psychological terrain and the multiculturalism of our planet's terrain, psychotherapy practices could demonstrate a morality that would challenge the dominant moral understandings and political arrangements of our era. By historically situating psychotherapy, and thus by acknowledging the ways that psychotherapy has unknowingly substituted for missing community tradition, has provided a covert moral framework about the proper way of being human, and has obscured the sociopolitical causes of psychological suffering, psychotherapy would model the ability to confront one's unconscious contributions to the political and philosophical problems of our time and to be freer to more explicitly present thoughtful, nuanced, moral conceptions of human being.

I do not mean by this argument that we should be one-dimensional, unreflective, or unpsychological. I am not at all suggesting that we lose the understandings about ourselves that make for a reflective, introspective, self-questioning, complex way of being. I wouldn't want to suggest for instance, that we reject concepts such as the existence of unconscious feelings, thoughts, or conflicts. But distinctions such as inner-outer, individual-society, society-nature are the products of a certain sociohistorical perspective, and as a result they have certain philosophical and political consequences. These distinctions are not the only distinctions possible; in other cultures and historical eras there have been and still are other distinctions. Why not frame our relationship with the world, with nature, with other cultures, with others in our own culture in a different, more *interrelated* way? Perhaps we can frame human being in a way that celebrates the interweaving of what we usually call individual, society, and nature. We don't have to think of ourselves as isolated, interior monads—that is not *the* unalterable truth about ourselves; it is just one perspective on ourselves, and perspectives can change. The tradition of isolation and interiority is embedded in a complex of traditions that have gained power during the modern age. It has brought us many helpful ideas, and some that have been harmful. Other traditions bring alternative perspectives into view—many of these traditions are not completely alien to us—we always live in the *intersection* of various traditions. Although we are not completely free to choose just any old tradition, or create any new tradition, we need not be strangers to other perspectives, some of which are also "ours."

GRINDING THE HERMENEUTIC AXE

This, then, is the axe I have to grind: I would like us to notice the moral and political consequences of our current way of being, the current configuration of the self. I would like for us to be aware of how social practices, such as psychotherapy, help shape the configuration of the self. After all, our current self, and the current configurations of race and gender, are not the only ways of being that are available to humans. We need to think about how we could shape our social practices, such as psychotherapy, so that we might begin configuring a slightly different, more cooperative, interrelated way of being that would have slightly different moral and political effects.

I have used the previous chapters to describe and contextualize certain trends in the history of psychotherapy. These trends have helped construct specific configurations of the self, which in turn have led to moral understandings and arrangements of power and privilege that seem unfortunate and in fact dangerous. Psychotherapy's current but unintentional compliance with the sociopolitical arrangements of our era could be reduced if the discipline as a whole would undertake and carry forward this hermeneutic project. Then we could better see how the correspondence theory of truth, the theme of domination-submission, the construction of isolated, interior individualism, the concept of the liberation of the enchanted American interior, the medicalization of emotional distress, the tokenism inherent in the "geographical strategy" of object relations theory, the reification and then commodification of self processes and the construction of the empty self have at various times led to the support and reproduction of negative aspects of the status quo, and thus a chronic lack of satisfaction, moral confidence, and meaning. Without a historical and cultural perspective, the field can't see what it is doing. The eye cannot see *how* it is seeing.

If psychotherapists could develop a historical perspective, perhaps we could get a sense of what framework we are seeing through. And then perhaps we could develop ideas about the philosophical soundness, moral rightness, and everyday effects of our theories on the lives of others. If we could do that, perhaps we could figure out whether we approve of the moral position we are taking and the political effect we are having on our patients. In other words, perhaps we could tolerate thinking of the work of psychotherapy as a kind of moral discourse that has political consequences. Since I believe that psychotherapy is unintentionally exercising a moral and political influence, we would do well to realize and acknowledge it. But how could we do that effectively? And where would it take us? What does the historical approach get us, when all is said and done?

Surprisingly, I believe, quite a lot. For many years of struggle I thought it unrealistic to expect a research approach to provide a different perspective for the practice of psychotherapy. But at some point I realized that, much to my surprise (and relief), it had. The constructionist, hermeneutic approach used throughout this book is, of course, more than just a social science "methodology." In fact, it is expressly *not* a methodology, not a set of techniques. It is instead a philosophy, a way of living—no, a perspective on living. At some point during all the years of *sturm und drang*, I noticed that, without realizing it, I had begun to think about the lives of my patients, and in fact my life as well, in a substantially different way. I had begun to apply the hermeneutic perspective I had learned while researching and studying the history of psychotherapy to my work as a psychotherapist. I am not sure whether the use of hermeneutics in psychotherapy will someday constitute a new practice or just a different way of describing and understanding already existing practices. It seems clear that hermeneutics is easily mixed with forms of interpersonal, constructivist, and intersubjective theory. So perhaps the second alternative will prevail. On the other hand, some hermeneuticists, such as Donnel Stern, believe this philosophy has an innovative, far-reaching potential we have barely begun to mine. In any case, it is to the beginning articulation of a hermeneutic perspective that I dedicate the remainder of this chapter.

POGO'S (AND GADAMER'S) HORIZON

There was an original Walt Kelly comic strip that pictured Pogo staring out into the swamp, peering out beyond where the trees stopped growing. He says, "I just thunk—Which horizon?" His companion, Howland Owl, lying with his hands behind his head, replies: "There's a old philosophiwockle thought—Which way lies the horizon—How far from here? Ne'er to be at hand—Ne'er to disappear—"[17]

When I recently saw this strip, I realized that something had changed in my work, some shift had taken place. I realized that I knew what this strip meant: I got the joke. And I also realized that, amusingly, so would some of my patients. They would get the joke because I have been using the language of philosophical hermeneutics with them, at least some of them, for the last couple of years. I remembered that old joke about how "coincidental" it is that Freudian patients have Freudian dreams and Jungian patients have Jungian dreams. My patients would get

Pogo's joke because I had been preparing them for it by the language I have used, by what I have shown interest in, and what I have ignored. I have prepared them for it because I have lived in it for a while now; it is my world, and by being involved with me, they have also moved into that world.

If my patients have been somewhat involved in this new world, then you, the reader, have too. Perhaps you got the joke, too. We laugh because the comic strip is funny, touching, troubling, paradoxical. It captures in a moment the hermeneutic idea of the clearing that philosophers Martin Heidegger and Hans-Georg Gadamer spoke of, the concept of the cultural clearing that I have used as the central metaphor of this book. Language, dress, religion, morals, class, hierarchy, manners, family rules and rituals, all those things that constitute our social world, all the experiences and institutions that are constituted by our everyday social practices make up what Gadamer called the horizon of understanding. Through our cultural beliefs and personal opinions we unknowingly make it possible in our clearing for certain things to be brought into view, and at the same time we exclude other things from showing up. Our culture does this by developing over time a certain placement of the horizon: it is situated in such a way as to make room for certain things but to deny space for others; to illuminate certain ideas, events, and relationships, but not to shed light on others. When the horizon is located in one place, there is only room in the terrain for certain things to show up; when the horizon moves out, farther away from the individual, there is room for new possibilities. But no matter where the horizon is located, when something is on the other side of the horizon, it is as if it is gone, as if it simply doesn't exist, because it can't show up: it has dropped off the face of the earth.

I have been thinking about this metaphor of the clearing for several years, using it in my writing to convey the shape of various historical eras and non-Western cultures. At some point it occurred to me that Gadamer did not restrict his use of the horizonal metaphor to historical research or complex, arcane philosophical disputes. Gadamer himself thought that the metaphor was potentially a good one for *all* human interaction. At some point in all this it occurred to me that I might be able to think of psychotherapy in the same way.

I was listening to a patient, a troubled mid-thirties male professional, one of the most tortured patients I have ever worked with.[18] We had been meeting for about four years at that time, twice each week. He was in a particularly excruciating experience that day, one that he sometimes slips into: he is certain that no one will want to know how he really feels, everyone will hate him and reject him for what he thinks, and no one will allow him what he needs. And it occurred to me that day that he was describing a world to me, the world that he lived in when he was in this particular state of mind. Suddenly, I saw that world, spread out before him on all sides, peopled with certain characters and voices from his past, from a time when the horizon was originally formed or significantly reordered. I thought of those pop-up books made for children: when we open them, a whole little world of mountains, cities, and individuals instantly pops up and comes to life before us.

Before I could think much about it, before I knew what would happen next, I told him it seemed to me as though a world had suddenly appeared before us, a world that encompassed him on all sides. In this world, the people of his young life live and interact, all according to the rules that he has described to me or enacted with me. These rules create positions in which certain people must live, and these positions determine destinies. I described some of these rules as I had come to understand them, especially those that pertained to how he felt that day.

"Well," he said, "that's life. That's all there is." He paused, cocked his head, and looked puzzled. "What do you mean—that there's some *other* world?" He paused, and then laughed, a relaxed, pleasant kind of laugh I have rarely heard from him. For a moment, he had glimpsed an alternative perspective, or the possibility of an alternative, and the experience momentarily released him from the tortuous imprisonment he experienced in that old terrain.

In the sessions that have followed we have come to that moment many times. Sometimes he has snarled at me, disgusted that anyone could be as stupid and naive as his therapist. There is only one world, the *real* world, and it is just a lie, a malicious trick on my part to get him to think that he could live some other way. Sometimes he has looked hurt and wistful, and remarked that he knows that others live in a different world, but it is a world that he is forever prevented from entering. He has come to believe that as a child he felt as though he should have died, or should never have been born, that he didn't deserve to live, that he was essentially "evil" (his word), and therefore he was denied the sense of entitlement others feel. This lack of entitlement was illustrated in a dream that he has referred to many times. He is a young child, perhaps two years of age. He is very hungry, and he finds himself at the table, wanting something to eat. But the surface of the table moves like a conveyor belt, and the wonderful food moves away from him, always beyond his reach. It is a supremely frustrating, maddening experience. Throughout the scene he has the pervasive sense that the reason the food passes him by is that he does not *deserve* it—he does not deserve to live—

because he is inherently evil. There is no doubt that the judgment he experiences is a *moral* judgment.

Sometimes, not often, but with increasing frequency, he has come to wonder about what other worlds he might have experienced in his past but hasn't let himself acknowledge, or other worlds—with other rules and thus other positions—that he could experience *now*, if only he could locate them or be free to experience them. He sometimes wonders if the therapy hour could be a different world for him, if in fact it *is* a different world for him. He wonders: if it is a different world, what does he do to construct it, what do the two of us do to co-construct it, what does he do to sabotage it, what do *I* do to sabotage it (this is a common topic), *why* does he sabotage it, and so forth. There seem to be a lot of good questions that can be asked about these worlds: the new ones, the old ones, the worlds that haven't yet been made, the worlds that could have been but weren't and now are lost forever.

We talk together about what is possible and what is prohibited in his old world; in other words, what the moral framework of that world is. We talk about what constitutes the mother position(s) and the father position(s) in that world. We listen to the stories and wonder about what was possible for that little boy in there, what he must have felt like, what he couldn't allow himself to feel, or what feelings were simply unavailable to him because they were on the other side of the horizon. These were feelings that might be called unconscious feelings, feelings that were unheard of, unnamed, too painful, too delicious (which was evil), or too threatening to the whole terrain, the whole cardboard stage, as Peter Berger[19] used to call it.

We talk about what positions are possible for humans to occupy in that world, what it means to be a man and what it means to be a woman. We notice what people cannot say, what they cannot even think, what they do to stop thinking in order to conform to the moral guidelines. Some psychodynamic theories, especially interpersonal psychology, stress these ideas; hermeneutics is in part simply a different, more direct way of talking about what some other theories have also described. But by placing an emphasis on the *moral* constellation of the psychological world, and by situating psychological processes in the social space *between* people, hermeneutics offers a new perspective, one quite relevant to the socially constructed nature of human being. In effect, we are continually asking the question "How are you treating others?" and "How are you treating yourself?" This sometimes leads to questions that might help answer an overall point such as what kind of world is the patient living in that would consider that kind of behavior proper or moral? These are, of course, not rhetorical questions carrying a disapproving tone, but real questions that both patient and therapist must cooperate to answer. Aspects of interpersonal technique, such as inquiring about how the patient thinks the therapist is feeling in the moment, or even (more rarely) the therapist disclosing how he or she is feeling, add to the material that can be used for these questions and are easily combined with the kind of interpersonal or intersubjective transference-countertransference analysis previously mentioned.

I have begun to think of our task as that of recognizing when the old world of my patient's past rises up, what it consists of, how it affects him, how he brings it into being, how he interacts with others because of it, what he evokes in others and how he influences them to join him in it, what he misses out on because he is immersed in it, and most difficult of all, what he gets out of it, what the benefits are for him to be in that world. Having been influenced by interpersonal theory, I consider the interaction within the therapy hour, including what the patient evokes in me and how the two of us cooperate in order to bring forth that old world, to be an important tool in this endeavor. Although at first we took the dream about the moving food to refer to the good, nourishing things he was deprived of by others, we are more recently also talking about the dream because it brings to my patient's attention what he is deprived of because of how he *currently*, *actively*, configures his world. Much of this we only get a sense of when he experiences the old world with me, or perhaps I should say when the two of us experience his old world, when he evokes that world for me too, and when I step into it. Occasionally, very occasionally, he can get a sense of what he does (or what I do) to summon that world. When he can do that, he gets very frightened, very angry, and for a moment almost hopeful.

He hates that hopeful, alive, joyful feeling, of course. It is the quintessence of evil in the old world. It has caused unbearable kinds of trouble. So then we wonder what it would be like to experience that feeling more often, how it would affect the terrain, what it would take to *move back* the horizon so that there would be room for that feeling, and why he resists knowing more about all that. Once, right after he was remarking about how drawn he is to the old world, and how guilty he feels if even for a moment he escapes it, lets the clearing open up, and resides somewhere else, I said to him: "You know, I wonder if this is what Freud meant when he talked about Oedipus?" He looked very sad, then, and quietly joked, "You mean I want to go to bed with my old world?" A small smile tugged at the side of his mouth. "I mean," I replied, "that I think you want to lie down with it each night." He looked up at me, eyes filled with longing: "It *is* so warm on a cold night." There are several potential meanings present in this type of exchange, including meanings related to a patient's feelings of love and sexual desire, which of course need to be explored in depth.

His response demonstrated one of the reasons why humans are driven to reproduce the old terrain, even though it is so destructive to us: my patient does to himself and to others what was done to him, in part to evoke the terrain that contained his relationships with those he loved and needed so desperately and the moral frame that explained and justified their particular pattern of relating. We unknowingly reproduce old ways of loving and being loved by sending a multitude of signals and cues to others, and by selectively attending and not attending to the signals and cues of others regarding what are permissible behaviors, feelings, and interactions. Through such not-conscious communication, the horizon of understanding gets positioned so that only the old terrain in which those old relationships and moral understandings were embedded has room to show up. Orthodox psychoanalysis would explain this phenomenon through the language of drives, and object relations theory would describe it as the wish to stay relationally connected to an *internal* part-object. But using the horizonal metaphor, we can describe the behavior without as much recourse to the interiorizing, hyperindividualistic language that unknowingly contributes to the reproduction of the empty self.

Through creative interpretations, the hermeneutic therapist can begin to sketch out the major psychological players and voices within the patient's world. But rather than locating these "positions" (that is, what is behaviorally and affectively possible) within the patient's psychological interior, this use of hermeneutics encourages the therapist to locate both self-conceptions and the various psychological configurations of "the other" in a cultural terrain conceptualized as spreading out on all sides of the patient. This theoretical tactic reminds the therapist and the patient that the split-off, disavowed, idiosyncratic representations generated by the patient are not naturally, necessarily located interiorly. They are currently thought to be interior because that is the way our cultural terrain designates them. More productively, they need to be construed as inhabiting the world *between* people. Therapists might find themselves making interventions such as, "You are describing a world in which 'the other' in your life is consistently angry and dissatisfied with you"; or "In your psychological world the one you love can only 'show up' as emotionally withdrawn"; or "In the world you are experiencing now with me, that we are enacting together, it seems as though there is no room in which to stand where you can be seen and understood by me, and there is no way that I can speak to you without bringing in the frustration and wariness that our interchanges evoke in me."

In this conceptualization of psychotherapy, the unconscious is not an interior "thing," but part of the patient's social landscape that contains potential feelings, thoughts, and experiences that are not able to "show up" because they lie on the other side of the patient's horizon of understandings. Defenses are not thought to be hydraulic mechanisms that manage the secret, dangerous id, but rather aspects of a moveable horizon. The horizon is configured in part through the exercise of linguistic, tropic strategies (see Nathan Adler, 1994, and Harold Bloom, 1975)— subtle uses of language that reflect understandings about what is considered possible and proper to see, feel, and give voice or movement to within a particular cultural clearing.[20]

This vision of human life is advantageous because it would help therapists talk about psychological emotions, urges, wishes, fantasies, and problems without locating them interiorly and thus reproducing and capitulating to the ideology of self-contained individualism. Also psychotherapists wouldn't be forced onto a path that has led to the consumerized metaphors that have saturated object relations theory and self psychology. This vision would also help therapists discuss psychological issues with less theoretical mystification. Hermeneutic theory sees the compulsive attempt to conceptualize and reproduce the world in a certain way as a basic human motive, an indispensable survival mechanism. This way of conceiving of motive might help us stay away from creating and theorizing about more esoteric, metaphysical, and needlessly complex motivational structures that run the risk of falling prey to highly technicized metaphors that have subtle political functions. Hermeneutics might therefore help therapists avoid some of the political pitfalls to which many twentieth-century healing enterprises have been vulnerable.

Through the hermeneutic approach repetitive self-destructive behavior is not conceived of as the return of the repressed or as an attempt to keep alive old attachment patterns, but as the product of the patient's unknowing efforts to reproduce a cultural terrain, usually an old terrain, in which it was correct to act in certain specific ways. Therapist and patient can then explore how the patient reproduces that terrain, what the patient does not attend to, forgets, exaggerates, reinterprets, manipulates, evokes, provokes, proscribes; what the patient and therapist do together in order to reproduce that terrain; and the toll all this takes on the patient's energy, perceptual faculties, well-being, and relational capacities. Such repetitive behavior is not considered by hermeneutics to be an occasional neurotic act but instead is the process by which each of us, each day, engages in the unconscious constructing and reconstructing of the parameters of our terrain. To live and survive in a world, we must constantly work at interpreting, anticipating, and influencing the social surround. Tropic strategies that disguise and hide from view unwanted feelings are essential in these maneuvers, because we use them to convince ourselves and others that we are thinking and acting in a proper manner, given the moral understandings that frame the particular world we inhabit.

USING HERMENEUTICS IN THE PRACTICE OF PSYCHOTHERAPY

I began using the same metaphor with my patients that I use in my history research: the metaphor of the cultural clearing. I started doing this because I wanted to limit my use of the metaphors, language, theories, and therapeutic interventions that have been so much in tune with the current sociopolitical terrain. I wanted my language to stop being taken over by the language of the masterful, bounded self. I wanted to stop reinforcing in an unquestioned, unqualified way what Foucault called the isolated individual with the "richly furnished interior," because I had come to realize that one of the *essential* ingredients of that interior was the absence of a vibrant connection with the social world of community and shared meaning. By the late twentieth century our richly furnished interiors are only furnished with *things*: our connection with others rarely shows up in our current clearing, our connection with consumer items often seems to be the only connection available to us, and an experience of our selves has been attenuated to the point that our interiors have become giant vacuums, making only great sucking sounds.

On the other hand, I didn't want to start sounding so weird that no one could understand me. I didn't want to start sounding like I was from Mars (or, more accurately, postmodern France). Probably, I remember thinking one day, this struggle is what is meant by the admonition to hold both sides of the dialectic. I want to resist negative aspects of the status quo, but I also know I can't, nor do I want to try to, singlehandedly do away with individualism. I know I live in this very Western, modern, individualistic world, and I know there are aspects of it that I enjoy and would not want to lose. So I asked myself what I could do to live in it and work in it with more integrity. It was soon after this that I began, selectively, to use the horizonal metaphor in therapy.

Slowly, I came to develop an interpretation of Gadamer's horizonal metaphor that I could live with in my work. It goes like this: at birth, each of us is thrown into a particular world. Growing up is the process of learning the background procedures, shared understandings, rules, and meanings of that very particular world, from the larger world of history and culture to the very particular, local world of families, friends, and communities that exists within and as a result of the larger cultural world. That world is communicated to us through myriad social practices and interactions that make up the little moments of everyday life. We must come to be a part of that background so fully, so completely, that we embody it—it is sedimented into our bodies. It comes to constitute us. We need to do that so that we can reproduce it instantaneously upon waking each morning, upon meeting and interacting with others, upon performing any of the innumerable but indispensable tasks we are called upon to perform each day. The world that we must reproduce shifts slightly according to the particular requirements of various situations, and especially with regard to particular persons within particular situations. Others, of course, are doing the same thing, and as a consequence of our shared social practices, we continuously co-construct a viable, understandable, predictable world. In other words, we are called upon to construct a particular world each morning and to recall and act according to specific procedural rules and moral understandings, depending on the individuals we encounter and the contexts in which we encounter them within the larger cultural clearing. We must learn which particular areas of the clearing we must emphasize or focus on at any one given moment.

We also, and here is the *most* difficult part, construct this world without being able to admit it or even be aware of it. There is something in the very nature of being human that makes it extremely difficult to differentiate what we are from what we construct, or what we can be from what our horizon permits us to be. We construct the social world in such a way so that we can consider it, experience it, as reality itself—the one, true, concrete truth. To do otherwise would be to open up the existential abyss for us, to force us to confront our own lacks, absences, and emptiness, to challenge the taken-for-granted power relations, economic privileges, and status hierarchy of our era, and to acknowledge the relational rules, alliances, and secrets of our family of origin. For various reasons, an awareness of the constructed nature of our world appears to be too difficult to acknowledge and too frightening to live with.

As a result, we have no conscious control over our part in the structuring of the world as we immediately know it and live it. This is good in that we can do many complex tasks without having to clutter our consciousness with questions pertaining to how we set the overall frame. (Imagine the trouble it would take to ride a bike, drive a car, or relate to the many strangers and acquaintances in our lives if each day we had to relearn the motor skills, relational rules, and selective inattention necessary to perform the required tasks and ignore the necessary dangers of these activities.) We can also go about our everyday life without confronting the lack of at-homeness that is necessary in the cultural construction of a world. But our lack of consciousness in structuring the world is also bad in that we experience the constructed world as an immutable, unchallengeable given: we can't imagine the possibility of changing it. Unfortunately, some aspects of the world that we have learned so much about and shaped our behavior in order to accommodate to—aspects of the world that we are perhaps most at home with—do not necessarily make for a very good world. This world may not be very compatible with the constructed world that *others* live in; it may not fit well with the present-day world that we, *as adults*, live in; and it may not be the kind of world we would *want* to live in. But as we saw in the earlier vignette with my patient, it is the world we cuddle up with, when it is cold outside and things go bump in the night. It may be a distant or mean parent we sidle up to, but we are drawn to him or her just the same. It may be a distasteful or irrational moral frame that we feel a strong, embodied allegiance to, but it may be the only one available or the only one we dare embrace at that given moment. It is precisely this conspiring, this unknowing, embodied collusion that psychotherapy is designed to reveal and undo.

There is a very subtle and complex dialectic at work in human life: the world we are thrown into constructs us, and then we must continually reconstruct it. It limits us by its givenness, and then we, in turn, limit it. Where does the givenness end, and our semiconscious collusion begin?

The task, in psychotherapy, is to confront our thrownness, discover experientially and cognitively how we cooperate in constructing the world the way we do, more fully experience the consequences of that construction, explore whether we want to continue constructing it, conceive of alternative configurations, and then develop ways of *letting* a different world emerge. I do not mean that this process is solely or even predominantly rational, calculating, cognitive, or conscious. I do not mean that this process is even entirely possible—the concept of the clearing implies not only the potential for change but also the very real limitations of givenness. But perhaps there is also a place for thinking and choosing, for will as well as feeling; a place for hope as well as resignation and compromise.

THE DISEMBODIED HAND

Once during a therapy hour a patient did something unusual. I had been seeing her for about two years. During this particular hour she had tried, unsuccessfully, to hide what she called a "stupid habit," which was to unconsciously pick at her skin or bite her cuticles until she drew blood. She was in her late forties at the time and had stopped her career at her husband's insistence after the birth of the first of several children. She reported a childhood that was the product of a marriage between a sadistic, sociopathic father and a long-suffering, exhausted, self-destructive mother. The therapy hour in question started as usual, with a description of various problems one or more of the children were causing. My patient became upset by something one of the teenage children had done, and then more upset still over something her husband had done in response to the child's behavior. She had begun picking at a wound in her arm, and, as I sometimes do, I commented on her behavior and asked her how she was feeling right then. She was embarrassed by being seen by me, flustered really, and as usual reported that she felt nothing and had been unaware of the picking. But this time she continued to get progressively more upset and was unable to put words to her feelings. She had always been inarticulate about her feelings, but on this day she literally ceased being able to speak. She sat, agonized, her mouth open in silent crying, her hand over her mouth, her eyes closed shut, her face contorted in pain and humiliation, her body shaking with suppressed sobs that made no sound.

In the year or so since that time, that scene has occurred a few times. It is not precipitated by the same events, nor does it take exactly the same form. But in most therapy hours, the self-wounding is reproduced, and occasionally the silent sobbing commences. For a long time, she had no idea what it meant; she reported an absence of feeling, a blank, almost trancelike state. But after witnessing it for some time, I began to develop some ideas about it, based on my own experience of being in the room with her when it happened, and I began to share some of my ideas with her.

I have noticed that she does not notice the self-wounding ritual, and she also does not expect me to notice it either. In fact, she might be angry with me for noticing, asking her about it, commenting on it, and causing her humiliation. I have noticed that she would start picking when I would expect her to feel angry and/or hurt about something that a loved one has done to her. The self-wounding, we might almost call it a kind of cutting, is very upsetting to witness; sometimes I don't think I can bear it. Sometimes I can't, and I have asked her to stop. I have always thought that one of the most important aspects of this enactment is that it affects me so viscerally, yet she expects me not to notice.

When I began to think about this in terms of the hermeneutic clearing, I told her that I thought she might be living in a world, or evoking a world with me, that seems to correspond to the world in which she lived as a child, the world she has described to me when she has words. In this world only her body can speak; somehow she is not allowed to put words, or tears, or shrieks to the grief that she is unconsciously experiencing. Only her body can speak, through what she writes upon it, the continual wounding that she suffers. Her body must be the text, because she is somehow commanded to be silent. She bleeds, quietly but continuously, from the wounds opened and reopened by a disembodied hand. And the hand, at least currently, is her own hand.

Sometimes as I watch her picking and rubbing the wounds open I think of the old saying "pouring salt into a wound." It seems to me as if sometimes her actions are like that. So I told her that I wonder if she is living in a world that is pouring salt into an old wound, continuingly picking at her, wounding her, reopening the pain. After groping for words, she finally said that her father was a terrible bully, always making fun of her, finding weak spots, and then picking and picking at her mercilessly. She has also mentioned ways that she thinks her husband criticizes and orders her about. But hers is, of course, a much more complicated experience than that, because it is actually her *own* hand that unconsciously inflicts or reopens the wound or administers the punishment or whatever it is that happens. I have asked her if that brings anything to mind. Over the course of time she has told me that for various reasons related to the poor health and behavioral problems of her siblings, and the serious economic deprivation the family suffered because her father was unwilling to work, her mother lived a life of constant harassment, confusion, and overwork, which was expressed through a series of debilitating psychosomatic illnesses. Because of her fears over her mother's physical and emotional condition, my patient remembers making a decision never to bother her mother with her own problems. She decided to take care of herself, to ask nothing and need nothing from her mother. At a relatively early age my patient began to work and volunteer at various community agencies after school and during evenings, in order to be out of the house, bring in some money, practice self-sufficiency, and I think also defend against thinking and feeling. These strategies made it possible for her to avoid the pain and resentment generated by being geographically close to her mother but unable to receive any help or comfort from her.

So perhaps the writing on her skin tells of a world in which, out of moral necessity, she had to wound herself, deprive herself of her mother's care, force herself to work when she might have wanted to play, isolate herself when she might have wanted to be involved, pretend to be directed and certain when in truth she needed guidance, act bravely and silently (although sometimes very resentfully) in the face of sorrow when she might have wanted to sob and be comforted. It is a lonely world that her acts demonstrate, one of cruelty, deprivation, and self-attack. Her only comfort, it seems, might come from her belief that she is helping her mother survive, that she is properly loving her mother by depriving and harming herself. Perhaps she also identifies with her mother by expressing her feelings the same way her mother expressed hers, through what Joyce McDougall has called the "theater" of the body.[21] If this is the case, then the wounds would feel comforting, the blood would be a sign of moral honor, the silent suffering a vindication of her self-righteousness. She might, during times of stress or family trouble, work even harder at causing herself pain, getting others to misunderstand and berate her, arranging ever more effectively to sacrifice yet go unseen and unappreciated. Her husband, weighed down by his own struggles and fighting his own demons, is sometimes quite willing to blame her and is unable to see his own role in their conflicts.

Of course the relations of gender in our society add immeasurably to my patient's frustration, pain, and self-condemnation. She embodies the taken-for-granted role of middle-class suburban wife and mother, a role that consists in large part of doing for others, caretaking, sacrificing, cooking and cleaning for them, running errands, volunteering, transporting them, often at the expense of her own wishes and needs. My patient's blood, I sometimes remember, is an image with which most mothers could identify. Also, adding to the salience of gender in my patient's marriage is the hierarchical implications of their two careers: my patient's career was in a secretary-like position in relation to her husband's attorney-like career. The two careers came complete with an automatic, taken-for-granted arrangement of hierarchy, privilege, and interactive rules that fit hand in glove with the world of her childhood. Her husband sometimes steps into her psychological world and stands in the place that she assigns him, the place of the one who blames and humiliates, the place in her world that lies waiting to be filled. Unfortunately, he is sometimes willing to step in and act the part, and she is willing to accept the blame, and so remarkably unwilling to see the way gender prescriptions contribute to her silent drama and the moral correctness of her bloody suffering. Because of the fit between the cultural arrangements of gender and my patient's private moral code, it is sometimes difficult to discern when it is her disembodied hand or when it is another's, her husband's or society's, that causes her suffering.

And what about my discomfort about her suffering? Might she interpret my reaction as an indication that the entire story about her young life and her choice to suffer silently was an unfortunate fantasy, unnecessary from the beginning except for the inadequacies of her mother and the malevolence of her father? For my patient, the web of meaning that defines her clearing is as much a spider's web, a deadly trap, as was Sullivan's. She is trapped in a perverse moral order, a world in which suffering was loving, needless bleeding honor, and self-inflicted deprivation equalled emotional closeness. My discomfort at her badges of honor might call into question the constructed meanings of her world, the family's shared understandings of what it meant in that world to be loved, to be a good daughter, to live a proper moral life. In other words, my discomfort might call into question the moral foundations of the particular, local clearing of her young life. No wonder my discomfort engenders feelings of shock, exposure, humiliation, rage, relief, gratitude. As I sit across from her, I guess that her reactions are constituted in part by anger at being disagreed with and intruded upon, and in part by relief and gratitude at being seen and cared about. But the overall impression she gives is one of being overwhelmed with undefined emotions. Many of those feelings would have no place to reside, to show up, within the horizon of her world. They would, for the time being, have to remain unnameable, because there is presently no frame of reference to illuminate them. They have not yet been constructed and thus drawn into the open. They are beyond the horizon: they are not conscious.

The other side of the dialectic, of course, is that this state of un-knowing is quite convenient for her: to know would cause some sort of change. This is illustrative of what some writers think Freud meant by the unconscious: the repository for that which is disavowed and dis-owned.[22] I sometimes notice that this state of unknowing might also be convenient for me. Perhaps she senses that I don't want to know what she doesn't remember—or maybe her wounds are symbolic of something I am doing or not doing to her. Am I sending her nonverbal signals that I don't want her to put words to her feelings? Or perhaps she expects me to send those signals and unconsciously thinks I am.

More recently, in response to my usual question about what she was feeling, she replied that she did, this time, have words for the sensation generated by her furious opening of the wounds. "I want to rub it out," she said intensely, "smooth it off." We were talking about how she felt about my observation that writing, which she seemed to have a facility for, appeared to help her understand herself better. It was with the compliment that her rubbing commenced. I wondered if she was perhaps trying to obliterate my comment, her feelings about my comment, or my feelings that she imagined caused my comment. I watched her finger-nails, gliding up and down her arm, seeking out, picking off, and then furiously rubbing her old wounds. I asked if she was uncomfortable because of my compliment. She replied that she was; she is always embarrassed when others compliment her. She tried to think about why she gets so embarrassed, but to no avail. I wondered if the contrast between someone in the present noticing her (and her willingness to let herself be seen) on the one hand, and her parents' inability to notice her, on the other, might draw attention to feelings (the old wound) that she preferred to avoid (rub out). The rubbing then, would be an acting out of the wish to do away with the scar, the reminder, of the old wounds. It would be a way of complying with the moral code dedicated to protecting mother from her childhood needs, observations, and complaints.

It was after listening to this idea that she was able to remember a feeling about the past: "I was angry all the time in high school! For instance, during Career Day at school, I needed my mother to be there and help me, but she didn't come, even at night. I had to go alone, and I was furious for days afterwards. I realized I had to decide for myself what to do. I had to make my own plans for graduation and beyond. . . . So when it came time for me to decide, I just told my mother I knew what I wanted to do and where I would go to school, even though I didn't have a clue as to what was best for me."

I remarked that that behavior released her from the necessity of asking for help or complaining about not receiving any, and absolved her mother of any responsibility for helping. "You never asked for help, so you never risked feeling angry and disappointed with her. These all seem like ways of avoiding your need for help and your wish for a better mother. Today you do the same thing: you rub out your needs, forget your anger and disappointment, erase good feelings that provide a contrast with old feelings, and don't notice the behavior of others that runs counter to your expectations of what people can do for you." In order to comply with the moral code that prohibited asking for help, she had to avoid her own needs, the awareness of what others could do for her, and her emotional response to a life of loneliness and bleeding. She smiled an old, ironic smile: "But, you know, it's self-defeating. I try to rub out the scar, but I know that just causes new bleeding. And then no one can ignore it—it sticks out like a sore thumb."

So we came to realize that the the bleeding is a way of avoiding and reexperiencing, both at the same time, without having to consciously feel the old wounds, be aware of them, put them into words, or break the secret promise to mother. The picking and rubbing help her comply with the old moral framework of silence yet at the same time draw attention to and act out the problem. It is a bloody, but effective, solution to an impossible moral dilemma.

Once during a session, while watching her unconscious self-attack, something came to mind. I thought of Adam Smith's concept of the "invisible hand," nature's hand, which the eighteenth-century philosopher believed would be forever vigilant, somehow manufacturing the best interest of the larger society out of the self-serving, ruthless strivings of each individual for private gain. This moved me to wonder after the session if one aspect of the damage unconsciously enacted on her body might be attributable to the larger political and economic arrangements of our era.

For instance, during a later session in which my patient was describing her childhood poverty, I remembered that her family home at that time in her life was not far from a large and famous Protestant church. Because she is now an active church member, I asked her if as a child she had ever had fantasies about the congregation helping her family in some way. She replied that the thought had never entered her mind—her family rarely attended worship services and was not active in the parish. Her mother was an exceedingly proud woman, painfully ashamed of their poverty, so they did not ask for help. In fact, they would never have thought of asking for help, nor did they consider themselves in need of help, even though, upon reflection, my patient did know that they were indeed quite poor. I remarked that, given her own current dedication to volunteer work within her religious community, it seems puzzling that the thought would never have occurred to her. How could she explain their plight, I asked, in a religious community known for its emphasis on communal aid? She said, "I just never thought of it, and no one ever mentioned it." Did she ever wonder, I asked, about the economic causes of her mother's exhaustion, her brothers' delinquency, and her own isolation? Did she ever feel overstressed by the economic system or angry about the injustice of it all? She replied no, it had never occurred to her; it could never have occurred to her, because her family prized an extreme form of self-reliance. "I guess," she replied after a pause, "my mother had a job, so she made too much to qualify for welfare. My father didn't hit us, so we were too unbruised [and unbloodied, I thought] to be reported to the police. And I was too busy to be considered depressed." "In other words," I said, "the wounding was unseen by others. Perhaps this is why you never expect me to notice."

I often think about her disembodied hand, and wonder what it means. Sometimes I wonder if she is on the verge of uncovering in her past some horrific physical or sexual abuse, thus uncovering the identity of the disembodied hand. This would seem to be an obvious possibility, and indeed it might turn out to be the case. But I also don't want us to be limited to that interpretation. Today, in our ahistorical world, we don't often attribute our suffering to the political structures that play such a powerful, determining role in our everyday lives. As Americans, steeped in the ideology of self-contained individualism, we pride ourselves in "rising above" the limitations of larger political arrangements, such as class. We pride ourselves in not bothering with what we cannot change, and focusing on what we can change, which, regrettably, has been reduced in most cases to one's individual "attitude." Nineteenth-century mesmerism (see chapter five) first transformed this ideology into a psychotherapy practice. Our American concept of freedom is a decidedly *personal* kind of freedom, a psychological freedom, one located *inside* each of us. Increasingly, the concept of freedom is often extended into the social realm in limited ways, such as in the freedom to choose which consumer goods and leisure activities to purchase and pursue, or which credit card to use. In the case of my patient, the exaggerated self-reliance she practiced as a child—outwardly unremarkable due to the ubiquity of individualism—seems self-defeating when contrasted with the desperate plight of her family. In this case, when placed within the context of the family, the "virtue" of self-reliance and compassion for her mother begins to appear counterproductive in relation to her family and destructive to her own development. The family needed help desperately, and her inability to cry out in pain, let alone directly ask for help, simply made matters worse.

Often we do not have words for the ideas or emotions that arise as a response to the political arrangements of our era. In the case of this patient I sometimes wonder if the symptoms she displays, which could be interpreted as post-traumatic stress from sexual assault, are not, in part, expressions of the trauma she experienced at the hands of a brutal and uncaring political system. Could it not be that the desolation and silent sobbing that she occasionally expresses is in part the result of being born into a situation from which there was no escape and no outside help? In the highly individualistic, isolated world of the postwar era, nuclear families have been left alone to struggle with their economic pressures and work out their own emotional problems, their fundamental "privacy" honored at all costs. For the family of my patient, there was little help to be found in extended family, community resources, religious tradition, school programs. They fell through the cracks of the few relief and community aid agencies that were available. All they had were only the social isolation, gender roles, and relentless economic pressures from which there was no escape, pressures that pounded at each of the family members, damaging the children and finally destroying the mother. With this in mind, it is perhaps easier to understand why my patient is so dedicated to volunteering her time to community and educational agencies, delivering food to the needy and self-help information to children. She is beginning to struggle with the idea of what her volunteering means. If the therapy can give her the opportunity to understand that her unseen, unnamed suffering is expressive of larger political complaints as well as complaints related to the personal interactions of an isolated, disturbed family, perhaps she will make increasingly better choices regarding personal behavior and community service.

But for now we must ask, "Why does she continue to re-create that old world?" Why do any of us repeat our old behaviors, reproduce and gleefully (sometimes vengefully) live in the old moral world of our earlier life, with the limitations of an inadequate, malicious, or unnecessarily painful clearing? I guess every psychotherapy theory, and perhaps every individual, practitioner and patient alike, probably has a tentative answer to that question. When all is said and done, that is probably *the* question in psychotherapy. Every theorist has an answer to that, and every theorist thinks his or her answer is the one correct answer.

Let us remember that every answer to that question is simply a metaphor for a local, moral, always interpersonal process that we really don't know very much about. Every answer to that question might be interesting, clever, insightful, complex, even brilliant; some will be persuasive and some confusing. But ultimately, one will seem convincing because it fits better with the world as *you* know it, not because it is the one correct answer, the universal truth.

The question that asks why do we reproduce our old clearing goes hand in glove with the other major theoretical question in psychotherapy, which could be phrased: "How does psychotherapy help a patient shift the horizon of the old clearing?" That is the hermeneutic version of the old question "How does psychotherapy cure?" It strikes me as a decidedly political question, because for psychotherapy to justify its status in a world framed by the empirical sciences and the Enlightenment era power agenda, it must be able to predict and explain. But hermeneutics suggests that the horizon is *always* moving. That is its nature, that is why Gadamer chose the metaphor in the first place, because it is moveable. Humans can only see so far at any one time. If we walk forward, our perspective changes; if we travel up a tall mountain, we can see more; if we are located in a low valley, we see less. The horizon shifts all the time, according to one's perspective. In other words, the positions we take regarding what is possible and proper human behavior, the moral ground available to us, the moral stance we strike and the political commitments we make in part determine where the horizon is located and when it shifts.

THE HIDDEN SUBWAY: A GADAMERIAN DREAM

The question of how the horizon shifts probably can never be answered. Moral and political shifts just can't be explained in medical-like terms. But we do know that the horizon can shift, because we can witness it shifting, in our world and in the worlds of others. Perhaps the shifting can be better discussed as taking place as a result of the development of new moral ground, terrain that will adequately support the weight of the individual or community in question. In other words, how the horizon shifts is not a mechanical or technological question of how a therapist can cause a horizonal shift; instead, perhaps the horizon moves precisely *because of*—that is, in response to—the new moral terrain that has emerged.

For instance, I see a male patient, now in his late thirties, in once-a-week individual therapy. His most identifiable characteristic is a certain facial expression: a half sneer, half suspicious look. Many years ago, when he was a young man, we had worked together for a couple of years with adequate results on various problems including the unexpected death of his father. But we both had the feeling something important hadn't yet been worked on. His most familiar feeling growing up was that somehow he was inadequate, that things weren't right and he was at fault. He remembered a fantasy he used to have as a young elementary school student: once the principal called an assembly for the kids at school and told them all an important secret about life—but my patient had been absent that day, so he never learned the secret, and no one was allowed to tell him. Sometimes during the therapy hour he would get a look of pure, unadulterated cynicism on his face, yet he reported being unaware of suspecting or mistrusting me of anything, or of being wary or angry. He decided to leave therapy temporarily, having accomplished the changes he initially sought treatment for, and I didn't hear from him for a while. Then several years later he made an appointment, walked into the office, and announced that during a recent visit to his mother, she had told him something that had been kept from him all his life: he had been adopted at birth. He was then thirty-four years old.

Needless to say, this revelation caused immense turmoil in his life. His communal, familial, and genetic identity was instantly thrown into question. He felt disoriented and dislocated. But he also began to understand more about his experience of life: about his omnipresent sense that he was failing at something; his characteristic cynical suspiciousness; his belief that everybody knew something crucial that he didn't know. His parents' difficulties with psychologically separating from him began to make more sense to him—for him to be psychologically separate, and therefore have differences from them, must have had a particular meaning for them that they couldn't tolerate, given his adoption and their fear of acknowledging it. He marveled at the pathology of an extended family that could keep such a secret from him without even so much as a hint or a regret. He started to remember things like staring into the mirror and noticing that he didn't look like either of his parents but never wondering why. Now he started to allow himself to wonder, very occasionally and timidly, what his birth parents were like. He started to allow himself to wonder what his life would have been like had they not arranged for the adoption. He experienced strong feelings of betrayal about and mistrust of his extended family and his imagined birth parents. Mostly he began to understand why cynicism was such an intense yet unknown aspect of his terrain.

Often, with this second round of treatment, we would talk about what I now think of as the moral shape of his old clearing, about what was possible and impossible, what could appear and what was not permitted to show up, what was revealed and what was secret, what could be spoken and what must never be named. He began to notice the statements he could not make straightforwardly, the answers he could not request, the truthful self-reporting he could not bring himself to utter. And we began to be curious together as to why he kept silencing himself, why he would do to himself what was done to him, why he would reproduce the old terrain that had been so harmful to him. Slowly he began to notice the character of his attachment to his adoptive mother and the shape of the family's moral code: he would tolerate her self-centered, dishonest behavior, and her characteristic forgetfulness about her promises or agreements with him, but he would not, under any circumstances, ask anything of her or be honest with her about his own needs. He began to realize that an expression of his needs in the old terrain was interpreted by his mother, it showed up as, *his* betrayal of *her*. In this moral frame, his needs showed up as disloyalty. He began to characterize this relation by the phrase "Hey, your feelings don't count!" In his dreams and memories this phrase was spoken by his mother; he identified the phrase as a composite experience of his mother's reaction to his wishes when they were in conflict with her own. It was easy to see how that had all begun, now as he began to sense his current wish to find his birth mother. He cannot, to this day, bring himself to mention his curiosity about his birth mother to his adoptive mother, let alone ask her for help in learning more about her. In the moral terrain of his childhood, honesty about his personal wishes that conflicted with his adoptive mother's wishes would have been a severe blow to her and would probably have precipitated her emotional withdrawal.

But at the same time other changes began to appear. My patient became more aware of wanting to stretch himself in his business, to branch out and try new and more demanding activities, to take more risks, to try to respect his skills more and let himself interact and work with a more accomplished level of colleagues and competitors—to work in a new world. And he kept wondering who his birth parents were, and who he would have been had he been allowed to stay with them. His adoptive mother volunteered no more information, and my patient became aware of how much he was procrastinating by not asking her for more, by not gathering more himself, by not deciding whether or not to try to find his birth parents. He also noticed how he sometimes treated me as if I was his adoptive mother, and we both noticed that I *do* occasionally act like her, especially by unconsciously pushing him to act in ways that he resists. At a certain point in the therapy, we seemed to hit a dead spot. We were stuck: he was handling work problems somewhat better at this time, but he was unable to take the big creative step in business that he needed to; he seemed to be reproducing passive-aggressive or avoidant patterns with his wife similar to those he exhibits with his mother; and he was unable to face the emotional issues about his birth parents. We faced transference-countertransference enactments when they arose; we explored the meanings of the interactions and their concomitant feelings, guided as much as possible by the interpersonal concept that the therapy could be best served if we faced the truth about my sometimes strange behavior (such as the times I ignore him or pressure him to act in certain ways). And I expected the same from him.

Some time passed, and he and his wife were about to have a baby. This seemed to shake things up, and he began to feel more about what his childhood was like from the perspective of knowing about his adoption. At work one day he solved a problem by taking a step back and looking at the problem from a different angle. And then a month later he had a dream. He was in the passenger tunnels of the New York subway, and he saw a peculiarity in one of the walls. He was puzzled by it and took a step back from the problem to look at it from a "different angle." He saw the "other side" of the problem, and found an opening in the wall that had been closed up. He climbed in and found an old abandoned subway station that had been closed off for years, walled off from the public, unused and unappreciated. It was an absolutely beautiful old terminal, majestic and impressively crafted. It looked like a turn-of-the-century design, with high arching ceilings and stunning columns. He felt comfortable, interested, and engaged, something he hadn't felt at work in some time. He wondered where the tunnels led to, what parts of the city they transported their passengers to. And then he discovered a cluster of circular mail slots, set in a wall off to the side. In the holes were rolled-up blueprints—just what he needed. He took one out to examine it, and sure enough, it was the floor plan for the old abandoned terminal he had just located. He felt excited and hopeful, wondering what tunnels the other floor plans led to, and what he would find there.

When asked what the dream brought to mind, he answered quickly that he thought of the approaching birth of his child (who the sonogram indicated was male). "I don't want to do to him what happened to me. I don't want him to be limited by secrets, lies, and unspoken rules." He thought the birth might help him act a bit differently, because he will be watching as his child-to-be enters a whole new world of possibilities. He also thought of his life as a child and wondered about what possibilities might have been available for him at the beginning of his life, and what might be possible now. Maybe, he thought, a new terrain might open up for *him*. The symbolism of the subway tunnel, the birth canal, and a psychological passage into a new terrain seemed rich with possibilities.

One week later, his wife gave birth to a healthy baby boy. The dream, of course, did not transform my patient. Two weeks later he reported himself exhausted with new childcare responsibilities and bogged down at work. He was unable to come up with a new plan about his work, or to activate the plan that he had tentatively developed. "What happened," I asked, "to the new room in the subway?" "I don't know," he said, "I can't find it again." But he has referred to the dream many times in the two years since. And, in truth, while there has been no brilliant transformation, no "breakthrough" into a new room, the world he now lives in is vastly different from his old world, or even from his world at the time of the dream. He enjoys his son immensely, he has found out a bit more about his own birth mother, and he and his wife have found the courage to enter couples therapy, something that he was instrumental in arranging. He is also restructuring his work into a vastly more challenging, effective, and creative set of activities. These are significant changes, but they have appeared very slowly, with great suspicion and doubting, with the sneer sometimes apparent.

In looking back over the dream, I think it significant that the visual image of the newly discovered room was associated in the patient's mind with his hopes and dreams for his son, and with his *moral commitments* to his son. Perhaps in being able to commit to constructing a more honest, open life for his son, he was also able to tolerate a slightly new, more open, adventurous, and committed terrain for himself as well. Perhaps the way he and I have been able to develop a way of discussing the transference-countertransference enactments, so that he had an opportunity to complain about me and watch me listen to, respect, and learn from his complaints, has helped him borrow some new moral ground, a ground where it is permissible, even admirable, to tell the truth, complain, and challenge the other, and influence the other to act in ways more in line with his wishes and needs. And, I hope, he is also developing ways to see his own actions in a different light, and to notice how his silence contributes to the very disappointments he complains about. This hermeneutic approach offers a different way of conceptualizing where psychological life and psychological change is located—not in hypothesized psychic structures thought to be located interiorly, but in the social terrain located in the space between patient and therapist.

There are many issues that the subway dream brings up that we have not yet been able to discuss. It would be instructive to discuss how the arrival of a new person in his life, someone to attach to and love, has effected my patient's ability to give up a bit of his need to reproduce the old terrain and thus the old attachment pattern with and moral code of his adoptive family. Also the act of being able to conceive a child and assist in the *birth* of his child probably has had a powerful impact on him, perhaps helping him distance himself a bit from his adoptive parents, who could not conceive, and his birth parents, who did not keep him. Perhaps he feels a sense of achievement or revenge in that, a surpassing of them, that has helped him be less dependent on his pattern of attachment with both sets of parents, real and imaginary, in the old terrain.

I'm sure that therapists of different stripes will have very different ideas about how to interpret his dream. If I were a self psychologist, for instance, I would be dying to get my hands on this dream, which would seem to be an obvious self-state dream about the nuclear self. The same, no doubt, for a Winnicottian, whose ideas about the true self, waiting to be discovered, would by now be bursting to be told. Jungians would probably want to talk about the explorer archetype, and Joseph Campbell would undoubtedly imagine the hero myth in the bowels of the New York subway system. And God knows what a past-life therapist would do with the idea that the terminal had come from a time before my patient's birth.

These are all fine stories, of course, but this is my chapter, and I want to tell the story in such a way so that we don't have to reconstruct in my patient the empty self in order to explain the dream and his subsequent psychological changes. I do not believe that I have the one, true way of interpreting the dream, but I do believe that the dream can be interpreted to illustrate several hermeneutic principles. The important issue, from my point of view, is that the dream speaks to us about someone who is in the process of making room for new possibilities, possibilities that are social in nature and that somehow have their roots in another, earlier time in his life, a time that had not, until that moment, been able to show up in his consciousness.

My patient, of course, has not been able to remember the first few hours of his life outside of his birth mother, nor what the womb was like for him. But I sometimes think of that almost-to-be-born fetus, in a beautifully designed room with a high ceiling, feeling the by then familiar, intimate movements, the inner sounds, the muffled voice of a mother whom he would suddenly be separated from, never to see or be seen again. He was severely premature, and evidently placed in an incubator for several weeks. I imagine that infant, so terribly alone, with no familiar sounds or smells, no one to touch him, no one to sing to him or rock him. When he was able to leave the incubator he was given to two people he did not know. These particular parents did as well as they could, I'm sure, but their efforts were inadequate. The promise of that old majestic room had been lost forever; it had been boarded up and closed off from sight, until it was somehow reconstructed anew by my client, in ways that neither he, nor I, nor anyone, I trust, could ever adequately explain. But we do know this: the room appeared in part because a new life (perhaps two new lives) had to be served, and my client felt a moral commitment to these new lives and to the relationship between them. His commitment transcended the secrets and limitations located in a world too small for the possibilities my client could now embrace. The newly exposed terminal, the starting place, led to new, interesting, unknown worlds. My patient felt a stirring, a wish, to travel to new places and see what might happen when he got there. The dream indicates that somehow new possibilities have been opened up for my patient—the horizon has been moved back away from him, and new territory, or at least the possibility of traveling to new territory, has shown up for him. How did he do it?

Some, especially self psychologists, might say that what I am describing is the result of the therapeutic use of empathy. That is, the beginning of therapeutic healing occurred when I was able to empathize, to feel the feelings, to experience what the patient experienced. The experience of being emotionally "held," self psychologists would say, is the foundation of the building of the self. But Gadamer would disagree. He has argued that since the patient possesses no one concrete, uncontaminated feeling state, no one true memory set about the past or the present, and since it is impossible for the therapist to set aside his or her own clearing, pure empathy as we sometimes mean it in psychotherapy is not possible. We cannot, in some decontextualized way, feel what the other is feeling. But we can be aware of the contrast between our clearing and the clearing of the patient; that experience will help us be aware of some of the prejudices and limits of our own clearing, the horizonal configuration of our immediate world. As we come to understand and recognize our own context as it unfolds in the therapeutic hour, Gadamer believed we will have an improved capacity to understand the *context* of the patient's world—the configuration of the patient's taken-for-granted clearing.

Sometimes, perhaps most times, this experience of the other's *world* takes place during a transference-countertransference enactment. The enactment is what Donnel Stern has called "a wholehearted experience of countertransference,"[23] which, if acknowledged and properly discussed, can be of central importance in the development of the treatment. The analyst can gain a particular experience—not of the patient's inner feelings, but of the patient's *context*, his or her *way* of seeing. This, in turn, will move the analyst to gain a new perspective on his or her *own* way of seeing. Donnel Stern, Georgia Warnke, and Joel Weinsheimer have suggested that this is what Gadamer means by his concept of the "fusion" of horizons: the fleeting moment in which the therapist can live in the patient's terrain or get a better understanding of what it is like to live in that terrain.[24] In this moment the therapist not only comes to understand the patient's feelings; the therapist experiences the overall frame that constructed those feelings so that they could show up the way that they do. In so doing the therapist models the process of moving the horizon and demonstrates to the patient possibilities, alternative ways of being, and conceptions of the good not previously available to the patient. The degree to which the patient can be startled at alternative possibilities available in the therapist's terrain, and curious about the therapist's ability to experience, however imperfectly and fleetingly, the patient's terrain, is the degree to which the patient is also beginning to move his or her horizon, to develop the capacity to experience for a moment the therapist's terrain, and thus to be open to new possibilities about the proper way of being, possibilities that were not available previously.

Psychotherapist and writer Jane Burka has mentioned to me that it seems exactly right to use dreaming as an illustration of the moveable nature of the horizon. "After all," she remarked, "what is dreaming if not an *experiencing* of alternative terrains, an experimenting with different realities, a following of unusual rules? In our dreams cars fly, cats talk, gender changes with the moment. Dreams are a realignment of things."[25] Burka is suggesting that dreaming is thinking the unthinkable; it is an illustration of what we have available to us but don't know. In dreams we allow ourselves to see what has previously been too important, subversive, or mundane to remember. While dreaming we somehow shift or rearrange the horizon in a deeply imaginative way, unknowingly experiencing, rehearsing, or practicing the *process* of reconstructing the clearing. While dreaming, we play with what is on the dark side of the moon.

More recently in my patient's life, an old problem with a new twist has emerged. Often in the past he has worked for business clients who turned out to be remarkably similar to his mother. They ignore his advice, forget what was mutually agreed upon, change their minds and forget having thought any other way, and worst of all, accuse *him* of misremembering. All in all, they have acted as though he exists so they can use him, and all the while they consider his feelings or opinions to be irrelevant. It is, I'm sure, not surprising to you that despite his best intentions my patient finds himself relating to this type of customer in ways similar to how he relates to his mother. Although he banished almost all clients of this type, one still remained. She was maddening to him, but he endured and, mercifully, the project finally ended. But then the customer wanted to start a second, even bigger job, fraught with even more pitfalls than the first. My patient has been quite troubled by whether or not to take the job—it meant good money in a depressed market, but it also meant immeasurable trouble. Characteristically, at first he decided not to take the job, but then he began to procrastinate and avoided telling her the truth. Had he told her the truth, he would have been unable to reproduce the old moral terrain and the old parent-child relationship, and he would have been prevented from doing the "right thing" (which in the old terrain meant denying his wishes in favor of hers). During sessions with me he began to smirk a lot, and he noticed he was feeling angry much of the time without knowing why.

Hoping to find others to encourage him to refuse the job, my patient began asking his colleagues what they thought he should do. Contrary to his hopes, each of them, without hesitation, advised him to take the job. The money, they thought, was too good to turn down, no matter how damaging it might be to him emotionally. In a session he explained: "It was like they stood up and spoke with one voice! The voice was my mother's voice, and it said, 'Hey, your feelings don't count!' " We looked at each other for a moment, and I hesitated to talk about the political idea that leapt to mind, so I compromised: "Well," I said, "it sounds like your mother isn't the only one who thinks that money is more important than emotional well-being." My patient smirked, looking the epitome of contemptuous cynicism: "Maybe it's everyone—hell, it's the system. That's the voice." His response made it easier for me to take the next step. I said something like, "I think the voice you heard speaks through all these people, because it's sedimented in each of us. [I had used this idea with him before.] The way we value money over emotional health and capital over labor, the way we automatically accept degrading and damaging work, our belief that our only responsibility is to our own, individual livelihood—that's our taken-for-granted world."

My patient was silent for a moment. Had I gone too far? He is an intelligent college graduate with an interest in economic theory, but did I become too intrusive, too political? "It's speaking through everyone," he said angrily, "my buddies, my competitors, everyone. It's not just my mother, as much as I'd like to blame it on her. It's the whole system." He thought for a while, then he looked up and smiled: "This is going to be more difficult than I thought. How are we going to get the whole damn system into the room?" We laughed together and I said, "You know, if it's all the same to you, I'd rather you take your ideas out *there*, instead of bringing the system in *here*. Would that be okay with you?"

In a more recent session my patient, still struggling with his disgust with the potential work project and his seeming inability to directly and straightforwardly refuse his client, realized something new. In order to take this new job, which he disagrees with and in fact despises, he will have to "detach" himself from the work, pretend that he isn't involved with its production and doesn't care about the client, the project, or *anything*. He said, "This is a lot like I was as a teenager—I had this overriding sense that I didn't care about anything. Nothing mattered. I hate that feeling, its so, so . . . cynical. If there's one thing I've learned in therapy, its that if I cut out my feelings about one part of my life, a lot more of the caring in me gets cut out. That's when I end up with that shapeless anger." And then later in the session he went on: "Okay, now I see something else. At the same time I have to emotionally detach from the project in order to get the job done, I have to pretend that I care, I value the project, and that I'll do a very good job. So I'm going to have to detach and pretend at the same time! I've never realized that before."

We have come to realize that that situation places him in the same moral predicament from which he suffered in childhood. He is in the position of being both victim and perpetrator: he is a victim because he is forced to live in a framework he never agreed to and that he hates, and a perpetrator because in order to emotionally survive he must not care even though he has promised to care, and because he has promised to do, properly, a job that ultimately cannot be done properly, given his standards. "In other words," I responded, "you are in the middle of a moral conflict. According to the moral code of your family and the society, you should accept the double bind: detach and yet pretend to care, work conscientiously and yet know that the work is impossible to accomplish, and all the while pretend not to notice that you are feeling enraged, unsatisfied, and deadened."

We came to realize that he is in the process of building a new understanding of what is moral. He has the sense that if he takes the job, he will be cheating the client, living a life of detachment, denial, and falseness. And now he thinks that is the wrong thing to do. But to refuse is to break the old family rules, to act in ways that they would think immoral. He is caught in a dilemma.

I sense that my patient is moving toward a resolution of his troubles. He is on one of the last laps of his journey. It is this moral dilemma that is one of the final issues to be resolved. Does he stay attached to his parents and observant of the old moral understandings, or does he embrace those that have emerged in the course of the therapy? If he can do the latter, he can free himself to relate to people who are better able to see him and respond to him, structure his work so that he will make money more effectively, be an equal partner in the decision-making of his business partnerships, have work that is more creative, pleasant, and less stressful, and be proud of what he produces. If he stays committed to the moral frame of his parents he will continue to seek out clients who ignore and dismiss him and relationships that require him to consistently abandon his needs in favor of others.' He will seek out work that is inefficient, burdensome, demeaning, supremely irritating and stressful, work he will be embarrassed by and from which he will have to emotionally detach and about which he will have to pretend. Because of his growing sense of the toll it takes on him, and the moral perspective that he is developing, I sense that he is moving toward a different way of living. The old moral code is about to be a thing of the past.

Now I know this hermeneutic way of thinking doesn't sound very complicated, in the way psychotherapy theories usually are. It's not. I am not offering this way of thinking as a fully developed theory of psychotherapy or in an attempt to convince psychotherapists to give up their old theory and their preferred ways of practicing and to start to use this as a substitute. I'm not sure exactly what this is, especially in light of Gadamer's horror at the thought of trying to turn hermeneutics into a new methodology, a set of technological procedures that can be applied *to* anyone *by* anyone. I think of hermeneutics more as a *way of thinking* about human being, a *perspective* on human being and on all human activities, including social practices such as psychotherapy. Perhaps it is best thought of as a way of thinking about current psychotherapy techniques, a perspective that, if used in concert with a certain less interiorized vocabulary, might help the therapist resist reproducing as directly or unquestioningly the current configuration of the self.

This hermeneutic way of thinking about psychotherapy is, of course, above all a way of thinking about the stories, joys, and agonies of our patients without locating all the action in the patient's deep, secret, somewhat empty interior. Instead, hermeneutics locates human being in the social surround, the horizonal space that encompasses us all, the space that has been "cleared" by language, dress, religion, politics, rituals, and nonverbal communications, by the shared understandings of our culture and the traditions of our communities, by the more particular customs of local neighborhoods and nuclear families, and even more minutely by the private exchanges of friends and lovers. The individual, with all his or her feelings, unconscious wishes and motives, envies, hatreds, loves, dreams, hopes, and fears is, of course, also located in the social clearing. So, little of the historic project of depth psychology is really *lost* in this hermeneutic conception of human experience. It is just *relocated*, out of the all-encompassing private interior, which has had such an important political part to play in the industrialized capitalism of the modern era. Instead, the complex intertwining of individual, society, and nature, the awe-inspiring web of meaning, the double-edged nature of Sullivan's web, the mysterious mix of conscious-unconscious, the frustrating, never-to-be-solved but-never-to-be-given-up-on dialectic; in short, the all-encompassing world of human being, is, in the hermeneutic metaphor, located in the social, historical realm. This seems to me right where it belongs.

A TALE OF TWO BRIDGES

But, with all this optimism, I have a cautionary note to strike. This book began with a saying about a bridge. It was Reb Nachman who said, "Life is a very narrow bridge between two eternities—do not be afraid." I took that occasion to interpret the saying in such a way as to encourage psychotherapists, and in fact all of us, to commit ourselves to being a connection between our ancestors, who live now only in our histories, and our children's children, who will only come into being through our diligent efforts to keep our communities and the earth safe for them. I suggested that the dim past and the unknown future are two kinds of eternity, and that we have obligations and responsibilities to each. Only by historically situating our social practices, such as psychotherapy, by making contact with our history and understanding where we fit within that history, and simultaneously by being free to face the moral dimensions and political consequences of our work as psychotherapists and human beings, can we walk Reb Nachman's narrow bridge, can we be alive (which is to stay aloft over the abyss). We make connections with our ancestors by honoring their traditions and by struggling with, challenging, and sometimes shifting those traditions. We hold on to our link with those who will come after us by currently fighting for what we believe in, by struggling for what we believe to be right and true, so that we can secure a future for them, for those we can never know.

In various ways I have suggested that we would be assisted in our dual task of securing both sides of the bridge (holding both sides of the dialectic?) by using Gadamer's notion of the cultural clearing and the moveable horizon. Perhaps, I have intimated, this metaphor will help us keep the bridge aloft. But let us also remember that life is *just* a bridge— and a narrow one at that. It is shaky, and when there is a storm it swings back and forth too much. In times of trouble we will want the bridge to be more than a bridge; we will try to pretend that it is solid ground. We might even, to assuage our fears, try to build a permanent house on it, as Acbar foresaw in the quote at the beginning of this chapter. Once the Israelites tried to do that, with a golden calf. Ultimately, as Acbar warned, this is not a good idea.

No theory, no matter how elaborate, beautiful, complex, or brilliant it might appear, no matter how well anchored to the past and the future, will ultimately be able to transform the bridge into solid ground. No theory can be a permanent house.

So let's not get overexcited about using constructionist and hermeneutic ideas in psychotherapy. These ideas might help us build and maintain our bridge, for a while. But let us remember that the two ends of the bridge, when you get right down to it, are not really anchored to much of anything. The memories and ideas of our ancestors and our dreams about our children are precious indeed, but not much, I think, to build a permanent house on. We walk from one eternity, one absence, to another. Below is the abyss. Better we should build a *temporary* shelter, perhaps a sukkah, and keep wandering.

A sukkah is a ceremonial replica of the nomadic huts the biblical Israelites used during their wanderings through the desert. It took them forty years after their slave rebellion to shift the horizon so that a new way of being, a new terrain of communal identity, moral commitment, and political freedom, could "show up" for them. During the days and nights of celebrating Sukkot, Jews are encouraged to build and actually live in a sukkah. The tradition says that a sukkah should be built so that one can look up through the palm leaves of the roof, into the night sky, and see the stars. By sleeping under the stars, the rabbis hoped to emphasize the wandering, impermanent, and fleeting moment that is a human life, to confront the dangers and material deprivations involved in revolution, and to acknowledge the ultimate values of human relationship (which we are encouraged to partake of in the sukkah), and freedom (which we are encouraged to seek, always).

This, then, is life on the narrow bridge: If we look down we see the abyss; if we look up we see stars through the roof. We are anchored only to memory and hope, and all the while our little plot of ground sways from side to side. It is not a comforting vision, but it is all we have. Living is a passage untamed by our yearnings for certainty and permanence.

Ours is an uncertain and impermanent fate, but one that allows us room to struggle, fight, imagine, dream, wish—to build, ever anew, the cultural bridge that keeps us aloft. We must build and rebuild it, even as we walk upon it, depending upon it for support. Our limitation, then, is also our strength: we live in an interdependent, interpenetrating world of tradition and change, communalism and individuality, confidence and confusion, authority and uncertainty. The source of our confusion and fear is also the source of our significance. If we are going to live imaginatively and meaningfully, we must simultaneously embrace what is morally and politically given, contend with it, and shift it. And all this in a world that has no definitive guarantees, certainties, or permanence. We give ourselves over to building that which must be continually resculpted and reconfigured. We must build bridges, not idols. Life is in the wandering.

CHAPTER TEN

The Politics of the Self

*Cry, the beloved country, for the unborn
child that is the inheritor of our fear.*
—ALAN PATON
CRY, THE BELOVED COUNTRY

Nine chapters have been written about the self. In one way or another each of these chapters has been about politics, because the self is *all* about politics. We use the term *politics* to refer to many events and activities within our late twentieth-century world: there is the politics of the American electoral process; the politics of race, gender, and class; the politics within the field of psychotherapy, the community, the family, the office, the romantic couple, and so on. In general *politics* refers to the exercise of power. But what embraces and frames each struggle, the bedrock of all political struggles, is the ongoing moral negotiation over what it means to be human: the self. The self is configured in ways that both reflect and influence the very foundations of social life and everyday living. Without the guidance set by a particular set of ideas about what it means to be human, political conflict would be impossible. The shape of the self in a particular era indicates which goals individuals are supposed to strive toward, and how individuals are to comport themselves while striving; it indicates what is worthwhile, who is worthwhile, and which institutions determine worthwhileness. In other words, the self emerges out of a moral dialogue that sets the stage for all other political struggles. Once the self is set, the rest of the struggles begin to appear in the clearing: they materialize.

When we speak of the self, our discourse is like the Zen adage of the "finger pointing to the moon"; we are signaling about something familiar yet beyond comprehension, luminous yet dark. The moral meanings that constitute the self are continually interwoven with the political structures of the social world—interwoven, intermingled, interchanged. The ongoing social construction of our world is not a linear, mechanistic struggle between the social and the biological as two discrete entities. It is more like the continuing dynamic interchange and mutual substitution of DNA chains—the fecund intermingling, interdependent, mutual forming and transforming of the most basic, elemental units of the reproduction of life. Where does one chain begin and the other end? What starts the process of genetic exchange and what stops it? And all of this—for what purpose? The same questions can be asked of social life. It is not possible to tease out and separate where culture ends and nature begins, where the moral starts and the psychological no longer exists, where the political takes center stage and the economic fades from sight.

POLITICAL MEANINGS OF SELF AND OTHER

Hermeneutics calls upon us to question and examine the distinctions of the modern age, those central to the moral understandings, power relations, and professional territories of the last five hundred years. These include the boundaries between discrete academic departments in the social sciences and humanities, the intellectual differences between intrapsychic and interpsychic, mind and body, self and other, rational and irrational, subjectivity and objectivity, history and narrative, scientific discovery and poetic metaphor, the one truth and a multitude of falsehoods. As a result, hermeneutic, interpretive views encourage us to *embrace* the entanglements of the social world. The self is not a thing; it is a constant process. It is not narrowly psychological; it is a foundational aspect of the overall cultural clearing. It is like Churchill's Russia, "a riddle wrapped in a mystery inside an enigma." If we do not open ourselves to the multiple and ever changing complexities of social life, we will never be able to develop understandings of our plights and joys that equal their solutions and celebrations. Only by embracing the entangled nature of human being can we articulate the truths of our world.

Entanglements, hermeneutics suggests, are unavoidable, pervasive, inevitable, omnipresent. Yet we are also called upon to *notice* our entanglements, become aware of and comment on them, and find ways of expressing our experiences and the meanings we make from them. In this way we can develop interpretations about our world and the political functions of various artifacts, such as the self and its healing technologies, that prosper in our time. Discourse about the self is never removed from the political realm. For instance, psychologists might dress in white coats, work in what is called a "laboratory," and refer to their work as science, but what they are unintentionally doing is using the approved of practices of their era to carry on a disguised moral discourse to justify a particular view about what is the proper way of being.[1]

The basic point is that it is impossible to step outside the entanglements of the social world and see one pure, uncontaminated truth. The language we use, the issues that we deem worthy of examination, the happenings we identify as problems and solutions, the information we consider data, the procedures we believe to be scientifically proper—all are embedded in a specific, entangled cultural terrain. Although we might claim to have "discovered" a scientific truth about being human, our results, as Jan Smedslund has suggested, are inevitably "necessary and true," a product of the cultural frame that had already been set long ago.[2]

It should not be a surprise that the taken-for-granted belief in self-contained individualism has influenced social psychologists to such a degree that they would not notice that the results of their work "proved" the properness of an inner, as opposed to an outer "locus of control" (that is, "inner direction" as opposed to "outer direction"). Similarly, developmental psychologists have consistently overlooked the fact that many laboratory experiments and observations in natural settings "discovered" that the qualities of mastery and boundedness are universal, natural, and the most proper an infant can develop. These are findings too similar to the configuration of the self of our time to be accepted uncritically. By uncritically accepting their colleagues' findings, psychologists have time and again aided current political arrangements of power and privilege through their scientific practices. A more historically situated approach to psychotherapy theories would ask questions such as "From where does this current configuration of the self originate?" Historians would, of course, look to the history of Western society to develop an answer. But this answer would reveal the historically embedded nature of theories of the self and thus unmask psychology's claim to own the universal truth about an objective, ahistorical human nature. Therefore most psychotherapy theorists have avoided historically situating their ideas. They have had to cast about to develop a new creation story about the self, one that would have unquestioned scientific credibility and at the same time be decidedly ahistorical. And they found it in some of the new infant development research. The birthplace of the self has been relocated: in the "scientifically" observable moments of infant development. In some of these laboratories, researchers claim to have discovered the essence of human nature. Not surprisingly, the essential qualities they have found are often the qualities of the Western self: masterful, bounded, and subjective. The origin of the self has been described in such a way as to leave intact psychotherapy's universal truth claims. The conformist, sometimes self-serving, though unintentional, nature of this enterprise seems obvious.

A philosophical hermeneutic approach flies in the face of the comfortable, in-house, Whig historiography our discipline has a tendency to produce.[3] Whig history conceives of theory building as the progressive development of a body of knowledge achieved through the unproblematic culling of the "best" from each theory, dropping that which was "mistaken" or "outdated," and moving ever closer to the one, "correct" theory. Mitchell Ash, Kurt Danziger, Laurel Furumoto, Ben Harris, Jill Morawski, and Franz Samelson,[4] among others, have referred to this as the "origin myth" or "community myth" style of historical scholarship. It seems puzzling that a discipline that prides itself on unflinchingly confronting the ambition, greed, hunger for power, perversity, and murderous rage of *individuals* can unquestioningly accept a *disciplinary* history devoid of similar motivations. It is surprising that a discipline governed by a set of uncompromising practices based on the suspicion of the merely obvious and an insistence on plumbing hidden depths could so deftly produce a history that conceives of the primary motive of the discipline to be the unproblematic, unself-interested search for an on-the-surface, readily available, highly sanitized scientific "truth." We routinely expect our individual patients to exhibit prejudice and practice self-deceit, and we believe individual practitioners to be capable of the same foibles. But when we write history we seem to consider our discipline, *as a discipline*, beyond such practices.

Occasionally, a historian might apply a dose of suspicion to the personal life of an individual theorist, but that seems as far as we can go. Only on rare occasions do our Whig historians look for the political involvements and cultural limitations of our discipline as a whole. We seem unable to conceive of unseemly, "unbourgeois" motives beyond the skin of the individual bourgeois. Motives related to power, political advantage, or domination, and limitations related to cultural understandings, seem beyond our collective ken. The hermeneutic turn is an attempt to rectify these omissions. If we could write a more comprehensive hermeneutic history, we would write a history in which the discipline is framed by the larger cultural vision, limited by the shared understandings of its sociohistorical era, influenced by the political forces that propel massive historical change, and moved by "unscientific" motives such as the wish for power and economic security.

If we believe that the psychological laboratory can and is producing an objective, unimpeachable truth about a universal human nature, and if we believe that laboratory results prove that the late twentieth-century Western self is the one, universal way of human being, then how do we evaluate cultures that do not configure the self in the way we do? Do we think they are misguided, primitive, disabled? If we think them less than us—less civilized, accomplished, moral, learned—will we then believe ourselves justified in trying to dominate them and make them more like us? Will imperialism, racism, cultural chauvinism, or noblesse oblige be considered justified once the one scientific truth about infant development is thought to be the property of one profession? If psychology can prove that separation-individuation is *the* universal process of psychological maturation, then how do we evaluate communities that do not envision a world in which the individual separates from family and clan, communities that instead value the well-being of the group over that of the individual? If psychology can prove that autonomy and personal agency are the cornerstones of the universal self, then how will this affect our ideas about unemployment benefits, welfare, social security, and national health care? If psychology can prove that the highest form of morality is an expression of unattached monads who have no moral commitments to one another beyond their own subjective sense of good and bad, then what are we saying about group solidarity, discipline in the ranks of striking workers, or personal sacrifice for the good of the whole? If psychologists can prove that each individual possesses a unique self the potential of which is present at conception or soon after, and that the self is a natural entity that grows organicistically with the proper nourishment, will that putative scientific truth be used to justify banning abortion?

One can see how vitally important the configuration of the self is in these political debates. If psychology is one of the guilds most responsible for determining the proper way of being human, then psychology wields a significant amount of power, especially in our current era, in which the moral authority of most religious and philosophical institutions has been called into question. By unknowingly propping up the hegemony of individualism through laboratory findings, psychology is preventing individuals from having the ability to see into how political structures impact the individual and how much these structures are responsible for the suffering of the victims and the crimes of the perpetrators. These opinions will determine our response to future political crises. Should we interpret a petty burglary solely as a manifestation of the criminal's psychopathology, or also the result of economic desperation? Should we interpret the increased popularity of African-American, Asian, and Latino youth gangs as a genetic defect that causes young people of color to be unable to develop a "mature" psychological autonomy, or a reflection of the consequences of centuries of racial discrimination, economic exploitation, community devastation, and the youths realistic appraisal that they have little chance for a reasonably safe and secure future if they play by the rules of white society? Should we interpret family violence solely as a product of the psychologically dysfunctional family system of the perpetrator, or also the absence of meaningful moral traditions, communal support, gratifying work, and extended family aid and advice?

THE DISAPPEARANCE OF THE CITIZEN AND A TWO-PERSON PSYCHOLOGY

Currently, the outer limits that most psychotherapy theories can conceive of as the social realm is the isolated parent-child or patient-therapist dyad, or at most the nuclear family.[5] This vision of the social is what is referred to as "two-person" psychology. In many ways it is a welcome improvement over older, more extreme forms of self-contained individualism, so-called "one-person" psychologies. But, ultimately, several forms of two-person psychologies, such as object relations theory and self psychology, fall short of what is needed: they are a kind of intellectual tokenism. If, under the influence of individualism, this myopia continues, it will be difficult for us as a nation to address problems that appear as a result of larger political arrangements and the cultural frame of reference. If we psychologize and medicalize every human action by ridding it of any significant political cause, we condemn ourselves to denying the effects of the macro structures of our society. Therefore we will leave those structures intact while we blame the only positions in our cultural clearing that shows up as responsible, culpable entities: the individual and the dyad. If we cannot entertain the realistic possibility that political structures can be the cause of personal, psychological distress, then we cannot notice their impact, we cannot study them, we cannot face their consequences, we cannot mobilize to make structural changes, and we will have few ideas about what changes to make. We will become politically incompetent. Perhaps we already are.

Ultimately, the hermeneutic critique is important to us because of the ways late twentieth-century populations are controlled by the state: less by military repression, and more by the state's ability to set and exploit the cultural frame of reference. The battles of our era are not joined at the barricades but in the corporate boardroom. They are battles fought through the manipulation of words, symbols, and electronic images; by the power to describe "the other," define gender, and determine the particulars of consumer desire. Today political lines are drawn in protracted white-collar battles over the content of the nightly news, judicial decisions regarding the meanings of sanity and culpability, expert opinion regarding causes of crime and homelessness, the personality of the latest soft drink mascot or celebrity spokesperson, the ideological positions of radio talk show hosts, the direction of a new beer advertising campaign, or the shape of this year's fashion trends. The process by which "the other" is constructed, defined, and used is the face of war in our time. The constructed content of "the self" and the determination of what is split off, disavowed, and then relocated into the unconscious and onto "the other" goes a long way toward legitimizing political decisions regarding the identity of the enemy, the content of major political issues, the distinctions between male and female and white and black, the understandings of right and wrong. The addict, African American, Asian, criminal, female, homeless, Jew, or Latino carries what is despised and disavowed; these distinctions, and the intellectual discourse that follows them, then justifies previous injustices and present or future governmental policies.

An adult male patient is sitting across from me in my therapy office. He has recently learned that several female relatives, including his mother and his older sister, suffered serial sexual abuse by his grandfather. He is afraid he either witnessed the sexual abuse of his sisters or was himself abused. For months he has been trying to remember events in his childhood that he believes happened but for which he cannot find images or words. What is it that moves him to think that these events happened? He is not sure. Two days ago his mother asked him how he was feeling, and when he replied by saying that therapy was difficult, she said nothing and changed the subject. Although she now remembers her abuse, she has never received adequate treatment. That night he dreamt that they were talking together in the house of his childhood; he told her he had been sexually abused, and she refused to talk about it. The day after the dream the mother called on the phone and left a frantic message asking her son how to clean a certain household furnishing that he had once delivered and installed for her.

My client suddenly begins to cry. For a moment, he realizes that he was angry with his mother because she did not encourage him to talk, disclose how she is currently feeling, talk about the childhood abuse that she had suffered at the hands of her father, or allow him to arrange for family therapy so they could all talk about what had happened. She did little but avoid the subject, and then symbolically attempted to erase the subject, her son's pain, and perhaps her own guilt, by scrubbing and cleaning. For a moment he feels angry and hurt. Then he feels nothing, and, characteristically, he cannot recapture the feelings he has felt so intensely just moments before. I remark that in the psychological terrain he describes so often to me, there is no room for him to stand so that he can face his memories and the feelings that they generate. Perhaps the feelings would be so frightening, feelings generated from being so unhelped and unsafe, that as a young child he could not bear to face them. And now, even though he is not a child any longer, he reproduces the old terrain, gets close to the horrible feelings, and then avoids all feeling. In the old terrain there was no one available to hear him; perhaps those who could have didn't want to know what happened to him and discouraged him from speaking. Perhaps they acted shocked or disgusted when he tried to speak about what had happened. But now he somehow reproduces that old terrain, and the moral rules that frame it. As a result, his memories and feelings disappear beyond the horizon; there is no room for them to appear in the old world that he unconsciously summons up.

In response to my remark, my patient makes one association to an old newspaper photo published during the Vietnam War. It is a well-known photo in which a young girl, perhaps seven or eight, is running, stumbling down a dirt road. She is naked, sobbing, in desperate pain, with a dazed, horrified look on her face. Her village had been destroyed by an American air strike, her parents killed, her skin burned and disfigured by the napalm. Her arms are held out from her body, in a gesture that appears to be both an attempt to avoid the agony of burned skin touching burned skin, and a desperate plea for help. "I was in college then. I remember that photo because I cried when I saw it, and that was unusual. I didn't know, then, why I cried. I never used to cry, it was something I never did."

I asked if he had an idea about why he was remembering the photo now. He said, yes, he felt like the girl. But he couldn't put it into words. I said, "Attacked, disoriented, betrayed?" He said, "That's it."

Since then, I haven't been able to get that picture out of *my* head. This is not just about my client, it is about all of us. Sometimes I think that is how we feel, as a country: attacked, disoriented, betrayed— grieving and enraged. My patient related this image to me during the 1992 presidential primaries. The country appeared confused and bitter, the candidates flawed and inadequate. They attacked one another; they produced sound bites; they defended their damaged integrity. Sufficient discussion of the issues, such as the inequities of race and gender, the financial scandals, taxation, the attack on education, or the rollback of abortion rights had been abandoned because none of the candidates knew how to adequately address them. We have enormous political problems that burn and disfigure us, and no one is there to help. We avoid facing how we feel, but if we didn't avoid it, we'd feel as though we were stumbling down the road, crying out, dazed, and alone.

We have difficulty solving our political problems today in part because we do not experience ourselves as political beings. Our cultural clearing is configured in such a way as to exclude the social connectedness of the commons, the public meeting place where citizens exercise their political obligations to their community and experience a sense of common purpose and group solidarity. The only place available for us in our current terrain is one that defines us as discrete, isolated individuals who have few loyalties and identities beyond our individual selves and families, and few available activities beyond acquiring and consuming. We cannot develop communal commitments because we cannot think of ourselves as citizens—as active, involved, caring political beings. In our world, a world in which the individual is pictured as separate and apart from, actually opposed to, a dangerous, potentially controlling state and rigid, authoritarian traditions, "freedom" is defined as the *absence* of social influence and political allegiances.

Although psychologists do not intend to do so, our practices reflect the current terrain by producing theories that glorify individuation, proclaim separation as the ultimate goal of child development, view psychological boundaries as essential to proper adjustment, and consider their absence or permeability a major cause of pathology. In the late twentieth-century clearing, caring is likely to show up as "codependence," and a sense of responsibility as an "obsessive-compulsive" trait.

Current Child Abuse

For these reasons moral dialogue and political activity are almost completely foreclosed. It is difficult for most of us to think politically, consider political activity honorable, follow through on political commitments, or retain hope for the future. One way to understand how the particular antipolitical shape of our cultural terrain affects us is to consider the increased and particular uses of the concept of child abuse as it relates to explanations of adult psychopathology. There has been a huge increase in reports of child abuse during the last twenty years. Accordingly, concepts of abuse have become increasingly prominent in psychotherapy theories, especially those which rely on seeing trauma as the primary or sole cause of adult psychopathology. This trend, in combination with the coming-of-age of addiction theory, has spawned many new treatment techniques in mainstream psychotherapy, a proliferation of twelve-step groups on a variety of subjects not directly related to drug abuse, and an explosion of how-to, pop psych books. Trauma theory, and especially abuse as a synonym for trauma, has even affected mainstream psychoanalytic theory in aspects of object relations theory and self psychology.

Several important questions arise in response to this phenomenon. Historians wonder if the increase in reported cases of child abuse is primarily attributable to increased public awareness and responsiveness. This implies that occurrences of child abuse have been relatively stable over time. Others believe that various sociohistorical changes have led to a breakdown in the moral commitments of modern society and the psychological well-being of individuals, causing adults to be significantly less protective of children and more willing to use and abuse them. This implies that the actual occurrences of abuse, not only reports of abuse, have increased over time. Some argue that the particular ways that society has changed have caused specific kinds of pathology, such as the social ineptness, isolation, and absence of reality testing or moral constraints that are often found in pedophilia, or the lack of communication skills and the profusion of rage and frustration that are often found in family violence. This again implies that it is the occurrence of abuse that has increased.

Each of these theories seems to have merit; as in most complex issues, the tragic prevalence of abuse in our society has been overdetermined by a combination of factors. However, recent social psychology research pertaining to the controversy over the definition of adult repressed memory and the induction of false memory, and recent psychoanalytic concern over the therapeutic implications of theory based primarily or solely on a trauma model of pathogenesis have been combined with philosophical and sociological concerns over the consequences of a psychology of victimization, all of which have produced a new awareness of the problems associated with the trauma-addiction paradigm. One concern, broadly stated, is that so many symptoms and wounds are being collapsed into the category "abuse" that the meaning of the term is shifting. Abuse may be becoming a catchall phrase, a symbol for other unnamed, unnoticed, unarticulated problems, both within the family and in society, that we would do well to acknowledge and learn more about. Another concern is that many practitioners are losing sight of the idea that psychological problems are rarely unicausal and never machinelike—how the victim *reacts* to trauma is a significant element in any psychological problem. Finally, a historically situated approach suggests that the current popularity of trauma theory might be related to the prominent ideology of our time, consumerism.

Trauma as Consuming the Bad Object

The concern that an exclusive reliance on trauma theory is an expression of consumerism goes like this: the post–World War II era has been dedicated to building a masterful, bounded self, which many psychological theories believe develops through the ingestion and metabolism of proper emotional supplies provided from external sources, especially the parents. Most current theories about psychopathology are focused on the success or failure of that goal. Many psychodynamic theorists believe that pathology is caused primarily by the consumption (internalization) of improper supplies (the bad parental object) before which the individual is powerless. In this view of pathogenesis, the commodity (the abusing or abandoning parent) controls the consumer's (the child's) development, and the victim, even as an adult, is helpless to prevent post-traumatic reoccurrences or events similar to the original trauma that result from interpersonal interactions in adulthood. Pathology that derives from the trauma is thought to be manifested in one of a few stereotypic and somewhat mechanistic ways. The child is condemned to consume the poisonous commodity automatically, and, as a result, to repeat self-defeating behavior and post-traumatic experiences in adulthood. Some writers are concerned that the discipline's excessive reliance on victimhood encourages passivity and helplessness, makes it the major constituent of identity, and encourages a definition of the self that highlights entitlement rather than moral responsibility and focuses on a self-absorbed preoccupation with personal wounds rather than communal commitments.

Historically situating the discipline's reliance on trauma theory highlights psychotherapy's involvement with the consumerism of our era. By unknowingly conceptualizing psychopathology as a manifestation of improper consumption, these theories unquestioningly rely on the idea that consuming is a basic, universal, natural human behavior. It is thought to be caused by the biochemical structure of our genes—human nature—not the particular political arrangements of twentieth century capitalism. Thus it is foolish and ultimately ineffective to blame, and then advocate resisting, current social structures. Twelve-step groups for the treatment of chemical addiction, or putative addictive processes such as "love and sex addiction," explicitly use the metaphor of helplessness. The addict is said to be helpless in the face of drugs—the ultimate commodity—and is told to surrender to a "higher power" in order to cease consuming. The idea of the commodity as all-powerful makes sense to late twentieth-century Americans because it is couched in the taken-for-granted understandings and power relations of the era; but like any uncritical, ahistorical healing technology, some addiction theories also unknowingly reproduce those understandings and power relations. The exclusive reliance on trauma theory thus joins certain types of addiction theory as another unintentional conveyor of consumerist ideology.

This is not to say that trauma does not exist or that child abuse and drug addiction are not tragic and significant problems—they most certainly are. It is only to suggest that psychotherapy theories that explain adult psychopathology *solely* through a combination of trauma and addiction theory have certain political consequences. Is there not a way that we could conceptualize emotional ills so that we could develop an understanding of the part the individual plays in his or her own troubles, in this case his or her power vis-à-vis the commodity? For example, in a hermeneutic view, trauma is re-experienced and abusive relationships repeatedly risked—unconsciously—by the patient in relations with others for various emotional reasons related to the necessity of staying involved with the (now absent) perpetrator or reproducing the (now absent) abusive terrain in order to act in a way that was considered moral within that terrain. This view of pathology does not perpetuate the person-as-consumer view, and it does not ignore the role the victim and current attackers play in the post-traumatic re-experiencing or reproducing of trauma or traumatic memory in adult life. For instance, by conceptualizing human interaction as including the constant reproduction of the cultural clearing, hermeneutics acknowledges—with compassion—the patient's role in the creation of dissociative states, avoidance, denial, self-sabotage, and acting out behavior in adult life. In this way the patient is less likely to be romanticized, sanitized, and degraded as a powerless consumer-automaton.

Abortion-as-Holocaust Metaphor

There are cases in which it seems improbable that there was abuse in the patient's past, and yet the vague, unspecific "feeling" of abuse lingers, unattached to specific memories. In these cases hermeneutics could help us wonder about how fitting the term abuse is in describing the patient's history. Concurrently, we could wonder about which unnamed experiences in the adult's current life might be expressed through the term. One way to characterize our era is to say that the cultural horizon is situated so that individuals are configured as consumers, not citizens. Honorable political activity is rarely possible in such a clearing; it is on the other side of the horizon. One of the few available activities is the act of consuming. The ideology of self-contained individualism is so dominant today that attributing personal pain or failure to the political "system" is generally considered to be an unacceptable excuse, a cop out. We do not think in terms of the political causes of personal problems because in a way we do not see the political at all; it does not show up in our terrain as a real-life influence. At most it is a removed, faraway process thought to be exercised by corrupt politicians and soulless bureaucrats in some untouchable Kafkaesque castle in the sky.

What does show up as the social realm in our terrain is the dyad, which is the container for many current two-person psychologies. We attribute political happenings to the dyad, because that is usually as social as we get. It is permissible in our individualistic world to claim that one other person, especially someone close, has had an impact on us. It is permissible to blame parents for one's depression, or a lover for an eating binge. It is understandable to blame one's boss for a headache or an upset stomach. But it is not okay to suffer from a psychological complaint if one attributes it to sexism, the pervasive profit motive of capitalism, or the increased economic stratification brought on by the political policies of Republican "trickle-down" economic policy. Psychological complaints only show up in our world if we depoliticize them and medicalize them (for example, "I'm stressed out") or if we attribute them to a dyadic relationship (for example, "the foreman is giving me an ulcer").

If this is the case, then it seems reasonable to wonder whether the only way the attacks, degradations, and betrayals visited upon us by the political arrangements of our world show up in our terrain, the only way we recognize and can give voice to them, is by conceiving of them as emanating out of a dyadic interaction. In other words, perhaps the only way we can experience and protest the political insults of our world is by experiencing them within a two-person psychology. Because of our alienation from productive political discourse and activity, some tend to situate these dyadic relationships in a time frame that would symbolize helplessness and powerlessness—in utero. We cannot find the words to protest our political alienation, our sense of degradation and betrayal, unless we unconsciously symbolize it by using figures who do show up in our terrain and are considered proper objects of fear and accountability. Perhaps the virulent hatred that the antiabortion movement focuses on "mothers who murder," and its extravagent claim that abortion practices have caused a second holocaust, can be attributed to this dynamic. The socioeconomic conditions of our world today do move many of us to feel as though either we are victims of atrocities or atrocities are happening all around us. How do we name and characterize these threatening acts, and who is available to be held accountable? Because the sociopolitical issues are so complex and appear so overwhelming, and because we are not skilled in thinking politically, we unknowingly use the words and people who are available and understandable to us. Mothers are prominent figures in our terrain, and mothering is an understandable metaphor. Therefore, all number of political crimes become displaced onto the act of abortion, and mothers show up in a narrow terrain as one of the few available perpetrators.

None of this is to say that abuse and addiction don't happen, or that abortion is not tragic and unfortunate; in fact, it is probable that abuse and addiction are happening more or we are properly defining them in a more inclusive manner now than at earlier times in our history. This is just to say that the way these issues have gripped the imagination of our society, the way they are being understood by some theories, and the unquestioned way they are sometimes accepted, is a puzzling phenomenon. It deserves study and examination. It presents new opportunities for understanding our society and is an instructive example of how psychotherapy theorizing can have important political consequences, in this case the furthering of political myopia and passivity.

RACE, GENDER, AND THE CONSTRUCTION OF AMERICAN IDENTITY

By psychologizing the effects of political structures, by conceiving of the social terrain as being peopled only by isolated, internally driven individuals or at the most politically insular parent-child or romantic dyads, and by claiming ownership of a special, objective, privileged, scientific method for producing truth about those monad/dyads, psychology has fortified its position as the guild most responsible for determining the proper configuration of the self, and thus has become an important cog in the wheel of late twentieth-century global capitalism. By conceiving of social life in a way that supports the economy, psychology is responsible for helping to bring about several serious problems.

By being part of the intellectual movement that has discredited historical and religious traditions, dismissed moral discourse in favor of a putatively objective scientism, and by standing by silently as industrial capitalism first manipulated the worker and then hypnotized the public, seducing both into the emptiness of consumerism, psychology has been a party to perpetuating a cultural clearing in which, among other features, racism and sexism are foundational elements. There are many complex political and economic reasons for the hegemony of discrimination based on race and gender, but none of them would have attained sufficient power in American society if it weren't for the characteristic American process of constructing a psychological identity by projecting that which is considered bad—and thus disowned and disavowed—onto "the other." The disrepute into which historical and religious traditions fell as a result of the Enlightenment era power agenda, and the systematic destruction of community occasioned by the onward march of industrial capitalism and urbanization, combined with the enormous disorientations and disruptions caused by westward immigration from Europe, created an unsettling absence of communal identity in the newly formed United States. One way Americans addressed this absence was by developing a negative identity. American society developed a concept of the self, the proper way of being human, by constructing "the other"—the Negro slave, the Native American, the Jew, the Irishman, the woman—in such a way as to define and justify the white self by demonstrating what it was not.

The particular political situation in which white Americans found themselves aided in both the destruction of old cultural meanings and the construction of new ones. It seems that wherever there are humans, there are usually forms of rivalries, conflict, discrimination, and warfare. But with each historical era and/or cultural frame of reference the meanings and functions of conflict and discrimination change. In the nineteenth and twentieth centuries in particular, racial and gender discrimination were powerful political forces because they served vital psychological functions related to identity formation and enculturation. The dominant white and especially Anglo-Saxon Protestant culture developed a configuration of the self that met their political and economic requirements by defining what was the improper way of being human, and locating it in "the other." They reinforced their own sense of personal worth and at the same time vicariously experienced dimly felt alternative ways of being (and expressed their inevitable self-loathing) by attributing disowned aspects of their own thoughts, feelings, wishes, urges, and old cultural identity prescriptions onto the despised "other." Personality traits that were considered to be negative, such as sloth, lack of ambition, inability to work, and sexual preoccupations, were often located on the African American. Personality traits such as avarice, dishonesty, "tribal" mentality, and a lack of proper Christian faith were located on the Jew, as were the lack of personal ambition, tribalism, and heathen beliefs on the Native American. Traits such as uncontrollable emotionality, physical weakness, a lack of business sense, and uncivilized and mysterious sexuality were located on the female.

In other words, the psychological processes of projection and displacement (and attendant processes such as avoidance, dissociation, and selective inattention) unconsciously work in combination with the political needs of the dominant population so as to configure the self, prove the correctness of the new configuration, provide an escape valve for unconscious guilt, self-hatred, and disowned emotional wishes, and maintain economic stratification. This combination of political strategies and unconscious psychological processes functions, to this day, to keep various discriminated-against populations in low paying, physically destructive, intellectually deadening jobs, in poorly financed, disease-infested, dangerous geographical locations, and in unending political impotence.

For these reasons, concepts such as the inferiority of the African American, the unindividualistic Indian, the greed of the Jew, and the untrustworthiness of the female became more important in the cultural clearing. They became deeply implicated in the configuration of the self, and thus in the sense of self-worth and moral rightness of the dominant population. These concepts not only served political and economic purposes, such as the creation of the Victorian bourgeois family and a permanent underclass, they also served psychological functions, such as the construction of identity and the maintenance of self-esteem and self-worth in the dominant population. Of course, distaff thoughts and experiences within the white population would often be redirected back through the psychological process of projection and displacement, and thus serve as more fuel for increased misogyny or racial hatred. Psychologists who use two-person theories, to their credit, are able to study and treat dyadic processes such as projective identification (see chapter seven). But they are unable to historically situate these psychological processes and relate them to crucial political struggles such as the creation of American identity. Therefore, ultimately, two-person theories do us little good when cast against the backdrop of the larger cultural canvas.

The concept of a two-person psychology was articulated and elaborated on by radical interpersonalists such as Edgar Levenson and Merton Gill. It was meant by them to emphasize the importance of a non-hierarchical, nonmechanistic, interactional Sullivanian process between patient and therapist in a spirit similar to that of the previously discussed comprehensive interactionist approach by Gadlin and Rubin in 1979. However, as a result of various shifts and misconceptions in the history of psychotherapy during the post–World War II era, the concept of a two-person psychology has often been identified more with an ahistorical, politically accommodating object relations-self psychology-limited interpersonal mix than with its more radical originators. Levenson's and Gill's innovative, nonmainstream perspectives were framed by a courageous free-thinking posture that is more critical and philosophically sophisticated, in fact closer to the three-person approach introduced in this book, than what the discipline has come to accept as the mainstream two-person approach. Object relations theory and self psychology— usually considered two-person approaches—have been unable to develop a historical perspective on their practices; this violates the central tenet of the three-person, hermeneutic approach I have proposed in previous work. Perhaps this is why Gill and his colleague Irwin Hoffman have turned increasingly to a "social constructivist" vision,[7] and why Levenson, in a recent 1991 article, has referred to his work as "an *at least* [emphasis mine] two-person psychology."[8]

TOWARD A POLITICALLY SUBVERSIVE HERMENEUTICS: A THREE-PERSON PSYCHOLOGY

The preceding discussion of the psychological functions of race and gender highlights a view of human being that has been used throughout this book. Philosophical hermeneutics helps us learn more about the power of the political structures of our landscape, and how that power shows up in a particular shape as a result of the moral understandings that frame that landscape. However, hermeneutics does not rely on a deterministic view of cultural influence, nor does it conceive of the individual as passive and powerless in relation to cultural prescriptions and the status quo. Instead, hermeneutics encourages us to become aware of and emphasize the ongoing psychological processes that we unknowingly use as a means of maintaining compliance with a particular cultural terrain. These unconscious processes are indispensable to the individual as he or she attempts to fit into and be considered an approved of member of a particular society.

The hermeneutic stance is important because it is an attempt to formulate a psychology that does not conform to our dominant consumerist frame. As has been argued throughout this book, many post–World War II psychotherapy theorists have unintentionally developed theories that are consumerist in nature. Object relations theory and self psychology reflect views of human being that are dependent on the metaphor of consuming: infant development is conceptualized as growth through the process of taking in (consuming) and finally internalizing (metabolizing) parental supplies. The sixties health food adage "you are what you eat" is a simplistic but not altogether inaccurate way of characterizing their view of infant development. Of course, clinicians aren't aware of, and would not want to be complicit in, this reproduction of a consumerist status quo. But because we are not trained to historically situate our theories, and to interpret the *political* functions of our theories, psychotherapists do not usually notice our subtle contributions to the continuing reproduction of the current way of life.

By describing the self as being "built" by the ingestion of supplies, psychopathology as the consequence of ingesting improper supplies or the consequence of the absence of supplies, and psychotherapy as an activity that provides the proper supplies, object relations theory and self psychology seem to be unknowingly enacting a covert strategy not unlike that used by nineteenth-century mesmerism. Mesmerism (see chapter five) provided a covert, compensatory response to a political problem—the loss of community—by describing an invisible spiritual substance that connected the patient with all humankind and with the cosmos, and by providing a healing technology that featured an ongoing group experience. However, although it provided a compensatory response to a political problem, it did so covertly; it was unaware of doing so, and it did not help patients recognize the political nature of their distress and challenge the political arrangements that caused it.

Could the current emphasis on providing supplies to neglected, deprived selves in psychotherapy be a covert, compensatory response to a political problem? By blaming parents (especially mothers) for the development of poorly built or dysfunctional selves, could we be drawing attention away from the larger culprit, a sociopolitical system in which the concept of the self is so riddled with contradiction that it is impossible to achieve? Could the culprit be a sociopolitical system that is structured in such a way so as to deprive the majority of the population of the emotional guidance and security provisions it needs, and then to convince people that what they need is to be found in empty calories, new electronic gadgets, and glitzy clothes? By conceiving of the self as a structure that can be properly built by the proper parents, and by conceiving of psychotherapy as the activity in which proper supplies are offered or a proper environment for the true self provided, are we unknowingly providing a covert, compensatory solution to a political problem best attacked directly? And by doing so are we preventing our patients from understanding the political nature of their distress and challenging the political structures that cause it?

Mesmerism provided a compensatory connective "glue" to a world that was falling apart, while at the same time remaining silent about the political causes of the wreckage. Is object relations theory and self psychology providing a small measure of compensatory emotional sustenance and safety, while at the same time not adequately relating emotional ills to their political sources. Are current psychotherapists making the same mistakes mesmerists did?

Philosophical hermeneuticists draw our attention to the historical and cultural and thus to the moral implications and political functions of various discourses and practices. An awareness of these implications could move psychotherapy toward adopting a more comprehensive hermeneutic perspective, which I propose we name "three-person psychology," in keeping with the current one-person/two person designation.

The third player I refer to is the the ever present, interpenetrating social realm. By "three-ness" I intend to convey that the individual, the dialogic partner, and the historical-cultural context are inextricably intertwined, that moral understandings are a foundational aspect of a culture, and that our discipline needs to be concerned with how various psychotherapy theories affect political structures and activities. By emphasizing the "givenness" of the cultural terrain and the powerful psychological processes that, outside of awareness, reproduce features of that terrain, philosophical hermeneutics demystifies psychopathology and grants a certain respect and efficacy to persons that is sometimes lost in other terrains. With a three-person psychology might also come an increase in hope and a willingness to continue to fight for the very thing that most of us have dispaired of, institutional change.

A three-person psychology encourages us to think of psychotherapy as a set of social practices shaped by its historical-cultural habitat and unable to be bracketed away from moral discourse. It reminds us that humans exist only in a culture, and that cultures simultaneously potentiate opportunities and limit possibilities. It presumes that every era and every culture develops images of the proper way to be human ("the self"), that each era's self has its idiosyncratic vulnerabilities, which must be healed by those designated as healers. Because humans *must* accommodate to their settings, each society develops practices that lessen suffering or remove it from view and return persons to their place in society. The question is not whether healers work hand in glove with a specific terrain, and thus with a particular set of moral understandings and political arrangements. This is a given. The question is only what kind of terrain do they work within, how can they make use of their knowledge and awareness of the terrain in their work, and how much power do they have or can they generate to shift the terrain?

In other words, hermeneutics argues that there are two types of healers. One type scrutinizes and owns up to the political consequences of therapy, and the second avoids that task and pretends that therapy is apolitical. The hermeneutic view is a measured but hopeful one: if as therapists we determine that our work has been unknowingly colluding with political forces that we oppose, then we can shift our practices so that our work does not support that with which we disagree and perhaps even add to the construction of social relations or political arrangements of which we approve. If we abstain from this overt, active role, then we become accomplices in social arrangements that run the risk of creating some of the very ills we are responsible for healing.

The hermeneutic stance is also important because by emphasizing the relationship between thrownness and the individual's unconscious complicity in maintaining the cultural status quo, and one's personal troubles, it can aid in undoing the mechanistic, passive, helpless view of human being that tends to be unknowingly reflected and reproduced in current psychotherapy theories that rely on addiction metaphors and trauma theory as the sole causes of adult pathology. If clinicians conceptualize adult pathology as a mechanistic process that is determined solely by what prominent figures in an individual's life did or did not do to the individual, patients will never come to understand what they unknowingly do in order to remember and reproduce the old cultural/moral/relational terrain of their youth, and they will not be able to develop understandings about how they currently collude with or even construct situations that risk further trauma, and thus they will not be able to protect themselves against the malicious or violent behaviors of others. The issue becomes more important when we consider that an exclusive reliance on trauma and addiction theory doesn't prepare individuals to think of themselves as active moral agents, who live in a world constructed by political arrangements and moral understandings about those arrangements. Instead it pictures a world of helplessness and mechanistic, reactive emotions. Let us remember what hermeneuticists such as Blaine Fowers, Charles Guignon, and Frank Richardson think of as the main point of the hermeneutic argument: because political arrangements and theories are embedded in and reflective of certain traditions, attempts at political change are only effective when activists put forth a believable moral framework that is capable of guiding the population in determining what is good and proper. Significant changes in political structures, they believe, will only be achievable and sustainable if the proposed changes are grounded in a moral stance that is situated within, and engaged in an ongoing dialogue with, existing historical traditions.

For instance, some forms of feminism, through their critiques of the arrangements of gender and class, have developed an understanding of the negative effects of individualism. This, in turn, has moved some writers to posit, and rightly so, alternative constructions of gender that would lead to a new configuration of the self less individualistic than the current configuration. Yet it is important to notice that feminism also grows out of aspects of the same traditions that it critiques. In fact, some forms of feminist discourse (for example, the current legal rationale for abortion rights, which is founded on the inalienable "right" to individual privacy) are strongly influenced by individualism.

Political battles are framed by larger moral understandings of the good. When it comes to the attempt to institute serious, sustainable social change, easy answers or simple, polarized alternatives are counterproductive. Political arguments that invalidate and dismiss Western traditions paint a picture too simplistic to be of help in facing the complex issues of our time and in developing realistic solutions that have a chance of creating political change that is sufficiently nuanced and sustainable. In opposition to a one-dimensional and simplistic rhetoric, a hermeneutic perspective would encourage us to see in any debate the complexities and the multiple aspects of historical traditions. Instead of grasping at trendy, extreme solutions, hermeneuticists call upon us to struggle with both communal and individualist strands in the traditions of the modern era, and to recognize their similarities as well as their differences. Hermeneuticists call upon us to acknowledge that ultimately the larger questions regarding what traditions identify as the good determine the choices societies make regarding what is expedient. Those who want to bring about radical change in the political structures of our society would do well to attend to the philosophical underpinnings of their arguments and make known their place within the traditions from which their arguments grow.

Rather than imagine political conflict as a winner-take-all competition between an old tradition and a new ideology, hermeneuticists encourage us to envision the political process as a dialogue between various aspects of one large tradition, or between two or more traditions. It is in the struggle, the grappling with moral issues, and in the experimenting, sifting through, blending, reformulating, and reconstituting of the moral frame that we can develop a clarity about what is right and proper for us at this time; out of this could emerge a renewed sense of inspiration and purpose. It is through the hermeneutic process that we might be able to affect a *significant* shift in the social terrain, one that is both understood and supported by the communities of citizens that make up the nation.

It is assuredly true that the structural arrangements of our society cause many in our world—especially people of color, women, and children—to be hated, attacked, and abused. Our current arrangements of power and privilege create many victims in the course of everyday life. But if our ways of understanding these attacks rob us of our ability to conceive of ourselves as persons who can join together into groups that can work to stop the emptiness, violence, and abuses of our era, then our theories are unhelpful. No, then our theories add to the oppression. There are other, more effective identities besides victimhood that we can use to fight back and create a better world. Hermeneutic's dialectical vision of humans as swimming in a sea of culture that is both given to us and continually reconstituted by us is a vision filled with equal parts awe, terror, and hopefulness. It is true that we suffer, some much more than others, but it is also true that we can make use of alternative traditions that are available to us in our everyday lives, develop ways of shifting the parameters of our vision, and in the process make more moral ground, and thus more behavioral possibilities, available to us. For instance, the moral understandings and communal practices handed down from our ethnic traditions are available but usually disowned sources of alternative guidance. The same might be said for some forms of alternative dialogue, when mothers and other female elders convey alternative ideas about human being that oppose dominate male views. And there are aspects of Western tradition that oppose the power-obsessed, greedy, control-oriented strains of Western culture. By adjusting our cultural horizon we can allow room for alternative traditions to show up, and then we can use those traditions to create a dialogue with the dominant tradition, thus informing our everyday life. We can then, armed with an enriched perspective, fight against the forces that oppress us. If various individuals have joined forces to manufacture and execute the *existing* political forces that oppress us, then it is also conceivable that other individuals can form into groups that can develop alternative, perhaps more compelling, forces.

THE IMMENSE *ALEPH*

If we can develop an increased understanding of how social worlds are constructed and reconstructed, perhaps we will be able to notice our unintentional contributions to the status quo, be less naive and seducible about claims of truth and scientific authority, better able to enter into effective collective efforts with community members and colleagues, and finally empowered to address the structural arrangements of our time. Everyday social interaction calls upon us to develop a multitude of interpretations about the immediate social context, and philosophical hermeneutics challenges us to become more effective at noticing those daily interpretations, those we are aware of, and those that we are not aware of; those that help us open our awareness to new possibilities, and those that close off possibilities; those that help us see the forbidden, and those that shut off, or help us disown and avoid, the forbidden; those that reproduce an old, destructive terrain, and those that help us develop a world in which new possibilities have the opportunity to emerge.

Are we really so powerful? Do interpretations really have such an important part to play in human experience? Steven Joseph, psychiatrist and Jewish scholar, tells this story alluded to by Gersholm Sholem in 1971:

> Once the rabbis meant to decide what in the the entire body of
> the centuries of Jewish learning was the direct word of God,
> and what was the human *interpretation* of God's word. They

argued for many weeks about this. Some took the position that the entire corpus of Jewish law and commentaries were the direct word of God, while others argued that only the Holy Books could be considered God's word. Finally, one faction argued that that was too large a body of work for God to have been directly, personally responsible for; instead, they argued that the Ten Commandments were all that God *actually* dictated; the rest was interpretation. This was a compelling arguement, and as a result, several factions relunctantly agreed. But then another group began to argue that even this idea was too broad. With sadness, they decided that only the *first* commandment was the direct word of God, and all the rest of the Ten Commandments, let alone the rest of the Torah, was interpretation. Finally, one old rabbi stood up and began to talk, and by the time he stopped talking and finally sat down, all were in agreement with him. It was decided that, if they were really honest with one another, all they could say with certainty was that the first word of the first commandment, *Anoche*, "I," was the direct word of God. But instead of ending the debate, that just occasioned more. Finally they came to one, final understanding, one with which they could all concur. In the whole of Jewish literature, in the entire body of Jewish commentary, throughout the vast tomes of the Holy Bible, scrutinizing every word of the Torah, only one letter could actually be said to be the one, direct communication of God. And that one communication was not even the word *Anoche*; instead, it was the first letter of *Anoche*, the letter *aleph*. Finally the rabbis had made a decision! The sound of the letter *aleph* was the only direct communication that God has ever made to humankind. Because it is the only sound that we have ever heard God make, the rabbis decided that that one moment of sound contained all the truth of all the literature in the entire body of Jewish learning. In that one sound, God captured for all time the immense truth of his word. All the rest, all except for that one sound, was commentary, was human interpretation. For that reason, the rabbis have referred to that first *aleph* as "the Immense *Aleph*," because it contained all the wisdom of the holy voice. The sound of the Immense *Aleph*, awe-inspiring and terrible, pregnant with a meaning beyond human comprehension, must have been filled to the breaking point with the overwhelming intensity of the direct experience of God. That one sound was God's—all the rest is interpretation.[9]

The irony and paradox of that rabbinic decision is instructive for us, as we discuss the meanings and possibilities of a more hermeneutic conception of interpretation, psychological process, and political action. The letter *aleph*, the first word in the Hebrew alphabet, is a silent letter. It has no sound.

The Immense *Aleph* contained all sound, but it made no sound. It contained all truth, directly spoken from God to Moses, in one immense silence. There is a great deal that the world offers, an immensity, we might say, but it makes no sound until humans interpret it. The potentiality of all understanding and experience is out there, waiting to be heard and comprehended, but first it must be interpreted by a human voice, imperfect but hopeful, limited and prejudiced but full of ideas, grand plans, and high ideals. Our human voice is easily corrupted by power, riches, and desire, but it is also, on occasion, noble and kind. Even God's voice, the rabbis understood, was unhearable, until generations of nondescript, anonymous Jewish scholars in poor European *shtetls* put pen to paper and interpreted God's silences through the understandings of their cultural clearing. Only then did God's voice speak.

That is how important, how powerful, human interpretation is. It is good news, the rabbis' decision, because it demonstrates to us the power of the interpretive frame. But it is also bad news, of course, because our cultural frame is always, unavoidably, limited, flawed, and constructed out of an unholy mix of human, historically situated motives. Interpretation is both grand and mundane, ennobling and corrupting, an opening and a shutting out. It is the description of God's voice, and yet it can never capture the totality of what is possible. The Immense *Aleph* is without end, pregnant with what is possible; but it can only be communicated through human understandings, and thus some, perhaps much, of what the *aleph* contains is then lost from sight.

Our landscape is littered with the consequences of what is continually being lost from sight. Often, in our world, the only way we can touch what has been lost from sight is to lust after the newest commodity or to hate and revile "the other" in public and then to masquerade—secretly— as "the other" in private. Unable to develop ways of changing our political structures, and thereby shifting the horizon, we are consigned to use destructive means of making contact with that from which we are otherwise closed off. Are there not new configurations of the self that we could develop, new ways of being human, that could help us live in a different terrain, a terrain that might allow new moral understandings of ourselves and others to emerge? Must we be trapped forever in the prison of our commodified, scientistic, projection-filled world, one that traps us into a much too narrow and hate-scarred vision of ourselves and others? How can we, as a nation, become more aware of the centrality of our moral concerns, the importance of our political stands, and the power of our interpretations?

When, Alan Paton first asked in 1948 about South Africa, will the dawn of our emancipation come, an emancipation "from the fear of bondage, and the bondage of fear"? The task of the post–World War II generation is not to build individual selves that conform to the requirements of our consumerist, stratified clearing. Instead, the task is to shape a new configuration of the self, one that leads to a citizenship based on realistic mutual regard and a moral commitment to economic justice and the well-being of all citizens, rather than a citizenship vulnerable to manufactured hatreds based on blood, race, and gender. When the day comes that we can develop a national identity that is not based on disowned projections, perhaps then we won't be required to hate and fear in order to feel worthwhile.

Can—and should—psychotherapists, as therapists, actively involve themselves in such an adventure? How can we avoid it? The one concept underlined in chapter after chapter of this book is that psychotherapy, throughout its history, unavoidably has been and continues to be saturated by that adventure. It is a good adventure, a proper adventure, and one well worth the effort of both therapist and patient. It is a proper adventure, that is, if it is entered into with eyes and minds open to the remarkably intertwined nature of the cultural, moral, political and psychological in human being. If our eyes are closed to all that, psychotherapy is nothing more than an effective tool of the status quo. But if we can open our eyes, or rather lift them and see more of what is possible, we will be able to move toward a critical, subversive, and perhaps even occasionally "constructive" moral discourse.

That would be a good adventure, one our present-day world is much in need of. We would fall short of grand deeds, of course, but our communities might be slightly better off for our efforts. Psychotherapy is a rickety, ultimately impossible bridge, but it is one of the few dialogic opportunities available to us. Perhaps, as our bridge sways to and fro below the stars and above the abyss, we can stop fighting the inevitable, take up our moral and political role, and enjoy the ride, in the winds of time.

The Self in Western Society

To-morrow, and to-morrow, and to-morrow,
Creeps in this petty pace from day to day
To the last syllable of recorded time,
And all our yesterdays have lighted fools
The way to dusty death. Out, out, brief candle!
Life's but a walking shaddow, a poor player
That struts and frets his hour upon the stage
And then is heard no more. It is a tale
Told by an idiot, full of sound and fury,
Signifying nothing.
　　　　　　　—WILLIAM SHAKESPEARE
　　　　　　　　MACBETH

For contemporary Westerners who prize above all geographical mobility and freedom of choice, who are suspicious of the influence of traditions and personal identities based on ancestry, the emphasis that non-Western cultures place on tradition and history seems strange indeed. But, of course, this was not always the case even in Western society. The masterful, bounded self of today, with few allegiances and many subjective "inner" feelings, is a relatively new player on the historical stage. Most historians place the emergence of this self in the modern era, beginning in the sixteenth century, although some have seen the beginnings of this form of the self as early as the twelfth century.[1] There have been many configurations of the Western self over the course of the last 2,500 years, and most of them have resembled more the communal self of non-Western cultures than the highly individualistic self of our current era.

GREEKS, HEBREWS, AND ROMANS: THE SELF IN THE ANCIENT WORLD

For instance, in his trilogy *Oresteia*, the classical Greek playwright Aeschylus portrays an Athenian self that is radically different than today's configuration.[2] In the course of waging war on Troy, King Agamemnon is forced by the gods to kill his daughter, Iphigeneia, and when he returns to Argos he is himself slain by his wife, Clytemnestra. Clytemnestra and her lover, Aegisthus, in turn are murdered by Agamemnon and Clytemnestra's son, Orestes, with help from Electra, their daughter. Although Orestes had been commanded by the god Apollo to kill his mother, the Furies (thought by Heidegger to be symbolic of the old, pre-Homeric gods) demand retribution under the old law of blood-revenge. The god Athene comes to Orestes' rescue and appoints a democratic jury to decide his guilt or innocence. Athene herself casts the deciding ballot, absolving Orestes of guilt.

One interpretation of this play, based in part on an analysis by Hubert Dreyfus and Jane Rubin, is that it is a kind of explanatory tale—an origin myth—describing the founding of the city-state Athens.[3] The old understandings that framed an earlier era in Greek history were breaking down under the pressures of new social conditions. The old law of retribution (the death of a family member was to be revenged by the death of an individual from the family that killed the victim) was no longer useful in this society; it was perpetuating the cycle of killing, not preventing it. Athene, one of the new gods, is a kind of synthesis figure, being neither one of the Furies nor one of the traditional Olympic gods. Her solution to the never ending cycle of violence and revenge was to found the city of Athens, dedicated to a configuration of the self that was inclusive of all Athenians: the city-state was to think of itself as a family. Therefore, no one in the city could commit murder or revenge a killing with another killing, because they were all of one family. Furthermore, as befit the new group self framework, Athens was to be built on a democratic foundation, symbolized by the jury of peers that Athene appointed.

The self in these plays is not a self that experiences intrapsychic conflict in the way we do today. It is not a self that is firmly bounded, nor is it one focused on individuality, personal autonomy, and freedom, the way the current self is. When the gods speak, the humans obey. When the Furies scream, the humans react as if they themselves *embody* what the Furies are feeling and thinking. The humans are aware that fate has decreed a certain place for them, and they comply. We could call this self a communal, nondeep, horizontal self. It was an inclusive self; the gods and the Furies embodied and articulated its feelings, were in a way part of the self. One of the principle illnesses from which this self suffered was the urge for revenge. The playwright Aeschylus (through the goddess Athene) was a kind of healer, and the technology used was the yearly Athenia theater festival and the playwright's artistic ability to define the city-state in a way that developed a new cultural clearing.

At approximately the same time the Hebrew culture was developing in the neighboring eastern Mediterranean region. As articulated in the early Genesis stories, such as the patriarch story cycle, the Hebrews developed a concept of the self that was also communal and inclusive. Although more individualistic than the Greeks, the Hebrew self had fluid self-nonself boundaries and was controlled in part by an external force, the Hebrew God Yahweh. In several of these early stories the protagonists Abraham, Isaac, and Jacob were confronted with decisions to make regarding their commitment to the particular God. For instance, each was asked to make a specific commitment, to involve himself with this God in a singular way. Abraham watched as the fire of God walked on earth between the split bodies of various animals that Abraham had been commanded to arrange (Gen. 15:9–15:21). The ritual is thought to be an embodiment of the dual, mutual commitment that was made between the Hebrews and their particular God: the Hebrews agreed to obey and be loyal to this God, and Yahweh agreed to protect the Hebrews and make of them a great nation. We could describe this self as a committed *partner* with a particular God. The dual nature of this partnership, or covenant, was enacted as Abraham argued with God before the destruction of Sodom and Gomorrah (Gen. 18:16–18:33). Contrary to usual eastern Mediterranean practices of the time, Abraham stood and argued with his God, using the covenant as a rhetorical weapon. "Should not the judge of all the earth," Abraham asked, "do justly?" In other words, Abraham called upon God to remember *His* part of the bargain, and God had to agree. The Hebrew self was one that has some fluidity in its self-nonself boundary. For instance, in a famous passage, the reader is told that "Jacob was left all alone—and a man wrestled with him until the break of dawn. . . . Jacob [said] 'I have seen a divine being face to face. . . .' " (Gen. 32:25, 32:31). It is sometimes difficult in Genesis to determine the boundary between the individual and Yahweh or the individual and the tribe. The most dangerous illness in the social terrain of the Hebrews was idolatry—that is, the act of treating God as though He was a thing, a creation of their own hands, an inert statue upon whom the Hebrews could project their alienated, renounced qualities, rather than a living, nameless, invisible being. God appeared as a kind of healer, who treated their idolatrous tendencies by entering into a covenant with them, teaching, threatening, and protecting them.

As time went on, new societies—featuring new selves—sprang up. The Athenian synthesis flowered and then began to disintegrate. In Plato's writings we can see that the self of his time (ca. 416–385 B.C.E.) was quite a bit less communal and embedded in certainty than was the self of Aeschylus' plays. The self of *The Symposium* was somewhat isolated and more removed. This was a self that was a thinker, a contemplator, an arguer. At this point the gods were not in control in the same way they were in the Oresteia trilogy. The self of the philosopher sought the universal Good, not the particular, local communal rules laid down by local gods. A certain kind of certainty and safety has been lost, and with it a certain kind of communality. By the time Petronius wrote *The Satyricon*, in 68 C.E., the Roman Empire was in full stride and the understandings of classical Athens were in a shambles. In a descriptive and despairing moment, Petronius has his character Seleucis proclaim, "What are men anyway but balloons on legs, a lot of blown up bladders?"[4] Some of the men and women at this dinner party, including the host, Tramalchio, were ex-slaves, wealthy but lacking social status, economic security, political rights, and religious convictions about an afterlife. Petronius portrayed the self of his time as an empty, hollow self, desperate for communal meaning but able to attain meaning only through purchasing, consuming, and overindulging. The self in Petronius appeared to have a much less fluid self-nonself boundary than the selves of earlier eras, to be more personally in control than controlled by the field, and to be defined more by exclusion than inclusion.

By 401 C.E., when St. Augustine finished *The Confessions*, the Roman Empire was in the process of total collapse. He is identified with the city of Hippo, located in North Africa. The intellectual and artistic glory of the Greeks, the disciplined military force of the Romans, as well as the communal cohesion and territorial integrity of the Hebrews, were but memories. Out of the ruins of the old understandings Augustine borrowed a bit from the Hebrews, a bit from the Greeks, and a bit from the early Christians, and revealed his own struggles for meaning. He built from the ruins of the old understandings new religious concepts and reflected a new configuration of the self. As Augustine wrote about his life he sketched for us a portrait of the confusions and emptiness of a communal world torn apart and unable to establish itself once again on local meanings and renewed social structures. Augustine used the Hebrew idea of a particular commitment to a particular God, the Greek ideas of philosophical dispute and the pursuit of the universal Good, and combined these with the experience of his own personal disappointments and miseries. From all this he shaped a form of Christianity that was attractive to the uncertain, confused souls of his time and place.[5]

Augustine described an empty, desiring, deceptive, hungry, lustful, and at bottom inadequate self. God begins, he explained, as an absence. This absence is located *within* each individual. Here there is no talk of a living community, no vibrant relationship with one's family or tribal ancestors, no strong Abraham-like individual arguing with God. Here there is just absence, emptiness, and self-hatred. Out of this, Augustine fashioned a religion for his time. The self as reflected in *The Confessions* is a self that is empty like a house and needs to be first cleansed by God (through confession and forgiveness) and then inhabited (furnished) by God. The only thing that is good in the self is a gift from God; all the rest, the deceit, the desire, the hunger, that which is naturally of the self, is bad. When individuals make choices by asking what is best for themselves, they will automatically fail to choose properly. The only way for them to make proper choices is to let God enter and transform them. The text is permeated with Augustine's self-loathing.

The self is empty, naturally hungry, lustful, and without meaning. Turning to others, Augustine explained, is equally ineffective. Humans always have ulterior motives such as greed, lust, and deceit, and therefore they cannot find meaning through personal relationships or political activity. The only relationship they can turn to is that with God. And the only possible way for individuals to relate to God is to realize that there is an absence in them, and then to let Him come into their hearts, to cleanse them, and to take them over. In other words, this is a self that is a potential container for God. It is a personal, inner, deep self whose sole purpose is to be filled with God. Slowly, as one tells the story of one's life to God, using God as the reference point, God fills the confessor. With Augustine, God begins within the self as a lack, and through narrative and memory God fills the self.[6]

The historical context of Augustine's era, I think, is obvious. The people of this time were deeply confused, isolated, cynical, disoriented. They were bereft of the community and tradition that distinguished certain non-Western cultures and certain eras in the West. With the relatively deep, empty, desiring, feeling, deceitful self of Augustine's time comes the need to be directed, guided, transformed, and finally saved. They fit hand in glove. Augustine explained that in order to be repressed, subdued, controlled, one had to submit to being surveyed and understood by something suprahuman. The emptiness and confusion of the sociohistorical era has, with Augustine, become decontextualized. In his writing the reasons for his fear and dissatisfaction have begun to take on an early, rudimentary form of being individualized and psychologized.

The healing experience of community and the aid of tradition have been erased in his cultural clearing: they simply don't seem to exist. Socio-political issues such as the desire for status, certainty, security have been reduced in *The Confessions* to the universal sins of autonomy and lust.

ROLAND, THE CRUSADING CHRISTIAN SELF, AND THE HIGH MIDDLE AGES

The Song of Roland, an eleventh-century French epic poem, describes a warrior society. Although it describes a battle in 778 c.e., scholars such as W. Merwin believe it was written at about 1090, the time of the first Crusade.[7] *The Song of Roland* is a story featuring Roland, the famous French knight who was vassal to the Emperor Charlemagne. They were out doing battle with the Spanish Sarasans, the Muslim infidel. Roland and a small band of Christian knights were betrayed by Roland's cousin, who set a a trap expressly for them. Pride and the code of chivalry moved Roland to refuse to sound the warning horn that would alert the Emperor and the bulk of his army that Roland was in need of assistance. By the time the horn was sounded and the Emperor rode to Roland's rescue, the gallant knight, all of his army, and all of the enemy were dead.

The epic reflects several elements of medieval European society: the entangling alliances of Church and State, the political obligations of feudal life, the importance of battlefield violence, the behavioral codes of the chivaric court, and the slowly emerging individualism in the middle and late medieval era. The epic poem tells the tale with a sense of impending doom, as if Roland's death and the entire catastrophe were preordained by God. Unlike Augustine's era, when religious confusion and uncertainty were the norm, the modern reader is shocked by the epic's depiction of the knights' absolute certainty about their raison d'être, especially in the face of the bloody violence they are involved in. In fact, it is the obsessive descriptive detail of the knight's dress and weaponry, and the same loving attention to gory detail in the violent war scenes, that is so striking. The text can be interpreted as conveying the religious significance of killing: killing on the field of battle, doing God's work against the infidel, was portrayed as a religious, sacramental act. The self portrayed in this epic poem is a warrior for God, God's vassal. If we recall that in this era the body was considered to be the container for the soul, then the violence and focus on killing makes more sense. Just as the heavily ornamental Empire protected and contained the Christian Church, and just as the heavily ornamental armor and weaponry pro-tected and contained the warrior's body, the body protected and contained the soul. The job of the Christian knight was to protect God's realm, both by defending it against intruders and by delivering the souls of the infidel into God's control. Using an interpretive formulation, we might say that the body was a container for the self, and the self was a resting place for the soul (remembering Augustine) that existed within the larger, corporate container.

The medieval self depicted in *The Song of Roland* could be said to have a relatively firm self-nonself boundary, in that these were fairly distinct, individual persons. However, the self was definitely field controlled, since the code of chivalry, the feudal oath, and ultimately God's wishes were all powerful. The self was defined primarily by exclusion. The knight was defined by what he was not: the infidel. The primary illness of the self of Roland's epic, epitomized by Roland's cousin who betrayed him, was greed driven by the desire for *individual* recognition outside of the feudal structure. He could not be healed, except to be killed, and then he was delivered to the devil. But other knights could be healed and thus saved from their illness, by joining the crusading Christian armies, giving their lives to God's struggle against the infidel. By participating, by protecting the realm and by dispatching the souls of the infidel, the errant knight could reorient his faith and alligiance to the corporate feudal structure, bond with his fellow warriors and with God's right hand on earth, the Emperor Charles. The Crusade, for the Christian knight, was a healing technology of the self.

Several important characteristics of the High Middle Ages, usually dated from 1000 to 1300 C.E., can be seen in *The Song of Roland*. The hierarchical nature of the society (its "corporate" structure) can, of course, be seen throughout the poem, as can the religious nature of the distinctions and bonds between classes and families. "Just as there was a universal hierarchy from God to angels to man to animals to matter; so was the church a hierarchy from pope to archbishop to bishop to priest to layperson; as was society from king to vassal and subvassal to serf."[8] Roland and his fellow knights lived in a material world reflective of God's heavenly world; what was of value in the everyday was what was beneath its veneer; the real truth, God's invisible truth, could be "read." This was as true for humans as for nature: Roland looked inside himself in order to know *God* rather than to know *himself* as a unique individual. The material world was a mirror of spiritual reality: When the sky storms and thunders in the Emperor's dream, in book CLXXXV, the reader knows that God is upset and something terrible is about to happen on earth. Visions, prophecies, and techniques of spiritual divining, such as alchemy, astrology, and dream interpretation, were commonly employed to discover and decipher God's message, which was embedded in the tiny entrails of a pigeon as well as in the immensity of a lightning bolt.

Philosophy in the Middle Ages was an exercise in accommodating what was already known, God's truth as revealed in the Bible and interpreted by the Church, with creative ideas and solutions to the puzzles of everyday life. Philosophers believed that a synthesis of all knowledge was naturally possible. Knowledge in the Middle Ages was conceived of as fixed and given: it was cyclical, rather than linear (which is how we think of it today). Time was also cyclical: the day, the week, the seasons, the years—all succeeded one another and then rolled on, attached to one another through membership in the great wheel of God's universe. What was important in human life was not the particular, the precise, the concrete; what was important was the universal, the essence, the spiritual.[9] Thus individuals might not know the year of their birth, but they might know under which astrological sign or on which Saint's day their birth fell.

Many developments occurred in the High Middle Ages that, although at first delayed during the late Middle Ages, eventually led to the decline and then the fall of the feudal system. Prominent among these were the beginnings of capitalism, the growth of larger cities, the beginnings of the concept of romantic love (first only at court, and in a most idealized and unpersonal form), and most important, the beginnings of individualism. We can see the beginnings of individualism in a myriad of small changes, such as portraits that began to reflect personal idiosyncracies as well as one's place in the social hierarchy; the concept of personal friendship rather than corporate feudal bonds; the philosophical growth of mysticism that emphasized personal communion, rather than a solely institutional, mediated relationship with God; the shift in art from a fixed to a moveable perspective; and literary forms such as the biography and autobiography. Peter Abelard, in an unusual individualistic move that would become important to the field of psychology hundreds of years later, maintained that it was not the act, but the individual's internal *intention* behind the act that constituted sin.

MARTIN GUERRE AND THE RENAISSANCE: THE SELF IN BOTH MEDIEVAL AND MODERN WORLDS

In the late Middle Ages the social trends of feudal times combined with severe economic problems and the spread of bubonic plague to devastate the population of Europe. The growing intellectual openness and creativity of the High Middle Ages was closed off as pessimism, crime, violence, and Church corruption, infighting, intellectual rigidity, and physical violence against heretics, witches, and Jews increased. But in the late fourteenth century in Italy the trends seen in the High Middle Ages began to reappear, coalescing in the broad shift to the philosophical movement known as Renaissance humanism. It spread slowly into northern Europe over the course of the next two hundred years. The poems of Petrarch (1304–1374) are often used to illustrate the ideas of the Renaissance, even though the poet was actually quite ahead of his time. The Renaissance emphasized an interest in human rather than divine truth, in the earthly, material world rather than the heavenly world, in many perspectives instead of God's singular truth. Whereas the unknown, the fearful, the sense of impending doom characterized the Middle Ages, an optimism and celebration of individual strength was often seen in the Renaissance. However, these were gradual changes, and it is important to remember that the Renaissance was still part of the Middle Ages. It was an era obsessed with signs and portents, and it relied on the technique of resemblance to determine truth. The Renaissance interest in secular human acts and the human body, and in the human body as machine, did eventually lead to empiricism and modern science, but the changes came about very slowly.

An example of the dual nature of the Renaissance, having one foot in the Middle Ages and one foot in the modern era to come, is the remarkable story of *The Return of Martin Guerre*. The acclaimed historian Natalie Zemon Davis researched an unusual legal episode from sixteenth-century France and expanded it into an excellent film and finally a historical novel.[10] In her writing we can see the process of the slow movement from feudalism to early capitalism, from a group self to an individual self, from the concept of the individual as embedded in the community to the individual as chooser of allegiances: from medieval to modern life.

In a small French village in the 1540s a man who had, at the age of twenty-four, abandoned his young wife and child, returns to them and wants to retake his rightful place in the community. He has been absent for fifteen years. The village, composed almost entirely of his extended family, is overjoyed at his return. His wife, although at first confused and timid, is finally overwhelmed with relief and happiness. Martin explains why he had left, quickly proves to everyone's satisfaction that he is indeed Martin Guerre, and is immediately integrated into the daily routine of the village. It is said that Bertrande de Rols, the wife, has never been happier. But after several years he becomes somewhat demanding of his uncle and nephews regarding some back rent he claims is due him, and two traveling strangers begin to whisper that Martin is an impostor, Arnaud du Tilh, who was known to them when they were in the army. Events lead to a trial, in which Arnaud is tried for "imposture, false supposition of name and person, and adultery." Bertrande appears confused and afraid but continues to stand by Martin, claiming that if anyone should know her husband, she should. He is exonerated. But then, in an unusual second trial, another Martin Guerre shows up, and it is obvious that he is indeed the real, surly, unpleasant Martin Guerre of years past. Arnaud confesses and is executed—loquacious, loving, and charming to the end.

The story illustrates several qualities of Renaissance-early modern life that are important to our brief exploration of the history of the self. First, it is impossible to imagine this set of events occurring in feudal Europe: roles could not be exchanged or appropriated, family networks could not be penetrated, selves, to use Stephen Greenblatt's phrase, could not be "fashioned."[11] Also it is difficult for post–World War II readers, who are so attuned to individual differences, to imagine that the members of this family-village could not immediately realize that the man was not their husband, son, brother, nephew, cousin Martin Guerre. How were individuals identified and recognized in this era? Third, the story raises questions related to the configuration of the self at this time. What were the distinctions and understandings that created the cultural clearing of this era, that created the definition of what it meant to be human?

Davis, after careful study, developed an interpretation about how the imposture came about. She argues that Arnaud, a vagabond and thief, had met the real Martin Guerre in the war and had tricked Martin and two other men who knew the village of Artigat into teaching him in detail about the family Martin had left behind. He had begun trying to leave his old life of disrepute, and latched onto the idea that he could start a new life by passing as Martin, since Arnaud and Martin resembled one another facially. But to do this Arnaud would have to trick the villagers and, of course, especially Martin's family, into believing he was *their* Martin. This would prove to be a difficult thing to do, since Arnaud and Martin were not at all alike in temperament, body shape, or accent. Davis argues that Arnaud is able to accomplish this feat, to convince the village that he is the returned Martin, because (1) he is able to imagine it and carry it off, due to the changing nature of the culture and his personal abilities as an actor, and (2) Bertrande and the family want to believe it for personal reasons and need to believe it for socioeconomic reasons. These two reasons illustrate the remarkable changes moving Renaissance Europe toward the modern era.

First, Arnaud's capacity to imagine pretending to be another person

was not exactly an aberration by this time in the West. Acting, imposture, switching places, as Greenblatt and others have argued,[12] was
becoming characteristic of the Renaissance. Lionel Trilling has described
the Renaissance preoccupation with "sincerity," which was thought to be
the degree of correspondence between the hidden thoughts or feelings of
an individual, and their public portrayal.[13] How different this is from
feudal conceptions of identity and the self. For the Middle Ages, identity
was given and fixed, a part of the Divine plan of the universe. One's
identity was determined by one's place in the corporate religious hierarchy, in the local community, in the family. One *was* one's place. In this
way identity was unproblematic. But with the breakup of the feudal
arrangements of allegiance, land, and locale, questions regarding identity
and proper behavior began to appear—as Roy Baumeister has put it, the
self became a "problem."[14]

These questions, and an uncertainty regarding who had the authority to answer them, were influenced by the trends of individualism and
Church reform. The attack and finally the overthrow of the Church's
absolute authority with regard to such matters in this same century,
known as the Reformation, were reflections of these trends. (Arnaud, in
fact, appears to have been a Protestant, and Davis suggests that his
apparent wish to make himself over into a new person is consistent with
some forms of Protestant ideology of this time.) As the feudal arrangements weakened, and as a revitalized mercantile capitalism began to
influence how individuals conceived of their position in the world, people began to become more mobile geographically, more independent
about religious matters, and more economically entrepreneurial. Men of
letters became obsessed with the act of wearing masks, playacting,
fashioning the self. As Montaigne wrote, "Men form and fashion themselves . . . , for dissimulation is among the most notable qualities of this
century."[15] "We [play roles]," explained Philibert de Vienne, "to please
others[. It is] an easy way to attract benevolence, honor, and good
reputation."[16] Thus, Arnaud du Tilh's idea to trick the villagers into
believing he was Martin Guerre, to refashion himself, was an imaginable
act, marginally within the bounds of the social understandings of the
time.

It was possible, then, for Arnaud to *imagine* doing this. But how was
it possible for him to *be able* to do it? How could he accomplish such a
seemingly impossible task? How was it possible to trick family and
friends, those who had known Martin so well, so intimately, all his life?
To understand this is to understand the era. First, we must turn to
historian Donald Lowe, who has argued that every era has a predominant communications medium, which develops a particular perceptual

sense, which fits with a corresponding epistemic order (that is, a way of "determining" the truth).[17] Lowe argued that in the Middle Ages the communications medium of orality waned and the written word came into vogue, hearing and touching predominated over seeing, and the principle of analogy was used to determine what was true. In the Renaissance the predominant communications medium shifted from the written to the printed word, hearing/touching slowly shifted to the primacy of sight, and the concept of resemblance helped determine what was true. In the Martin Guerre story we can imagine how the passage of time and the age at which Martin left the village combined with the prominent sensing hierarchy of hearing and touch to make it difficult for villagers to imagine his current appearance. Lowe's schema can also help us understand how the villagers could accept Arnaud as Martin because Arnaud remembers what Martin should remember, that is, he *possesses* Martin's memory. French country peasants at this time were not empiricists as we are today; that is, they did not believe in the existence of concrete data points that could, by being identified, observed, and counted, determine the truth. They thought of truth in terms of analogy and similarity: Arnaud acts as if he is Martin, therefore he is Martin. Arnaud possesses Martin's memory, therefore he *is* Martin.

This brings up perhaps the most important quality of the time that makes Arnaud's imposture possible. The family and village want desperately to believe that Arnaud is Martin, for both emotional and socioeconomic reasons. Davis suggests that Bertrande colludes with, in fact becomes an active partner in the conceit:[18] she makes it possible for Arnaud to learn and commit to memory all the little details of family history, personal idiosyncrasy, and physical appearance that make the scheme possible. And why does Bertrande join with Arnaud to deceive the community? And why is the community so easily deceived? Because Bertrande needs a husband. She needs a husband not only personally, which appears to be true, but also socioeconomically; and the community needs her to have a husband. Martin is important not so much because of the unique individual person he is (in fact it appears as though he is a pretty obnoxious individual), but because of his *place* in the community. Martin Guerre's place as husband, son, father, nephew-cousin, and land holder has been vacant, and that vacancy has caused a problem for the whole community. Economic questions of land use, rent, inheritance, and family politics related to decision making, authority, and protection have been vastly more problematic because of Martin's absence. These questions were initially answered when Martin and Bertrande got married, and their family's lands and wealth were combined and solidified; probably this is why the marriage was arranged, especially when both of them were at such an early age. Martin's absence has caused the family alliance to be shaken, and probably has led to the marriage of Bertrande's mother to Martin's uncle after the death of Bertrande's father. This marriage was an attempt to partially solidify the economic-political instability caused by Martin's continued absence. But it was not a complete solution; Bertrande and her children continue to float out of context, as it were, because the Martin Guerre *place* is not being occupied.

Here we see the meaning of what we might call the self as place holder. Bertrande, and her family, and the community, need someone in the Martin Guerre place. By leaving and not returning, by not dying and not ending the marriage, the person Martin Guerre left the place Martin Guerre unfilled and unable to be refilled. Thus, Davis argues, when Arnaud arrives at an inn outside of the village and asks for Bertrande, claiming to be Martin, she decides after a couple of days to help him prove that he is Martin. Without her, Davis argues, Arnaud does not have a chance of success.[19] By helping Arnaud, Bertrande runs the risk of being declared an accomplice, should they be found out. The penalty would have been severe, if not the ultimate—excommunication and death. Why, then, does she join in the conceit? Because her life has become increasingly problematic: She is in danger of becoming a nonperson, without political power and economic status within the family. Women at that time played important roles within the rural family economy, working side by side with the men, but they had little authority, could not own property, and had no legal clout.[20] "Weighing and calculating," Davis explains, "provide a mode of resistance for wives who, in their legal status as subject to their husbands, have few other means of getting their way."[21] Without the Martin Guerre place filled, Bertrande is becoming uncontextualized and increasingly precarious. The risks she takes are great, but the consequences of the continued status quo would be worse.

In response to the challenge of historian Robert Finlay,[22] Davis convincingly argued that a simple peasant woman of that time and place was indeed capable of such self-conscious calculation, independence, and proactive behavior.[23] "There is," historian Pierre Goubert noted, "something of a merchant in every [French Renassiance] peasant."[24] We see in the Martin Guerre story the growing self-consciousness of individuals who must increasingly shift for themselves economically. They live in a world more fluid and suggestive of promise than the Middle Ages, yet a world of greater insecurity and danger. Arnaud takes it upon himself to sell some of his inherited land, and to lease other family holdings. This upsets Martin's uncle Pierre Guerre, and starts the uncle to questioning and then doubting Arnaud's story. These economic actions are a bit troubling to the little Artigat community, but not so unusual to be considered illegal or immoral. A new economic age is developing, and with it the need to be more calculating, more active in service of one's own individual economic needs.

The new economy and the trend toward individualism are not the only new features of the changing cultural scene that the Martin Guerre story illustrates. An increased loosening of the feudal ties has also brought about another change: romantic love. In *The Song of Roland* Roland appears to be deeply in love with the beautiful Lady Alde, and she with him. But his betrothal to her does not stop him from fulfilling the vows of fealty to the King and especially to the codes of knighthood. Roland is more committed to fulfilling his chivalric vows than his romantic vows: in effect, he commits suicide. When one takes into consideration the lack of information about Lady Alde, their relationship, or Roland's feelings about her, his choosing his feudal vows over his life and his future with Alde indicates that he is more involved with Alde's position and status as the Emperor' sister, than with Alde as an individual.

Contrast Roland's relationship with Alde to the growing relationship between Arnaud and Bertrande. Something appears to happen to them and their *personal* relationship during the three years they lived together as husband and wife. Bertrande is reported to be happier than she had ever been in her life, and Arnaud settles into life as Martin Guerre and stays (!), even though he could have, at some convenient time, taken the money and run. During the first trial, when the decision is very much in question, Bertrande does not panic and distance herself from Arnaud, even though she is under great pressure from her mother and uncle to denounce him. At the end of the scheme, when the imposture is at last found out, Arnaud protects Bertrande, and makes sure she is safe, even though he is declared guilty and is about to die. Even though the self as place holder has brought them together, the self as *unique individual* has kept them together and protected Bertrande in her moment of greatest danger. They act together as a self-conscious unit, in opposition to the community in which they live. The husband-wife unit, bound in romantic love, cannot be possible without some semblance of unique individualism, without a self that stands apart from the community. It is only when the self was conceived of as separate from the community, that a romantic union between two unique individuals could be possible.

This is what is so fascinating about the Martin Guerre story. It illustrates a moment of change as the Middle Ages configuration of the self changes to the modern era configuration. Arnaud and Bertrande stand with one foot in each world. We see the self becoming configured as a self that could be consciously "fashioned," shaped, even changed. Yet we see the self as place holder. Without the possibility of individualist self-fashioning and imposture, they could not have imagined the scheme. But without the concept of the self as place holder and possessor of memory, the scheme would not have been necessary: Bertrande would not have been motivated to risk everything to join in the scheme, and the family would not have been motivated to believe it. We see the beginnings of an economically entrepreneurial self, yet we see the self immersed within and bound by family and community. We see the beginnings of the self as the arbiter of religious and ethical decisions, yet we see the remorse and guilt of two community members who are embedded in a world still anchored by belief, communal responsibility, and Church authority. We see the beginnings of a romantic union between two individuals isolated and set off from the community, yet we see the merging of the political needs of two place holders whose entire existence is dependent upon the community. Arnaud's and Bertrande's in-betweenness, their freedom and their limitations, their imaginations and their limited goals, hint at and illustrate some of the vast changes people are about to confront in the modern age and with the increasingly individual configuration of the self. They foreshadow the vastly expanded freedoms, and confusions, of our time.

THE EARLY MODERN AND ENLIGHTENMENT PHILOSOPHERS: THE POWER STRATEGY OF SCIENCE, FREEDOM, AND INDIVIDUALISM

Not surprisingly, with the newly found beginnings of the modern concepts of the freedom and fluidity of the self came a great deal of uncertainty. Without an unquestioning loyalty to feudal oaths, the one Church, and an extended family embedded in centuries-long community traditions, resting in the loving, all-knowing hands of God—how is one to live one's life? How is one to know right from wrong, proper from improper, the cause of God's approval or His eternal wrath? What does it mean to be a human being, when old distinctions and understandings have been undermined and finally lost? These questions are the fruits of the modern age, just as are the more celebrated discoveries of medicine, science, and political freedom. The consequences of an increased interest in humanity and man as the measure of all things; a growing belief in "progress" and the ability to quantify, count, and understand all things; a conviction that the way to truth is to question every traditional notion and defy every authority led to an uncertainty and a confusion that had to be addressed. The early modern and Enlightenment philosophers undertook that task.

But of course their discourse was more than just a response to a philosophical dilemma. As we shall see, it was also a means of promoting a political agenda: concepts such as individual freedom, empiricism, and scientific objectivity were not simply neutral philosophical concepts. They were weapons in a political battle that eventually wrested power from the hands of the Church and Monarchy by shifting the entire cultural frame of reference of Western society. It was a monumental victory, one from which the West is still profiting and by which it is still scarred.

The thinkers and writers of the early modern age, such as Descartes, Locke, Hume, Montaigne, Rousseau, and Kant were all writing within the context of the explosion of interest in scientific learning that marked that era. They struggled with disturbing new questions, such as what type of knowledge can humans realistically be able to discover, how can they come to attain it, and how can they be certain that it is correct, accurate knowledge? This in turn led them to discuss issues such as the nature of truth and reality, the existence of good and evil, and the nature and proper place of humans in the cosmos. In other words, the configuration of the self was the subject of explicit debate. As the new science grew and its authority spread to all intellectual subjects, philosophers began to ask questions about what we would now call psychology. They wondered about the relationship between mind and body, how humans could attain "true" knowledge, if it was possible to accurately represent the "real" world, how ideas were generated and interrelated, and if it was possible to develop a science of psychology.[25] These questions, framed with this particular type of intellectual freedom and with fewer constraints, could not have been asked in the Middle Ages. The enthusiasm for the new science and the optimism it engendered, the freedom to call tradition and (certain types of) belief into question, the willingness to discuss truth, morality, and reality without direct recourse to God and the Church—these all marked the philosophical discourse of the early modern era.

During the Renaissance and the early modern era, the Church was becoming increasingly fragmented, and finally it divided over the Reformation; mercantile capitalism was becoming more prominent, and early forms of individualism were becoming increasingly influential; all of this influenced the breakup of the religious-military-economic arrangements that had been the foundation of feudalism. With the increased interest in humans for their own sake, the material world became a more interesting topic of study, and innovative, critical ideas were generated. This naturally threatened the intellectual privilege and authority of the Church, which struck back with the weapons at its command. The new interests also threatened the power of the new nation states, which countered with new forms of punishment and new strategies of control. Thus there was a need to develop an intellectual justification for the new science of empiricism, to explain why its techniques should be used in the moral deliberations that heretofore had been the sole domain of the Church. Society was thus increasingly less certain about questions regarding how to live a proper life, about what constituted good and evil and how to distinguish between the two.

In other words, people of the time required moral guidance and an intellectual justification for the overthrow of the authority and power relations that had been dominant throughout the Middle Ages. Onto the historical stage came the early modern philosophers, armed with an optimistic belief in the new science of empiricism and/or innate rationality, emboldened by the early success of the physical sciences, and excited by the opportunities created by the demise of the old order. There was in the sixteenth, seventeenth, and eighteenth centuries a strong sense that science would solve the confusion: it would lead to discoveries about the universal laws of human nature, equivalent to the universal laws of the nature of matter, which would ultimately reveal the answers to the perplexing questions about proper human living. Some, like Locke and Hume, believed that scientific empiricism would discover the truth about human being. Others, such as Descartes, Leibniz, and Kant, argued that human rationality was the cornerstone upon which the new human science must be built. Still others, such as Montaigne and Rousseau, favored using the mirror of nature as the guiding force over using the techniques of science. But to varying degrees they all believed in the explanatory capacities of the human mind, the efficacy of reason and nature, and the ultimate triumph of observation and logic over tradition and intellectual compliance.

Amusingly, the major psychological debate of this era, that of Hume versus Kant, ended with both deciding that an empirical science of psychology was an impossibility. Hume, the radical empiricist, argued that we cannot accept explanatory concepts such as "causality" or "the unified self" because they can not be demonstrated empirically. Kant reported that when he realized what Hume meant, he was awakened from his "dogmatic slumbers" and he leapt into action. In response to Hume he came to argue that although humans cannot empirically demonstrate certain concepts, they certainly perceive them; therefore, the capacity to perceive certain relationships and concepts must somehow be implanted *within* the mind. In this way Kant "invented" modern structuralism, the great-grandparent of some forms of learning theory, cognitivism, and even psychoanalysis. He argued that we possess by nature certain intrapsychic perceptual psychological structures that allow us to categorize the material (phenomenal) world. The noumenal world, however, is beyond our grasp. Therefore, because humans can only see "through" their innate perceptual structures, perfect scientific clarity into the workings of the human psyche is not possible. Bertrand Russell, the twentieth-century empiricist, wryly remarked that, although Kant did, initially, awaken from his slumbers, his activity only resulted in the invention of a new "soporific" that quickly put him back to sleep again.[26] In any event, regardless of Kant's sleep patterns, he and Hume had both decided, for different reasons, that the science of psychology was not possible. It was then, after their negative conclusions, that psychology as a field began to develop, disregarding Hume's warnings and Kant's limits.

In any event, the philosophers began the arduous task of developing an intellectual justification for the use of the new science in human affairs and a program of moral guidance based on the new science's potential findings and discoveries. Behind all of this was an implicit power strategy: philosophers not only decried the repressive aspects of the Church and the Monarchy; concurrently they also helped construct a new cultural clearing with an entirely new and more compatible power structure. This new structure was better suited to the exercise of power by new political regimes whose style and allegiances were favored by the philosophers. Their power strategy, which wrested control from the Church and the old regimes in part through the "positive" or "constructive" use of discursive power, to use Michel Foucault's terms, was marked by the valorization of terms such as *freedom, scientific truth, objectification, independence,* and *personal responsibility.* Their discourse was not only an attack on traditional authority; it was also the *creation* of a new framework, with a new set of power relations, founded on what in hermeneutic circles has come to be known as the modern era's program of self-surveillance, self-fashioning, and self-transformation. The program, it was thought, could only be brought about through the self processes of objectification, disengagement, inwardness, and radical reflexivity.[27] The gauntlet had been thrown down, and a new struggle had begun, a struggle over the shape of human being and the justifications, means, instruments, and objects of the exercise of power. It was to be a struggle waged with words as well as torture chambers, with concepts as well as swords, with "positivity" (that is, the construction of a new self) as well as repression. At stake was the power to control the modern populace and to harvest the unimagined wealth and riches that the new science, in partnership with industrial capitalism, was about to produce.

The slow changes in the configuration of the self that marked the shift from the Middle Ages to the modern era were both reflected and produced by philosophy. René Descartes' contribution to that debate was considerable. Philosopher Charles Taylor has shown how several of the hallmarks of the ontological framework of the dawning age, such as the removal of God *out* of the material world, the development of an objective stance toward the world and toward oneself, the universalizing of doubt, the extension and elaboration of the concept of interiority, and the valorization of rationality were all begun or advanced by Descartes.[28]

The broad intellectual change in the modern era, which resituated the geographical *location* of "the order of things," to use Taylor's phrase,[29] from the external world to the internal, intrapsychic world of the mind, was first articulated by Descartes. Whereas the Hebrews located God and His laws, and Plato the realm of pure forms, in the external world, Descartes found order and truth through the interiorized searching of the individual, logical thinker. By doubting everything, even his own existence, Descartes began the process by which he could arrive at a certainty that his calculations were true. Through the exercise of the private capacities of doubt and logic humans could construct a conceptual order that they were absolutely certain of; they could then live their lives in harmony with it. "Truth," Taylor suggested, "ceases to be something we *find* and becomes something we *build*."[30] This is all crucial to the new age of science. The most important capacity in the world, the ability to order the universe and direct human behavior, has been relocated *inside* each modern individual. In order for Descartes to be able to conceive of such a monumentally different geography, and in order for his contemporaries to tolerate and in fact embrace such a radical concept, a new cultural framework must have been forming.

The foundation upon which this new framework was predicated can be found in another of Descartes' ideas the disenchantment of the material world.[31] He took issue with the most basic concept of the medieval clearing: the belief in the indwellingness of God in the world. During the Middle Ages it was believed that the form and order of God's divine realm was reflected in the forms and happenings contained in the material world on earth; everything was a reflection of and an unfolding of God's eternal plan. The interpreter and thus the "keeper" of the divine plan was, of course, the Church. Thus, to hold to the concept of the indwelling of God in the material world was to submit to the ultimate authority of the Church and the power of its vassals.

The obverse was also true: to challenge the concept of the indwelling of God was, ultimately, to refuse to be governed by the Church. And that was exactly, although implicitly, what Descartes did. In his actions we can see the subtle, "positive" uses of intellectual discourse. He couched his ideas in the ideals of "freedom" and "certainty." He thought that people were confused and violent because they were trapped in the confusion between the soul and inert matter. The two realms, that of the spirit and the material, the mind and the body, were two distinctly different realms of reality. There were, he argued, two kinds of things, the kind that takes up space and the kind that doesn't. Although the two realms interact with one another, spirit and matter are not identical or coterminous.

When matter is disenchanted, Descartes suggested, it must be interacted with differently. Descartes advocated a scientific attitude toward the material world, one that necessitated an objectifying stance. He advocated that individuals emotionally remove themselves from the world of matter in order to study it mechanistically and learn its functions. The discipline of inwardness and logic also required a type of self-objectivity in the form of the self-discipline of logic. The emotionally removed stance meant that no traditional body of knowledge (for instance, the Church's scholasticism and the folkways of particular rural communities) had a prior claim over the scientist. Universal doubt and logic were the first priority and demanded one's strongest loyalty. One's body was of the material world, and as such in order to properly understand it and interact with it one had to objectify it, remove oneself from it and from any prior body of knowledge about it or moral laws regarding it. By taking this objectifying stance toward one's body, logic could be applied and ultimately the passions could be controlled by the logical categories that one developed. Thus the body can be brought under the domination of the mind. Here we see the beginning of the philosophical justification for self-mastery, upon which the modern era's self-surveillance is built. Martin Guerre's self-fashioning, and later Jeremy Bentham's nineteenth-century reform prison the Panopticon (see chapter four), could not have been conceived nor carried out without some belief in this type of self-objectification and self-mastery.

According to Descartes, not only is the logical order of the universe to be found in the innate functions of the mind, but so is the source of morality. With Descartes has come the articulation of a strange new configuration: inwardness and interiority, not the external and the outward-oriented, was becoming the seat of order and morality. Au-

gustine also looked inward, but when he looked inward he found emptiness and an intolerable absence of God—a lack of self-sufficiency. When
Descartes looked inward he found innate logic, certainty, and a supreme
self-sufficiency.[32] Somehow, the location of the center of the universe
was in the process of changing, and Descartes captured it, and advanced
it, in words. Ironically, just as science was "proving" that the earth was
not the center of the physical universe, the Enlightenment philosophers
were arguing that the center of the moral universe was located within
each individual.

Descartes' ideas, as radical as they were, seemed tame when com-
pared to the quintessential early modern scientist John Locke. Locke took
some of Descartes ideas, such as objectification, and radicalized them,
applying them to the human psyche in ways that ultimately led to the
disciplines of psychology and finally psychotherapy. Locke applied the
concept of objectification not only to the material world but also to the
mind. He proposed a radical disengagement, a stance that would objectify and instrumentalize the self: one must disengage from the self in
order to remake the self. This "work on the self" could be done, Locke
asserted, through the methodical application of scientific discipline.[33]
Here again we see the modern power strategy at work: the scientific
method of objectification, and not a traditional body of knowledge or the
authority of the Church, sets the norm. The criteria of the new science,
instrumental control, determines what is to be considered the truth.
When a specific concept or process is determined through the empirical
method to predict and control human behavior, it is considered to be the
truth. During the early modern era, just as the modern state was attempting to develop new methods of controlling a new, more individualistic
populace, Locke argued that scientists know they have found truth when
a concept or theory can control and predict activity in the material world.
The link between the needs of the state and the arguments of the
philosophers, inadvertent though it may have been, seems too advantageous to be a coincidence.

Locke differed from Descartes in various ways; he was a radical
empiricist who believed that the empirical theory applied to everything,
including human mental activity. He advocated a "radical reflexivity" that
required that the individual withdraw from ordinary experience, including business-as-usual mental activity.[34] The purpose: to destroy and then
reconstruct the self based on the objective findings of sense experience.
For Locke, this was not as difficult as it sounds, because ideas, like
everything else in the world, were of the material realm, and humans
could control matter. Reason, freed from the bonds of tradition and
authority, could choose the scientifically correct alternatives. Taylor has

seen in Locke a powerful moral force that insists that humans must not rely on tradition but must think independently; for Locke all traditional and preempirical knowledge was suspect. What produced pleasure was good, what caused pain was evil.

Locke described a self that was "the object of a far reaching reformation."[35] Why were Locke and his contemporaries so focused on reforming the self? What was it about the modern era that necessitated the reconstruction of the self? Taylor has suggested that the identifying characteristic of Locke's self was the power to disengage from and remake itself.[36] It was a self that was pure, independent, disengaged, instrumental consciousness. Locke developed an ideal of self-responsibility, an implicit moral theory of scientific objectivity. One should always strive to think and remake oneself by disengaging from how one conceives of the world and how one acts in the world. In the words of Charles Taylor, one should "take charge of one's own representations."[37] Some current forms of psychotherapy theory, such as object relations theory and cognitive theory, seem to echo Locke's concern with the morality of representations. There is an implicit strategy at work here that will have an enormous impact on Western culture: the attempt to locate supreme power and agency *within* the individual. By remaking the self into the final arbiter of truth and the center of initiative, individualism becomes entrenched and the dominance of the Church and folk traditions become severely undermined.

The above early modern philosophers used the claims and the findings of the new science in order to justify their previous departure from the Church and to further delegitimize the authority of the Church in public debate. But other early modern literary figures took a different tack. "Naturalist" writers such as Montaigne and Rousseau anchored their arguments in the transparent truth of nature rather than the new science. Instead of promoting disengagement and objective observation, these precursors of romanticism argued that they could learn the truth about human being by delving ever deeper into their interior subjectivity. Although the naturalists are usually thought to have been rebelling against the Enlightenment's valorization of rationality and the new science, they too were part of the vanguard that advanced the power strategy of the new era. For instance Montaigne, although seeing instability and confusion where the new scientists perceived orderly law, clearly came down on the side of the new individualism as against the authority of the Church. He advocated a radical inwardness, a subjective looking and seeking inside the individual in order to discover one's particular uniqueness. When he began his introspective study, Montaigne expected to find the cohesive stability that one would expect from the ideas of the new science. To his shock and dismay he "discovered" inner chaos and instability instead. However, in a move characteristic of his time, Montaigne recovered, treated his experiments as producing scientific data, and used them to further delegitimize traditional authority. He juxtaposed the "truth" of inner instability with the moral demands of the Church, arguing that the terrifying chaos of the interior disproves the possibility of one universal set of moral laws of human nature. Since each person is uniquely different inside, and since each is chaotic and many sided rather than stable and universal, self-knowledge is (a) achieved by learning about one's individual characteristics through subjective introspection, and (b) marked by an awareness of one's personal limitations. One of Montaigne's central points was that external standards of morality were not applicable to humans; the demands of traditional authority showed a contempt for the inevitable yet wonderous differences of each individual's natural being. It was only by discovering one's personal uniqueness and by accepting one's idiosyncratic limitations that humans could realize and respect their true nature. Montaigne's concept of the self as "unrepeatable difference"[38] led him to a process different than that of Descartes. Whereas Descartes suggested the process of radical, objective *disengagement* from the material world and from the self, Montaigne advocated an ever deeper subjective *engagement* in order to discover the truth of nature and of natural being. A second path to the discrediting of the Church and the development of a new cultural framework was thus begun by Montaigne; the new science watchwords such as *freedom, autonomy,* and *truth* were used by the naturalists but with a new twist. With the naturalists came an increasing emphasis on subjectivity and inwardness that ultimately led to an increased valorization of individual uniqueness. The isolated search for individual identity has begun in earnest. Montaigne didn't know quite who he was, but he knew who he was not: the universal man.

If Montaigne began to articulate the concept of individual uniqueness, Rousseau perfected it; if Montaigne described inwardness, Rousseau turned it into a kind of early modern self-therapy. For Rousseau, to be engaged in the inward search for self-discovery meant not only to know one's limits (as with Montaigne), but to be able to learn from nature what one *truly is,* and when one is able to hear that voice one will know how to live. "To live in conformity with this voice," as Taylor explained Montaigne, "is to be entirely ourselves."[39] The valorization of individual autonomy, as against traditional authority, had taken a quantum leap. The ultimate source of unity and wholeness had been located definitively *inside* the individual self. Augustine looked inward and found absence, which eventually led to and was filled by God;

Rousseau looked inward and found the sole source of unity and goodness, the individual, radically autonomous self.

It should not be difficult for us to understand Kant's main concern
with the Enlightenment and naturalist philosophers. He looked at the
intellectual trends that they represented and saw the absence of the
moral dimension of human being. He argued that the laws of morality
were limited by the very nature of reason, which was itself embedded
within the innate internal structures of the human psyche. Morality, Kant
argued, did not spring automatically from the objective workings of the
new, empirical science (as the empiricists thought), or naturally unfold
from the subjective inward encounter with the transparent truth of
natural being (as the naturalists thought). Instead, morality is a product of
the rational will, one of the internal structures implanted within each
individual. He agreed with Montaigne and Rousseau regarding the necessity of following what is generated from within. He also agreed with
Descartes and Locke that it is only out of universal doubting and the
exercise of rationality that humans can determine how to live; and with
Hume when he argued that sense experience alone cannot help humans
generate intellectual concepts and moral laws. Kant then took each of
these ideas and combined them into a radical critique: he argued that the
moral knowledge that is generated from within is not pure, natural
impulse, the mirror of nature, nor is it perceived from without by pure,
natural perceptions that demonstrate that morality is determined by
pleasure or pain. Instead moral knowledge is produced from innate
forms, especially the innate natural structures of rationality and agency.

Humans, Kant believed, are the only animals that can use the logic of
their innate structures to generate moral laws and then choose through
the exercise of their will to live up to those laws. It is in this way, Kant
suggested, that humans have dignity. Like Hume and Montaigne, Kant
believed that freedom is constituted by living in accord with what one
truly is. But he differed with them by holding that individuals are not
only *limited* by, respectively, an empirical or unstable nature; he also
believed that individuals are *liberated* by their nature because they have
been naturally "given" the internal structures and will that could lead
them to the true moral laws. Thus freedom from traditional authority
was still maintained, radical autonomy was reaffirmed, and personal
uniqueness upheld. Kant thought he had saved the modern and Enlightenment eras' power strategy from the jaws of its own contradictions.
Like Augustine, Kant believed that a transformation of the will is the
therapeutic that saves the empty individual. But unlike Augustine, it is
not God that fills the internal void and transforms the will; the universal
structure of rationality does the transformative deed. Kant rescued the

early modern power strategy, but in the process he took one more step in constructing the valorization and mystification of an increasingly isolated, interior individualism.

The self of the early modern era was a departure from the self of the Middle Ages. It was a self that was powerful and autonomous (and confused and isolated) in ways the medieval self was not. It was an inner self that was essentially removed from the outer world. It was a self that was capable of building the order of the universe from sense impressions and inner logic. It was a self that achieved independence from traditional authority through the exercise of the capacities of doubt, observation, and objectification. It was a self that lived in a world in which spiritual was divided from material, mind from body—a disenchanted world. It was a self that could disengage from this divided, disenchanted world and thereby achieve a scientific self-certainty and self-sufficiency. Most importantly, it was a self that was instrumental; that is, it could manipulate the material world and transform it. Miraculously, the self could also manipulate and transform *itself*: it was pure, independent, instrumental consciousness. From the naturalists we learned that it was a self that was inward, deep, and unique. It was the container of instability and limitation, yet it was also the ultimate source of unity and wholeness. From Kant we learned that the self was a container of internal structures that were capable of producing moral laws. The early modern self was capable of prodigious feats of scientific observation, logic, and inward subjectivity; it was a kind of radically independent self. It had to be, because it was responsible for producing what heretofore had been entrusted to tradition and community. It was a self that was all alone, with the weight of the world on its shoulders.

All this talk about isolated individuals independently determining their own behavior and developing moral law *on their own* does not explain why these pursuits and particularly the solitary nature of the process were so very salient. It would seem to be a reasonable assumption that the loss of feudal arrangements and understandings, the religious divisions and subsequent wars that swept through Europe (particularly England), and the internal political revolutions about to errupt in late eighteenth-century America and France combined to produce a strong sense of the bankruptcy of traditional knowledge and the necessity of determining new social rules. The intense philosophical focus on self-sufficiency and certainty could be interpreted to mean that, contrary to the philosophers' protestations, persons of this era did not always feel quite so optimistic about their ability to achieve the lofty heights of autonomy and independence. Puritanism and to a lesser extent other Protestant religions at this time developed a notion of the self that stressed an increased self-consciousness and a deep self-suspicion. Baumeister has noted that the recognition of self-deception in Puritan ideology added to the increasingly problematic nature of the early modern self.[40] If the above Foucaultian interpretation has merit, the power strategy of the philosophers of the early modern era achieved a certain independence from the Church, but at the expense of a sense of community and moral certainty.

Enlightenment rationality, of course, was not the only contributor to individualism and the late modern era. The romantic era, set in the late eighteenth and early nineteenth centuries, is often described as a rebellion against the scientific rationalism of the Enlightenment, and indeed in many ways it was. However, it also incorporated various Enlightenment ideas about the self, particularly a belief in the autonomous individual who had the capacity to determine his or her own destiny. This Romantic vision of the autonomous, all-powerful self became an influence throughout Europe. Rousseau's Enlightenment era emphasis on inward uniqueness found full expression with the romantic poets such as Byron, Keats, and Whitman. And the realm of the mysterious, mystical, hidden self, what Quentin Anderson called the "hypertrophied self,"[41] was expanded and promoted by the romantics. What had begun in the sixteenth century as a concept of the inner, hidden, private realm of individuality that is different from public appearance and social behavior became for the romantics a mystical source of vitality and self-potential. They accomplished what the Enlightenment philosophers only dreamed of doing: they created a believable kind of secular salvation.[42] For the Early Modern power strategy to work it eventually needed to supplant one of the most powerful coercive elements of Church power: the monopoly on salvation. Wordsworth's worship of a mystical, eternal nature, and Keats's description of the eternal beauty of the figures on a Grecian urn led the way to a concept of secular salvation, eternal life through the achievements of passion, love, and art. The romantic tradition, with its focus on interior mysticism, would become institutionalized in the United States, first through Emersonian transcendentalism, and then, more recently, through some forms of secular psychotherapy (see chapters five and eight).

THE VICTORIAN AGE: CULMINATION OF THE ENLIGHTENMENT AGENDA

If the romantics extolled the eternal, transcendent qualities of love and art, it was up to the Puritans to combine salvation with work. And they did that with a vengeance. But the Victorian age in Europe was the true inheritor of the Enlightenment's power strategy, the romantics' secular but mystical salvation, and the Puritans' religious valorization of work. In many respects the era shaped by the class interests of the bourgeoisie was the culmination of the modern agenda. The bourgeois self was a secular, rational, subjective, divided, sexually conflicted, linear self that viewed the world as objectifiable and quantitative.[43] By the early decades of the nineteenth century the Industrial Revolution had transformed the economies and class structure of western Europe, and the French Revolution had forever made its political and emotional mark. The Enlightenment trends of objectifying and quantifying the material world, an increased secularization and cynicism—which was a consequence of the Reformation—and the romantic emphasis on a this-worldly preoccupation with love and passion can all be seen in the prominent trends of the Victorian age. With the ascendance of the bourgeoisie, everything was thought to be reducible, knowable, understandable, and figured into the calculations of everyday living. The force of religion became increasingly circumscribed, and hard work assumed an almost transcendent value. As the workplace had changed from the rural farm or medieval guild to the urbanized, industrialized factory or business office, workers and managers alike came to suffer from an increased alienation. The proletariat was forced into repetitive activities and/or hard labor; they had been forced off the land of their families and communities and lured to the larger cities, where living conditions were noxious and working conditions dangerous. Mass-production factory jobs created a numbing alienation and hard labor jobs such as coal mining were life-threatening. The industrialization of the last century and the accumulation of capital caused enormous social changes in the industrial cities. The middle class had white-collar jobs available to them; these jobs forced workers to adopt a pseudoscientific attention to detail, a repressed, conservative stance toward work, and a staunch, deferred gratification approach to life. A stern, rigid sexual morality developed that reflected what Lowe has called "the unspeakable gulf between subjectivity of the self and the objectivity of the world."[44] There has been much speculation about the nature of sexual practice in the Victorian age. Freud maintained that sexual repression was the major social force of the age. But Steven Marcus, studying Victorian literature and pornography, found that sexual literature was racy and voluminous.[45] He concluded that there was little repression of the literature, probably not as much repression in sexual practice as is commonly thought, and little or no repression in the proletariat. His interpretation fits with Foucault's argument, discussed in previous chapters, that the "repressive hypothesis" was itself a way of exercising power: by setting the cultural frame-of-reference, intellectual discourse influences and thus has an unknowing hand in controling society.

No matter what the actual sexual behavior of the bourgeoisie, the mores and proscriptions of the age reflected if nothing else the vast gulf between the sexes in the Victorian age. Women in the modern era were increasingly restricted, desexualized, and kept from positions of power. Their primary responsibility in the middle class was thought to be the protection of the family as a "haven in a heartless world."[46] The division between the genders widened and became more distinct. Some historians have argued that it was the sociopolitical position in which women were placed that produced the psychosomatic symptoms synonymous with the Victorian era and the psychotherapy theories that treated them.[47] It was, I argued in chapter four, an unknowingly political act on the part of male Victorian physicians to mystify sociopolitical ills by medicalizing, individualizing, and pathologizing the symptoms of their mostly female patients.

Before the modern age, the unknown was thought to reside in the external world. Slowly, however, with the growing belief in rationality, science, and calculation, the unknown became increasingly removed from or calculated out of the external physical world, and relocated. By the time the bourgeoisie was firmly in control, the unknown was believed to be a thing of the past; science and strict business practices had triumphed. In a move typical of the modern era and reminiscent of the inwardness of the early modern philosophers, Freud "discovered" the unknown in the interior of the deep Victorian self, hidden and secret: the unconscious.

We could describe the Victorian self, then, as interiorized, rational, secular, hardworking, self-disciplined, frugal, split along gender lines, and secretly sexual and aggressive. Four predominant psychological illnesses of the Victorian European self were hysteria, neurasthenia, sexual perversion, and violent criminal behavior such as murder and rape.[48] The causes of these illnesses were thought to be located in the private unconscious in the form of uncontrollable, uncivilized impulses. Importantly, hysteria was understood to be primarily a female disease, whereas sexual perversion and criminal violence primarily afflicted males. There is much more to this Victorian story, especially as it emerged in the United States, and more yet to the history of the twentieth century. For a more detailed discussion see the main body of the book.

INDIVIDUALISM AND THE LOSS OF COMMUNITY:
THE JEWISH COMMUNITY AS CASE EXAMPLE

Ironically, the fate of the most unrepresentative community in all of Europe, the Jews, illustrates the general fate of community in Europe during the modern era. The fate of the Jews demonstrates the effects of the forces of the modern era, such as urbanization, secularization, and especially individualism, in the brave new world of the new science, the Enlightenment philosophers' power strategy, and the needs of the modern state to control an individualistic, isolated populace. The story of how the Jews agreed to give up a communal identity to join the modern French state is a story that could illustrate the opportunities and dangers inherent in the social and cultural changes that peoples all over Europe experienced in the modern era.

One of the problems of a sociocultural system as cohesive and sealed off as that of the Christian Middle Ages was that alternative ideas and unenfranchised communities had no credence, safeguards, and power. This was certainly the case for European Jews in the Middle Ages, except for a few eras of notable exception, such as the "golden age" in Spain. For most of their history during the feudal age, Jews were mercilessly persecuted and attacked. Anti-Semitism was institutionalized in Europe to the point where violent attacks were considered commonplace, laudable occurrences. However, after the French Revolution, and with Napoleon's ascendence to power in 1799, the western European Jewish community was offered a new life. "Liberty, Equality, and Brotherhood," the watchwords of the French Revolution, was still the slogan of the day; some European governments, under great pressure from France, moved to wipe out the centuries-old laws that discriminated against and oppressed the Jews. The ghettos were to be liberated, Jews were granted equal rights and legal protection and allowed into occupations and schools previously denied them. This new opportunity was referred to as "the Emancipation" by Jews who were eager to join the new postrevolutionary world order.[49] That this never happened, or that this happened in an incomplete and ineffective manner, or that it lasted such a brief period of time, is one of history's great tragedies. For what came after "the Emancipation" were many new decades of oppression, humiliation, and violence, culminating in the death camps of Nazi Germany.

There were segments of the Jewish population, notably the orthodox traditionalists of Eastern Europe, who rejected the possibility of becoming "Westernized." However, many Jews already living in Western

Europe had been attempting to transform themselves into Western citizens for decades without the benefit of official laws or decrees.[50] They had been speaking in the tongue of their adopted country, studying European thought, and appreciating European art. Moses Mendelssohn was their leader and great champion.

Those were the two extremes: Mendelssohn in the far West, extolling Western culture, and the Vilna Gaon to the east, supervising the whole of Orthodox Jewry as the head of the rabbinate. But there were also a great many Jews, leaders and followers, who were positioned between those two extremes. It was a time of unparalleled explosion of Jewish thought and learning. A literary movement sprang up that argued that the great works of Europe should be translated into Yiddish, so that Jews everywhere could share in European culture. There was a literary movement that argued that Jews should give up Yiddish and Hebrew and use only the language of the country of their habitation; it was from this group that the Reform movement grew. There were also the political movements of the Socialists, Communists, and Laborites. There were the lyrical songs and stories of the mystical Hasidic movement. And, of course, there was the zionism of A'had Ha'am and Hertzl.

But what lurked in the background was the price that had to be paid. The French legislature asked one question to the Jewish representatives who stood before them. The Jews would be granted full citizenship, with all the privileges and protections of the realm, if they would agree to consider themselves individual French citizens first, and part of the Jewish people second. By answering yes to the question, the French Jewish community hoped to free itself from centuries of violent persecution and oppression, and to be granted the opportunities then opening up to all citizens of the new scientific modern state. However, by answering yes, the Jewish community would also lose something. It would lose an important aspect of its communal identity. It would then become susceptible to the same social ills and moral confusions that were plaguing all modern Europeans. As Rudavsky explained: "In bestowing equal civic rights upon the Jews, the French Assembly implicitly recognized them as free, independent persons, associated with the state directly, rather than as formerly through the mediacy of a corporate group which was not an integral part of the body politic."[51] Count Clermont Tonnerre publically declared "To the Jews as a nation we must deny everything. To the Jews as individuals we must grant everything."[52] The result, Rabbi Eugene Borowitz has noted, was that their decision relegated Judaism to being just "another church of Western man. . . . It [ceased to be] an all-encompassing way of life, a people."[53] The amalgam of learning, spirituality, ethics, law, storytelling, and singing peoplehood that formed the organic unit of medieval European Jewry was broken.

Perhaps the single most distinguishing characteristic of the Jewish community was its non-Western sense of the multifaceted, intertwined nature of communal life. For medieval Jews there was no point at which religion stopped and everyday life began; each person was whole, and his or her communal life was a unity. But it was exactly this sense of communal reality that so troubled the French Assembly and Western Europeans everywhere. Europe, in the modern era, was built on exactly that Enlightenment, Cartesian split between body and soul, secular and spiritual. One was a citizen, a businessperson, a scientist, a political party member, a religious soul—but all separately and apart. The Western self had become split, compartmentalized, and isolated. That splitness, more than any other single item, was what was demanded of the Jew. In Borowitz's words, "one learned that there were large and significant areas of existence where one's Jewishness was completely irrelevant. . . . [This was] the beginning of the divided Jewish self."[54]

In the end, of course, the denial of Jewish communal identity was shockingly unsuccessful in emancipating the Jew. It was the non-Jewish European culture that was the final arbiter of the Jews' fate, and it eventually condemned to torture and death millions of Jews, many of whom had decided to become Europeans instead of Jews. Despite the enshrinement of rationality, individuality, and freedom, or perhaps in part because of it, not only the Jews but all of Europe was caught in the insane conflagration of Nazism, the death camps, and World War II. One wonders what it was about the particular shape of the Western clearing that caused such madness.

Notes

Chapter One: Psychotherapy, the Impossible Bridge

1. Franz Samelson, "History, Origin Myth and Ideology: 'Discovery' of Social Psychology," *Journal for the Theory of Social Behaviour* 4 (Fall 1974): 229.
2. Telephone interviews with the Board of Behavioral Science Examiners and the State of California Medical Association, Sacramento, California.
3. Joel Freeman (producer), *Love at First Bite* (Melvin Simon Productions, 1979).
4. J. H. Van den Berg, *The Changing Nature of Man: Introduction to a Historical Psychology* (New York: W. W. Norton, 1961), 19.
5. Mark Twain, *Adventures of Huckleberry Finn* (New York: W. W. Norton, 1962), 72–73.
6. Richard J. Bernstein, *The Restructuring of Social and Political Theory* (New York: Harcourt Brace Jovanovich, 1976).

Chapter Two: Selves, Illnesses, Healers, Technologies

1. Berke Breathed, *Penguin Dreams and Stranger Things* (Boston: Little, Brown, 1985), 97, 107.
2. Frank C. Richardson and Robert L. Woolfolk, "Social Theory and Values: A Hermeneutic Perspective," *Theory & Psychology* 4 (May 1994).
3. Martin Heidegger, *Being and Time* (New York: Harper & Row, 1962); Hans-Georg Gadamer, *Truth and Method* (New York: Continuum, 1975). For a discussion of the concept of the cultural clearing (*Lichtung*) and its "horizontal" nature see Hubert L. Dreyfus, *Being-in-the-World: A Commentary on Heidegger's "Being and Time,"* *Division I* (Cambridge, Mass.: MIT Press, 1991), especially chapter nine; and Georgia Warnke, *Gadamer: Hermeneutics, Tradition and Reason* (Stanford, Calif.: Stanford University Press, 1987).
4. In the last decades of the twentieth century, moral issues rarely show up directly in public debate as aspects of moral discourse. An example of the absence for moral discourse was the 1993 controversy over revelations regarding the gambling debts of the great professional basketball player, Michael Jordan. The issue was framed by the sports media as a concern over whether or not Jordan had a *psychological* sickness, i.e., compulsive gambling. Public debate did not center on— in fact rarely mentioned—moral questions related to betting enormous sums of money on a single round of golf, when a significant percentage of our population

is suffering from insufficient food and shelter. The issue showed up as a medical-psychological question; the moral issues had no room in which to show up.

5. For instance, in Genesis 4:10, after Cain killed his brother Abel, God confronted Cain saying "Your brother's blood cries out to Me from the ground." Yet later rabbinic commentators noticed that, in the original Hebrew, the word *blood* is written in the plural (*dammim*). In puzzling over this, they remembered a common medical understanding of that time: that every individual carries within his- or her veins blood from his or her ancestors and their successors. Therefore, the rabbis decided, God used the plural form of the word *blood* to teach us about the sacredness of life, the value of each individual person, and the significance of the prohibition against murder. Individuals are so valuable, killing even a single person is an act as serious as if one has destroyed the whole world. Conversely, because human life is so sacred, saving even one person is equivalent to saving the entire world.

6. Paul Heelas and Andrew Lock, eds., *Indigenous Psychologies: The Anthropology of the Self* (New York: Academic Press, 1981).

7. Kenneth J. Gergen, "If Persons Are Texts," in *Hermeneutics and Psychological Theory: Interpretive Perspectives on Personality, Psychotherapy, and Psychopathology,* ed. Stanley Messer, Louis Sass, and Robert Woolfolk (New Brunswick, N.J.: Rutgers University Press, 1988).

8. Louis Sass, "Humanism, Hermeneutics, and the Concept of the Human Subject," in Messer, Sass, and Woolfolk, eds., *Hermeneutics and Psychological Theory,* 250.

9. Martin J. Packer and Richard B. Addison, Introduction to *Entering the Circle: Hermeneutic Investigation in Psychology,* ed. Martin J. Packer and Richard B. Addison (Albany, N.Y.: SUNY Press), 13–36; Anthony Stigliano, "Hermeneutic Practice," *Saybrook Review* 7 (1989).

10. Fortunately, others have done so, such as Heelas and Lock, *Indigenous Psychologies;* Bambi B. Schieffelin and Elinor Ochs, eds., *Language Socialization across Cultures* (New York: Cambridge University Press, 1986); Geoffrey M. White and John Kirkpatrick, eds., *Person, Self, and Experience: Exploring Pacific Ethnopsychologies* (Berkeley: University of California Press, 1985).

11. Jean Smith, "Self and Experience in Maori Culture," in Heelas and Lock, *Indigenous Psychologies,* 145–59. The following discussion is informed by Smith's work.

12. Ibid., 152.

13. Charlotte Hardman, "The Psychology of Conformity and Self-Expression Among the Lohorung Rai of East Nepal," in Heelas and Lock, *Indigenous Psychologies,* 161–180. The following discussion is informed by Hardman's work.

14. Ibid., 164.

15. Natalie Zemon Davis, *The Return of Martin Guerre* (Cambridge, Mass.: Harvard University Press, 1983).

16. For a detailed discussion of the modern era in the West see Charles Taylor, *Sources of the Self: The Making of the Modern Identity* (Cambridge, Mass.: Harvard University Press, 1989). The following discussion of the Enlightenment era philosophers, and issues related to the configuration of the self in the modern era in general, is informed by Taylor's work.

17. Adam Smith, *Inquiry into the Nature and Causes of the Wealth of Nations* (New York: Modern Library, 1776/1965).

18. For instance, Donald Lowe, *History of Bourgeois Perception* (Chicago: University of Chicago Press, 1982), 23.

CHAPTER THREE: THE SELF IN AMERICA

1. L. P. Hartley, *The Go-Between* (New York: Knopf, 1953), prologue.
2. Richard L. Bushman, "Jonathan Edwards as a Great Man: Identity, Conversion, and Leadership in the Great Awakening," in *Our Selves/Our Past: Psychological Approaches to American History*, ed. Robert J. Brugger (Baltimore: The Johns Hopkins University Press, 1981), 48–74. The following discussion is informed by Bushman's work.
3. Ibid., 48.
4. Ibid., 68.
5. Ibid., 63.
6. For the concept of the "problem" of the self, see Roy F. Baumeister, "How the Self Became a Problem: A Psychological Review of Historical Research," *Journal of Personality and Social Psychology* 52 (1987).
7. Quoted in Carl Wittke, *Tambo and Bones: A History of the American Minstrel Stage* (Durham, N.C.: Duke University Press, 1930), 28.
8. Joseph Boskin, *Sambo: The Rise & Demise of an American Jester* (New York: Oxford University Press, 1986), 75–76.
9. Wittke, *Tambo and Bones*, 27.
10. Ibid., 7.
11. Ibid., 51.
12. Ibid., 64.
13. Frank Dumont, *The Witmark Amateur Minstrel Guide and Burnt Cork Encyclopedia* (Chicago: M. Witmark & Sons, 1899), 8.
14. Wittke, *Tambo and Bones*, 8.
15. *New Minstrel and Black Face Joke Book* (Baltimore: I. M. Ottenheimer, 1907), 36.
16. *Minstrel Gags and End-Men's Handbook* (New York: Dick and Fitzgerald, 1875), 54.
17. Ibid., 45.
18. William De Vere, *Negro Sketches, End-Men's Gags and Conundrums* (Chicago: Charles T. Powner Co., n.d.), 19.
19. Ibid., 19.
20. *Minstrel Gags*, 14.
21. *Hi Henry's Premium Minstrel Songster* (New York: New York Popular Publishing Co., 1881), 53.
22. Francis P. Gaines, *The Southern Plantation* (New York: Columbia University Press, 1925), 198.
23. Dailey Paskman and Sigmund Spaeth, *"Gentlemen, Be Seated!"* (Garden City, N.Y.: Doubleday, Doran & Co., 1928), 51.
24. See De Vere, *Negro Sketches*, 14, 16, 39, 80–81, 104, 125–26; Dumont, *Witmark Amateur Minstrel Guide*, 83; *Minstrel Gags*, 8, 26, 48, 70.
25. See De Vere, *Negro Sketches*, 22, 25, 33, 56; Dumont, *Witmark Amateur Minstrel Guide*, 84, 89; *Minstrel Gags*, 8, 47; Paskman and Spaeth, *"Be Seated!"* 112, 115.
26. See De Vere, *Negro Sketches*, 24, 49, 57–58; Dumont, *Witmark Amateur Minstrel Guide*, 102; *Minstrel Gags*, 50.
27. Paskman and Spaeth, *"Gentlemen, Be Seated!"* 187.
28. *Hi Henry's Songster*, 50.
29. Byron Christy, *Christy's New Songster and Black Joker* (New York: Dick and Fitzgerald, 1963), 32.

30. Frank Converse, *Frank Converse's Old Cremona* (New York: Dick Publishing Co., 1863), 9.
31. Bob Hart, *Bob Hart's Plantation Songster* (New York: Dick and Fitzgerald, 1862), 6.
32. Joseph Boskin, "The Life and Death of Sambo: Overview of an Historic Hang-Up," *Journal of Popular Culture* 4 (Winter 1971): 648.
33. George M. Beard, *American Nervousness* (New York: Putnam's, 1881).
34. This section is drawn in part from the work of Dee Brown, *Bury My Heart At Wounded Knee* (New York: Holt, Rinehart & Winston, 1970); Angie Debo, *A History of the Indians of the United States* (Norman: University of Oklahoma Press, 1970).
35. Brown, *Bury My Heart*, 298.
36. Laurence F. Schmeckebier, *The Office of Indian Affairs: Its History, Activities, and Organization* (Baltimore: The Johns Hopkins University Press, 1927), 58.
37. Robert Winston Mardock, *The Reformers and the American Indian* (Columbia: University of Missouri Press, 1971), 65.
38. Schmeckebier, *Office of Indian Affairs*, 56.
39. *Congressional Globe*, 42nd Cong., 2d sess., 1871–1872, 780.
40. Ibid., 718.
41. Ibid., 714.
42. *Congressional Globe*, 41st Cong., 3d sess., 1870–1871, 1501.
43. Ibid., 736.
44. Ibid., 1500.
45. Ibid., 765.
46. Ibid., 1112.
47. Ibid., 1501.
48. Ibid., 732.
49. See Lowe, *History of Bourgeois Perception*.
50. Richard Slotkin, *The Fatal Environment: The Myth of the Frontier in the Age of Industrialization, 1800–1890* (Middletown, Conn.: Wesleyan University Press, 1985), 3–47. The following discussion is informed by Slotkin's work.
51. Frederick Jackson Turner, "The Significance of the Frontier in American History," in Frederick Jackson Turner, ed., *The Frontier in American History* (New York: Henry Holt & Co., 1893/1920), 1–38.
52. Slotkin, *Fatal Environment*, 47, 52.
53. Ibid., 80.
54. Robert Park, "Human Migration and the Marginal Man," *The American Journal of Sociology* 33 (1928), 131.
55. Warren I. Susman, *Culture as History: The Transformation of American Society in the Twentieth Century* (New York: Pantheon Books, 1973); T. J. Jackson Lears, "From Salvation to Self-Realization: Advertising and the Therapeutic Roots of the Consumer Culture, 1880–1930," in *The Culture of Consumption: Critical Essays in American History, 1880–1980*, ed. Richard Wightman Fox and T.J. Jackson Lears (New York: Pantheon Books, 1983), 3–38. The following discussion is informed by their work.
56. Henry Laurent, *Personality: How to Build It* (New York: 1915), iv. Quoted in Susman, *Culture as History*, 277.
57. Theodore T. Munger, *The Appeal to Life* (Boston, 1887), 33–34, as quoted in T. J. Jackson Lears, *No Place of Grace: Antimodernism and the Transformation of American Culture 1880–1920* (New York: Pantheon Books, 1981), 42.

58. Rollo Ogden, "Some Blessings of Intolerance," *Nation* 52 (28 May 1891): 434–35. Quoted in Lears, *No Place of Grace*, 46.
59. Vida D. Scutter, "Democracy and the Church," *Atlantic Monthly* 90 (October 1902), 521–27. Quoted in Lears, *No Place of Grace*, 46.
60. Lears, *No Place of Grace*, 50.
61. H. Addington Bruce, "Insanity and the Nation," *North American Review* 187 (January 1908): 70–79. Quoted in Lears, *No Place of Grace*, 50.
62. Lears, "From Salvation to Self-Realization," 4.
63. Ibid., 6.
64. Scutter, "Democracy and the Church," 521–27.
65. Munger, *The Appeal to Life*, 33–34.
66. Lears, "From Salvation to Self-Realization," 11.
67. Philip Rieff, *The Triumph of the Therapeutic: Uses of Faith after Freud* (Chicago: University of Chicago Press, 1966), 261.
68. Ibid.
69. Lears, "From Salvation to Self-Realization," 19.
70. See Stuart Ewen, "Advertising and the Development of Consumer Society," in *Cultural Politics in Contemporary America*, ed. Ian Angus and Sut Jhally (New York: Routledge, Chapman and Hall, 1989), 82; Roland Marchand, *Advertising the American Dream: Making Way for Modernity 1920–1940* (Berkeley: University of California Press, 1985).
71. Rieff, *The Triumph of the Therapeutic*, 13.
72. Lears, "From Salvation to Self-Realization," 27.
73. Royal Cortissoz, "Egotism in Contemporary Art," *Atlantic Monthly* 73 (May 1894): 644–52. Quoted in Lears, *No Place of Grace*, 49.
74. *Diagnostic and Statistical Manual of Mental Disorders, III.* (Washington, D.C.: American Psychiatric Association, 1980), 317.
75. Marchand, *Advertising the American Dream*, 347, 360.
76. Joel Kovel, "The American Mental Health Industry," in *Critical Psychiatry: The Politics of Mental Health*, ed. David Inglesby (New York: Random House, 1980), 72–101.
77. For a cultural history perspective on the Hawthorne research done by Elton Mayo, *The Human Problems of an Industrial Civilization* (New York: Macmillan, 1933) and F. J. Roethlisberger and W. J. Dickson, *Management and the Worker* (Cambridge, Mass.: Harvard University Press, 1939), see Richard Gillespie, "The Hawthorne Experiments and the Politics of Experimentation," in *The Rise of Experimentation in American Psychology*, ed. Jill G. Morawski (New Haven, Conn.: Yale University Press, 1988), 114–37.
78. "Gasoline Alley" *Los Angeles Times*, 22 December 1949.
79. Telephone interviews by author on 9 May 1989 with Bernard Lansky, *San Diego Tribune* cartoonist, and William Blackbeard, curator, San Francisco Academy of Comic Art.
80. "Gasoline Alley" *Los Angeles Times*, 7 January 1949; 27 July 1949; 2 August 1949.
81. Ibid., 2 January 1949; 8 January 1949; 28 July 1949.
82. Ibid., 2 January 1949; 6 January 1949.
83. Ibid., 2 February 1949.
84. Ibid., 27 March 1949; 7 November 1949; 28 December 1949.
85. Ibid., 5 May 1949.
86. Ibid., 1 June 1949.

87. John M. Blum et al., *The National Experience: A History of the United States* (New York: Harcourt Brace Jovanovich, 1973), 441, 808.

88. Erich Fromm, *The Sane Society* (New York: Holt, Rinehart and Winston, 1955); Christopher Lasch, *The Culture of Narcissism: American Life in An Age of Diminishing Expectations* (New York: W. W. Norton & Co., 1978).

89. Many writers have discussed this. For example, see Robert Bellah et al., *Habits of the Heart: Individualism and Commitment in American Life* (Berkeley: University of California Press, 1985); David Michael Levin, "Clinical Stories: A Modern Self in the Fury of Being," in *Pathologies of the Modern Self: Postmodern Studies on Narcissism, Schizophrenia, and Depression*, ed. David Michael Levin (New York: New York University Press, 1987), 479–537; Edward E. Sampson, "The Debate on Individualism: Indigenous Psychologies of the Individual and Their Role in Personal and Societal Functioning," *American Psychologist* 43 (January 1988): 15–22; Eli Zaretsky, *Capitalism, the Family, and Personal Life* (New York: Harper & Row, 1976).

90. Frances E. Korbin, "The Fall in Household Size and the Rise of the Primary Individual in the United States," in *The American Family in Social-Historical Perspective*, ed. Michael Gorden (New York: St. Martin's Press, 1978), 71.

91. Robert Jay Lifton, *The Protean Self: Human Resilience in an Age of Fragmentation* (New York: Basic Books, 1993).

92. Edward E. Sampson, "Psychology and the American Ideal," *Journal of Personality and Social Psychology* 32 (1977): 309–20.

93. Benjamin J. Friedman, *Day of Reckoning: The Consequences of American Economic Policy under Reagan and After* (New York: Random House, 1988); Alfred L. Malabre, *Beyond Our Means: How Reckless Borrowing Now Threatens to Overwhelm Us* (New York: Random House, 1987).

94. Malabre, *Beyond Our Means*, 4, 21.

95. Ibid., 27.

96. See Cushman, "Why the Self Is Empty: Toward a Historically Situated Psychology," *American Psychologist* 45 (May 1990); Stewart Ewen, *All Consuming Images: The Politics of Style in Contemporary Culture* (New York: Basic Books, 1988); Fox and Lears, *Culture of Consumption*; William Leiss, Stephen Kline, and Sut Jhally, *Social Communication in Advertising: Persons, Products, & Images of Well-Being* (New York: Methuen, 1986).

97. Baumeister, "How the Self Became a Problem."

98. Philip Cushman, "The Politics of Vulnerability: Youth in Religious Cults," *Psychohistory Review* 12 (Spring 1984); Philip Cushman, "The Self Besieged: Recruitment-Indoctrination Processes in Religious Cults," *Journal for the Theory of Social Behavior* 16 (March 1986).

99. Philip Cushman, "Iron Fists/Velvet Gloves: A Study of a Mass Marathon Psychology Training," *Psychotherapy: Theory, Research, Practice, & Training* 26 (February 1989); Jan Haaken and Richard Adams, "Pathology as 'Personal Growth': A Participant Observation Study of a Lifespring Training," *Psychiatry* 46 (1983); Steven Hassan, *Combatting Cult Mind Control* (Rochester, Vt.: Park Street Press, 1988); Margaret Thaler Singer and Janja Lalich, *Cults in Our Midst: How They Capture Individuals, Families, and the Workplace* (Jossey-Bass, in press).

100. Heinz Kohut, "Creativity, Charisma, Group Psychology: Reflections on the Self-Analysis of Freud," in *Self Psychology and the Humanities: Reflections on a New Psychoanalytic Approach*, ed. Charles B. Strozier (New York: W. W. Norton, 1985),

171–211; Charles B. Strozier, "Heinz Kohut and the Historical Imagination, *Psychohistory Review* 7 (Spring 1978).

101. Louis J. West and Margaret T. Singer, "Cults, Quacks and Non-Professional Psychotherapies," in *Comprehensive Textbook of Psychiatry*, vol. 3, ed. Harold I. Kaplan, Alan M. Greedman, and Benjamin J. Sadock (Baltimore: Williams & Wilkins, 1980).

102. Teresa Boulette and Sharon Anderson, " 'Mind Control' and the Battering of Women," *The Cultic Studies Journal* 3 (Spring 1986).

103. Clifford Geertz, *The Interpretation of Cultures* (New York: Basic Books, 1973).

104. Ewen, "Advertising and Consumer Society," 85.

CHAPTER FOUR: HEALING THROUGH SELF-DOMINATION

1. John Demos, *A Little Commonwealth: Family Life in Plymouth Colony* (New York: Oxford University Press, 1970).

2. In 1775 Franz Anton Mesmer, a representative of the modern practice of hypnosis, and Johann Gassner, a Catholic priest who practiced exorcism, appeared before the German medical academy. They each presented a demonstration of and an argument for their respective medical practices. The academy was to decide which practice seemed the most scientific. Mesmer won, and a new, psychological way of thinking about illness and deviance gained a bit more legitimation. For a fuller discussion of this event, see Robert C. Fuller, *Mesmerism and the American Cure of Souls* (Philadelphia: University of Pennsylvania Press, 1982), 3–4.

3. Historians such as Richard Fox, *So Far Disordered in Mind* (Berkeley: University of California Press, 1978) and Ingleby, "Understanding 'Mental Illness,' " and Andrew Scull, *Social Order/Mental Disorder: Anglo-American Psychiatry in Historical Perspective* (Berkeley: University of California Press, 1889) have reminded us that a complex social concept such as madness does not suddenly appear out of nowhere, or out of a simple-minded conspiracy created by a few greedy or power-hungry individuals in high places. A concept such as madness is constructed by the moral understandings and the political arrangements of its time, and as such is a product of mutually influencing, interdependent forces and traditions.

4. Some saw in psychiatry the progressive march of ameliorative science. Others rightly perceived the machinations of institutions and guilds but failed to place the subjects of study, such as psychiatry, within the larger sociopolitical forces of their time and place. Historians such as Fox, *So Far Disordered*; David Ingleby, "Understanding 'Mental Illness,' " in *Critical Psychiatry: The Politics of Mental Health*, ed. David Ingleby (New York: Pantheon, 1980), 23–71; and Scull, *Social Order* have taken a critical cultural approach, and thus I draw upon them in the following discussion.

5. Various laws and court trials, such as the case of *Nottidge* v. *Ripley and another* in 1849, slowly defined the criteria for the institutionalization of the mad in England. See Scull, *Social Order*, 282–83.

6. Andrew Scull, *The Most Solitary of Afflictions: Madness and Society in Britain, 1700–1900* (New Haven, Conn.: Yale University Press, 1993), 181.

7. George Man Burrows, *Commentaries on the Causes, Forms, Symptoms, and Treatment, Moral and Medical, of Insanity* (London: Underwood, 1828), 601. Quoted in Scull, *Social Order*, 73.

8. Benjamin Rush, *The Letters of Benjamin Rush*, vol. 2, ed. L. H. Butterfield (Princeton: Princeton University Press, 1951), 1052. Quoted in Scull, *Social Order*, 73.

9. Smith, *Wealth of Nations*.

10. Scull, *Social Order*, 219.

11. See Michael Foucault, *Discipline and Punish: The Birth of the Prison* (New York: Pantheon, 1977).

12. Jeremy Bentham to J. P. Brissot, in Jeremy Bentham, *The Works of Jeremy Bentham*, vol. 10, ed. J. Bowring (Edinburgh: Tait, 1843), 226. Quoted in Scull, *Social Order*, 218.

13. See Scull, *Social Order*, 112, n. 78.

14. Ibid., 231.

15. Ibid., 230.

16. Ibid., 228–31.

17. J. Mortimer Granville, *The Care and Cure of the Insane*, vol. 1, (London: Hardwicke and Bogue, 1877), 8. Quoted in Scull, *Social Order*, 238.

18. Scull, *Social Order*, 76.

19. Louis Sass, "Schreber's Panopticism: Psychosis and the Modern Soul," *Social Research* 54 (1987).

20. See Elaine Showalter, *The Female Malady: Women, Madness, and English Culture, 1830–1980* (New York: Pantheon, 1985); Edward Shorter, *From Paralysis to Fatigue: A History of Psychosomatic Illness in the Modern Era* (New York: The Free Press, 1992).

21. Scull, *Social Order*, 272.

22. Ibid., 273.

23. J. Mortimer Granville, in Andrew Wynter, *The Borderlands of Insanity*, 2d ed. (London: Renshaw, 1877). Quoted in Scull, *Social Order*, 275.

24. Florence Nightingale, *Cassandra* (Old Westbury, N.Y.: Feminist Press, 1979), 41–42. Quoted in Showalter, *Female Malady*, 128.

25. George Frederick Drinka, *The Birth of Neurosis: Myth, Malady and the Victorians* (New York: Simon & Schuster, 1984), 17–59.

26. See Ibid., 47 ff.

27. James George Frazer, *The Golden Bough* (New York: New American Library, 1890/1959).

28. Although at first trained in neurology, fascinated by Charcot, and befriended by Joseph Breuer, Freud was after a time able to bypass these mainstream theorists. He was perhaps influenced by other, less fashionable realms of medical theory, such as the psychotherapy theories of the Leipzig group (especially Paul Mobius and Adolf Strumpell), Hack Tuke, Hippolyte Bernheim, Frederick van Eden, Paul Dubois, Jules-Joseph Dejerine, and Wilhelm Griesinger that posited the psychogenesis of neurotic symptoms (see Shorter, *From Paralysis to Fatigue*). He most probably was also influenced by the cultural and artistic currents of his age, such as those expressed by Henrik Ibsen, Arthur Schnitzler, and Hippolyte Taine (see Gunnar Brandell, *Freud: A Man of His Century*, trans. I. White [Atlantic Highlands, N.J.: Humanities Press, 1979]).

29. Nathan Adler, "The Polyvocal Psyche: A Dialogue with Dr. Nathan Adler," *Northern California Society for Psychoanalytic Psychology Newsletter* (Spring 1994): 1–11; Barnaby Barrett, *Psychoanalysis and the Postmodern Impulse: Knowing and Being Since Freud's Psychology* (Baltimore: The Johns Hopkins University Press, 1993); Era A. Loewenstein, "Psychoanalytic Life History: Is Coherence, Continuity, and

Aesthetic Appeal Necessary?" *Psychoanalysis and Contemporary Thought* 14 (Spring 1991): 3–28; Thomas H. Ogden, "The Dialectically Constituted/Decentered Subject of Psychoanalysis, I. The Freudian Subject," *International Journal of Psycho-Analysis* 73 (Autumn 1992): 517–25.

30. See Shorter, *From Paralysis to Fatigue*, esp. 245–53.
31. Sigmund Freud, New Introductory Lectures on Psycho-analysis. *The Standard Edition of the Complete Psychological Works of Sigmund Freud*, vol. 22, ed. and trans. James Strachey et al., (London: Hogarth Press and Institute of Psychoanalysis, 1953–1974), 7.

CHAPTER FIVE: HEALING THROUGH SELF-LIBERATION

1. Robert Darnton, *Mesmerism and the End of the Enlightenment* (Cambridge, Mass.: Harvard University Press, 1968).
2. Fuller, *Mesmerism*, 15. The following discussion is informed by Fuller's work, and by Donald Meyer, *The Positive Thinkers: Religion as Pop Psychology from Mary Baker Eddy to Oral Roberts* (New York: Pantheon, 1980).
3. There was a type of psychotherapy active in the United States before mesmerism arrived: pastoral counseling. For the first three centuries of European-American communities, the ministers were the official dispensers of the "cure of souls." Their talking cures were shaped by techniques originally developed by the medieval Church and then the Protestant reformers. The object of their healing was the soul. Early pastoral counseling consisted of guiding colonists in seeking salvation, and in recognizing and following the signs that demonstrated salvation. However, over time Enlightenment ideas regarding the value of self-preservation and economic ambition became accepted as the motivating principle of moral living. What had once been thought to be the devil's work and a sign of damnation became the bedrock of the social order. The Enlightenment era notion of the moral goodness of the "invisible hand" of the marketplace combined with the romantic era notion of the natural morality of the emotions to form a new conception of the self, which was founded on the selfishness and subjectivity of the autonomous individual. In the early nineteenth century, new clinical theology, featuring a case-studies approach, became popular among the clergy. A new homiletical style developed, which included emotional narratives, instructions on how to be one of the elect, and aids for self-examination. Pastors referred to this as a "science of the will." Over the course of time, the colonial and eighteenth-century concern over the state of the soul and predetermined salvation changed to a preoccupation with the self—the terror of eternal damnation changed to a fear of the fragmentation or devitalization of the self. Self-love, ministers began to argue, if under the influence of the conscience, was indeed religiously proper and good. However, mesmerism soon entered onto the American stage and proved more adept at developing and spreading this secular gospel, as we shall see in this chapter. By the beginning of the twentieth century the talking cure had become a completely secular activity, intent not on "breaking" the "proud heart," but on constructing and maintaining it. For more information on early pastoral counseling, see E. Holifield, *A History of Pastoral Counseling in America* (Nashville: Abingdon Press, 1983); Richard Lind, "Pilgrim's Progress: Progressive

Development and the Transitional Self" (Ph.D. diss., California School of Professional Psychology, 1992).

4. See Christopher Lasch, *Haven in a Heartless World: The Family Besieged* (New York: Basic Books, 1977).

5. See Nancy F. Cott and Elizabeth H. Pleck, eds., *A Heritage of Her Own: Toward a New Social History of American Women* (New York: Simon & Schuster, 1979); Carl N. Degler, *At Odds: Women and the Family in America from the Revolution to the Present* (Oxford: Oxford University Press, 1980).

6. Thomas Lake Harris, quoted in R. Laurence Moore, *In Search of White Crows* (New York: Oxford University Press, 1977), 12.

7. Fuller, *Mesmerism*, 129–31.

8. Ibid., 137.

9. Ibid., 139.

10. Warren Felt Evans, *The Primitive Mind Cure: The Nature and Power of Faith, or Elementary Lessons in Christian Philosophy and Transcendental Medicine* (Boston: H. H. Carter, 1885), 87. Quoted in Fuller, *Mesmerism*, 150.

11. Ralph Waldo Trine, *In Tune with the Infinite* (New York: Crowell Co., 1897), 172. Quoted in Fuller, *Mesmerism*, 153.

12. Emile Cady, *Lessons in Truth* (Lee's Summit, Mo.: Unity Press, 1894), 62.

13. Henry Wood, *Ideal Suggestions through Mental Photography* (Boston: Lee and Shepard, 1893).

14. Fuller, *Mesmerism*, 159.

15. For example, Frank Haddock, *Power for Success through Cultivation of Vibrant Magnetism* (Auburndale, Mass.: Power Book Library, 1910).

16. Orestes Swett Marden, *Every Man a King, or Might in Mind Mastery* (New York: Thomas Y. Crowell Co., 1906); Napolean Hill, *Think and Grow Rich* (Greenwich, Conn.: Fawcett Publications, 1961).

17. Fuller, *Mesmerism*, 160.

18. Horatio W. Dresser, *Health and the Inner Life: An Account of the Life and Teachings of P. P. Quimby* (New York: G. P. Putnam's Sons, 1906), 179.

19. Phineas P. Quimby, *The Quimby Manuscripts*, ed. H. W. Dresser (New York: Thomas Crowell, 1921), 180.

20. See *The Quimby Manuscripts*.

21. Ralph Waldo Trine, *In Tune with the Infinite.* Quoted in Fuller, *Mesmerism*, 155.

22. Evans, *Primitive Mind Cure*, 87. Quoted in Fuller, *Mesmerism*, 150.

23. Fuller, *Mesmerism*, 149–50.

24. Cady, *Lessons in Truth*, 62.

25. Fuller, *Mesmerism*, 160.

26. Meyer, *Positive Thinkers*, 120.

27. Ibid., 111.

28. William James, *Varieties of Religious Experience* (Cambridge, Mass.: Harvard University Press, 1902/1985), 259.

29. Henry Wood, *New Thought Simplified* (Boston: Lee and Shepard, 1908), 10. Quoted in Fuller, *Mesmerism*, 176.

30. For a detailed discussion of this malady see Drinka, *The Birth of Neurosis*; F. G. Gosling, *Before Freud: Neurasthenia and the American Medical Community, 1870–1910* (Chicago: University of Chicago Press, 1987); Tom Lutz, *American Nervousness, 1903: An Anecdotal History* (Ithaca, N.Y.: Cornell University Press, 1991); and Shorter, *From Paralysis to Fatigue.* The following discussion draws from their work.

31. Shorter, *From Paralysis to Fatigue*, 117–26.
32. Gosling, *Before Freud*, 80.
33. Ibid., 37, 111–20.
34. J. S. Greene, "Neurasthenia: Its Causes and Home Treatment," *Boston Medical and Surgical Journal* 109 (1883): 77. Quoted in Gosling, *Before Freud*, 85–86.
35. George M. Beard, "Cases of Neurasthenia (Nervous Exhaustion), with Remarks on Treatment," *St. Louis Medical and Surgical Journal* 36 (1879), 345–46. Quoted in Gosling, *Before Freud*, 36–37.
36. See especially Drinka, *Birth of Neurosis*, 152–83.

CHAPTER SIX: STRANGE BEDFELLOWS

1. Carl Jung and Sandor Ferenczi, two of Freud's most trusted colleagues, accompanied Freud on the trip. They consulted with him throughout the trip, especially about the content and delivery of Freud's five lectures. The forced intimacy occasioned by an ocean voyage of this length caused many noteworthy events, including one incident in which Freud became so upset at Jung that he fainted. For more information on the trip see Demos, "Oedipus in America: Historical Perspectives on the Reception of Psychoanalysis in the United States," in *Ourselves/Our Past: Psychological Approaches to American History,* ed. Robert J. Brugger (Baltimore: The Johns Hopkins University Press, 1981); Nathan G. Hale Jr., *Freud and the Americans: The Beginnings of Psychoanalysis in the United States, 1867–1917* (New York: Oxford University Press, 1971); and Saul Rosenzweig, *Freud, Jung and Hall the Kingmaker: The Expedition to America (1909)* (Seattle: Hogrefe & Huber, 1992). The following discussion is drawn in part from these sources.
2. Ernest Jones, *The Life and Work of Sigmund Freud*, vol. 2 (New York: Basic Books, 1955), 57.
3. John M. Blum et al., *The National Experience: A History of the United States* (New York: Harcourt Brace Jovanovich, 1973), 441, 808. This trend, of course, would increase at a high rate. See chapter eight for more details about twentieth-century trends.
4. Frances S. Kobrin, "The Fall in Household Size and the Rise of the Primary Individual in the United States," 71. Again this trend toward fewer and fewer individuals in each house would continue throughout the twentieth century: by 1950 the percentage had declined to 5.8 percent.
5. Carl N. Degler et al., *The Democratic Experience* (Glenview, Ill.: Scott, Foresman and Co., 1973), 436.
6. George E. Mowry, *The Era of Theodore Roosevelt and the Birth of Modern America 1901–1912* (New York: Harpers and Brothers, 1958).
7. Freud, New Introductory Lectures, *Standard Edition*, vol. 22, 7.
8. Frederic V. Grunfeld, *Prophets without Honor: A Background to Freud, Kafka, Einstein and Their World* (New York: McGraw-Hill, 1980), 37.
9. Much has been written regarding these defections/rejections. For more details see Edith Kurzweil, *The Freudians: A Comparative Perspective* (New Haven, Conn.: Yale University Press, 1989). She suggests that differences between disciples were owing to cultural differences and political disagreements as well as to theory or personality clashes.

10. Philip Rieff has suggested that Freud's rejection of Jung could be attributed to Freud's disagreement with Jung's basic program: Jung's attempt to forge a wholistic theory of spiritual transformation. In Jung's world, unified, transformative spiritual theories were possible; but in the psychological terrain Freud inhabited they were not possible and in fact were viewed as deceptive betrayals, mystifications and failures of will. See Sigmund Freud, *The History of the Psychoanalytic Movement*, ed. Philip Rieff (New York: Crowell-Collier, 1963), 16–22.

11. For a treatment of the issue of Jung's involvement see Clarence J. Karier, "The Ethics of a Therapeutic Man," in *Varieties of Psychohistory*, ed. George M. Kren and Leon H. Rappoport (New York: Springer, 1976), 333–63; and Aryeh Maidenbaum and Stephen A. Martin, eds. *Lingering Shadows: Jungians, Freudians, and Anti-Semitism* (Boston: Shambhala, 1991).

12. Demos, *Oedipus to America*, 304.

13. Ibid., 299.

14. Turner, "The Significance of the Frontier." See chapter two for more details.

15. See Clifford Whittingham Beers, *A Mind that Found Itself: An Autobiography* (Pittsburgh: University of Pittsburgh Press, 1907/1981); Kovel, "American Mental Health Industry"; and John M. Reisman, *A History of Clinical Psychology* (New York: Irvington, 1976). The following discussion draws upon their work.

16. Albert Deutsch, *The Shame of the States* (New York: Arno, 1973), 300–11.

17. Kovel, "American Mental Health Industry."

18. Ibid., 81.

19. A few other writers have argued that Freud's theories carry aspects of a politically radical and historically situated theory that remain mostly unrecognized by American historians of psychotherapy. For instance, see Adler, "A Polyvocal Psyche"; Russel Jacoby, *Social Amnesia: A Critique of Contemporary Psychology from Adler to Laing* (Boston: Beacon Press, 1975); and Richard Lichtman, *The Production of Desire: The Integration of Psychoanalysis into Marxist Theory* (New York: The Free Press, 1982).

20. Kovel, "American Mental Health Industry," 82; italics in original.

21. See Lears, "Salvation to Self-Realization"; Susman, *Culture as History*.

22. Kovel, "American Mental Health Industry," 81; italics in original.

23. See Franz Samelson, "Putting Psychology on the Map: Ideology and Intelligence Testing," in *Psychology in Social Context*, ed. Allan R. Buss (New York: Irvington, 1979), 103–68.

24. See Reisman, *A History of Clinical Psychology*, 135.

25. See Samelson, "Putting Psychology on the Map."

26. See Jill G. Morawski, ed. *The Rise of Experimentation in American Psychology* (New Haven, Conn.: Yale University Press, 1988).

27. For details about the growth of psychology as an academic discipline in American universities, see Kurt Danziger, "The Social Origins of Modern Psychology," in Buss, *Psychology in Social Context*, 27–45.

28. John B. Watson, "Psychology as the Behaviorist Views It," *Psychological Review* 20 (1913): 89–179. Quoted in Reisman, *A History of Clinical Psychology*, 133.

29. Edward L. Bernays, *Propaganda* (New York: H. Liveright, 1928), 50–52, 63. Quoted in Lears, "Salvation to Self-Realization," 20.

30. Reisman, *A History of Clinical Psychology*, 135.

31. This shift in the philosophy of personnel management can be seen in the famous Hawthorne experiments, in which "scientific" researchers "discovered" that the

"feelings" of the workers, that is, their attitude about work, was a greater predictor of production than material working conditions. This issue is also briefly discussed in chapter seven. For more details see Gillespie, "The Hawthorne Experiments and the Politics of Experimentation," 114–37.

32. Kovel, "American Mental Health Industry," 82.

CHAPTER SEVEN: THE ROAD NOT TAKEN

1. To some extent Freud seemed to believe that psychic events were governed by the same laws of physics that governed all matter. These laws were associated at that time with Isaac Newton's prerelativity physics. Events in the material world could be explained, Newton thought, by calculating the operations of various forces—or vectors—and determining their influence on matter. Because the mind was thought to be a material aspect of nature, it was thought to be governed by these same laws. Thus, Freud hypothesized that the psychic energy generated by the id, for instance, was governed by the natural laws of the physical world, and would affect and be affected by other pressures in the psyche, as they collided and joined forces while engaging in the conflicts natural to the mind. The emergence of dreams, slips of the tongue, and psychosomatic symptoms could be explained in part through the analysis of the various forces at work on the conscious and unconscious systems of the mind of the patient. By determining which force was strongest at a given moment, one might be able to understand why a certain thought or feeling was repressed, sublimated, or expressed in a symptom. Just as liquid or gas could exert pressure on an object during movement, so too could psychic energy exert a "hydraulic" pressure through its flow from one "place" to another.

2. See Howard Zinn, *The Politics of History* (Boston: Beacon Press, 1970) 79–101.

3. See Joseph Boskin, *Urban Racial Violence in the Twentieth Century* (Beverly Hills, Calif.: Glencoe Press, 1968), 30–37. For a general discussion of American racism see Gary B. Nash and Richard Weiss, eds., *The Great Fear: Race in the Mind of America* (New York: Holt, Rinehart, and Winston, 1970).

4. See Howard Zinn, *A People's History of the United States* (New York: Harper & Row, 1980), 350–67.

5. For a detailed account of their conflict see Phyllis Grosskurth, *Melanie Klein: Her World and Her Work*, (Cambridge, Mass.: Harvard University Press, 1987), especially pp. 279–362. For details about their respective theories see *The Writings of Anna Freud*, 8 vols. (New York: International Universities Press, 1966–1980); *The Writings of Melanie Klein*, 4 vols., ed. R. E. Money-Kyrde, in coll. with B. Joseph, L. O'Shaughnessy, and H. Segal, (London: Hogarth Press and the Institute of Psychoanalysis, 1975).

6. Blum et al., *The National Experience*, 589–653; Degler et al., *The Democratic Experience*, 421–91.

7. Modris Eksteins, *Rites of Spring: The Great War and the Birth of the Modern Age* (Boston: Houghton Mifflin, 1989).

8. See Zinn, *People's History*, 247–367.

9. Degler et al, *The Democratic Experience*, 436–38, 443–44.

10. For a detailed account of his life and work see Helen Swick Perry, *Psychiatrist of America: The Life of Harry Stack Sullivan* (Cambridge, Mass.: Harvard University

Press, 1982); and A. H. Chapman, *Harry Stack Sullivan: The Man and His Work* (New York: G. P. Putnam's Sons, 1976). The following discussion is drawn from their work.

11. Perry, *Psychiatrist of America*, 243.

12. See Charles H. Cooley, *Social Organization: A Study of the Larger Mind* (New York: Scribner's, 1909); Anselm Strauss, ed., *The Social Psychology of George Herbert Mead* (Chicago: University of Chicago Press, 1934); Warren I. Thomas and Florian Znaniecki, *The Polish Peasant in Europe and America* (New York: Knopf, 1918).

13. Harry Stack Sullivan, "The Illustion of Personal Individuality," in *The Fusion of Psychiatry and Social Science*, ed. H. S. Perry (New York: W. W. Norton, 1964), 220–21. (Originally presented as a paper to the Society on the Theory of Personality, New York Academy of Medicine, 3 May 1944); first published in *Psychiatry* 13 (1950).

14. See Harry Stack Sullivan, *The Fusion of Psychiatry and Social Science*.

15. Harry Stack Sullivan, "The William Alanson White Psychiatric Foundation—An Editorial," *Psychiatry* 1 (1938): 136.

16. Harry Stack Sullivan, "Introduction to the Study of Interpersonal Relations," *Psychiatry* 1 (1938): 123 n.3.

17. Harry Stack Sullivan, "Security of the American Commonwealth—An Editorial," *Psychiatry* 1 (1938): 420.

18. Ibid.

19. Harry Stack Sullivan, "The Cultural Revolution to End War—An Editorial on the Second William Alanson White Memorial Lectures by Major-General G. B. Chisholm," *Psychiatry* 9 (1946): 81.

20. Ibid., 84–85.

21. For an insightful treatment of this general problem see Howard Gadlin and Susan H. Rubin, "Interactionism: A Nonresolution of the Person-Situation Controversy," in *Psychology in Social Context*, ed. Allan R. Buss (New York: Irvington, 1979).

22. Their group was so named because they were accused of emphasizing the effects of the sociocultural realm to the exclusion of the intrapsychic. This demonstrates how thoroughly embedded in the Cartesian split between material-spiritual (and thus individual-society) was mainstream American psychoanalysis.

23. Aldo Carotenuto, *A Secret Symmetry: Sabina Spielrein between Jung and Freud*, trans. Arno Pomerans, John Shepley, and Krishna Winston (New York: Pantheon, 1984).

24. See Karen Horney, *The Neurotic Character of Our Time* (New York: W. W. Norton, 1937); Karen Horney, *Neurosis and Human Growth* (New York: W. W. Norton, 1950).

25. See Erich Fromm, *Escape from Freedom* (New York: Farr and Rinehart, 1941); Erich Fromm, *The Sane Society* (New York: Holt, Rinehart, and Winston, 1955).

26. Erich Fromm, *You Shall Be as Gods: A Radical Interpretation of the Old Testament and Its Tradition* (New York: Holt, Rinehart and Winston, 1966).

27. Quoted in Edgar A. Levenson, "Harry Stack Sullivan: From Interpersonal Psychiatry to Interpersonal Psychoanalysis," *Contemporary Psychoanalysis* 28 (July 1992): 459.

28. For an excellent illustration of this concept see Edgar A. Levenson, "Harry Stack Sullivan: The Web and the Spider," in Edgar A. Levenson, *The Purloined Self: Interpersonal Perspectives on Psychoanalysis* (New York: William Alanson White

Institute, 1991), 142. Originally published in *Contemporary Psychoanalysis* 20 (1984).

29. Harry Stack Sullivan, *Schizophrenia as Human Process* (New York: W. W. Norton, 1962).

30. Harry Stack Sullivan, *The Psychiatric Interview* (New York: W. W. Norton, 1954).

31. Harry Stack Sullivan, *The Interpersonal Theory of Psychiatry* (New York: W. W. Norton, 1953).

32. Sullivan, "Illusion of Personal Individuality."

33. In a recent article, psychoanalyst and writer Donnel B. Stern noticed that Sullivan's idea about the "illusion" of personal individuality is Sullivan's one idea almost universally abandoned by the interpersonalists who succeeded him. See Donnel B. Stern, "Social Construction of Therapeutic Action," *Psychoanalytic Inquiry* (in press).

34. For example, see Merton M. Gill, "The Distinction between the Interpersonal Paradigm and the Degree of the Therapist's Involvement," *Contemporary Psychoanalysis* 19 (1983); Irwin Z. Hoffman, "The Patient as Interpreter of the Analyst's Experience," *Contemporary Psychoanalysis* 19 (1983); Irwin Z. Hoffman, "Discussion: Toward a Social-Constructivist View of the Psychoanalytic Situation," *Psychoanalytic Dialogues* 1 (1991); Edgar A. Levenson, *The Ambiguity of Change* (New York: Basic Books, 1983); Edgar A. Levenson, "Mistakes, Errors and Oversights," *Contemporary Psychoanalysis* 28 (October 1992); Stephen A. Mitchell, *Relational Concepts in Psychoanalysis: An Integration* (Cambridge, Mass.: Harvard University Press, 1988); Harold Racker, *Transference and Countertransference* (New York: International Universities Press, 1968); Donnel B. Stern, "A Philosophy for the Embedded Analyst: Gadamer's Hermeneutics and the Social Paradigm of Psychoanalysis," *Contemporary Psychoanalysis* 27 (January 1991); Donnel B. Stern, "Conceptions of Structure in Interpersonal Psychoanalysis: A Reading of the Literature," *Contemporary Psychoanalysis* 30 (April 1994).

35. Levenson, "Harry Stack Sullivan: From Interpersonal Psychiatry to Interpersonal Psychoanalysis," 465.

36. Levenson, "The Web and the Spider."

37. Perry, *Psychiatrist of America*, 189–90.

38. Levenson, "The Web and the Spider."

39. Sass, "Humanism, Hermeneutics, and the Human Subject," 250.

40. Kovel, "American Mental Health Industry," 100.

41. Sullivan, "Introduction to the Study of Interpersonal Relations," 123.

42. Sullivan, "Cultural Revolution to End War," 86.

43. Ibid., 84.

44. Ibid., 85.

45. Leston Havens and Justin A. Frank, review of *Psychoanalysis and Interpersonal Psychiatry*, by Patrick Mullahy, *American Journal of Psychiatry* 127 (1971): 1705; Mary-Joan Gerson, "Sullivan and Family Therapy: An Unconsummated Affair," *Contemporary Psychoanalysis* 24 (October 1988); Jay R. Greenberg and Stephen A. Mitchell, *Object Relations in Psychoanalytic Theory* (Cambridge, Mass.: Harvard University Press, 1983).

46. Harry Stack Sullivan, "This Journal—An Editorial," *Psychiatry* 1 (1938): 141.

47. Reuben Fine, *A History of Psychoanalysis* (New York: Columbia University Press, 1979); Heinz Hartmann, *Essays in Ego Psychology* (New York: International Universities Press, 1964).

48. See for example Michel Foucault, *The History of Sexuality* (New York: Random House, 1978); Michel Foucault, "Technologies of the Self," in *Technologies of the Self: A Seminar with Michel Foucault*, ed. Luther H. Martin, Huck Gutman, and Patrick H. Hutton (Amherst: University of Massachusetts Press, 1988).
49. Adler, "The Polyvocal Psyche," 3.
50. For a detailed inquiry into the immigration of European analysts and their effect on psychoanalytic theory, see Russell Jacoby, *The Repression of Psychoanalysis: Otto Fenichel and the Political Freudians* (New York: Basic Books, 1983).
51. See the discussion about the mental hygiene movement in chapter six.
52. For example, see Robert A. LeVine, "Infant Environments in Psychoanalysis: A Cross-Cultural View," in *Cultural Psychology: Essays on Comparative Human Development*, ed. James W. Stigler, Richard A. Shweder, and Gilbert Herdt (New York: Cambridge University Press, 1990); Edward E. Sampson, "Cognitive Psychology as Ideology," *American Psychologist* 36 (1981); Richard A. Shweder, Manamohan Mahapatra, and Joan G. Miller, "Culture and Moral Development," in Stigler, Shweder, and Herdt, eds., *Cultural Psychology*.
53. The following discussion is informed by Grosskurth, *Melanie Klein*.
54. Ibid., 279–362.
55. Thomas H. Ogden, *The Matrix of the Mind: Object Relations and the Psychoanalytic Dialogue* (Northvale, N.J.: Jason Aronson, 1986).
56. Thomas H. Ogden, *The Primitive Edge of Experience* (Northvale, N.J.: Jason Aronson, 1989), 83–108.
57. Ogden, *Matrix of the Mind*, 150–65.
58. *The Diary of Virginia Woolf*, ed. Anne Olivier Bell, vol. 5 (London: Hogarth Press, 1984), 209.
59. Grosskurth, *Melanie Klein*, 96.
60. Ibid., 97.
61. Ibid., 83.
62. Ibid., 96, 97.
63. Ibid., 97.
64. Ibid., 95.

CHAPTER EIGHT: SELF-LIBERATION THROUGH CONSUMERISM

1. Donald W. Winnicott, "Transitional Objects and Transitional Phenomena: A Study of the First Not-Me Possession," *International Journal of Psychoanalysis* 34 (1953); Donald W. Winnicott, *The Maturational Process and the Facilitating Environment* (New York: International Universities Press, 1965); Donald W. Winnicott, "Mirror-Role of Mother and Family in Child Development," in *Playing and Reality* (Middlesex, England: Penguin Books, 1971), 111–18; Donald W. Winnicott, *Holding and Interpretation: Fragment of an Analysis* (New York: Grove Press, 1986).
2. Heinz Kohut, *The Analysis of the Self* (New York: International Universities Press, 1971); Heinz Kohut, *The Restoration of the Self* (New York: International Universities Press, 1977); Heinz Kohut, *How Does Analysis Cure?* (Chicago: University of Chicago Press, 1984).
3. The following discussion of Kohut's life story is drawn from Charles B. Strozier, "Glimpses of a Life: Heinz Kohut (1913–1981)" in *Progress in Self Psychology*, vol. 2, ed. Arnold Goldberg (New York: Guilford Press, 1985). See also *The Curve of Life:*

The Correspondence of Heinz Kohut, 1923–1981, ed. Geoffrey Cocks (Chicago: University of Chicago Press, 1994).

4. Strozier, "Glimpses of a Life," 6.

5. Charles B. Strozier, telephone interviews with author, February 18, 1993, and September 16, 1994.

6. The following discussion was drawn from Blum et al., *The National Experience*; Stephanie Coontz, *The Way We Never Were: American Families and the Nostalgia Trap* (New York: Basic Books, 1992); Degler et al., *The Democratic Experience* (Glenview, Ill.: Scott, Foresman, 1973); Eric F. Goldman, *The Crucial Decade—And After: America, 1945–1960* (New York: Random House, 1960); Howard Zinn, *Postwar America: 1945–1971* (New York: Bobbs-Merrill, 1973); Howard Zinn, *A People's History of the United States* (New York: Harper & Row, 1980).

7. Samuel Goldwyn (producer), *The Best Years of Our Lives*, (Samuel Goldwyn Productions), 1946.

8. Behind the cold war there lurked the threat of a socialist society, the ultimate challenge to a capitalism that veered between plenty and economic depression. American foreign policy was driven by the continuing imperative that the Soviet Union must be contained so that capitalism could survive. Some have hypothesized that behind British Prime Minister Neville Chamberlain's unsuccessful appeasement strategy was his hope that Hitler, if unthreatened by the West, would first turn east and eradicate the threat of socialism. Similarly, some historians have wondered whether Truman's decision to use the bomb on Japan was as much an attempt to end the war before the USSR could invade and control Japan and a veiled warning to the Soviet Union, as it was an attempt to convince the Japanese of the utility of unconditional surrender. After the war, the nation that was the first to use the atom bomb had a troubled conscience and needed to justify itself and project its own guilt by ascribing to the communist "other" evil motives. The West's fears of the Soviet Union appeared more immediate after the end of the war. The democracies, impelled in part by their fear of expanding socialism, refused to extend postwar credit to the Soviets and the Eastern European nations they occupied in the hope that that would prevent those countries from producing or at least decrease their ability to produce consumer goods. The West's military-economic organization, the North Atlantic Treaty Alliance, excluded the USSR. In return, the USSR formed its own alliance, the Warsaw Pact. To further its own geopolitical strategies and in response to NATO's pressures, the USSR eventually turned to excessive military production in an attempt to invigorate the economy, expand into and exploit foreign markets, and protect its borders. Recently it has become obvious that this worldwide game of chicken has bankrupted the Soviets and damaged, perhaps incapacitated, the ability of the United States to effectively attend to pressing domestic issues.

9. Degler et al., *The Democratic Experience*, 530. According to Zinn, *Postwar America*, 125, even by 1965, eleven years after the first desegregation order, more than 75 percent of Southern school districts were still segregated.

10. Goldman, *The Crucial Decade*, 301.

11. Coontz, *The Way We Never Were*, 171.

12. Goldman, *The Crucial Decade*, 300–303.

13. Blum et al., *The National Experience*, 747.

14. Degler et al., *The Democratic Experience*, 560.

15. Goldman, *The Crucial Decade*, 328–30.
16. Ibid., 329.
17. As the era progressed, political meanings and religious transcendence were increasingly subsumed under the metaphor of consumption. This trend increased and was unmistakable by the eighties. For instance, the Minolta camera company has a model named "Freedom." A 1993 California billboard for a radio station encouraged listeners to tune in to their station by using a St. Augustine quotation: "Change What You Can." A window display in California during a July 4th Independence Day sale featured a mannequin as the Statue of Liberty standing under a large gaudy sign that read, "Life, Liberty, Shopping." Another California window, this time during the bicentennial celebration of the Constitution in 1987, featured a naked statue of liberty draped only in paper that proclaimed "SALE! SALE! SALE!" A commercial for General Motors service centers lets the viewer in on a conversation between a father and his young-adult son. The son is busily packing a GM car; he is about to go on an extended trip. The father nervously asks if the car has been recently serviced, and where the son is traveling. The son answers that the car has indeed been serviced, and that he doesn't know where he is going, he just needs to go. The voice-over gently croons: "It's not just your car, it's your freedom."
18. Goldman, *The Crucial Decade*, 261–94.
19. Degler et al., *The Democratic Experience*, 540.
20. See Zinn, *A People's History*, 120–97.
21. Nathan Adler, *The Underground Stream: New Life Styles and the Antinomian Personality* (New York: Harper & Row, 1972), xviii.
22. For the event itself see "Gasoline Alley," *Los Angeles Times*, 1 June 1949.
23. John Demos, "Oedipus and America," 298.
24. See Donald L. Bartlett and James B. Steele, *America: What Went Wrong?* (Kansas City: Andrews & McMeel, 1992); Kathleen Hall Jamieson, *Dirty Politics: Deception, Distraction, and Democracy* (New York: Oxford University Press, 1992); Michael Rogin, *Ronald Reagan, the Movie: And Other Episodes in Political Demonology* (Berkeley: University of California Press, 1987).
25. For instance, see Nathan Schwartz-Salant and Murray Stein, eds., *The Borderline Personality in Analysis* (Wilmette, Ill.: Chiron Publications, 1988).
26. For instance, see James Hillman, *Revisioning Psychology* (New York: Harper & Row, 1975); James Hillman and Michael Ventura, *We've Had a Hundred Years of Psychotherapy—& the World's Getting Worse* (San Francisco: Harper, 1993).
27. For a comprehensive history of family therapy see Philip J. Guerin, Jr., and David R. Chabot, "Development of Family Systems Theory," in *History of Psychotherapy: A Century of Change*, ed. Donald K. Freedheim (Washington, D.C.: American Psychological Association Books, 1992); Lynn Hoffman, *Foundations of Family Therapy: A Conceptual Framework for Systems Change* (New York: Basic Books, 1981).
28. John Elderkin Bell, *Family Therapy* (New York: Jason Aronson, 1975), 3, 392 n. 1.
29. Charlotte Buhler and Melanie Allen, *Introduction to Humanistic Psychology* (Monterey, Calif.: Brooks/Cole, 1972), 1.
30. James F. T. Bugental, "Humanistic Psychology: A New Break-Through," in *Clinical Psychology in Transition*, ed. J. R. Brown (Cleveland: The World Publishing Co., 1966), 359.
31. Ibid., 363.

32. For a preliminary discussion, see Mark Poster, *Existential Marxism in Postwar France: From Sartre to Althusser* (Princeton, N.J.: University of Princeton Press, 1977).

33. Jack Gaines, *Fritz Perls: Here & Now* (Millbrea, Calif.: Celestial Arts, 1979), 153.

34. James F. T. Bugental, *Psychotherapy and Process: The Fundamentals of an Existential-Humanistic Approach* (Menlo Park, Calif.: Addison-Wesley, 1978), 142.

35. See Richard Adams and Janice Haaken, "Anticultural Culture: Lifespring's Ideology and Its Roots in Humanistic Psychology," *Journal of Humanistic Psychology* 27 (Fall 1987); Cushman, "Iron Fists/Velvet Gloves"; Janice Haaken and Richard Adams, "Pathology as 'Personal Growth': A Participant Observation Study of a Lifespring Training," *Psychiatry* 46 (1983); Carol Lynn Mithers, *Therapy Gone Mad: The True Story of Hundreds of Patients and a Generation Betrayed* (Reading, Mass.: Addison-Wesley, 1994).

36. Joe McGinniss, *The Selling of the President, 1968* (New York: Trident Press, 1969).

37. See J. Bouhoustsos, J. Holroyd, H. Lerman, B. Forer, and M. Greenberg, "Sexual Intimacy Between Psychotherapists and Patients," *Professional Psychology: Research and Practice* 14 (1983); J. Holroyd and A. Brodsky, "Psychologists' Attitudes and Practices Regarding Erotic and Nonerotic Physical Contact with Patients," *American Psychologist* 32 (1977).

38. John Clark, "On the Further Study of Destructive Cultism," in *Psychodynamic Perspectives on Religion, Sect and Cult,* ed. David A. Halperin (Boston: John Wright PSG Ltd., 1983); Steven Hassan, *Combating Mind Control* (Rochester, Vt.: Inner Tradition Press, 1985); John Hochman, "Iatrogenic Symptoms Associated with a Therapy Cult: Examination of an Extinct 'New Psychotherapy' with Respect to Psychiatric Deterioration and 'Brainwashing,' " *Psychiatry* 47 (November 1984); Margaret Thaler Singer with Janja Lalich, *Cults in Our Midst: How They Capture Individuals, Families and the Workplace* (San Francisco: Jossey-Bass, 1995); Maurice Temerlin and Jane Temerlin, "Psychotherapy Cults: An Iatrogenic Perversion," *Psychotherapy: Therapy, Research, and Practice* 19 (1982); Madeleine Landau Tobias and Janja Lalich, *Captive Hearts, Captive Minds: Freedom and Recovery from Cults and Abusive Relationships* (Alameda, Calif.: Hunter House, 1994).

39. Cushman, "Iron Fists/Velvet Gloves"; Haaken and Adams, "Pathology as 'Personal Growth.' "

40. Heinz Kohut, "Introspection, Empathy and the Semi-Circle of Mental Health," *International Journal of Psycho-Analysis* 63 (1982): 339.

41. See also Philip Cushman, "Confronting Sullivan's Spider: Hermeneutics and the Politics of Therapy," *Contemporary Psychoanalysis* 30 (October 1994).

42. Madeline Davis and David Wallbridge, *Boundary and Space: An Introduction to the Work of D. W. Winnicott* (New York: Brunner/Mazel, 1981), 102.

43. Ogden, *Matrix of the Mind,* 200.

44. Greenberg and Mitchell, *Object Relations,* 190.

45. Ogen, *Matrix of the Mind,* 195.

46. Ibid.

47. Greenberg and Mitchell, *Object Relations,* 201.

48. Strozier, "Glimpses of a Life," 6–8.

49. Kohut, *Restoration of the Self,* 99.

50. Greenberg and Mitchell, *Object Relations,* 365.

51. For an insightful discussion of the historiographic implications of self psychology

see Charles B. Strozier, "Heinz Kohut and the Historical Imagination," *Psychohistory Review* 7 (1978).

52. Heinz Kohut, "Creativeness, Charisma, Group Psychology: Reflections on the Self-Analysis of Freud," in *Heinz Kohut Self Psychology and the Humanities: Reflections on a New Psychoanalytic Approach*, ed. Charles B. Strozier (New York: W. W. Norton, 1985), 171–211.

53. John Putnam Demos, *Entertaining Satan: Witchcraft and the Culture of Early New England* (New York: Oxford University Press, 1982); Charles B. Strozier, *Lincoln's Quest for Union: Public and Private Meanings* (Chicago: University of Illinois Press, 1987).

54. Morris Eagle, *Recent Developments in Psychoanalysis: A Critical Evaluation* (Cambridge, Mass.: Harvard University Press, 1984); Lynne Layton, "A Deconstruction of Kohut's Concept of the Self," *Contemporary Psychoanalysis* 26 (July 1990); Louis A. Sass, "The Self and Its Vicissitudes: An Archaelogical Study of the Psychoanalytic Avant-Garde," *Social Research* 55 (Winter 1988).

55. The casebook Layton refers to is *The Psychology of the Self: A Casebook*, ed. Arnold Goldberg (New York: International Universities Press, 1978).

56. Layton, "A Deconstruction of Kohut's Concept of the Self," 427.

57. Greenberg and Mitchell, *Object Relations*, 111, 382.

58. Kovel, "American Mental Health Industry," 81.

59. Ibid.

60. Virginia Satir, *Self Esteem* (Millbrae, Calif.: Celestial Press, 1975), 37–42, 48–49.

CHAPTER NINE: PSYCHOTHERAPY AS MORAL DISCOURSE

1. See Gadlin and Rubin, "Interactionism."

2. Ibid., 219.

3. Irwin Z. Hoffman, "Discussion: Toward a Social-Constructivist View of the Psychoanalytic Situation," *Psychoanalytic Dialogues* 1 (1991); Donnel B. Stern, "Conceptions of Structure in Interpersonal Psychoanalysis," *Contemporary Psychoanalysis* 30 (April 1994).

4. Irwin Z. Hoffman, "Expressive Participation and Psychoanalytic Discipline," *Contemporary Psychoanalysis* 28 (March 1992); Lane Gerber, "Intimate Politics: Connectedness and the Social-Political Self," *Psychotherapy: Theory/Research/Practice/Training* 29 (Winter 1992).

5. Daniel N. Stern, *The Interpersonal World of the Infant: A View from Psychoanalysis and Developmental Psychology* (New York: Basic Books, 1985). For a more detailed critique see Philip Cushman, "Ideology Obscured: Political Uses of the Self in Daniel Stern's Infant," *American Psychologist* 46 (May 1991).

6. See Bernstein, *The Restructuring of Social and Political Theory*.

7. See Gary Greenberg, *The Self on the Shelf: Recovery Books and the Good Life* (Albany, N.Y.: SUNY, 1994); Wendy Kaminer, *I'm Dysfunctional, You're Dysfunctional: The Recovery Movement and Other Self-Help Fashions* (Reading, Mass.: Addison-Wesley, 1992) for detailed critiques of recovery literature.

8. For instance, see Donald W. Winnicott, "Ego Distortion in Terms of True and False Self," in *The Maturational Processes and the Facilitating Environment*, ed. John Sutherland (London: Hogarth Press, International Psychoanalytic Library, 1960); Donald W. Winnicott, *The Maturational Process and the Facilitating Environment*

(New York: International Universities Press, 1965); James F. Masterson, *The Search for the Real Self: Unmasking the Personality Disorders of Our Age* (New York: The Free Press, 1988).

9. See Layton, "A Deconstruction of Kohut's Concept of the Self," cited initially in previous chapter, note 54.

10. See Ben S. Bradley, "Infancy as Paradise," *Human Development* 34 (1991); William Kessen, "The American Child and Other Cultural Inventions," *American Psychologist* 34 (1981); Stephen Seligman and Rebecca S. Shanok, "Subjectivity and Complexity in Adult Development: A Reconsideration of Erickson's Identity Concept in Light of Contemporary Psychoanalytic Theories," *Psychoanalytic Dialogues* (in press).

11. This process must, of course, be balanced by an understanding of the dangers inherent in an isolated, solipsistic, narcissistic process in which the researcher ignores, denies, or lies about that which does not fit with his or her frame of reference. Again we see the dialectic: our frame of reference is crucially important, but it does not *create* the world, although it does cause new things to "show up" in it. Also, for a general study of the history of the discipline, see Freedheim, ed., *History of Psychotherapy*. For a history of behavior therapy see Daniel B. Fishman and Cyril M. Franks, "Evolution and Differentiation within Behavior Therapy: A Theoretical and Epistemological Review," in Freedheim, ed., *History of Psychotherapy*; for a history of cognitive therapy see Diane B. Arnkoff and Carol R. Glass, "Cognitive Therapy and Psychotherapy Integration," in Freedheim, ed., *History of Psychotherapy*. For an innovative, interpersonal approach to cognitive therapy see Jeremy D. Safran and Zindel V. Segal, *Interpersonal Process in Cognitive Therapy* (New York: Basic Books, 1990).

12. Rachel Hare-Mustin, "An Appraisal of the Relationship between Women and Psychotherapy: 80 Years after the Case of Dora," *American Psychologist* 38 (1983); Rachel Hare-Mustin, "The Problem of Gender in Family Therapy Theory," *Family Process* 26 (1987); Rachel Hare-Mustin and Jeanne Maracek, "Autonomy and Gender: Some Questions for Therapists," *Psychotherapy: Theory/Research/Practice/Training* 23 (1986); Lynne Hoffman, "A Reflexive Stance for Family Therapy," in *Therapy as Social Construction*, ed. Sheila McNamee and Kenneth J. Gergen (Newbury Park, Calif.: Sage, 1992); Deborah Ann Luepnitz, *The Family Interpreted: Feminist Theory in Clinical Practice* (New York: Basic Books, 1988).

13. Merton M. Gill, "The Distinction Between the Interpersonal Paradigm and the Degree of the Therapist's Involvement"; Greenberg and Mitchell, *Object Relations*; I.Z. Hoffman, "The Patient as the Interpreter of the Analyst's Experience"; I.Z. Hoffman, "Discussion"; I.Z. Hoffman, "Expressive Participation"; Mitchell, *Relational Concepts in Psychoanalysis* (1988); Stephen A. Mitchell, *Hope and Dread in Psychoanalysis* (New York: Basic Books, 1993); Donnel B. Stern, "Courting Surprise," *Contemporary Psychoanalysis* 26 (October 1990); D. B. Stern, "A Philosophy for the Embedded Analyst."

14. See Greenberg, *The Self on the Shelf*; Kaminer, *I'm Dysfunctional, You're Dysfunctional*.

15. See Rom Harre, ed., *The Social Construction of Emotions* (Oxford: Basil Blackwell, 1986).

16. Blaine J. Fowers and Frank C. Richardson, "Psychology and the Modern Identity"

(paper delivered at the ninety-ninth annual meeting of the American Psychological Association, San Francisco, 17 August 1991); Frank C. Richardson and Blaine J. Fowers, "Hermeneutics and Modern Psychology," (paper delivered at the one-hundredth annual meeting of the American Psychological Association, Washington, D.C., 17 August 1992); Frank C. Richardson and Blaine J. Fowers, "Beyond Scientism and Constructionism," (paper delivered at the one-hundred and second annual meeting of the American Psychological Association, Los Angeles, 14 August 1994); Blaine J. Fowers and Frank C. Richardson, "Why Multiculturalism Is Good" (paper delivered at the one-hundred and second annual meeting of the American Psychological Association, Los Angeles, 16 August 1994).

17. Reprinted in the *New York Times*, 23 May 1993.

18. In the clinical vignettes that follow, I have used material from therapy sessions in order to discuss various hermeneutic concepts and to illustrate ways in which they might be utilized in the therapeutic hour. I do not offer them as examples of "successful" outcomes brought on by a transformative technology. The patients featured in these scenes have given their permission for their words to be used in this book, and I have taken care to protect their identities. To the degree that I have been able to portray their therapeutic courage and their willingness to contribute to our store of common knowledge, this chapter will come alive and make some sense. As always, the learning that goes on in the therapy hour is first of all dependent upon what the patient is able to teach the therapist.

19. Peter L. Berger, *The Precarious Vision: A Sociologist Looks at Social Fictions and Christian Faith* (Garden City, N.Y.: Doubleday & Co., 1961). I realize that, although I attribute this approach primarily to Gadamer, Gadamer himself comes out of an existentialist-phenomenological-hermeneutic tradition in Europe that includes many other philosophers. It has been pointed out to me, for instance, that my description of patients sometimes sounds like it is influenced by Ludwig Binswanger's work. I'm sure this is true in certain ways, because Binswanger was part of that larger philosophical movement that also included the hermeneuticists. At first glance, Binswanger's concept of the *Mitwelt* (the social world), *Umwelt* (external world), and *Eigenwelt* (private world) seems germain in this chapter (for example, see Ludwig Binswanger, "Existential Analysis and Psychotherapy," in *Progress in Psychotherapy*, vol. 1, ed. Frieda Fromm-Reichman and J. L. Moreno [New York: Grune and Stratton, 1956]). However, Binswanger's ideas took a decidedly individualist and asocial tack—similar to Edmund Husserl's attempts to understand "intuitional essences" through a removed, transcendent process—which I try to avoid whenever possible. It is Gadamer's particular genius that warned us against forgetting history and culture and cautioned against talking about human being as though individuals can invent their own idiosyncratic world. The world is socially constructed, Gadamer would argue, but through the continuing historical and cultural traditions that are given to us, that we are "thrown" into. Traditions conflict with one another, and we continually sift through them in order to make decisions about how we are to act. This issue will be discussed further in chapter ten.

20. Adler, "The Polyvocal Psyche," 10; Harold Bloom, *A Map of Misreading* (New York: Oxford University Press, 1975), 84.

21. Joyce McDougall, *Theaters of the Body: A Psychoanalytic Approach to Psychosomatic Illness* (New York: W. W. Norton, 1989).

22. For instance, see Adler, "The Polyvocal Psyche"; Walter A. Davis, *Inwardness and Existence: Subjectivity in Hegel, Heidegger, Marx, and Freud* (Madison: University of Wisconsin Press, 1989).

23. Stern, "A Philosophy for the Embedded Analyst," 69.

24. Stern, "A Philosophy for the Embedded Analyst"; Georgia Warnke, *Gadamer: Hermeneutics, Tradition, and Reason* (Stanford, Calif.: Stanford University Press, 1987); Joel C. Weinsheimer, *Gadamer's Hermeneutics: A reading of "Truth and Method"* (New Haven, Conn.: Yale University Press, 1985). For a similar, but more Heideggerian, treatment of psychotherapy, see Charles B. Guignon, "Authenticity, Moral Values, and Psychotherapy," in *Cambridge Companion to Heidegger*, ed. Charles B. Guignon (Cambridge: Cambridge University Press, 1993).

25. Jane Burka, Ph.D., conversation with author, Berkeley, Calif., 28 July 1993.

CHAPTER TEN: THE POLITICS OF THE SELF

1. Several researchers have pointed this out about the practices of a number of psychological pursuits: on social psychology, see Lita Furby, "Individualistic Bias in Studies of Locus of Control," *Psychology in Social Context*, ed. Allan R. Buss (New York: Irvington, 1979); Kenneth J. Gergen, "Social Psychology as History," *Journal of Personality and Social Psychology* 26 (1973); Susan Hales, "The Inadvertent Rediscovery of the Self in Social Psychology," *Journal for the Theory of Social Behaviour* 15 (October 1985); Edward E. Sampson, *Justice and the Critique of Pure Psychology* (New York: Plenum, 1983); on personality psychology, see Kenneth J. Gergen, Andrea Hepburn, and Deborah Comer-Fisher, "Hermeneutics of Personality Description," *Journal of Personality and Social Psychology* 50 (1986); Jon Smedslund, "Necessarily True Cultural Psychologies," in *The Social Construction of the Person*, ed. Kenneth J. Gergen and Kenneth Davis (New York: Springer-Verlag, 1985); on cognitive psychology see Isaac Prilleltensky, "On the Social and Political Implications of Cognitive Psychology," *Journal of Mind and Behavior* 11 (1990); Edward E. Sampson, "Cognitive Psychology as Ideology," *American Psychologist* 36 (1981); on organizational development see Gillespie, "The Hawthorne Experiments"; on intelligence testing see Franz Samelson, "Putting Psychology on the Map"; and on developmental psychology see Bradley, "Infancy as Paradise"; Cushman, "Ideology Obscured"; Kessen, "The American Child".

2. Smedslund, "Necessarily True Cultural Psychologies."

3. Leahey, *A History of Psychology*, 87.

4. Mitchell Ash, "The Self-Presentation of a Discipline: History of Psychology in the United States Between Pedagogy and Scholarship," in *Functions and Uses of Disciplinary Histories*, ed. Loren Graham, Wolf Lepenies, and Peter Weingart (Boston: D. Reidel, 1983); Kurt Danziger, "The Social Origins of Modern Psychology," in *Psychology in Social Context*, ed. Allan R. Buss (New York: Irvington, 1979); Furumoto, "The New History of Psychology"; Ben Harris, "Ceremonial versus Critical History of Psychology," *American Psychologist* 35 (1980); Morawski, Introduction to *The Rise of Experimentation in American Psychology*, ed. Jill G. Morawski (New Haven, Conn.: Yale University Press, 1988); Franz Samelson, "History, Origin Myth, and Ideology: Comte's 'Discovery' of Social Psychology," *Journal for the Theory of Social Behaviour* 4 (1974).

5. Even group therapists, who one would think would be the most social of theorists, usually conceive of the social as constituted—and limited—by the boundary of the group. Some group therapists—such as those who practice a combination of gestalt and transactional analysis—think of the group as being composed of a mix of individuals, who are to be understood according to psychotherapy theory saturated with individualism.

6. See Michael Bader, "Looking for Addictions in All the Wrong Places," *Tikkun* 3 (November/December 1988); Greenberg, *The Self on the Shelf*; Kaminer, *I'm Dysfunctional, You're Dysfunctional.*

7. See Gill, "The Distinction between the Interpersonal Paradigm and the Degree of the Therapist's Involvement"; and Hoffman, "Dialogues."

8. Edgar A. Levenson, "Character, Personality, and the Politics of Change," in *The Purloined Self: Interpersonal Perspectives in Psychoanalysis* (New York: Contemporary Psychoanalysis Books, 1991), 241. It is true that Levenson has recently taken issue with aspects of Hoffman's constructivist position, at one time referring to it as "the tarpits of constructivism" [Levenson, "Shoot the Messenger: Interpersonal Aspects of the Analyst's Interpretations," *Contemporary Psychoanalysis* 29 (July 1993): 385], but as Irwin Hirsch has recently suggested ["Extending Sullivan's Interpersonalism," *Contemporary Psychoanalysis* 28 (October 1992): 741–42], this seems to be more an intramural disagreement among members of the same family, than a crucial theoretical impasse. Levenson has been, and will continue to be, a courageous and original voice reminding us of the nonhierarchical, semiotic implications of the interpersonal approach. Although Levenson is not as focused on a historical perspective as I might wish him to be, I believe he is the most creative and inspiring interpersonalist of the postwar era.

9. Stephen Joseph, M.D., personal communication, October 1992.

APPENDIX: THE SELF IN WESTERN SOCIETY

1. Colin Morris, *The Discovery of the Individual 1050–1200* (Toronto: University of Toronto Press, 1972).

2. Aeschylus, *Oresteia*, ed. David Greene and Richmond Lattimore, trans. Richmond Lattimore (Chicago: University of Chicago Press, 1953).

3. Hubert Dreyfus and Jane Rubin, "Oresteia" (paper delivered at workshop "Inventing the Modern Self," Berkeley, 1987).

4. Petronius, *The Satyricon*, trans. J. P. Sullivan (Middlesex, England: Penguin, 1986), 50.

5. Dreyfus and Rubin, "Augustine of Hippo" "Inventing the Modern Self."

6. Ibid.

7. W. S. Merwin, introduction to *The Song of Roland* (New York: Modern Library, 1963).

8. Thomas H. Leahey, *A History of Psychology: Main Currents in Psychological Thought* (Englewood Cliffs, N.J.: Prentice-Hall, 1987), 62.

9. William J. Brandt, *The Shape of Medieval History: Studies in Modes of Perception* (New York: Schocken, 1966); Johan Huizinga, *The Waning of the Middle Ages* (Garden City, N.Y.: Doubleday, 1954).

10. Natalie Zemon Davis, *The Return of Martin Guerre* (Cambridge, Mass.: Harvard University Press, 1983).

11. Stephen J. Greenblatt, "Psychoanalysis and Renaissance Culture," in *Learning to Curse: Essays in Early Modern Culture* (New York: Routledge, 1990).

12. Ibid.

13. Lionel Trilling, *Sincerity and Authenticity* (Cambridge, Mass.: Harvard University Press, 1971).

14. Baumeister, "Why the Self Became a Problem."

15. Cited in Davis, " 'On the Lame,' " *American Historical Review* 93 (June 1988): 589, where it is referenced as follows: Michel de Montaigne, *Essais*, Book 2, chapter 18: "Du Dementir" in *Oeuvres completes*, ed. A Thibaudet and M. Rat (Paris, 1962), 649, trans. by Donald Frame, *The Complete Works of Montaigne* (Stanford, Calif.: Stanford University Press, 1948), 505.

16. Philibert de Vienne, *Le Philosophe de Court* (Lyon: Jean de Tournes, 1547), 63. Cited in Davis, " 'On the Lame,' " 589.

17. Lowe, *History of Bourgeois Perception*, 9–12.

18. Natalie Zemon Davis, " 'On the Lame,' " 584–87.

19. Ibid., 592–97.

20. Ibid., 584.

21. Ibid., 585.

22. Robert Finlay, "The Refashioning of Martin Guerre," *American Historical Review* 93 (June 1988): 553–71.

23. Davis, " 'On the Lame,' " 584.

24. Pierre Goubert, *Paysans francais au XVII siecle* (Paris, 1982), 92. Cited in Davis, " 'On the Lame,' " 585.

25. Daniel N. Robinson, *An Intellectual History of Psychology* (Madison, Wis.: University of Wisconsin Press, 1986). See especially chapters seven through ten.

26. Bertrand Russell, *A History of Western Philosophy* (New York: Simon & Schuster, 1972), 704.

27. See Michel Foucault, "Technologies of the Self" in *Technologies of the Self*, ed. Luther H. Martin, Huck Gutman, and Patrick H. Hutton (Amherst: University of Massachusetts Press, 1988); Louis Sass, "Schreber's Panopticism: Psychosis and the Modern Soul," *Social Research* 54 (1987); and Charles Taylor, *Sources of the Self: The Making of Modern Identity* (Cambridge, Mass.: Harvard University Press, 1989).

28. Taylor, *Sources of the Self*. The following discussion is drawn from Taylor's work.

29. Ibid., 144.

30. Ibid.

31. Ibid., 17.

32. Ibid., 156.

33. Ibid.

34. Ibid., 163.

35. Ibid., 169.

36. Ibid., 171.

37. Ibid., 174–75.

38. Ibid., 181.

39. Ibid., 362.

40. Baumeister, "Why the Self Became a Problem," 163.

41. Quentin Anderson, *The Imperial Self* (New York: Knopf, 1971).

42. Baumeister, "Why the Self Became a Problem," 166–67.
43. Lowe, *History of Bourgeois Perception*, 21–23.
44. Ibid., 21.
45. Steven Marcus, *The Other Victorians: A Study of Sexuality and Pornography in Mid-Nineteenth-Century England* (New York: W. W. Norton, 1964).
46. Christopher Lasch, *Haven in a Heartless World: The Family Besieged* (New York: Basic Books, 1977).
47. See Charles Bernheimer and Claire Kahane, eds., *In Dora's Case: Freud-Hysteria-Feminism* (New York: Columbia University Press, 1985); Sander L. Gilman et al., *Hysteria Beyond Freud* (Berkeley: University of California Press, 1993).
48. Drinka, *The Birth of Neurosis*.
49. David Rudavsky, *Emancipation and Adjustment* (New York: Behrman House, 1967).
50. See Lucy S. Dawidowicz, *The Golden Tradition: Jewish Life and Thought in Eastern Europe* (New York: Holt, Rinehart, and Winston, 1967); Cecil Roth, *A History of the Jews* (New York: Schocken, 1970); Rudavsky, *Emancipation and Adjustment*.
51. Rudavsky, *Emancipation and Adjustment*, 81.
52. Count Clermont Tonnerre, cited in Eugene B. Borowitz, *The Masks Jews Wear: The Self-Deceptions of American Jewry* (New York: Simon & Schuster, 1973), 30.
53. Borowitz, *Masks Jews Wear*, 30.
54. Ibid.

INDEX